ALEXANDRIA

EDITED BY DAVID FIDELER

D1452795

5

PHANES PRESS
2000

ALEXANDRIA

David Fideler
EDITOR

Melanie Brawn Mineo
PROOFREADING

Port City Fulfillment
Andy Harwood
Cynthia Weber-Brownell
SUBSCRIPTIONS

The Alexandria Society
FUNDING

Words Distributing Company (USA)
Airlift Books (UK and Europe)
DISTRIBUTION

PUBLISHED BY

Phanes Press
PO Box 6114
Grand Rapids, Michigan 49516
USA

Web site: *www.cosmopolis.com*

ISBN 1-890482-75-7

Contents

Beatrice and Dante Ascend to the Sphere of the Sun.
Engraving by Botticelli.

Dante and the Comic Way

JOSEPH MEEKER

DANTE ALIGHIERI, the fourteenth-century Italian poet, called his great poem simply *The Comedy*. Theologians later mistook Dante's intentions and added *Divine* to the title. The mistake has since led readers to see the work as a textbook of medieval religious beliefs. But Dante said that his purpose was "to remove those living in this life from the state of misery and lead them to the state of felicity."[1] To accomplish this, Dante believed that he must present the world in all its complex multiplicity so that people could better understand where they were in relation to everything else, material and spiritual. Misery, according to Dante, is the result of mistaking or distorting one's vision so that only a fragment of reality can be seen, and then taking that fragment for the whole. Felicity becomes possible as the eye learns to see the millions of fragments that make up the universe interacting with one another to create a cosmos. Misery arises from simplified and narrow vision; felicity lies in participation in systemic complexity.

Dante's *Comedy*, like all truly great literature, describes concrete instances of human universals. Dante was writing about the particular people and events of fourteenth-century Florence, yet he does so in a way that illuminates human experiences that could as easily be found in fifth-century Peking or twentieth-century San Francisco. His cosmology is derived from Ptolemy and Thomas Aquinas, yet its essence and complexity are compatible with modern quantum theory and complex dynamic systems. Dante provides one of the rare instances of deep insight into the concrete realities of the present that reveals timeless and universal qualities. This poet from seven hundred

From Joseph Meeker, *The Comedy of Survival: Literary Ecology and a Play Ethic* (Tucson: University of Arizona Press, 1997).

years ago speaks in a modern voice, and will no doubt do so seven hundred years hence.

The view of life presented in the *Comedy* can be called ecological in the largest sense of the term. Dante's Hell is a sink of noxious gasses, polluted water, and denuded forests. The people there have caused their own misery and have created the miserable environment in which they are trapped. They all suffer an impairment of vision that causes them to exaggerate their selfish rights and to satisfy themselves at any cost to others or to the world around them. Purgatory is a place of learning, where souls discover what else there is in the world beside themselves. As they increase in understanding and perspective, they begin to see the causes of misery and degradation, and so gradually become free of them. Paradise is an extremely complex place, physically and intellectually. The inhabitants see themselves as part of the intricate physical, spiritual, and social life of the world, and they are intensely aware of their own relationships to what they see. Paradise is where human awareness expands to comprehend and to participate in the complexity of things.

Fully as important as the human souls who inhabit Dante's three symbolic environments are the environments themselves. Hell, Purgatory, and Paradise are settings that correspond to the moral and psychological states of the people within them. Since all souls have chosen the particular circumstances that define their lives, they have contributed to the creation of an environment that perfectly mirrors their values. In Dante's imaginative vision, human actions build their own most appropriate environment.

Inferno

Hell is an image of both moral and biological pollution. Its physical conditions are the environmental equivalent of moral error. The imagery is strikingly similar to that of the modern industrialized, overpopulated, polluted world. Hell is a familiar environment for anyone who feels at home in New York or Los Angeles.

Hell's air is clouded with contaminants and foul odors. The carnal sinners of the second circle whirl in a storm of "dark air."[2] Further down, Dante discovers that "his eye could hardly journey far / across the black air and heavy fog."[3] Everyone in Hell squints because of the stinging air and its failure to pass enough light for clear vision. As Dante descends, the air pollution index rises until at the tenth level of Malebolge he is reminded of an ancient disaster at Aegina "when the air was so infected that / all animals, down to the little worm, / collapsed."[4] Cocytus, the frozen lake at Hell's greatest depth, is clouded by a "dense and darkened fog"[5] that all but prevents both breathing and sight.

Hell's waters never run pure. From a spring on the fifth circle the River Styx spurts forth its waters "even darker than deep purple,"[6] that Dante follows downhill past various stagnant bogs notable for their smells and muck. Other rivers run blood or salt tears. All are without nourishment for the barren land through which they pass. Their banks are either lined with stone or, like the channels of Malebolge, coated with "exhalations, rising from below, / stuck to the banks, encrusting them with mold, / and so waged war against both eye and nose."[7] When Dante looks deeper he sees "people plunged in excrement that seemed / as if it had been poured from human privies."[8] Literal and figurative sewage is the burden of all infernal waters. The rivers Styx, Acheron, and Phlegethon drain toward the center of Hell, increasing their burden of tears, blood, sin, and excrement at each descending level. Later on the Mountain of Purgatory, Dante also learns that the River Lethe, which originates in the Garden of Eden, collects the cleansed sins of Purgatory before it, too, makes its way to Hell. The sins and excretions of penitent and impenitent alike mingle in the frozen cesspool of Cocytus where Dante's great sewage-laden rivers converge. In Hell, the polluted rivers become instruments of torture for those who have polluted them.

Hell's most distinctive characteristic is its hostility to life. Dante's last view of earthly wildlife is an encounter with a leopard, a lion, and a wolf shortly before entering Hell. Although they seem threatening, Dante reacts only in fear of their power and is not repelled by their appearance. The leopard is "very quick and lithe" and has a "spotted hide"; the lion is a dignified animal with its "head held high and ravenous with hunger"; and even the she-wolf is not hideous, but merely seems "to carry every craving in her leanness."[9] The lean agility of these predators is in sharp contrast to the obese and malformed animals that occupy Hell. The few animals in Hell are grotesque mythical beasts with humanoid features such as Cerberus, the three-headed doglike creature whose "eyes are blood-red; greasy, black, his beard; / his belly bulges, and his hands are claws";[10] the harpie birds whose "wings are wide, their necks and faces human; / their feet taloned, their great bellies feathered";[11] or the Monster Geryon whose face was "that of a just man" but has a serpent's trunk with a scorpion's stinger at its tail.[12] Hell's fauna are grotesque fusions of animal and human forms; genuine animals are not to be found there.

The flora of Hell is similarly maimed. Like its animals, Hell's plants are stunted, deformed, leafless, and lifeless. The third circle is "an open plain / that banishes all green things from its bed," and is surrounded by "a wood of sorrow."[13] Such scenes are frequent in Hell, reminding the reader of the absence of light and water required by plant life. Hell's most memorable plants are perhaps the trees that encase the suicides on the seventh circle: "No green leaves in that forest, only black; / no branches straight and smooth, but knotted, gnarled; / no fruits were there, but briers bearing poison."[14] Like the animals of Hell, these plants are images of distorted humanity. When Dante plucks a twig, words and blood bubble forth together to reveal the vegetative soul of Pier della Vigna, a statesman who had taken his own life when his political fortunes fell. Suicide means refusing to face the changes and difficulties that go with being a human being. This tree is a man who has sought and attained a stunted vegetative existence. Aside from such images, Hell is without greenery or flowers.

All landscapes in Hell are bleak, and all natural processes are diseased. Natural elements normally associated with beauty have become ugly reminders of human destructiveness. Although Hell is an alpine setting that taxes the climbing skills of Dante the Pilgrim, scaling its crags provides no more satisfaction than climbers would find from exploring an open-pit mine. Such anachronistic comparisons are hard to avoid when reading the *Inferno*. Modern oil slicks are suggested by Dante's description of the boiling pitch in which the barrators suffer, especially when Dante compares the souls to wild ducks, falcons, and hawks and shows them trapped in petroleum: "there was no way they could get out; / their wings were stuck, enmeshed in glue-like pitch."[15] We need not speculate on Dante's mystic premonition of twentieth-century problems; it is enough to recognize that his fourteenth-century attempt to imagine the worst possible human environment describes many of the environmental features that have only recently been realized.

Hell is also overpopulated. Overcrowding is the first misery Dante encounters on his guided tour. Just inside the gate he sees the mob of neutrals: "so long a file / of people—I should never have believed / that death could have unmade so many souls."[16] As his journey continues, Dante discovers that everyone in Hell is crowded, spaceless, jammed together with others from whom there is no escape. Trapped togetherness is one of Hell's most characteristic images, repeated on many levels among souls whose torment is to share a small space with one another: Farinata and Cavalcante in their tiny tomb, Ulysses and Diomede as forked tongues of a single flame, Ugolino and Ruggieri gnawing one another while frozen fast in the ice. High population density is one of Hell's most painful miseries.

As citizens are said always to get the kind of government they deserve, Dante provides his characters with the kind of environment they have earned by their actions. The inhabitants of Hell are people who would make the headlines in any century: political and religious leaders, businessmen and scientists, sex queens, heroes and cowards, and freaks. They have in common a single-minded egotism that sets them apart from others and makes their actions seem abnormally significant or dramatic. They are people who have focused their attention upon some fragment of the world, either in an admirable or reprehensible way, and made it their own.

Readers are often troubled to find some of their favorite mythical or historical figures in Dante's Hell. Achilles, Dido, Cleopatra, and several famous popes are there, together with others whose names are not well known but whose characters are easily admired: Farinata, the competent and powerful politician who puts the welfare of his party above all else; Francesca, the beautiful woman whose passionate love has made her the victim of murder by a jealous husband; Cavalcante, the dedicated parent who sacrifices himself for his son; Pier della Vigna, the faithful and dedicated civil servant who lost his identity when a bureaucratic shakeup cost him his job. The reader's easy sympathy for such people expresses the recognition that most of us are equally susceptible to such misfortunes, but it also obscures for many reasons the essential fact that all of these souls have limited their vision of the world to the confines of their personal interests and activities. They all assume that their private experience of the world is somehow definitive of its basic nature. That is why the sign at the gate says "Abandon every hope, who enter here." The souls in Hell are those who have lost the capacity for seeing themselves in the context of a larger perspective. They will never discover the true reasons for their suffering.

The people in Dante's Hell do not really know they are there. Like many moderns, their creation of a joyless environment results from the actions in which they take greatest pride, and they fail to see any causal relationship between those actions and their consequences. The souls do not know they are in Hell any more than Dante's contemporaries knew that the Earth revolves around the Sun, for recognition of either fact would necessarily lead to the correction of error. They are prevented from knowing their true state by the pride they take in their uniqueness and specialized talent. Francesca loves being in love, Farinata is proud of his political party, Ugolino lives only to punish his enemy. They feel the pain of their existence, but are at a loss to explain its source. Some, like Francesca and Pier, think they are punished unjustly by a tyrannical God and so solicit pity; others, like Farinata and Satan himself, are proud figures who nobly bear their pain and show only contempt for their surroundings. Scorning the condition of one's soul is one of the meanings of Hell. Many are like addicts in denial, unable to take responsibility for their own addiction, and facile at explaining their unhappiness by pointing to everything except its cause. Hell is a colossal image of spiritual irony, where the means for relief from pain are not discernible because the pain is so intense.

Souls in Dante's Hell are not punished by God because they have broken the rules of medieval Christian morality. No God and no rules appear in the *Comedy*. Technical sin is of small interest to Dante, who is concerned about the motivations of human actions and their appropriateness to the context in which they occur. Suicide damns Pier because it is an abdication of responsibility, but Cato, also a suicide, has a place of honor in Purgatory because he sacrificed his life in the service of human freedom. Sexuality becomes a prison for Francesca but is the power that Beatrice uses to lure Dante toward Paradise. No action or event in Dante's poem has any meaning apart from its context, and it is the context itself, not any external authority, that governs its consequences. The people in Hell are there because they have "lost the good of the intellect."[17] The mind permits humans to understand the world and to act for its welfare and their own. The refusal to understand is its own punishment.

It would have been easy for Dante to represent Hell as a fearful wilderness setting where nature is symbolic of evil and hostile to humans. Much precedent for such an image was ready at hand in medieval tales and legends and in church dogma. Dante's decision to describe Hell as an environment polluted by people and excluding all wild or natural forms is a deliberate innovation that he executes with care and consistency. It is necessary to his idea that humans are the responsible creators of the world in which they must live.

Purgatorio

The first line of the *Purgatorio* proclaims that Dante's journey now moves "across more kindly waters." He has also "left behind the air of death / that had afflicted both my sight and breast,"[18] and the sky is now clear from zenith to horizon. Purgatory is an environment congenial to life where trees give shade, dew falls, and grass grows. Air, water, and vegetation are in a healthy state, not cultivated and managed by human gardeners, but self-maintained.

Purgatory is a real mountain. The souls Dante meets there are fellow climbers who share together a common cause, ascent, and who collaborate to achieve it. They work hard together all day and gather in the evening for friendly conversation. Like good climbers everywhere, they know that the purpose of climbing is to master oneself, not to conquer the mountain. Purgatory is "the mountain whose ascent / delivers man from sin"[19] not because it has magical powers but because climbers increase their strength as they ascend by their own efforts.

Hell was shaped like a funnel where vision was directed increasingly inward with each stage of descent; on Purgatory perspectives become broader with each higher level. Dante exploits the relationship between optical and figurative vision to show that Purgatory is a place of learning. The pilgrim's meetings with groups of souls become impromptu seminars on some aspect of nature or experience, moderated generally by professor Virgil, Dante's guide. The curriculum of Purgatory includes whatever can be understood by the intellect.

Virgil is a person "who ponders as he labors, / who's always ready for the step ahead."[20] He is a competent scholar and a well-informed scientist. In addition to his running commentary that explains the phenomena of Purgatory and includes excursions into such topics as anatomy and physiology, Virgil frequently instructs his pupil in the techniques and limitations of intellectual investigation. His characteristic admonition to Dante is "your mind must not attend to just one part"[21] as he emphasizes the multiple aspects of knowledge and the subtle relationships among its many parts. His lectures are factual expositions of what is known about humanity and the world, not speculation into mysteries. His advice is "confine yourselves, o humans, to the *quia*"[22]—with the *that* of facts and experiences—rather than searching for the *why* of final causes.

Short of the mountaintop, Virgil pauses to conduct a graduation ceremony for his pupil. "I crown and miter you over yourself,"[23] he tells Dante as he bids him farewell. "I've brought you here through intellect and art; / from now on, let your pleasure be your guide."[24] There is a limit to the help that professors can give, and Virgil has reached it. Only when he is fully knowledgeable about the world does

Dante become free to let his instincts guide him.

Dante often expresses a belief that instincts govern the behavior of living creatures, including people. The exposition of this idea occurs first in one of Virgil's lectures on love, and is later expanded by Beatrice in Paradise. Virgil first equates love with pleasure, explaining that "the soul, which is created quick to love, / responds to everything that pleases."[25] Dante is troubled to hear that love is a manifestation of innate desires, for that suggests to him that humans are not responsible for their actions and therefore that no free will exists. Virgil cannot solve this problem, but he explains it as best reason can manage:

> Every substantial form, at once distinct
> from matter and conjoined to it, ingathers
> the force that is distinctively its own,
>
> a force unknown to us until it acts—
> it's never shown except in its effects,
> just as green boughs display the life in plants.
>
> And thus man does not know the source of his
> intelligence of primal notions and
> his tending toward desire's primal objects:
>
> both are in you just as in bees there is
> the honey-making urge; such primal will
> deserves no praise, and it deserves no blame.[26]

As plants produce leaves and as bees make honey, so humans behave according to innate desires, the origins of which are unknown. "Innate" (*innata*) is Dante's word, not an imposition of modern terminology upon Dante's text. Virgil has more to say about the role of intellect, which has an influence upon innate desires, but leaves the fuller exposition of that matter to Beatrice, as we will. Virgil merely distinguishes between two types of love, "natural or mental," and specifies that "the natural is always without error, / but mental love may choose an evil object / or err through too much or too little vigor."[27] The sins suffered from in Hell and Purgatory are all results of excessive, defective, or misdirected love; that is, of the harmful use of the mind to distort natural behavior. Virgil sounds like a modern cognitive ethologist in this and in his assertion that the actions of organisms arise from within the organisms themselves and are not the products either of divine will or of environmental determinism.

Souls rise in Purgatory when they succeed in reconciling their minds with their instincts, or in Dante's terms, their will with their desire. No jailers watch over them and no rules of penance are imposed to determine their qualifications for ascent. Statius, a soul just freed from the circle of prodigality, explains to Dante that "the will alone is proof of purity / and, fully free, surprises soul into / a change of dwelling place"[28] as soon as its innate desires are consonant with its conscious will concerning the particular sin with which it has been afflicted. All human suffering in Hell and Purgatory is the consequence of misusing the powers of the mind to limit or distort natural processes which are "always without error." The main difference is that souls in Purgatory have accurately recognized the source of their suffering, and so can seek to correct it, while souls in Hell remain blind to the causes of their pain.

The final environment of Purgatory is the Earthly Paradise on the mountaintop. Dante finds there no pastoral pleasure garden or mani-cured rural landscape, but a "forest—alive with green, divine."[29] It is like a dense tropical forest where the sun never reaches the ground. Something prompted Dante to avoid the standard Christian image of a cultivated and sunny Eden where nature is subordinate to humanity and to describe instead a complex landscape which, "depending on / the nature of its land and sky, conceives and bears from diverse powers, diverse trees."[30] Diversity is the clearest feature of Dante's Eden, felt in everything from the ground "full of every seed"[31] to the intricate pageantry that displays the entire medieval bestiary of symbolic griffons, foxes, eagles, and dragons, along with the complicated forms of church and state on Earth and the spiritual transcendence repre-sented by Christ and the heavenly eyes of Beatrice. This Eden is no place of quiet repose, but a busy meeting ground where the processes of nature coalesce with those of society, the human intellect, and the powers of spirit in active interchange. It is here that Beatrice, called by Virgil "the light between your mind and truth,"[32] takes over the guidance of Dante through the even more complex experiences ahead of him.

Paradiso

Dante's Paradise is not properly an environment at all, but a state of being experienced by those who know themselves to be in harmony with the principles and processes of creation. For this reason it is the most difficult part of the poem for many modern readers to understand. Paradise represents principles and ideas freed from their dependence upon particular entities: love that transcends attachment to things, process without active agents, relationships without objects, plurality without singularity, truth without facts, comedy without tragedy, play without games, and pure light perceived directly rather than reflected from surfaces. "On the sun I set / my sight more than we usually do,"[33] Dante announces at the beginning; Paradise is where he learns to look directly at the sources of life, not by wearing protective glasses or studying reflected images, but by perfecting his vision.

Virgil conducted Dante as far as good scientific analysis can conduct human beings, to the point of factual understanding of the structure and meaning of the world. The vision of integration that Dante finds in Paradise is suprascientific, although inclusive of the science of Dante's time and consistent with it. It is also suprahuman in the sense that it passes beyond the levels of human experience that language is suited to describe. Dante reminds his readers that "passing beyond humanity (*transhumanar*) cannot be / worded,"[34] because words, however figurative or abstract, depend upon their relationships to things and events. Virgil, the inquiring and comprehending mind, is no longer enough to serve Dante's needs, and he is superseded by an image that combines rational knowledge with spiritual insight and wordless wonder, the beautiful woman Beatrice.

The role played by the historical Beatrice in Dante's life and her symbolic role in the *Comedy* are subtle and complex. In the *Paradiso*,

Dante uses her to represent a fulfilled human being who has realized intellectually and spiritually her true relationship to reality and who thus radiates beauty united with intelligence. She has everything that Virgil had, plus the powers of emotional and aesthetic attraction that make her loved as well as respected.

Like a good scientist, Beatrice believes that "all things, among themselves, / possess an order."[35] Her concept of order, however, is a rich synthesis of material and spiritual reality that has nothing mechanistic about it. Beatrice is a vitalist who believes that there is an instinct (*instinto*) in all things: "This is the motive force in mortal creatures; / this binds the earth together, makes it one."[36] Her doctrine is derived from scholastic theology, which defines God's love as a kind of divine mucilage holding the world together and governing all change and growth. Unlike some church dogmatists, Beatrice emphasizes that the instinct for order is *internal* to the creatures of the universe, not regulated by a divine intelligence, and that it operates the same in all forms of life: "Not only does the shaft shot from this bow / strike creatures lacking intellect, but those / who have intelligence, and who can love."[37] The metaphor that likens instinct to a bow and creatures to arrows reaffirms the belief expressed throughout the *Comedy* that the power of life is internal to living creatures, and that humans alone have the ability to misdirect that power through errors of the intellect. As the souls in Hell aimed toward selfish aggrandizement and those in Purgatory learned of higher targets, so the souls in Paradise have achieved the unity of the bow of instinct (desire) and the arrow of intellect (will) centered on the target of universal order.

Throughout the *Paradiso*, great emphasis is placed upon diversity as a necessary condition for stability and order. When Beatrice instructs Dante in the complex organization of Paradise, she reminds him that "diverse virtue makes diverse alloy"[38] and that he should not expect to find here the relative simplicity of Hell and Purgatory. The soul of Charles Martel later extends this principle to include behavioral as well as structural diversity, arguing that humans must "live in diverse ways for diverse tasks"[39] as other natural creatures do. He concludes his explanation of diversity with an admonition: "If the world below would set its mind / on the foundation Nature lays as base / to follow, it would have its people worthy."[40] Although this argument is often interpreted as an instance of the medieval effort to hold people in the social status of their birth, it is evident from the context that Dante intends also to establish diversity of human and natural elements as a necessary condition for stability.

Dante's *Paradiso* is not an abstract conception that rejects the validity of physical or sensual experience. Much medieval literature shuns the senses and the world, but not Dante. His Paradise is a place where bodily experience is perfected, not rejected. However spiritual or symbolic Beatrice may be, Dante never lets the reader forget that she is also a beautiful woman whose appearance thrills him as often as do her words. And when Beatrice explains the resurrection of the body, she is happy to assure Dante that on Judgment Day, "the body's organs will have force / enough for all in which we can delight."[41] Paradise is no ascetic retreat, but a completed experience in which sensuality is appreciated for its full meaning and context and therefore enjoyed more fully than when it is pursued only for personal gratification.

Dante never rejects the world even when he perceives its smallness from the threshold of the Empyrean. His astronaut's view of Earth, like those we have acquired technologically in our time, reminds him that the Earth is a small element of a larger system, a dependent part rather than an end in itself. "I saw this globe in such a way that I / smiled at its meager image,"[42] says Dante. There is no scorn in this view, but rather compassion for the Earth's inhabitants on their "little threshing floor."[43] Dante's entry into Paradise is not an escape from the Earth, but the acquisition of a larger perspective from which to understand it.

Even Dante's final beatific vision is an integration of the world's parts, one of which is humanity. There is no ordering deity in human form controlling the universe from the upper reaches of Paradise, but only pure light, dazzling in its clarity and intensity. Dante's visual schooling as he has passed through the realms of being has prepared him to gaze at the source of light directly, and even to make out some images within it:

> O grace abounding, through which I presumed
> to set my eyes on the Eternal Light
> so long that I spent all my sight on it!
>   In its profundity I saw—ingathered
> and bound by love into one single volume—
> what, in the universe, seems separate, scattered:
>   substances, accidents, and dispositions
> as if conjoined—in such a way that what
> I tell is only rudimentary.
>   I think I saw the universal shape
> which that knot takes; for, speaking this, I feel
> a joy that is more ample.[44]

The universal form is a complex of relationships, inclusive of all life, thought, and spirit. As Dante stares, his vision improves further and he begins to see circles and colors and movements that appear to be "painted with our effigy."[45] The image of humanity, in some obscure way, is a part of the image of universal form, and Dante strains in an effort to see "the way in which our human effigy / suited the circle and found place in it— / and my own wings were far too weak for that."[46] Humanity is somehow amidst the substances, accidents, and relationships of universal order, but Dante's vision and his poem end with the unanswerable question of how, precisely, humanity fits in.

Dante's Paradise, and especially the beatific vision at its height, resembles an ultimate climax ecosystem. Ecologists sometimes object to the use of the term *climax* because it suggests finality and completeness, states that are foreign to natural processes, and because it tends to encourage people to think of nature in static terms. But the climax of a literary work is the moment when all themes, moods, and ideas unite in a flash of insight and their genuine relationships suddenly become clear. It is not a sustainable insight, but is followed inevitably by a denouement, returning the reader once more to the more prosaic world of fragmentary events and their uncertain consequences. Literary, metaphysical, sexual, and ecological climaxes are not permanently frozen states of being, but momentary epiphanies from which less intense and less perfect events must follow. Dante must return from his high vision to a desk somewhere in tortured Italy so that he can write a poem telling of what he has seen.

Play in Paradise

Play is a dependable indicator of mental and spiritual good health. The souls in Dante's Hell are mildly neurotic to pathological people, all of them with compulsive goals, enemies, and agendas to fulfill. Souls in Purgatory work hard, too, trying to overcome their shortcomings and build their strengths. The souls in Dante's Paradise are also very busy, but their time is full of joy. They are without goals and objectives, and they are free of ambitions. Being in Paradise means feeling fully engaged, genuinely pleased with oneself, strong in relationships, with spirit, mind, and body bent on fulfilling themselves and those they love. Paradise is for the playful.

Modern experience confirms Dante's comic classification. Those with the least play in their lives are people like convicted felons, murderers, drunk drivers, and others who probably had little or poor play in childhood, and have long since lost the capacity to play for the sake of play. Somewhat above them, in the equivalent of Dante's Purgatory, are the hard-working people whose lives are devoted to tangible objectives, like wealth, property, power, or status. Their lives may be honorable, but they are subject to great stress and endless pendulum swings of highs and lows.

The happiest people, those Dante would find in Paradise, are also some of the most successful and healthy people in our world. They are the Nobel Prize winners, the great artists and scientists, the leaders who act out of hope and vision. They are all those people who are continually astonished that they are paid for what they do, because they so love doing it. They are the happy people whose work is play.

To understand what it means to be in Paradise, we can begin by reflecting upon those times when life has seemed at its best. The souls in Dante's Paradise show states of being and feeling that many people have experienced at one time or another:

- They feel perfect clarity of mind, with no impediments between subject and object, and confidence in the accuracy of their perceptions.
- They feel perfectly understood and accepted by those around them.
- They feel genuine empathy for the joys and pains of others.
- They feel perfectly free to do and be what they choose.
- They feel that they are doing work of excellent quality that is almost effortless for them.
- They know that the work they are doing is exactly the right work for them.
- They feel unimpededly joyful.
- They experience a powerful sense of interconnectedness with others and with the world.
- They are aware that they are in the presence of great beauty.
- They experience complete sensual fulfillment.
- They feel fully loved and fully loving.
- They feel that they genuinely understand the meaning of their lives.
- They know that the things they most desire are really the things that they ought to have.
- Their best fantasies agree with their best judgment.

All of us know that experiences like these are possible, because we have felt them for ourselves at our great moments. Dante's *Paradiso* is simply a place where these are normal for everyone, all the time. This is the highest state of play.

Dante's Comic Way

The twentieth-century French philosopher Jacques Maritain spoke of Dante's "innocence" and of his "luck."[47] Dante was innocent in the sense that he unashamedly assumed that his private experience was symbolic of the life of all humanity. His love of Beatrice stood for all love, his life in politics illustrated the meaning of politics, and his vision of universal order was treated as a revelation of genuine cosmic integration. Dante's poem is unique in its fusion of the intensely personal with the highest levels of abstraction, and in its convincing demonstration that the two are compatible.

Dante was "lucky" because his life coincided with a climactic moment in medieval Christianity just prior to its disintegration. Dante's time made available what Maritain calls "existential certainties" that affirmed that the intricate complexities of the world are intelligible, and that all life is integrated according to principles that we must recognize and adapt to if we hope to attain fulfillment. Dante's world permitted these basic assumptions as no period since has been able to do, and permitted Dante to construct in his poem the last image of an integrated universe before the fragmentations of the modern world emerged.

From a modern, scientific perspective, Dante's medieval world appears to be drastically misinformed about the nature of things. Dante lived in a world that did not know about nuclear power, about the profound changes that technology was to make upon human perceptions, about indeterminacy in physics and neurosis in the subconscious, about space travel and the evolution of humans from animal origins. Nevertheless, modern readers discover that Dante describes accurately the specific characteristics of their own felt experience. The nature of human pain and joy has not changed in the seven centuries since Dante, but the world has come to resemble Hell more than ever before.

Medieval Christianity provided people with a way to think about the world and to respond to its conditions as participants in an order larger than themselves. However complex, the world appeared to have a meaningful structure, and a human being's welfare appeared to depend upon understanding that structure and the ability to coordinate one's own life with it. During the succeeding centuries, Western civilization has operated largely on the assumption that the world must be shaped and managed to conform to human needs and interests. The consequences of that assumption are evident in the disruption of the natural environment and in the disorder of the modern soul.

Dante explained the title of his poem by referring to the classic definition of comic form as the passage from pain to pleasure: "At the beginning it is horrible and fetid, for it is Hell; and in the end it is prosperous, desirable, and gracious, for it is Paradise." It is also comic in that its language is "lax and humble," as opposed to the elevated and dignified discourse of tragic poetry.[48] But the poem is also comic in the sense that it is an image of human adaptation to the world and acceptance of its given conditions without escape, rebellion, or egotistic insistence upon human centrality.

Thomas Mann's Felix Krull and Dante's pilgrim have in common their belief that life is an art form. Dante's love of all life causes him to see the cosmos as an all-encompassing work of art in which all creatures can find fulfillment. This is not the tragic-pastoral vision of a world of raw materials destined to receive artistic form through skillful human manipulation, but the comic-picaresque image of a beautiful world that human creativeness should complement. Felix Krull's motto, "He who truly loves the world must shape himself to please it," describes accurately the meaning of Dante's philosophy and the strategy of his art.

Notes

1. Dante, *Epistola* 10, *Letter to Can Grande della Scala*, trans. P. H. Wickstead, in J. H. Smith and E. W. Parks, *The Great Critics* (New York: W. W. Norton, 1951), 148.

2. Dante Alighieri, *The Divine Comedy*, trans. Allen Mandelbaum (New York: Bantam Books, 1980), *Inferno* 5.51. Quotations used are from this parallel translation; numbers refer to canto and lines in the Italian text.

3. *Inferno* 9.5–6.

4. *Inferno* 29.60–63.

5. *Inferno* 31.37.

6. *Inferno* 7.103.

7. *Inferno* 18.106–8.

8. *Inferno* 18.113–14.

9. *Inferno* 1.31–50.

10. *Inferno* 6.16–17.

11. *Inferno* 13.13–14.

12. *Inferno* 17.10–13.

13. *Inferno* 17.9–10.

14. *Inferno* 13.4–6.

15. *Inferno* 22.143–44.

16. *Inferno* 3.55–57.

17. *Inferno* 3.18.

18. *Purgatorio* 1.17–18.

19. *Purgatorio* 13.2–3.

20. *Inferno* 24.25–26.

21. *Purgatorio* 10.46.

22. *Purgatorio* 3.27.

23. *Purgatorio* 27.142.

24. *Purgatorio* 27.130–31.

25. *Purgatorio* 18.19–20.

26. *Purgatorio* 18.49–60.

27. *Purgatorio* 17.91–96.

28. *Purgatorio* 21.61–63.

29. *Purgatorio* 28.2.

30. *Purgatorio* 28.112–14.

31. *Purgatorio* 28.119.

32. *Purgatorio* 6.45.

33. *Paradiso* 1.53–54.

34. *Paradiso* 1.70.

35. *Paradiso* 1.103–4.

36. *Paradiso* 1.116–17.

37. *Paradiso* 1.118–20.

38. *Paradiso* 2.139.

39. *Paradiso* 8.119.

40. *Paradiso* 8.142–44.

41. *Paradiso* 14.59–60.

42. *Paradiso* 22.134–35.

43. *Paradiso* 22.150.

44. *Paradiso* 33.82–93.

45. *Paradiso* 33.131.

46. *Paradiso* 33.137–39.

47. Jacques Maritain, *Creative Intuition in Art and Poetry* (New York: Meridian, 1955), 264–81.

48. Dante, *Epistola* 10, p. 147.

An Ecology of Mind

DOUG MANN

IN HIS *The View from Nowhere*, Thomas Nagel wants to see the world from Nowhere by way of presenting a model of knowledge and the mind that encompasses both the objective and subjective poles of human awareness. His goal is to harmonize the insights of scientific reductionism and a phenomenological sense for the individual into one big happy philosophical family. I would like to argue that Nagel stands at the edge of the precipice of the modern, trying to complete an uncompleteable project, namely, to reconcile the two major models of mind endemic to modernist understandings of human existence, the Mind as Machine and the Mind as Culture (or as a cultural product). I would further like to argue that the latter arose by and large as a reaction to the former, and has been perpetuated in something akin to what C. P. Snow in his famous inaugural address called the "two cultures." Lastly, I would like to sketch out, with broad and perhaps inelegant strokes, a "premodernist" (or maybe even postmodernist!) model of mind that is at least worth considering as an alternative to the two principal modes of understanding the human psyche, a picture of the mind that is a view from everywhere. In short, I would like to present an *ecology of mind* that maps the psyche *not* with the symmetrical grids of Cartesian geometry but with the open-ended curve of the organic.[1] The strangeness of this option is for the most part a result of the anti-historical and anti-catholic sense found in modern metaphysics and epistemology, especially from the lack of much of a direct awareness and appreciation of artistic and cultural history amongst present-day university-trained philosophers.[2]

A Bit of Metahistory

We can see the chief technology of the self as the self of technology, a product of the modern (post-Renaissance) world. We puzzle over the self as dual, reduced, fragmented, a fiction, and so on because we see Mind as Machine or as a product of Culture. The technologization of the self led to such diverse phenomena as metaphysical dualism, utilitarian ethics, and libertarianism and scientific socialism in political theory. Yet there is a common thread here. As Susan Griffin notes, we have evolved into the historical position of seeing natural power as something to be dominated: "We try to break the heart and spirit of Nature which is our own heart and our own spirit . . . We belong to a civilization bent upon suicide, secretly committed to destroying the self that is Nature."[3] Griffin sees the mindset that seeks to maximize control over nature as a tragic delusion. This leads us to look for solutions not in the natural but in the cultural order, which for Griffin includes scientific culture. However:

> the more this mind learns to rely on delusion, the less tolerance this mind has for any betrayal of that delusion . . . this mind has denied that it itself is a thing of Nature. It has begun to identify not only its own survival, but its own existence with culture. The mind believes that it exists because what it thinks is true. Therefore, to contradict delusion is to threaten mind's very existence.[4]

At the dawn of modern science in the sixteenth and seventeenth centuries, the self was defined in terms of the way that the natural scientist objectifies the world, in terms of mechanistic laws. Western metaphysics from the seventeenth century on is by and large a response to this technologization of the self. The first stage of our dialectic is to see Mind as Machine (Hobbes and Locke), or, tightly connected to this, to see Mind as Anti-Machine (Descartes) or as a Shadow-Machine (Hume). The mechanical model of the mind popular in the seventeenth century (e.g. in Hobbes) was a reflection of a given process of mind-activity, the new physics (e.g., Bacon and Newton). The basic impulse came from Baconian and Galilean mechanistic science. This image is still alive in our own century: the New Baconians of cognitive science use the language of computer science to revivify the corpse of the theory of the Mind as a Machine which rises, vampire-like, all pale and bloodless and hoary, from its grave, flitting about in the region between philosophy and psychology, throwing streaks of light across this usually gloomy space. For example, in the last chapter of Keith Holyoak and Paul Thagard's *Mental Leaps: Analogy in Creative Thought*, the authors tell us that "the human mind, in all its subtlety and complexity, is in its essence a machine." The model of the Mind as Machine has been recycled time and again within academic consciousness.

In response to this first stage of our dialectic, there arose in the late eighteenth century and later a view of Mind as Culture, for example in the idealism of Hegel and in the historicism of Dilthey, Croce, Ortega, most of the existentialists, and to some extent in post-modernists like Rorty. The Mind was seen as a *cultural product*, not as a mechanistic engine. From this image sociology got its start in the work of eighteenth-century thinkers like Adam Ferguson and John Millar. By the twentieth century sociology had evolved, in thinkers like Peter Berger and Thomas Luckmann, to a radically constructivist position, which sees the self as "constructed" by culture. This constructivist position is echoed in postmodernist analyses of the self as a text with multivalent meanings. As Taylor notes, poststructuralist thought is attractive because it offers a complete license to subjectivity, "unfettered by anything in the nature of a correct interpretation . . . of either life or text."[5] It pretends to "construct" the self *ex nihilo*. This constructivist view of the self stands in radical but symbiotic opposition to the image of the mind as a machine.

But a third possibility exists: to see Mind as a Natural Entity. I mean by "natural" not the nature of the objective-mathematical worldview of modern science, but something closer to the lifeworld of Husserl. By staying within the mythic and poetic sense of nature, we can avoid the agony of a self separated from that nature, and thus divided against itself.

Thomas Nagel, in his *The View from Nowhere*, wrestles with the whole problem of the "objective self." He wants to include the subjective point of view within a framework of an objective understanding of the world. His alternation between a view of mind as machine (the objective self) and as culture (the subjective point and view) leads to an unhappy *angst*, to an attempt to see the world from nowhere. But the primordial background of this nowhere is the "everywhere" of an unobjectified nature. Heidegger had it right in the first place, although he was handicapped by his rather obtuse and pompous literary style. We approach the truth of our being through poetic creation. Nietzsche's Apollonian/Dionysian dualism provides an interesting framework for this creation: we probably come most directly to the primordial, natural ground of our existence in the most Dionysian art form, music. Whether one prefers the pounding rhythms of contemporary music, or the sweeter strains of classical, music is the art form that hints most strongly to our grounding in nature.

The "brain in a vat" scenario of the contemporary metaphysician illustrates all too well the distancing of the mind from its natural source. This bizarre scenario taken from the pages of science fiction points out the mechanistic presuppositions of many of the commonly used metaphysical thought experiments. The mind-as-brain can be plugged and unplugged at will. As one recent popular work puts it, we in the modern age are all bastards of reason. Reason is the central technology of the self, the one that allowed the building of modern economies, modern social and political structures, and the modern hope of continual progress. It also holds out the illusory hope of a final solution to the riddle of the mind.

An ecology of mind would have to rely heavily on metaphor and analogy as theory-building devices. This could quickly lead to the charge, perhaps from behaviorists or cognitive scientists, that it produces no "results," that it can have no practical applications. But in what sense does metaphysics ever produce "results"? What has 2500 years of questioning done to improve our understanding of the human mind? At best metaphysics can paint the backdrop for some other more pragmatically orientated activity going on at center stage. It is, to a large extent, to use R. G. Collingwood's formulation, the science of absolute presuppositions. The sort of understanding of the mind that I see as the central focus of metaphysical speculation is the one that leads to a self-knowledge that is at the same time a roadmap to social, scientific, or creative action. Metaphysics in this sense is a roadmap for the spirit; it is up to other forms of thought and action to choose to be guided by the map, or to reject it and look for another.

Seeing the mind as a machine, for example in the project of cognitive science, has powerful cultural, political, and sociological meanings. The *Geisteswissenschaften* for a century have been seen as the poor cousins of *Naturwissenschaften*. This is reflected in the structure of our educational institutions, especially in our universities, and also in the social capital adhering to the various professions in a liberal society. The scientists, engineers, and their loose allies, the social engineers (lawyers, social workers, bureaucrats) are accorded high levels of social status. Of course, the representatives of culture are also given their due, but only the most successful artists, musicians, writers, and film makers are able to "make it" in the same way that even the average manager of the "machine" social metaphor can. I now turn to a more explicit social understanding of how the dialectic of the Mind as Machine versus Mind as Culture works in one specific case.

The Social Dimension: The Case of the Narcissistic Personality

It has become almost trivial to say that science and technology have divorced most of the human race (especially the city dweller) from nature. Yet this is as true today as it was over a hundred years ago, when British social critics like Blake, Carlyle, Ruskin, and Morris vituperated against the dark satanic mills, whether built of brick and mortar or of mathematics and scientific theory. Carlyle saw as the sign of his times that:

> Were we required to characterise this age of ours by any single epithet, we should be tempted to call it, not an Historical, Devotional, Philosophical, or Moral Age, but, above all others, the Mechanical Age. It is the Age of Machinery, in every outward and inward sense of that word; the age which, with its whole undivided might, forwards, teaches,

and practices the great art of adapting means to ends. Nothing is now done directly, or by hand; all is by rule and calculated contrivance . . . Men are grown mechanical in head and heart, as well as in hand . . . Their whole efforts, attachments, opinions, turn on mechanism, and are of a mechanical character.[6]

These social critics revolted against mechanistic analogies for social and political action, for understanding history, and, perhaps most importantly, for understanding the self. Carlyle himself knew that the analogy of the machine was what the German idealists used to call a "world historical" idea, or what Thomas Kuhn was later to call (if we extend his analysis beyond science in its strictest sense) a paradigm. Carlyle vehemently rejected this idea:

The living TREE Igdrasil, with the melodious prophetic waving of its world-wide boughs, deep-rooted as Hela, has died-out into the clanking of a World-MACHINE . . . I, for my share, declare the world to be no machine! I say that it does not go by wheel-and-pinion "motives," self-interests, checks, balances; that there is something far other in it than the clank of spinning-jennies and parliamentary majorities; and, on the whole, that it is not a machine at all![7]

Yet this "organicist" critique has all but disappeared from the cultural mainstream.[8] This is part of a larger process, the internalization of the machine metaphor as a cultural given, and the reaction against this metaphor expressed in the idea of Mind as Culture, with its attendant problems (e.g., ethical and cultural relativism, the "absolute" tolerance and lack of communal direction of liberal societies, and, most importantly, the emptiness of inner life).

As a case in point, I turn to the notion of the narcissistic personality. At the end of the seventies Christopher Lasch, in a cunning diagnosis of post-sixties American consumer capitalism in decline, showed how much of the contemporary cultural scene (and I would argue much of more formally political, sociological, and philosophical thought) can be understood as manifestations of the narcissistic personality. Lasch saw the America of just a few years ago (and no, not that much has changed) as participating in the dying culture of competitive individualism, "which in its decadence has carried the logic of individualism to the extreme of a war of all against all, the pursuit of happiness to the dead end of a narcissistic preoccupation with the self."[9] A central element in our culture's bankruptcy is that in its forward-looking bias it encourages an active hostility to the past, leading to a general leveling and impoverishment of the psyche.[10] In his *The Culture of Narcissism*, Lasch traces the role that the narcissistic personality plays in various contemporary cultural phenomena. One of the more interesting cases can be found in his discussion of "the psychosociology of the sex war." For several reasons—e.g., the collapse of "chivalry," the liberation of sex from its old constraints, the pursuit of sexual pleasure as an end in itself, overloaded personal relations, and the male fear of feminism—Lasch sees the dominant cultural image of sexuality as involving a flight from feeling. This divorce of sexuality from Eros leads to a cynical detachment and protective shallowness in the relations between the sexes.[11] The results include promiscuity without emotional commitment, sexual separatism (e.g., ideologically motivated lesbianism on the part of feminists fed up with men), or even withdrawal from relationships altogether.

This case is interesting insofar as it illustrates one of the ways that the demystification of mind and body, allied to seeing the body as a mechanism that requires periodic "servicing" (i.e., the paradigm of commonsense mechanistic dualism), winds up perpetuating the image of the mind as machine. Just as we can, on a larger scale, scrape the Amazonian rainforest off the surface of the planet and replace it with a network of strip mines, we can satiate our bodily lusts without impeding our emotional or intellectual lives. In this sense the narcissist fully accepts the mechanistic image of the mind just as much as he or she accepts a mechanistic image of the body. We can split the whole into its parts, and give to each what it needs.

Shifting the train of my argument to an alternative but parallel track, Freud was quite right to draw aside the curtain of rationalism and show us how much thought and behavior was engineered by the unconscious Wizard of Eros. To borrow a phrase from Erving Goffman, just beneath the way the self is presented in everyday life is the surging subterranean stream of the sensual. It flows into and out of consciousness with a jerky, inconstant rhythm. Despite this wavelike surging of Eros into everyday life, sexuality has been traditionally seen as less than central to grand metaphysical questions. The way that our culture becomes aware of and presents sexuality (i.e., in terms of what is seen as morally acceptable, the way that sexual images are manipulated by the media and "commodified," and the way that sexual issues become tied to broader social and political issues) I would term "submetaphysical." Remaining in the central dining room of culture, in metaphysics proper, makes one short-sighted as to how the delicacies of High Intellectual Culture (HIC) are prepared and served by those working in the basement. As academics we live too much the lie of the exclusivity of HIC from human existence, happy not to know what's going on downstairs. My ecology of mind would involve a call for a new species of philosophers, for sub-metaphysicians, whose purpose would be to relate the goings-on downstairs to those upstairs, to relate this sub-culture to HIC.

Ways into the Natural Mind

There are ways into the natural mind, ways to tear off the veil of Maya. We must however remember that the ecology of mind is at the same time an ecology of the human organism, and thus does not separate off the body as something to which we must reduce mind (i.e. physicalism), nor does it assume that the mind is "plugged into" the body, although still independent of it (i.e. as in classical dualism). This dominant narcissistic personality of our times tries to "get in touch with" the body, with its feelings, with its psyche, or with others, all evidence of a prior rift between mind and body produced by the technologization of the self. How do we de-technologize the self? Surely not by using further technological fixes. I propose what may seem traditional (if not romantic) roads to the natural self, namely:

1) Being in the presence of non-human nature, whether vegetative or animal. An "understanding" (*Verstehen*) of this nature.

2) Visual art, music, poetry that draw us into nature, whether as a picture of the external world or a tapping of the wellsprings of our "inner selves." Embracing primal cultural archetypes.

3) "Spiritual" experiences unmediated by institutional authority. The personal, unguided, genuine experience.

4) Love combined with sexual fulfillment. *Not* the well-adjusted personality or relationship, but the romantic image of courtly love informed by a modern sense of the social, economic, and political equality of the sexes. This (along with the other three ways) is a self-conscious appeal to a "dead" paradigm, just as the revolutionaries of the German peasant rebellions, the English Civil War, and the French Revolution, gave shape to their rebellions by wanting to return to a past golden age, by appealing to age-old, traditional rights, or by attempting to recreate the classical idea of citizenship.

In formal thinking, it is clear that we cannot return to medieval paradigms such as the view of the cosmos as layers of crystal spheres. But we can bring back into our individual and collective consciousness past ways of thinking, modify them to suit our own needs, change our way of thinking, and thereby change our social reality. This is especially easy to do if these images are highly metaphorical and abstract, and we do not become overly concerned with the concrete content they had in the historical period from which they were taken.

When approaching the issue of how we can find our way back to the natural mind, we should remember that what Charles Taylor calls the second of his three malaises of modernity,[12] instrumental reason, is firmly tied to the mechanistic model of mind. Instrumental reason is a central technology of the modern self in the sense that it is a way of building and extending that self through time and space. It provides us with much of the physical landscape of modernity (modern technology, modern cities, communications, transport, information storage and retrieval, and mass production), along with its dominant metaphysical roadmap. As Taylor notes, this instrumental reason has grown alongside a view of the human subject as disengaged, tied to a view of human thinking divorced from any messy embedding in the body, emotions, our dialogical situation, or traditional life forms.[13] But I do not want to claim that this should be seen, purely and simply, as a moral evil. The world we all live in, whether we choose to retreat from it or embrace it, is built on the techonological, social, and economic foundation of instrumental rationality. The point, however, for the sub-metaphysician is not just to interpret the world, but to interpret it in a socially critical sense, as a *social choice*, and not just as a random conglomeration of unintended consequences.

Quentin Skinner reminds us that in the contemporary human sciences there has been a return to Grand Theory in its traditional and architectonic sense.[14] I see an ecology of mind as part of this general return to grand theory. The physical and mental structures erected on the scaffolding of the Machine and Culture metaphors of mind are still quite solid and in no danger of being toppled over by a spirited critique or two. There is something invigorating and creative about the sheer act of thinking critically, provided that thinking is grounded in an understanding of and an at least preliminary empathy for the author, point of view, or social institution under consideration.

So the utility of the grand critique comes from both the act of questioning itself (dialectics being the mental equivalent of gymnastics) and from the slight possibility that such a critique will effect a few cracks in the wall of a structure that, as a whole, is in little danger of tumbling to the ground. There's just too much at stake, too many institutions built on the metaphysical grounds laid out by the Machine/Culture dualism, for us to need worry about "philosophical" damage. There are always lots of underlaborers around to sort out the little philosophical puzzles that academic, especially analytic, philosophy values so highly. We could all lie back on our couches and imbibe liberal doses of Huxley's *soma*, but it should seem obvious to any thinker of spirit that an active intelligent questioning coupled with a willingness to assert, at least provisionally, clear moral, aesthetic, and political positions is a healthier philosophical state of mind than the near catatonia of the underlaborer, grubbing deep in the mines of pure scholarship.

Mind, Politics, and the New Idealism

What we might need in order to allow an ecology of mind to bloom most radiantly is a New Idealism. Under the sway of this idealism, we would see Mind as *real*, and not just as an epiphenomenon of matter. But the reality of this mind would be expressed not in terms of *culture* but in terms of *nature*. The natural mind would be seen as the primary phenomenon, spreading itself out through "others," through machines, through technology, through culture, into the wider natural world. It would be an *expansive idealism*, for by redefining mind as a natural entity it would automatically include ways of knowing and feeling that dualists would normally classify as bodily states. Yet it would not be the sort of idealism that Nagel criticizes in this *The View from Nowhere*: this is the idealism that claims that the real is circumscribed by what we can know. It *would*, however, be opposed to the anti-humanist *expansive rationalism* that Nagel defends, for it would collapse the unhappy tension between "objective reality" and the subjective self into the unified field of nature.

Seeing the mind as an open-ended curve doesn't especially commit one to any given color on the political spectrum, even though many of the nineteenth-century organicists took conservative stances. It is perhaps wary of abrupt and violent political change, but the very essence of the organic is growth, therefore making it hostile to simply leaving things the way they are. This is why I call for a new idealism: this is in recognition that men and women shape their future, including their political future, by acts driven by economic, social, and political ideas. We should not see politics on an analogic par with blind, mindless vegetative growth.

I see a legitimate extension of the organic metaphor into politics as a partial abandonment of the politics of unlimited industrial growth, of class, and of gender (which I see as the last gasp of the politics of class, transferred to the realm of social biology) in favor of a politics of limited and ecologically intelligent economic growth, an attention to human decency as expressed in some minimum level of well-being for all who are willing to play some economic role in society, direct communal participation in the political process, and tolerance for dissent and cultural diversity (although not state-managed multiculturalism). This would not involve a fatal blow being administered to the fatted calf of consumer capitalism, but instead a series of good wacks to its rump. Many liberal freedoms are essential here, including the freedom of speech, of the press, and of public assembly. But a sweeping right to private property is certainly not ecologically sound, taking the latter term either in its literal or its metaphysical sense. The transference of the idea of spiritual fulfillment into the consumption of mass-produced goods is the antithesis of my central claim here, and I would thus reject a definition of freedom founded solely on economic liberties.

As with other idealisms, this "new idealism" would make the claim that the fundamental reality is mental, but a mental reality that shoots out into the world like ivy-tendrils crawling up a stone wall. Art and nature would cease to be mere entertainments or ways of unwinding from the travails of the workaday world. Our mechanistic Eros would give way to an at least partial healing of the bond between Lust and Love. It would leave science to the scientists and engineering to the engineers, recognizing the epistemologically-constructivist nature of these disciplines. The fundamental distinction between philosophy and science I see as that between *drawing a picture* of the world and *manipulating reality* to *construct a new world*. But sometimes when one draws an appropriate picture, the phenomenological world shifts ever so slightly to accomodate this new picture.

Notes

1. See Frank Delaney, *The Celts* (Boston: Little Brown, 1986), on the use of the "open-ended curve" in classical Celtic art of the La Tène period. I believe that traditional Celtic culture (and its dim echoes in modernity in such forms as music, poetry, and the visual image) can be seen as one of the prime origins of what I mean by the expression "ecology of mind," especially in its loving attention to natural forms.

2. Other than the socially acceptable "high culture." Popular culture is seen by most academics (outside of a few sociologists and rebellious spirits like Camille Paglia) as analogous to sex: necessary, but not really a legitimate subject of inquiry outside of a narrowly-defined field.

3. Susan Griffin, quoted in "Ecofeminism is Voice of Political Conscience," *Kitchener-Waterloo Record*, Oct. 16, 1993.

4. Griffin, "Ecofeminism."

5. Charles Taylor, "Overcoming Epistemology," in *After Philosophy: End or Transformation?*, edited by K. Baynes, J. Bohman, and T. McCarthy (Cambridge: MIT Press, 1987), 482.

6. Thomas Carlyle, "Signs of the Times," *Collected Works* (New York: AMS Press, 1903), vol. 27, 59, 63.

7. Thomas Carlyle, *On Heroes, Hero-Worship and the Heroic in History* (Lincoln: University of Nebraska Press, 1970), 171.

8. Although modern pop culture can be accused as by and large guilty of trivializing life and reducing the self to a commodity, to an engine to be periodically fueled with amusement and pleasure, i.e. the consumption of goods (including food, sex, and visual and auditory images), we can unearth within it the occasional (usually unconscious) revolt against the two traditional models of the mind. For example, in "new wave" and punk rock of the late seventies we find highly charged layers of irony and "world-historical" pessimism about the whole modern experience. Note Jonathan Richman's song "Roadrunner":

I'm in love with Massachussets / The neon looks so cold outside / And the highway when it's late at night / With the radio on / I'm like a Roadrunner . . .

And then later on, in Johnny Rotten of the Sex Pistols' hastily improvised version:

> I'm in love with the Modern World / Out of touch with the Modern World / But still in love with the Modern World / Roadrunner Roadrunner / Going a thousand miles an hour / With the radio on

Needless to say, for those who know what I'm talking about, this irony and pessimism comes out most strongly in British punk, e.g. in the "no future" attitude and antisocial anarchism of the Sex Pistols, or the radical social critique of The Clash or Belfast's Stiff Little Fingers.

9. Christopher Lasch, *The Culture of Narcissism* (New York: Warner Books, 1979), 21.

10. Lasch, *Narcissism*, 25.

11. Lasch, *Narcissism*, 322–23, 330.

12. Charles Taylor, *The Malaise of Modernity* (Concord, Ontario: Anansi, 1991), 4–5.

13. Taylor, *Malaise*, 101–2.

14. Quentin Skinner, introduction, *The Return of Grand Theory in the Social Sciences* (Cambridge: Cambridge University Press, 1985), 14.

Science's Missing Half:
Epistemological Pluralism and the Search for an Inclusive Cosmology

DAVID FIDELER

From Wonder to Reductionism

Wonder—the cosmological impulse—is the seed from which philosophy, science, and religion emerge. As Socrates maintained, "Wonder is the beginning of all philosophy." At the dawn of Western civilization, this sense of the world's structure and beauty inspired the first philosopher-scientists to investigate the deepest nature of the world-fabric and our own innate relation to it. Philosophy, in its truest sense, emerges from a desire to grasp our relationship to the whole and constitutes the search for an integrated worldview.[1] Similarly, cosmology and science, in their truest sense, are a search to understand the common order that embraces both humanity and the larger universe.

Even today the cosmological impulse inspires the greatest philosophers and scientists, but over the course of time the scope of the cosmological imagination has become radically diminished due to the increasing proliferation of technical knowledge and academic specialization. For Plato, like the Pythagoreans, there could be no firm dividing lines between cosmology, epistemology, ethics, metaphysics, and social philosophy. All were part of an integral enterprise, rooted in a desire to understand our place in the cosmic pattern. For Plato, the discursive intellect was a tool that could lead beyond itself, and the rhapsodic intellect, too, could powerfully illuminate our bond with the deepest levels of reality. With Aristotle's emphasis on discrete

An earlier version of this paper was given at the Institute for Liberal Studies Conference on Science and Culture, Kentucky State University, Frankfort, April 2–4, 1998, and was subsequently published in *The Proceedings of Science and Culture*.

41

categorization, this all began to change. For Aristotle, the philosopher was a universal thinker who took all branches of human knowledge as his domain, but his desire to divide and categorize marks an important turning point that would decisively influence the trajectory of Western civilization. But if ethics and cosmology were closely related in the thought of both Plato and Aristotle, it is with Aristotle's successor, Strato of Alexandria, that we find the first example of "the pure scientist." Strato specialized in the study of applied technology, and in his researches ethical and social questions did not apply.

With the emergence of modern science, the worlds of fact and value became further divorced as technical knowledge began to proliferate. For Aristotle, every phenomenon possessed a "why" or a final cause, but with the advent of Galilean physics the universe became mathematicized and stripped of teleological qualities. Science limited itself to the functional question of "how," consciously ignoring the question of meaning. Yet despite this ever-growing divide between fact and value, the greatest minds of the Scientific Revolution were passionately inspired to grasp what they saw as the divine order of the cosmos. Science itself, in many ways, emerged from theology, and this new breed of natural philosophers—Copernicus, Galileo, Kepler, and Newton—saw themselves as probing the sacred mysteries of creation. Having discovered the mathematical key which unlocked the harmonious motions of the celestial spheres, Newton exclaimed, "O God, I think thy thoughts after thee!" In this sense, there was not yet much of a split between science and philosophy, and it was only in the late 1800s that the term *scientist* was first coined.

With the proliferation of technical knowledge following the Scientific Revolution, specialization became a necessity. In the nineteenth century the humanities—which in the Renaissance were resources to deepen human life—became professionalized. In the academic sphere, the humanities fell under the spell of Germanic scholarship, scientific methodology, and objectivized, disinterested specialization. Yet in all such specialization, the integrity of human life was jeopardized. The cosmological impulse to understand our relation to the whole is an essential part of human nature, and when it is compromised, our essential nature is compromised, too. Owen Barfield has spoken of "the accelerating increase in that pigeon-holed knowledge of more and more about less and less," while John Naisbitt once observed that we are "drowning in information but starved for knowledge."

Despite the trend toward specialization, I believe that science and philosophy remain at their core the search for an integrated worldview, inspired by the cosmological impulse. The greatest minds of both the historical and modern periods have been synthetic thinkers who, while not repudiating the need for analysis, have situated the quest for knowledge within a larger cosmological context. But, given the stunning discoveries of modern science and the general discrediting of various religious fundamentalisms (such as literalistic readings of symbolic creation myths), what would it mean today to engage in the search for an integrated worldview? How do we reunite the worlds of fact and value? What contributed to the split in the first place? Moreover, what are the limitations of science—that human invention that has so powerfully shaped our world? These are some of the questions that I would like to explore in this paper.

My analysis touches upon questions of epistemology but also draws upon psychology; in particular, I explore our sometimes anxious attraction to modes of thought which are reductionistic in nature. While science itself has undermined the myths of religious fundamentalists, science itself is no less a mythic enterprise than other world religions.[2] Moreover, if religious fundamentalists are often inflexible in thought, the same can be said of equally dogmatic reductionists who propound an ideology of scientific materialism, especially since the ultimate nature of "matter" remains quite unclear.

Science, religion, and philosophy all emerged out of the same primordial sense of wonder. But sadly, they have all contributed to our present state of crisis through a failure of the imagination and an insatiable appetite for rigid models and systems of thought, which are then naively assumed to explain the infinite depths of the cosmic mystery.

By saying this, I do not wish to demean the wonderful contributions that science, religion, and philosophy have made and continue to make to human life. But everything has its shadow. Philosophy may begin in wonder, but then the intellect's tendency to organize, systematize, and dogmatize begins to take over. As we grow older and mature, the ego begins to harden; we become estranged from our emotional and life energies. The living sense of wonder and the desire for exploration become eclipsed, weeded out, or crucified in the interests of regularity and predictability. Western science, religion, and philosophy have reflected both the very best and worst aspects of human nature. If we are to inhabit a more life-enhancing world, we need to carefully evaluate and reconsider the past, present, and future of our intellectual and educational traditions. We especially need to guard against the powerful human tendency to reduce the richness and complexity of life to simplistic, inadequate formulas which are then enshrined in textbooks, catechisms, or mathematical equations, only to be over-thrown as obsolete at a later date. Finally, we need to understand science, religion, and philosophy as human activities and the search for helpful metaphors. For should we see the universe as being infinitely deep, it is ultimately not reducible to a limited intellectual or theological system.

Exploring the Boundaries of Science

> The more we learn about the world, and the deeper our learning, the more conscious, specific, and articulate will be our knowledge of what we do not know, our knowledge of our ignorance—the fact that our knowledge can be only finite, while our ignorance must necessarily be infinite.
>
> —Karl Popper

In exploring the boundaries of science, I begin with two stories. The first comes from philosopher Jacob Needleman's delightful book, *A Sense of the Cosmos.*

Needleman asks us to imagine a man who discovered a gun. The man took the gun home with him, but had never seen a gun before, and had no idea what it really was. Nonetheless, he discovered that the gun was good for pounding nails into a board. After having used the gun as a hammer with repeated success, he assumed that he had discovered its true nature—even though, in reality, he was quite far from understanding it.

While a simple story, Needleman's tale strikingly illustrates a major limitation of science. Since its inception, the truth value of scientific theories have been seen in instrumentalist or operational terms. Like the man using the gun as a hammer, empirical science works in a repeatable way, but offers no guidance as to whether we have discovered the deeper nature of things or even if the questions we raise are nontrivial. Science proves that we live in an ordered universe of repeatable patterns, but cannot tell us whether the patterns we have decided to focus on are more than skin deep. Like the man who mistakes the gun for a hammer, science could easily blind us into thinking we had discovered the universe's essential nature, when in fact we had touched upon the shallowest of surface impressions.[3]

The second story comes from the great physicist Arthur Eddington. In this case, the story is about a marine explorer who would lower his net into the sea. His particular net had a two-inch mesh, and after lowering his net into the sea on many occasions, the explorer concluded that there are no deep-sea fish less than two inches in length. The point of the story is that the man's methods of fishing were incredibly limited and incapable of revealing the true richness of deep-sea life. So too, if science is selective, it cannot claim that its vision of reality is comprehensive.[4]

The correspondence theory of truth claims that there is an objective reality out there which we can faithfully model in a one-to-one way. But it also suggests that reality is frozen and simple, and that our minds are capable of actively or passively mirroring this reality in a fully comprehensive way.[5] However, if the world is conceived as being infinitely deep or multifaceted, no simple correspondence theory of truth is possible, because the world cannot be fully represented by a simplified conceptualization.

Newton believed that he had once-and-for-all peered into the mind of God and discovered the Absolute Laws of Cosmic Motion. Laplace claimed that "Newton was not only the greatest genius that ever had existed, but also the most fortunate; inasmuch as there is but one universe, and it can therefore happen to but one man in the world's history to be the interpreter of its laws."[6] But general relativity undermined his assumptions of absolute space and time, and accounted for anomalies that Newtonian theory could not explain. Thus, general relativity proved Newtonian theory to be a helpful, instrumentalist theory, but not a comprehensive model that corresponds to the nature of things in a one-to-one fashion.[7]

With the advent of quantum physics it became more and more apparent that the way in which we question the universe determines the type of answers we receive. In his *Philosophy of Physical Science*, Arthur Eddington raised the question of whether scientific experiments actually "discover" or "manufacture" results. In other words, he wondered if advanced scientific experiments tell us more about how we can *make* nature behave than how she cares to act on her own.[8] Similarly, quantum physicist Werner Heisenberg maintained that "natural science does not simply describe and explain nature; it is part of the interplay between nature and ourselves; it describes nature as exposed to our form of questioning."[9] And as Neils Bohr maintained, "It is wrong to think that the task of physics is to find out how nature is. Physics concerns what we can say about nature."[10]

In this sense, all science and philosophy is a creative undertaking, the task of which is to expand and explore the boundaries of our learned ignorance. As the British poet Peter Russell points out, "Knowledge increases ignorance," for as our sphere of knowledge increases, the outer surfaces of the sphere expand and come into greater contact with the surrounding space that represents the volume of our ignorance.[11]

Reductionism and the Monomythic Imagination

> Every man takes the limits of his own field of vision for the limits of
> the world.
>
> —Arthur Schopenhauer

The Greeks saw the world as both One and Many. In terms of religious symbolism, this allowed the Neoplatonists to envision a Supreme Source of the universe, but also allowed them to imagine a multitude of gods and goddesses as overflowing from the ineffable One that existed beyond Being. In this way, they were able to strike a harmonious balance between monotheistic and polytheistic imaginations, between simple unity and creative multiplicity.

The question of the monotheistic and polytheistic imaginations— the One and the Many—is a topic that transcends the religious sphere. The beginning of Western science with the Presocratics involved the search for the One Principle—the *archê*—that lies behind the multiplicity of cosmic phenomena. For Thales it was water, for Anaximenes air, for Heraclitus fire, and for the Pythagoreans number. But we must remember that there are different types of "Oneness": dogmatic theologians have tended to speak of "the one correct way of looking at things," while mystics have tended to speak of "an underlying oneness" that links all things together.

Related to this theme are the perspectives of reductionism and holism in science. Reductionism is the analytical tool first elaborated by Descartes in his *Discourse on Method*: take any problem, divide it into its smallest parts, figure out how the parts work independently, then add them back together, and *hope* that the sum of the parts will allow you to understand the whole.

Holism, on the other hand, recognizes that organisms and other emergent systems possess a central organizing tendency that exerts a form of top-down causation on the parts. In this view, the parts of an organism are inextricably intertwined, and it is impossible, for instance, to study the circulatory system without reference to the respiratory system, because they are interdependent—and co-emergent—aspects of a larger, self-regulating system, the parts of which cannot be understood in isolation from one another.

Commenting on the problem of reductionism, Gregory Bateson wrote that

> It is the task of every scientist to find the simplest, most economical, and (usually) most elegant explanation that will cover the known data. Beyond this, reductionism becomes a vice if it is accompanied by an overly strong insistence that the simplest explanation is the only explanation. The data may have to be understood within some larger gestalt.[12]

Yet aside from reductionism as a scientific methodology, the term *reductionism* is commonly used as a description of the human tendency to reduce reality to an overly-simple conceptual framework and then take the resulting model to be synonymous with reality. Alfred North Whitehead called this widespread phenomenon "the fallacy of misplaced concreteness" and charitably identified it as "the accidental error of mistaking the abstract for the concrete"[13]—but it is often a cognitive fallacy influenced by underlying psychological dynamics.

Every human desires and needs to simplify reality. But carried to an extreme, this basic need becomes pathological. The ambiguities and possibilities of life are then reduced to rigid theological or scientific certainties. Prediction and control must be maintained at any cost, and by simplifying reality in such a way, troubling uncertainties are held at bay. In his book on *The Psychology of Science*, Abraham Maslow characterized this objectivizing need for control as a cognitive pathology that attempts to reduce the anxiety caused by uncertainty or ambiguous situations.[14]

In such a way, the monotheistic imagination and the "theological desire" for absolute certainty are transposed into many spheres of life, which then becomes colored by the psychology of puritanism, a byproduct of the monomythic imagination. While single-minded focus is often demanded in life, individuals afflicted with puritanical attitudes fix their minds upon one ideal and then dismiss all else as unworthy of their attention. Other modes of thought and experience then become things to be defended against. Imagined psychologically, puritanism is associated with the fantasies of the monotheistic ego which wants everything to be crisp, controlled, well-ordered, and unambiguous. Yet as Emerson wrote, "insane persons are those who hold fast to one thought, and do not flow with the course of nature."[15]

I do not want to make a case for either the monotheistic or polytheistic imagination and say that one is better than the other. In healthy people both can fruitfully coexist, and both can have their drawbacks. The downside to the monotheistic imagination is a tendency toward one-sided absolutism. It proclaims that there is only one correct way of looking at things, "one true way" leading not only to God, but also one true way to envision the world and to relate to others. The potential failing of the polytheistic imagination is relativism, the belief that "one thing is as good as another," and that there are no ultimate values worth striving for or embodying in one's life. If people under the spell of the monotheistic imagination can be stern, harsh, and judgmental, people under the spell of the polytheistic imagination can lack focus, be wishy-washy, and be overly experimental. Yet in their positive manifestations, both "monotheistic" and "polytheistic" imaginations are necessary, interwoven strands in the fabric of a flourishing life.

More specifically, the quest for purity can be identified as a deeply archetypal and numinous desire that has expressed itself in both monotheistic *and* polytheistic religions. Yet if the numinous quest for purity can be negatively envisioned as a desire for monastic withdrawal from the world and its unsettling ambiguities, it can also positively be seen as prerequisite for the emergence of the self-reflective, autonomous self, which by definition conceives of itself as being separate from the world. Seen in this way, powerful archetypal factors have been at work in the long evolution of the Western psyche, with the emergence of the modern autonomous self being historically anticipated by the leading philosophical, theological, and scientific intellects of the Western tradition. Not coincidentally, behind this development stands the powerful and charismatic god-image of a monotheistic divinity which itself stands purely, clearly, and distinctly separate from the world. Thus, in terms of the evolution of consciousness, the emergence of the Judeo-Christian god-image that stands separate from (and in some ways opposed to) the world, provided an archetypal and highly-charged charismatic image of the rational, autonomous Cartesian self that would ultimately differentiate itself from the rest of the world and make its judgments according to the criteria of pure, intellectual clarity and distinctness. Moreover, in addition to precipitating the emergence of the modern self, the Judeo-Christian god-image (whether theist or deist), also uniquely sanctioned the emergence of Western science. For not only did modern science initially emerge from the theological tradition, but the central idea of "scientific law" is directly dependent on the Western, monotheistic conception of God as a cosmic lawmaker.[16]

Myth and symbol possess the power to deeply inspire and catalyze human action. Yet while the monomythic tendencies of Christian theology and scientific theory helped to sanction the emergence of the autonomous self, they did so at the expense of driving other spiritual and epistemological possibilities underground. In this way, I believe it is possible to draw a significant parallel between the emergence of Christianity as a world religion and the emergence of modern science, which I also see as being colored by distinctive mythological ideas.

Christianity arose in a pluralistic and polytheistic world, a world suffused with natural divinity. Theoretically, Christianity could have represented one spiritual path among many, and initially arose as a highly complex, pluralistic movement before assuming a monolithic structure through its ongoing process of self-definition. Due in part to both internal and external pressures that were perceived as threats, developing Christian orthodoxy isolated itself in a singular and essentially puritanical way from what it perceived as competing ideas, deemed other spiritual traditions to be irrelevant if not corrupt, and, when it came to inherit the political power of the Roman state, used that power to suppress other spiritual traditions. Emphasizing the transcendent image of God as a creator or architect who is distinct from the cosmos, early Church Fathers such as Lactanius encouraged a thoroughly desacralized vision of the natural world—cleansing it of all divinity and spiritual significance—and then, in a monomythic fashion, proclaimed the new faith as the only true way to salvation.

While the development of early Christian orthodoxy is a complex phenomenon and must not be oversimplified, I attribute early Christianity's success in establishing a doctrinal monomyth in large part to the charismatic image of the One God distinct from creation— a powerful, archetypal image that ultimately precipitated and sanctified the singular conception of "One God, One Church, and One Truth." Yet a similar analysis can be applied to modern science at its inception. Rather than being a neutral, objective quest for empirical knowledge, emergent science possessed a distinctive ethos highly colored by mythological ideas. This is most clearly seen in the writings of Francis Bacon (1561–1626). For Bacon, knowledge is power. Science represents a "new instrument" of investigation—"a new machine for the mind"—that, together with the mechanical arts, can help to "establish and extend the power and dominion of the human race over the universe."[17] Nature should be "bound into service," made a "slave," put "in constraint," and "molded" by human ingenuity.[18] Only then will true advancement be possible. Knowledge is cumulative and progressive, and science holds the power to usher in a new, utopian era in which nature can be controlled for human benefit. In the same way that the early Christians distanced themselves from the pagan past and looked forward to the coming kingdom of God, Bacon contrasted the "moderns" with the "ancients" and looked forward to a coming scientific utopia. Writing with a similar grandiosity and prophetic enthusiasm, René Descartes emphasized the puritanical need to make a "clean sweep" in philosophy; displayed a need for absolute, indubitable certainty; believed that the scientific method could solve any problem (given enough time);[19] and, like Bacon, held that science could "make ourselves masters and possessors of nature." In the same way that early Christianity proclaimed itself the one way to truth, the emerging mechanical philosophers exalted the discrete, analytical intellect as the one pathway to indubitable knowledge.

Continuing in the prophetic lineage, when Isaac Newton was able to predict the movement of the planetary bodies using a few simple laws, it seemed that the New Age of rational enlightenment was finally at hand. Born on Christmas Day, Newton saw himself in messianic terms, as a link in the Golden Chain of Hermetic sages.[20] Edmund Halley, in his "Ode to Newton," asked his readers to "Come celebrate with me in song the name Of Newton, to the Muses dear, for he Unlocked the hidden treasures of Truth. . . . Nearer the gods no mortal may approach." In the eyes of Enlightenment Europe, Newton's accomplishment was mythologically pictured in divine terms, and as Theodore Roszak succinctly notes, "In the figure of Newton, the traditional imagery of prophet, poet, sage, oracle, all merge to create a cultural identity of superhuman dimensions."[21] (See figure 1.)

The stunning success of Newtonian physics eventually led many to adopt a reductionistic worldview in which the entire universe was seen as following the strictly deterministic laws of a giant clockwork mechanism. However, as E. A. Burtt pointed out in his classic work on *The Metaphysical Foundations of Modern Physical Science*, the mechanistic premise that all reality consists of dead, inanimate matter in motion, which could be modeled by mathematical laws, constituted an a priori *metaphysical* premise that shaped the direction of modern science, but could not in itself be tested.[22] In other words, the fact that Newtonian physics worked, did not logically support the reductionistic move that followed. It just created a fallacy. Scientific materialism assumed that the universe is matter in motion that can be predicted by mathematics. But when the theory worked, the materialists made the unwarranted conclusion that *all* of reality can be *explained* from a quantitative and materialistic perspective, rather than merely concluding that, indeed, the universe possesses a *mathematical dimension*.[23] This reductionistic move constitutes a prime example of Alfred North Whitehead's fallacy of misplaced concreteness in which a reductionistic, conceptual model is taken to be more real than the sensuous world of lived experience. As Theodore Roszak notes, "scientific reductionism is swayed by an age-old zeal to find unity in nature— even at the expense of agonizing distortion."[24] Under the spell of reductionism, an aspect or part is mistakenly taken to explain the all-encompassing whole, and one type of explanation is taken to *exclude* any other kind of explanation.[25]

Figure 1.
The apotheosis of Newton.

Edmund Husserl also addressed this dilemma with his critique of Galilean physics in *The Crisis of the European Sciences and Transcendental Phenomenology*. Galileo assumed that matter, quantity, and motion were primary realities. When these factors could be modeled mathematically, the abstract, conceptual order became more real than the tangible universe, which now was seen as dead matter in motion. Galileo's physics left us with a world of "facts," whereas the experienced relationship of living beings to the lifeworld (*Lebenswelt*) is one of meaning and context: when we see a painting, we experience a work of art, not just a collection of chemical substances. Ultimately the disengaged, quantitative mathematicalization of the universe resulted in what Hans Jonas called an "ontology of death,"[26] for if matter was the primary reality then life itself could only be seen as a freakish accident, a "disease of matter,"[27] rather than an essential aspect of the cosmic pattern. Rather than seeing humanity embedded in a biocentric cosmos, under the spell of Newtonian physics and the second law of thermodynamics, life itself came to be increasingly seen as an anomaly or, at best, a mere epiphenomenon.

As Ian Barbour succinctly observes,

> Scientific materialism makes two assertions. The first assertion is epistemological: The scientific method is the only reliable path to knowledge. The second assertion is metaphysical: matter (or matter and energy) is the fundamental reality in the universe.
>
> In addition, many forms of materialism express reductionism. Epistemological reductionism claims that the laws and theories of all the sciences are in principle reducible to the laws of physics and chemistry. Metaphysical reductionism claims that the component parts of any system constitute its most fundamental reality.[28]

In the same way that monotheistic Christianity strove to eliminate multiple ways of imagining the divine, scientific materialism has tended to assume that it offers the only genuine way of viewing the deep structure of the world. Seen in this way, science becomes a "candle in the dark" that is invoked to cleanse the world of every

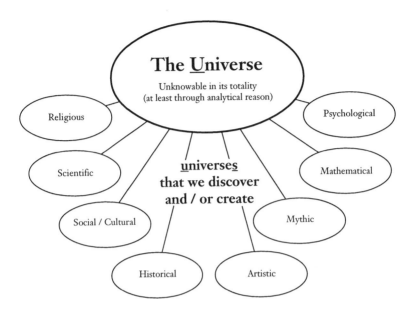

"*The image not only makes society, society continually remakes the image.*"
—Kenneth Boulding

Figure 2.
The idea of comparative cosmology.

superstition—except for the superstitious premise that scientific materialism represents the only true pathway to human knowledge.

Comparative Cosmology and Epistemological Pluralism

The ideas of comparative cosmology and epistemological pluralism provide us with the tools needed to move past the limitations of metaphysical and epistemological reductionism.

Physical cosmologist Edward Harrison suggests that the ultimate nature of the Universe itself—the Universe with a capital "U"—is unknowable in its totality, in both principle and in fact. Nonetheless, in our ongoing dialogue with the world, we humans discover and/or create multiple cognitive universes, which emerge from various ways of knowing and relating to the whole (fig. 2). In this sense, comparative cosmology is a study of the multiple ways of knowing and the universes that we discover and/or create.

Each worldview or way of envisioning our relationship to the universe sanctions and draws upon certain ways of knowing while ignoring others. In order to realize the fullness of what it means to be human, and in order to relate to the world in deeper ways, we need to develop the ability to look at the world from a variety of perspectives. Thus comparative cosmology points toward the idea of epistemological pluralism. We humans possess many ways of knowing, but no one way of knowing can fully encompass the whole. Rather than promoting epistemological relativism, comparative cosmology suggests that there are many valid ways of knowing and relating to the deep structure of the universe, and that *all modalities of knowledge contribute to our understanding of the whole*. In this sense, comparative cosmology can help us to revision epistemology itself by making a move away from the monomythic question, "How is rational knowledge possible?" to a more pluralistic inquiry of "What are the various ways of knowing and the relationships between them?"

In a practical sense, epistemological pluralism carries with it the suggestion that, if we truly wish to know and engage with the deep structure of reality, we need to become well-rounded, broadly-educated, and sensitive individuals. The more sophisticated our sensitivities, metaphors, and ways of knowing, the deeper our ability to comprehend the many faces of the whole. In the finest statement of epistemological pluralism I have seen, Goethe wrote that

> I, for my own part, drawn in many directions as I am, cannot content myself with one way of thinking. As poet and artist I am a polytheist; in my nature studies I am a pantheist—both in a very determined way. When I require one God for my personality, as an ethical being, this is provided for also. The things of heaven and earth contain such a wealth of value that only the organs of all beings jointly can encompass it.[29]

Epistemological pluralism also helps us to understand the place and limitations of empirical science. (See figure 3.) We can imagine the universe as a multidimensional object which can be viewed from a

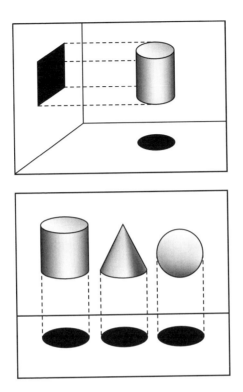

Figure 3.
The multidimensional universe.

variety of perspectives. Let us imagine that the circular shadow cast on the bottom is the view of the universe that quantitative science is capable of providing through empirical measurement. Let us further imagine that the vertical dimension is the qualitative, spiritual dimension of the lifeworld that can be grasped through the direct experience of beauty or creative participation on an aesthetic level. Quantitative science, by illuminating one important dimension of existence, provides a valid pathway to human understanding if seen in context, but misrepresents—and severely flattens—the essential nature of reality if we mistakenly assume that it provides the *only* valid window through which to view the world. More significantly, these diagrams show that the quantitative, spiritual, and aesthetic dimensions of knowing are not opposed to one another, but complementary. Multiple perspectives are necessary if we wish to deeply understand the nature of things. In this way, the idea that the world is infinitely deep liberates us from the anxious and reductive literalism of the monomythic imagination.[30]

Behind every epistemology there is a hidden anthropological assumption about the nature of humanity which the epistemological theory then attempts to justify. And, in modern philosophy, these assumptions have been highly dualistic, setting humanity at odds with the world. For empiricists like Locke, we are atomistic sense receptors adrift in a materialistic universe of discrete, impinging stimuli. For rationalists like Descartes, our minds reflect a divine, rational order—but it is the divine order of a white, male, European reasoner, in which the external world is merely a self-running logico-deductive machine, different in kind from our own essential nature. And for empiricists and rationalists alike, feelings are the grit in our cognitive wheels; they possess no real epistemological dignity, but tend to mislead the intellect. For Kant, the mind actively orders reality, but at the same time alienates us from grasping the true nature of the world, which we can never know "in itself." In each of these modern examples, we encounter an alienated vision of human nature, where the full range of human experience has been reduced to a limited way of knowing. For as William Barrett has pointed out, the error of modern philosophy has been to falsify the human self by abstracting the self into merely one modality or cognitive function, which then fails to correspond with our *actual experience* of the self and its relation to the world.[31] In short, modern philosophy itself has fallen under the spell of competing monomythic imaginations.

Thus in the world of academic philosophy, epistemology itself has embodied a suffocating reductionism through its predominate focus on the rational intellect. In so doing, it has tended to systematically exclude all other modalities of knowing, learning, and expression: art; love; intuition; empathy; compassion; immediate, nonverbal aesthetic appreciation of nature's underlying order and beauty; the dialectic of friendship, intimacy, and sharing; creative process as knowing and self-revelation—the list goes on. Rather than seeing epistemology as an integrative or pluralistic discipline that could illuminate the relations between the various ways of knowing, contemporary academic philosophy has sanctioned an amputation and fragmentation of the self into discrete categories which are not allowed to officially coexist.

Participatory Epistemologies and the Search for an Integrated Worldview

Philosophy and science arose from the cosmological impulse and the desire for an integrated worldview, but through the human appetite for system-building and conceptualization became mired in the sea of metaphysical and epistemological reductionism. In conclusion, I would like to suggest how a non-alienated, participatory epistemology can contribute to the ongoing search for an integrated worldview.

The starting point for all participatory epistemologies is the traditional idea of the microcosm, the idea that humanity is an embodiment of the world process. Because we embody the world, we are not alienated from the greater life patterns of the cosmos, but encapsulate them. This essential bondedness with the universe makes genuine, existential knowledge possible—deep knowledge that transcends the surface chatter of mere conceptualization. Or, as Wordsworth wrote, rebuffing the Kantian-like idea of epistemological alienation,

> How exquisitely the individual Mind
> . . . to the external World
> Is fitted:—and how exquisitely, too—
> Theme this but little heard of among men—
> The external World is fitted to the Mind . . .[32]

Similarly, for Schelling (1775–1854), mind and nature are just two aspects of a unitary whole. Humanity's estrangement from the world is a modern condition, for the growth of intellectual reflection has introduced a rift between the inner and outer worlds. But if we could penetrate through the remoteness of abstraction to the immediacy of feeling, we would experience our essential unity with Nature. For Schelling, Nature and Spirit—the "objective" and the "subjective" poles—are but different faces of the same underlying reality. Nature is "visible spirit," and spirit is "invisible nature." In humanity, nature's slumbering spirit awakens into self consciousness. But ultimately, "human knowledge" is *nature's knowledge of itself*, and nature and mind are only different aspects of one teleological unfolding. Schelling's non-dualistic, participatory epistemology thus stands in sharp contrast to the Cartesian epistemology of the Spectator.

One of the most fully developed participatory epistemologies is found in the scientific and philosophical writings of Johann Wolfgang von Goethe (1749–1832). While best known for *Faust* and his other literary productions, Goethe placed greater emphasis on his in-depth scientific studies which included research into geology, the nature of color, and the morphology of plants.

Goethe was a philosophical holist and a critic of scientific reductionism. In terms of his holism, Goethe saw all natural phenomena as related and co-implicated in one another.[33] In the tapestry of nature and living organisms, part and whole are intimately related.[34] "If you would seek comfort in the whole," he wrote, "you must learn to discover the whole in the smallest part."[35] In terms of understanding nature, "Theory," he wrote, "in and of itself is of no use, except in as far as it makes us believe in the interconnection of phenomena."[36]

While Goethe's orientation was holistic, he readily adopted and employed reductionism as a legitimate scientific method.[37] According to Goethe, reductionistic methodology is *necessary*, but becomes an impediment to true understanding if it becomes a one-sided ideology—if science become scientism. He writes,

> To be sure, what is alive can be dissected into its component parts, but from these parts it will be impossible to restore it and bring it back to life. . . . Thus scientific minds of every epoch have also exhibited an urge to understand living formations as such, to grasp their outward, visible, tangible parts in context, to see these parts as an indication of what lies within and thereby gain some understanding of the whole through an exercise of intuitive perception (*Anschauung*).[38]

Thus, in criticizing the emerging climate of scientific reductionism, Goethe wrote that

A century has taken the wrong road if it applies itself exclusively to analysis while exhibiting an apparent fear of synthesis: the sciences come to life only when the two exist side by side like exhaling and inhaling.[39]

As a proto-phenomenologist, Goethe articulated a form of "delicate empiricism" that strove to attend to the archetypal phenomena of the lifeworld while avoiding a retreat into abstract conceptualization. While not rejecting mathematics, Goethe wrote:

Number and measurement in all their baldness destroy form and banish the spirit of living contemplation.[40]

And, in a further reflection he notes

How difficult it is, though, to refrain from replacing the thing with its sign, to keep the object alive before us instead of killing it with a word.[41]

Theory does not explain, it merely describes. For Goethe, the true "theory" is present in the living phenomenon. The archetypal phenomenon does not stand above things like a Platonic idea, but is embedded in the world fabric. But in order to grasp this in its living completeness, the investigator of nature needs to purify his faculties to directly grasp the essential nature of the phenomenon. For Goethe, the ultimate goal is

to grasp that everything in the realm of fact is already theory. The blue of the sky shows us the basic law of chromatics. Let us not seek for something behind the phenomena—they themselves are the theory.[42]

While not rejecting experiment or quantitative analysis, an inclusive cosmology must transcend the merely quantitative and embrace the phenomenological. If the world is infinitely deep, all of our faculties of cognition must be brought into play. "The things of heaven and earth contain such a wealth of value that only the organs of all beings jointly can encompass it."[43] For Goethe, the idea that the world is infinitely deep—and the consequent necessity of epistemological pluralism—frees us from the deadly literalism of the correspondence theory of truth. Rational analysis is needed, but we must not depart from living experience into a disembodied realm of theory which is then deemed to be more real. "Contemplation, knowledge, divination, faith—all these feelers with which human beings reach out into the universe must set to work jointly if we are to fulfill our important but difficult task."[44]

Commenting on Goethe's philosophy of science, Jeremy Naydler notes that

> an object investigated by empirical analysis alone will reveal only as much of itself as the limitations of this method will permit. If we allow intuitive thinking, feeling and imagination a place in our scientific method, then—providing these are deployed in conjunction with exact observation and clear thought, and providing they are trained as thoroughly as our powers of observation and thinking—then a much fuller and more complete experience of nature will become possible.[45]

For Goethe, humanity is an embodiment of living nature. Since the world is deep and multivalent, we cannot know it completely through rational analysis or any other single faculty. But, by the same token, we are not alienated from nature, because humanity is a living organ of nature's self-revelation. Thus, "through an intuitive perception of eternally creative nature we may become worthy of participating spiritually in its creative processes."[46] It is this insight which makes Goethe's epistemology *participatory*. Goethe replaces Kant's epistemological skepticism with a living awareness that "there is a secret element of regularity in the object which corresponds to a secret element of regularity in the subject."[47] As for Schelling, in Goethe's perception we incarnate the world process, and the human act of knowing is Nature's own act of self-cognition. Nature awakens and inspires us to know her inner depths. Thus, writes Goethe,

> Had I not harboured the world within me by anticipation, I would have remained blind with seeing eyes, and all research and experience would have been a lifeless and futile effort.[48]

In this sense, the microcosm is bound to the macrocosm, an idea familiar to Goethe from his Hermetic studies. We are not alienated from the world, but inner self and outer world are reciprocal aspects of one underlying nature. Thus Goethe could write:

> Nothing "inside" or "Out there,"
> The "outer" world is all "In Here."[49]

In order to know the world in the very deepest sense, we must approach it in the deepest, most intimate way possible: "To know Nature, one ought to be nature itself."[50]

Strictly speaking, because all knowledge is participatory, the possibility of scientific "objectivity" is an illusion. We cannot intellectually stand outside of the universe as Descartes and Newton presupposed, because our organs of cognition are already saturated and colored by the archetypal energies and patterns of nature. In a quotation worthy of a quantum physicist, Goethe maintained that "the manifestation of a phenomenon is not independent of the observer—it is caught up and entangled in his individuality."[51] Through our perception, we participate in the creation of the world. But most importantly, in a participatory epistemology, the *observer* is changed and transformed by the encounter with reality, which further undermines the myth of objectivity. We cannot stand by as disinterested observers or pretend to be unchanged by the encounter without risking alienation from our very ground of being—and experiencing the terrible consequences that follow. Likewise, to understand the world in the deepest and most intimate way requires purification, training, reverence, and experiential engagement. Unlike Bacon, who sought to put nature on the rack and dislodge her secrets by force of torture, Goethe maintained that nature will reveal her deepest secrets only to those sincere individuals who approach nature in a loving spirit of reverence. Thus he writes:

> In the sciences, we find . . . innumerable attempts to systematize, to schematize. But our full attention must be focused on the task of listening to Nature to overhear the secret of her process, so that we neither frighten her off with coercive imperatives, nor allow her whims to divert

us from our goal.[52]

In summary, Goethe embraced holism where Descartes embraced dualism; he advocated epistemological pluralism where physical science championed reductionism; he saw the necessity of self-transformation in the quest for knowledge where the Enlightenment spirit adopted a mythos of detached objectivity; and where Francis Bacon defined knowledge as the acquisition of manipulative power, Goethe envisioned authentic knowledge as the development of insight, reverence, and contemplative understanding. Finally, and perhaps most importantly, Goethe provided an alternative to Kant's epistemology of alienation. For, as Richard Tarnas observes, while,

> like Kant, he recognized the human mind's constructive role in knowledge, he nevertheless perceived man's true relation to nature as overcoming the Kantian dualism. In Goethe's vision, nature permeates everything, including the human mind and imagination. Hence nature's truth does not exist as something independent and objective, but is revealed in the very act of human cognition. The human spirit does not simply impose its order on nature, as Kant thought. Rather, nature's spirit brings forth its own order through man, who is the organ of nature's self-revelation.[53]

Drawing on Goethe's participatory epistemology, Tarnas has proposed a participatory theory of scientific discovery. If the world is infinitely deep, no simple one-to-one correspondence theory of truth is possible. Nonetheless, in a limited way, scientific models do mirror the archetypal structure of the world fabric. Challenging Karl Popper's idea that scientific theories are merely a "lucky guess" which survive attempts to refute them,[54] Tarnas maintains that scientific theories emerge out of nature's own process of self-revelation. In his words,

> The bold conjectures and myths that the human mind produces in its quest for knowledge ultimately come from something far deeper than a purely human source. They come from the wellspring of nature itself, from the universal unconscious that is bringing forth through the human

mind and human imagination its own gradually unfolding reality. In this view, the theory of a Copernicus, a Newton, or an Einstein is not simply due to the luck of a stranger; rather, it reflects the human mind's radical kinship with the cosmos.[55]

In conjunction with this, Tarnas offers a participatory theory of paradigm shifts:

A paradigm emerges in the history of science, it is recognized as superior, as true and valid, precisely when that paradigm resonates with the current archetypal state of the evolving collective psyche. A paradigm appears to account for more data, and for more important data, it seems more relevant, more cogent, more attractive, fundamentally because it has become archetypally appropriate to that culture or individual at that moment in its evolution.[56]

Moreover,

The emergence of a new philosophical paradigm . . . is never simply the result of improved logical reasoning from the observed data. Rather, each philosophy, each metaphysical perspective and epistemology, reflects the emergence of a global experiential gestalt that informs that philosopher's vision, that governs his or her reasoning and observations, and that ultimately affects the entire cultural and sociological context within which the philosopher's vision is taking form.[57]

Thus, in both the emergence of scientific theory and the social context of shifting paradigms, powerful, archetypal attractors are at work. Scientific theories, philosophical ideas, and cultural movements are "socially constructed" in one sense, but in another sense even these social constructions are conditioned by archetypal, psychological realities—realities deeply rooted in the world-fabric and world psyche. More importantly, scientific theory is not arbitrary, but a genuine reflection of the world's archetypal structure, even though every scientific discovery remains, by necessity, limited and provisional.

Goethe's importance is that he does not reject modern science, but places science in a larger epistemological framework that *completes* it. Goethe provides us with science's missing half and allows us to move beyond instrumentalism and exploitation into a more life-enhancing, collaborative partnership with nature.

The Participatory Mind

In his book *The Participatory Mind*, contemporary philosopher Henryk Skolimoski presents a participatory ontology and epistemology fully congruent with Goethe's thought. Although Skolimoski does not cite Goethe and seems more directly indebted to later evolutionary philosophers such as Bergson and Whitehead, he is nonetheless clearly working in a similar vein to Goethe and offers a stunning critique of the modern scientific and philosophical project.

Skolimowski embraces epistemological pluralism and explicitly critiques the one-sided logocentrism of the Western philosophical tradition. Aristotle defined man as a "rational animal," but why not, Skolimowski asks, as a compassionate animal? For Skolimowski, all human sensitivities are evolutionary endowments, ways of knowing, and manifestations of mind. "Thinking is one of the many threads with which the tapestry of our sensitivities is woven,"[58] but it is only one aspect of our evolutionary heritage. Intuition, the moral sense, the capacity for deductive thinking, the aesthetic sense, reverence for life, and the power of creativity are likewise manifestations of the evolutionary mind incarnate within our being. While not rejecting the need for rational analysis, Skolimowski points out that the Western emphasis on logico-deductive thinking is more highly valued in the West than other cultures and is therefore culture-specific. By emphasizing rational intelligence above all other forms of intelligence, the effect of the Western tradition has been to impoverish and devalue other ways of being, knowing, and relating to the world.

Reality and mind are aspects of one another.[59] And both mind and cosmos are evolutionary. Life and mind are best pictured as "a growing tree of sensitivities. We have as many windows onto the world as sensitivities we have evolved and refined."[60] Because both mind and the universe are unfolding in a way that is at least partially nondeterministic, a simple correspondence theory of truth is untenable, because it is based on the idea of a static, unchanging world:

> As the universe is evolving, so it creates more knowable minds. As the mind becomes more knowable, it begets a more intelligent universe. In this process, truth does not remain static and frozen, but evolves with our evolving universe and knowledge. . . . Truth is a "happening"—not a frozen state of being.[61]

Despite the fact that reality is evolutionary and open, humans possess an anxious attraction to closed and deterministic models of thought: "Deterministic and mechanistic systems, such as science, subtly coerce us to close up, to cling to what is predictable, what includes no risk."[62] Moreover, "There is a congruence between the static (dead) universe that empiricism postulates and its concept of a static, entirely passive mind."[63] Nonetheless, true philosophy is an embodiment of courage and often revolutionary in intent. Philosophy is not an attempt to justify the rigid order of the status quo, even if it has frequently been subverted into systems of justification.

As our perceptions are refined and our sensitivities expand, so too does the universe we inhabit:

> We simply cannot find, see or envisage in reality more than our senses, our intellect, our sensitivities, our intuition (and whatever other evolutionary endowments we possess) allow us to find and see. The more sensitive and knowing we become, the richer and larger becomes our reality.[64]

Truth is a coevolutionary spiral in which we and the unfolding universe are intertwined. Truth is intersubjective and in some sense universal, but not objective or absolute because it is never finished.[65] It is species-specific, culture-specific, evolving, determined by the unfolding spiral of understanding, and an *event*.[66] Nonetheless, there does exist Absolute Truth:

> it is one gigantic truth about the whole universe in its transformation and unfolding. Depending on the context, we can distinguish various forms of participatory truth: religious, cultural, physical, formal, existential and practical.[67]

Truth is not handed to us ready-made on a platter, but the strength of our seeing lies with us, for "all perception, especially sophisticated forms of perception, requires rigorous training and development."[68] As William Blake wrote, "As a man is, so he sees."

With their emphasis on epistemological pluralism and the mind's active role in disclosing and thereby shaping reality, the participatory epistemologies of Goethe and Skolimowski undermine a simplistic correspondence theory of truth and help to illuminate what is needed in the search for an inclusive cosmology: not *one* way of seeing things, but *many ways* of seeing things simultaneously. For the more refined our sensitivities, the deeper our perception of the world, and the deeper our participation in the world's unfolding process. In this sense, we do not stand distinct from the world, but bring it to fruition in a collaborative, participatory endeavor. We are woven into the world fabric, and its unfolding is *our* unfolding and vice versa. The categorical imperative of epistemological pluralism is that we need to become well-rounded people in order to experience and understand the universe, and our own living relationship to it, in any sort of depth. In this sense, we cannot understand the universe without being changed, because the search for an integrated worldview necessitates our own transformation.

Notes

1. Many quotations could be given in support of this claim. As William James wrote, "In its original acceptation, meaning the completest knowledge of the universe, philosophy must include the results of all the sciences, and cannot be contrasted with the latter." Or, as Alfred North Whitehead wrote, "Philosophy is the endeavor to frame a coherent, logical, necessary system of general ideas in terms of which every element of our experience—everything of which we are aware, which we enjoy, perceive, will or think—can be interpreted."

2. As Karl Popper suggests in *Conjectures and Refutations*, "In a certain sense, science is myth-making just as religion is. . . . My thesis is that what we call 'science' is differentiated from older myths not by being something distinct from a myth, but by being accompanied by a second-order tradition—that of critically discussing the myth."

3. As Needleman notes, "When an idea or theory 'works' it always does so relative to what we are asking of reality. . . . I think the pragmatic successes of science need to be looked upon mainly as signs of the sort of questions we modern men are actually asking of reality" (*A Sense of the Cosmos* [New York: E. P. Dutton, 1976], 14).

4. Arthur Eddington, *The Philosophy of Physical Science* (New York: Macmillan, 1939). He writes: "Observationally grounded science has been by no means a failure; though we may have misunderstood the nature of its success. . . . The selection is subjective, because it depends on the sensory and intellectual equipment which is our means of acquiring observational knowledge. It is to such subjectively-selected knowledge, and to the universe which it is formulated to describe, that the generalisations of physics—the so-called laws of nature—apply" (17).

5. As Henryk Skolimowski notes, "When we adhere to the correspondence theory of truth, we assume that the universe is static, permanent, unchanging."

6. Quoted in E. A. Burtt, *The Metaphysical Foundations of Modern Physical Science* (London: Routledge and Kegan Paul, 1932), 18.

7. As Ian Barbour notes, the Newtonian worldview made three crucial assumptions: its epistemology was realistic, its physics was deterministic, and its outlook was reductionistic. All three assumptions have subsequently been

undermined by contemporary physics. Ian Barbour, *Religion in an Age of Science: The Gifford Lectures, 1989–1991, Volume 1* (San Francisco: HarperSanFrancisco, 1990), 96.

8. See Eddington, *The Philosophy of Physical Science*, chapter 7.

9. Quoted in Edward Harrison, *Cosmology: The Science of the Universe* (Cambridge: Cambridge University Press, 1981), 20.

10. Quoted in Ronald Pine, *Science and the Human Prospect* (Belmont: Wadsworth, 1988), 228.

11. Peter Russell, "Ruminations on All and Everything," *Alexandria* 4 (Grand Rapids: Phanes Press, 1995), 93–94.

12. Gregory Bateson, *Mind and Nature: A Necessary Unity* (New York: Bantam, 1988), 248.

13. Alfred North Whitehead, *Science and the Modern World* (New York: Free Press, 1925), 51.

14. Abraham Maslow, *The Psychology of Science* (New York: Harper & Row, 1966). See chapter three for a discussion and list of typical cognitive pathologies that are instigated as a means of avoiding anxiety.

15. Ralph Waldo Emerson, "The Method of Nature," in *The Works of Ralph Waldo Emerson* (New York: Charles Bigelow, no date), vol. 4, 136.

16. Thus while the Stoics had pictured divine law or intelligence as being immanent in the world, for the deists of the Scientific Revolution, divinity and divine law were envisioned as wholly transcendent.

17. Francis Bacon, *Novum Organum*, quoted in Carolyn Merchant, *The Death of Nature* (San Francisco: HarperSanFrancisco, 1980), 172.

18. Bacon, quoted in Merchant, *The Death of Nature*, 169.

19. As Anthony Kenny notes, "Descartes had immense confidence in his own abilities and still more in the method he had discovered. He thought that given a few more years of life, and sufficient funds for his experiments, he would be able to solve all the outstanding problems of physiology, and learn thereby the cures of all diseases."

20. For discussion see Morris Berman, *The Reenchantment of the World* (Ithaca: Cornell University Press, 1981), chapter 4, and David Kubrin, "Newton's Inside Out," in H. Wolf, editor, *The Analytic Spirit* (Ithaca: Cornell University Press, 1980), 96–121.

21. Theodore Roszak, *Where the Wasteland Ends* (New York: Doubleday, 1972), 211.

22. Thus, with the scientific revolution, there was a shift from the medieval scholastic categories of treating things in terms of substance, accident, causality, essence and idea, matter and form, potentiality and actuality, to viewing them in terms of forces, motions, laws, changes of mass in space and time, and so on (13). With the scientific revolution, there is a change in the prevailing conception of reality, causality, and the human mind. "The heart of the new scientific metaphysics is be found in the ascription of ultimate reality and causal efficacy to the world of mathematics, which world is identified with the realm of material bodies moving in space and time" (300). And, as Burtt notes, "These changes have conditioned practically the whole of modern exact thinking" (301). Summary and quotes from E. A. Burtt, *The Metaphysical Foundations of Modern Physical Science*.

23. As Burtt notes, the "founders of the philosophy of science were absorbed in the mathematical study of nature. Metaphysics they tended more and more to avoid, so far as they could avoid it; so far as not, it became an instrument for their further mathematical conquest of the world" (*Metaphysical Foundations of Modern Physical Science*, 303).

24. Roszak, *Where the Wasteland Ends*, 397.

25. Barbour, *Religion in an Age of Science*, 7.

26. For the ancient Greeks and other traditional peoples, the great mystery was that of death; for modern science, the great mystery is that of life. On this and the modern "ontology of death," see Hans Jonas, "Life, Death, and the Body in the Theory of Being," in *The Phenomenon of Life* (New York: Harper & Row: 1966). I am indebted to Paul Lee for his discussions of Jonas's work and Edmund Husserl's critique of Galilean physics.

27. Physicist Gerald Feinberg, quoted in Heinz Pagels, *The Cosmic Code* (New York: Bantam, 1983), 213.

28. Barbour, *Religion in an Age of Science*, 4.

29. Jeremy Naydler, editor, *Goethe on Science: An Anthology of Goethe's Scientific Writings* (Edinburgh: Floris Books, 1996), 46.

30. While multiple perspectives are thus called for, the type of epistemological pluralism I am advocating differs sharply from Nietzsche's

"perspectivism." For Nietzsche, there are no truths, only interpretations; but for the epistemological pluralist, multiple perspectives unveil multiple truths and expressions of truth, *all* of which contribute to a comprehensive understanding of the whole. My theory of epistemological pluralism also differs from William James's idea of a pluralistic universe, insofar as James's description of his "multiverse" implies a position of *ontological* pluralism. While an epistemological pluralist could accept James's idea of a multiverse as a metaphor, I find the idea of a single universe to be more economical, and prefer the metaphor that the single universe is "infinitely deep." In this way, epistemological pluralism does not inherently imply ontological pluralism.

31. For a full development of the argument, see William Barrett, *The Death of the Soul: From Descartes to the Computer* (Garden City: Anchor, 1987).

32. William Wordsworth, *The Recluse*, lines 816–821.

33. "Nature, however manifold it may appear, is nevertheless always a single entity, a unity; and thus, whenever it manifests itself in part, all the rest must serve as a foundation for the part, and the part must be related to all the rest" (*Goethe on Science*, 92).

34. "Nothing happens in living Nature that does not bear some relation to the whole . . . The question is: how can we find the connection between these phenomena, these events?" (*Goethe on Science*, 60).

35. *Goethe on Science*, 59.

36. *Goethe on Science*, 86.

37. See *Goethe on Science*, 57.

38. *Goethe on Science*, 49–50.

39. *Goethe on Science*, 55.

40. *Goethe on Science*, 66.

41. *Goethe on Science*, 33.

42. *Goethe on Science*, 91. Participatory epistemologies are phenomenological and Romantic, for as Theodore Roszak notes "Romanticism is the struggle to save the reality of experience from evaporating into theoretical abstraction or disintegrating into the chaos of bare, empirical fact" (*Where the Wasteland Ends*, 278).

43. *Goethe on Science*, 46.

44. *Goethe on Science*, 106.

45. *Goethe on Science*, 115.

46. *Goethe on Science*, 101.

47. *Goethe on Science*, 123.

48. *Goethe on Science*, 123.

49. *Goethe on Science*, 124.

50. *Goethe on Science*, 124.

51. *Goethe on Science*, 72.

52. *Goethe on Science*, 72.

53. Richard Tarnas, *The Passion of the Western Mind* (New York: Harmony Books, 1991), 378.

54. Karl Popper, *Conjectures and Refutations* (New York: Routledge, 1989), 95.

55. Tarnas, *The Passion of the Western Mind*, 437.

56. Tarnas, *The Passion of the Western Mind*, 438.

57. Tarnas, *The Passion of the Western Mind*, 439.

58. Henryk Skolimowski, *The Participatory Mind* (New York: Penguin, 1994), 23.

59. Skolimowski, *The Participatory Mind*, 39.

60. Skolimowski, *The Participatory Mind*, xiii.

61. Skolimowski, *The Participatory Mind*, 313.

62. Skolimowski, *The Participatory Mind*, 335.

63. Skolimowski, *The Participatory Mind*, 35.

64. Skolimowski, *The Participatory Mind*, 15.

65. Skolimowski, *The Participatory Mind*, 309.

66. Skolimowski, *The Participatory Mind*, 309.

67. Skolimowski, *The Participatory Mind*, xix.

68. Skolimowski, *The Participatory Mind*, 47.

The Northern Milky Way

This time exposure shows the northern Milky Way and the great rift starting in the constellation Cygnus. Photograph by Carter Roberts.

Negotiating the Highwire of Heaven: The Milky Way and the Itinerary of the Soul

E. C. KRUPP

As TRANSCENDENTAL TERRITORY, the sky is a destination for visionaries, shamans, and the dead. All require a route to heaven, and in many traditions, the Milky Way has functioned as the celestial superhighway. Cross-cultural analysis of Milky Way imagery outlines the abstract, philosophical, and religious dimension of the Milky Way and spotlights its role in the symbolism of spirituality. People grappled with the existence of death and the mysterious animating spirit of life, and found lessons in nature and references from the sky to integrate human experience with the rest of the cosmos.

As a zone of cyclic order and enduring structure, the sky has been allied with celestial gods. Through analogy, the Milky Way has been linked with the soul's journey beyond the Earth, beyond death, to the realm of the gods. The visual appearance of the Milky Way, its relationship to the rest of the sky, and its seasonal behavior inspire analogical relationships that link the domain of divine power with the destiny of the soul. Divine power is expressed, in part, in the pattern of seasonal renewal. For that reason, concepts of spiritual transformation are modeled, in turn, on the principle of cyclic renewal. Examples from Greek mythology, Finno-Ugric myth, California Indian ritual, European literature, and other traditions emphasize the worldwide appeal of the Milky Way as an Interstate on the itinerary of the soul.

Like a lost soul, the Milky Way is now abandoned and concealed in the light-saturated wilderness of our night sky. Most of us only know it casually or secondhand. When, now and then, we remember it, its

This paper was given at the conference on "The Inspiration of Astronomical Phenomena," Villa Mondo Migliore, Rocca di Papa, Italy, June 27–July 2, 1994.

name inspires the romantic imagery of a heaven where something pure and white streams through the stars and carries in its currents something as wholesome and filling as milk—milk, of course, flowing from no cows of this Earth.

A true measure of our loss of the stars was delivered at 4:31 A.M., Pacific Standard Time, on January 17, 1994. Everyone in Los Angeles, California, got out of bed together with the 6.7 Northridge earthquake, and fear of structural collapse prompted many of them to abandon their homes and apartments for yards and streets. In the week that followed, people telephoned Griffith Observatory to find out whether the strange night sky they had seen when they had rushed outdoors had had something to do with the quake. It was difficult, at first, to understand what these callers were talking about, but in time it became clear that they had seen the stars. The earthquake had knocked out the power all over southern California. The lights were out, and people not used to the starry sky had encountered an unfamiliar wonder.[1]

Because it is difficult these days to meet the Milky Way on its own stardusted turf, it is hard to appreciate its power to inspire our ancestors with visions of transcendence. For them, however, the Milky Way rippled and rolled through the night with memories of creation and guideposts to the gods. It was, in fact, a route to heaven, a celestial superhighway for souls on their way to exaltation.[2]

For ancient and traditional peoples, the sky is a transcendental landscape. It is a source of power and a zone of cosmic transformation. Those are the messages celestial objects telegraph to Earth. The stars and the Sun confer night and day. The Moon cartons the days with its monthly growth and decline. Together they all download the seasons, and the planets parade overhead according to their own marching orders. The cyclic changes of the sky seemed to drive and accompany events on the ground, and the heavens were recognized as a destination for shareholders on the stock exchange of transcendence. Those investors in revelations of divine power included visionaries, shamans, and the dead. All were pilgrim souls drawn like moths by the luminous attraction of the lights in the sky. Celestial elements, for example, in the myth of Adapa, from ancient Mesopotamia, illustrate, with

Figure 1.
In the northern hemisphere, the summer Milky Way emerges from the northeast, bridges the zenith, and plunges below the horizon a few hours after midnight. This all-sky photograph was taken by Dennis di Cicco in Australia and shows the great star cloud at the center of our Galaxy, located in the constellation Sagittarius, directly overhead.

economy, how the Milky Way linked the mysteries of the soul with the presence of the divine.

The story of Adapa,[3] who by tradition was one of the world's first sages, is preserved in second millennium tablets from Tel el-Amarna in Egypt, and from Assur, in Iraq. He resided in Eridu, which the Babylonians regarded as the world's first city. Adapa, then, belonged to the primordial time when the world was established in its present

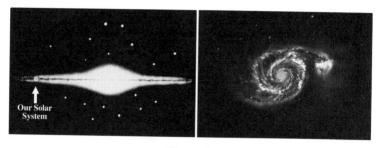

Figure 2.
The Milky Way is, of course, our edge-on inside view of the spiral galaxy in which we reside. Shown on the right is a photograph of M51, a typical spiral galaxy, looking down from the "top." The dark lanes or rifts in the Milky Way—shown in the accompanying photographs and clearly visible with the naked eye under very dark skies—are vast dust clouds that traverse the plane of our Galaxy.

order, and he personally played a part in setting things up the way they are now. His actions on Earth prompted Anu, the high creator god of heaven, to call him to the sky. In the sky, he encountered two gatekeeping gods, Tammuz and Gishzida. The theme of death's transformation is underscored by their presence, for they are seasonal dying gods of terrestrial fertility that have themselves traveled to heaven. Adapa's celestial journey is, at its core, the passage of death. To reach the celestial gatekeepers of life and death, Adapa takes the "road to Heaven," the Milky Way, and his encounter with them and with Anu denies him everlasting life. Accordingly he returns to Earth as a mortal soul. Although the motives of the gods are obscure, the story seems to account for human mortality and contrasts it with a realm of eternal life and divine power that is reached via the Milky Way.

I intend to explore this symbolic aspect of the Milky Way by sampling the character of Milky Way imagery, analyzing its content, and establishing its function. Cross-cultural comparison will, I hope, identify some primary themes of this imagery and clarify how the astronomical character of the Milky Way articulates those themes.

Graphic representation, mythic narrative, and ritual invocation of the Milky Way all are activated by analogy. Analogy organizes and classifies experience, and celestial analogy is primarily structured by the pattern of cyclical renewal. We see a resemblance between the cyclical pattern of celestial phenomena and the transformative character of nature. We also understand that human behavior, celestial phenomena, and seasonal change are directly and physically related. For these reasons, analogical relationships have linked spiritual transformation with celestial transformation and with the seasonal connotations of the sky.[4]

To understand the analogical use to which we have put the Milky Way, we have to isolate the aspects of the Milky Way that invite metaphor. The Milky Way is, of course, an element of the night and a companion of the stars. Although it, like the stars, glows with inner light, the stars themselves are numerous and dispersed. The Milky Way, on the other hand, is a continuous belt of light that arcs through the ranks of solitary stars. The stars are like fires, but the Milky Way is fluid. The stars are simple and elemental, but the Milky Way has a structure. Its relationship with Earth and its appearance in the sky are products of its placement, its shape, and its extent.

The Milky Way looks like a gossamer-white cummerbund on the black tuxedo of the night (fig. 1). It is a pale and frayed belt that rings the sky, but we only see half of it at any one time. It resembles, then, a ribbon thrown across the sky. It connects one side of the horizon with another by vaulting over the Earth, but the angle it makes with the ground depends upon where you are located and how the spinning Earth has lifted the Milky Way into the sky. Half of the circular band rolls out of the east like a great dark wave revealed by the stately folds and flows of a whitecapped crest that looks like it will take eons to break. As it rises, like a frosty rainbow, it slowly swivels with respect to the ground. At one point or another, the semicircle of Milky Way that has been brought into view crosses through the zenith, and the Milky Way truly bridges heaven. From there it drops steadily and quietly, with dignity and manners, down to the west, while another length of this loop of heavenly rope emerges in the east.

The exact configuration of the Milky Way at a particular time of night—say just after dark, at midnight, or just before dawn—varies seasonally, and so the Milky Way's posture in heaven has seasonal value. Because it completely encircles the sky, it intersects other great celestial circles, including the ecliptic. The ecliptic crosses the Milky Way in the general vicinity of the solstices, and these key seasonal stations of the Sun sometimes also associate certain aspects and arrangements of the Milky Way with seasonal transformation.

Of course, the Milky Way is really the inside, edge-on view of the Galaxy, the vast, spiral-armed swarm of 200 billion stars we ourselves inhabit (fig. 2). This system of stars, gas, and dust resembles a flat disk with a central bulge. It is about 70,000 light years in diameter, and we are located on a satisfyingly blue speck of debris in orbit around a modest star that is swimming its way through the rest of the pack about two-thirds of the way out from the center. Because most of the obvious (but nevertheless distant) stars of the Milky Way are confined to the disk, their light merges into the soft band that seems to surround us. Interstellar dust between us and the more distant stars obscures our view of the brilliant bulge in the center and sculpts the Milky Way with polyps, tendrils, and tears that make it look like it is sloshing through the sky. So the Milky Way connects heaven with Earth and provides a path for the journey. Although its light seems faint compared with the focused brilliance of single stars, it is huge. It belts the entire sky and completely embraces the Earth. It moves with a deliberate grandeur that suggests that somehow it, too, controls the decorum of heaven and affairs below.

Explicit links between the seasonal configuration of the Milky Way, the seasonal renewal of the natural world, and the transformation of the soul are evident in Finno-Ugric tradition.[5] For the Finns, the Lapps, Estonians, and other related peoples, the autumn Milky Way, as it is seen just after dark, signals and directs the path, to the south, of migrating birds. The Milky Way at this time has one end planted in the northeast. The band reaches high through the canopy of heaven and roots its other end in the southwest. Cygnus the Swan wings its way along this section of the Milky Way (fig. 3). Its flight path is southwest, and its stars are nearing the time when they will leave the night sky. The celestial swan is, then, departing heaven at the same time and in the same direction as the ducks, geese, swans, and other migrating birds of the world below are also leaving their summer home. Even the names of the Milky Way reflect this connection.[6] It

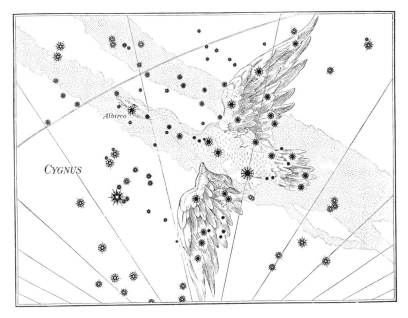

Figure 3.
Cygnus the Swan migrates through the seasons along with the Milky Way. The ancients placed the bird at the place where the Milky Way splits into two branches, and it appears to fly south along this starry trail. Engraving from Johann Bayer, *Uranometria* (1603).

is the "Birds' Road" to the Finns and Estonians (fig. 4). There are several Lapp names, and they all carry the same connotation—"Path of Birds," "Birds' Stair," and "Year Mark."[7] Voguls and Ostyaks, who reside in the Ob River Basin and the Urals of northwest Siberia, say the Milky Way is the "Ducks' Road" or the "Southern Birds' Road." Turkic and Tatar (Tartar) speakers of Siberia shared the same tradition, and among them we find names like "Birds' Way" and "Wild Ducks' Way."

Thus, the Milky Way's seasonal value as a herald of the winter to come is linked with the seasonal behavior of the migrating waterfowl. Their absence is, in fact, one of the elements that defines winter. This configuration of the Milky Way is also a component of the coming winter, and for that reason, the Milky Way operates, like the migrating birds, as an emblem of seasonal death and renewal.[8] This is, in fact, exactly what the Uralic peoples say. The birds are said to travel at night and are guided by the Milky Way back to their winter home, the "Land of Birds." To get there, they must vanish beyond "the edge of the sky." In their winter quarters, they are said to be killed, but by spring they are magically resurrected and return north for another season. The death and revival of migrating birds transforms their seasonal absence into an encounter with the supernatural forces that maintain world order through cyclic change.

The bittersweet Milky Way story the Estonians tell about Lindu, the Queen of the Birds,[9] extends the range of seasonal metaphor into territory traveled by the soul. It is a tale of abandoned love and forgotten obligation. Lindu was the daughter of Uko, the god of thunder and master of the sky. Lindu was a looker, and her admirers included Sun, Moon, and North Star. All of them courted her with extravagant gifts and attention, but she rejected these suitors as unsuitable and instead lost her heart to Northern Lights. They were engaged, but soon after her betrothal was announced, Northern Lights informed her that he had business to attend to back in his own neighborhood. Promising to return for the wedding, he departed for the north, and Lindu waited for him as the seasons turned. Dressed in her wedding gown, she remained on standby. Spring came and went, and the summer passed, too. By autumn, she realized that Northern Lights had left her at the altar. He was, of course, a poor marital risk— more style than substance. But that didn't comfort her broken heart.

Lindu's preoccupation with lost love distracted her from her duties to the birds. Their spring nesting had passed without her protective care. Now autumn had arrived, and Lindu's neglect threatened their passage south. Uko realized the birds needed her help, and so he solicited the South Wind, who quietly lifted Lindu into heaven. That wedding veil she had been wearing since waving goodbye to Northern Lights now ruffled across the sky. It is the Milky Way, and it guides Lindu's birds south for the winter.

Astronomical elements of this story make sense. The *aurora borealis* is fickle, but it can date the Milky Way only when the nights are dark and long and both can be seen. In these far northern latitudes, the short summer night provides little opportunity for the pair to meet in

Figure 4.
The Milky Way appears to be symbolized by a line of birds in flight on this Evenki (Oroqen or Tungus) shaman's drum from Siberia.

luminous love. And, of course, the seasonal arrangement of the early evening's Milky Way echoes the behavior of the migrating birds. Their seasonal departure and return reflected, in turn, the death and renewal of nature. Nature's capacity for seasonal renewal has been embodied in the concept of a primordial Mother Goddess since prehistoric times. Often associated with the life-giving, life-taking Earth, the vocabulary of her symbols included migrating waterbirds. They operated as emblems of death and rebirth. Lindu herself personifies the process and, as Queen of the Birds, is the Mother Goddess in yet one more disguise. Each year she brings the world back to life.

Migrating birds are like souls that depart this world for the realm of the dead, and the Lapps regard the soul as a bird. The Voguls called their high god the Guardian of the World, and adopting the shape of a swan, he conducted the souls of the dead to the south.[10] They traveled there *via* the Milky Way.

Winter, the Voguls say, is what happens when the Guardian of the World sleeps. In spring, when he wakes up, he sends the birds back to the north. Sleep is itself a kind of temporary death linked with dreams and shamanic trance. In the trance, the shaman flies, like a bird or a soul, to supernatural realms, the kingdoms of Heaven and Hell. He acquires spiritual knowledge and magical power on these journeys and "returns to life" when he emerges from the trance.

Seasonality and the Milky Way take on a spiritual connotation through Finno-Ugric beliefs about the fate of migrating birds. This network of meaning allows us to see the sequence of associations that have been layered upon a footing of celestial and seasonal transformation:

Milky Way	flight path of departing birds
Winter	absence of migrating waterfowl
Death	soul's departure from Earth
Shamanic trance	spirit journey to Other World
Initiation of youth	transformation to maturity

By extending the metaphor of migrating birds to the spirits of the dead, to the souls of the shamans, and to the personalities of adolescents, the Milky Way becomes a road for the dead, a route for supernatural travel to the spirit realm, and an emblem of ritual transformation to adulthood. Our own name for the Milky Way seems, however, to be unrelated to these concepts. It comes to us from the Romans, who called it *Via Lactea*, or Milky Way.[11] The Romans got the idea from the Greeks, who saw in it a celestial stream of spilled milk. Their word for it was *kuklos galaxias*, or milky circle.[12] In the earliest extant collection of Greek star myths, the *Katasterismoi* of the Pseudo-Eratosthenes (perhaps compiled in the first century C.E. from sources two to three centuries older), the "Galaxy," or Milky Way, is said to be "one of the heavenly circles," and is linked with the story of Heracles (*Katasterismoi* 43).[13] Immortality was conferred upon all who nursed at Hera's breast, but Hera, consort of Zeus and a Mother Goddess of Olympian proportion, had little inclination to offer a nipple to illegitimate children fathered by her husband on those easy Earth girls. Hermes, however, caught Hera napping and held Heracles to her bosom for a sip from the divine dairy. Awakened with the surprise of Heracles tippling at her teat, she spurned the child and spilled the milk (fig. 5). It rolled and flowed all down her breast and

Figure 5.

Greek myth attributes the Milky Way to spray from Hera's breast. She woke to find the infant Heracles sucking there and had no interest in mothering her consort's illegitimate children. Reflex kept her breast pumping even after Heracles was thrown off, and milk fountained into the sky. The painting is Tintoretto's *The Origin of the Milky Way* (National Gallery, London).

across the sky to create the Milky Way.

Although this story at first seems to share nothing in common with the spiritual dimension of the Milky Way in Finno-Ugric tradition, it does concern transcendence and immortality. The origin of the Milky Way (portrayed so romantically by Tintoretto) is, in fact, a tale that links the Milky Way to divine power and the character of the soul. Heracles is transformed by his contact with the fluid that runs in the Milky Way, and the myth in that sense tells us that the Greeks saw a connection between the immortal spirit of the divine and the Milky

Way. The theme is reiterated in another treatment of this tale in which the Milky Way spurts from the breast of Rhea, another primordial Mediterranean Mother Goddess. In *Poetica Astronomica*, the Latin poet Hyginus includes several versions.[14] In one, the milk flies as Juno fortifies Mercury with the milk of divine kindness. In another, Rhea nurses a stone she tells her child-eating husband Saturn is his son Jupiter. Unable to suckle a stone, Rhea gushes across the sky but still manages to fool her Saturn into swallowing the stone.

People all over the world, of course, have noticed the Milky Way and have described it in many ways. For the Greeks, it was a stream of divine milk. The ancient Hindus and the Aborigines of Australia said it was a celestial river. Others thought of it as a highway in the sky. In most cases, its affiliation with the power of the gods and destiny of souls is well developed.

Hindu names for the Milky Way include *Chhayapatha*, "the path of the shades of the dead," and *Somadhara*, "the stream of soma."[15] Soma was the elixir of divinity and immortality won by the gods in their tussle with the demons at the time of the creation of the present world order. Both names carry the connotation of the soul's transcendental journey. The ambrosial currents of heaven flow through the sky, pour through a hole at the top of the sky, ripple over the North Star, and cascade upon the summit of the central mountain of the world, Mount Sumeru. Sumeru, in turn, is the world axis and is associated with Mount Kailasa, the Himalayan peak at the source of the Ganges River. The celestial river is regarded as a heavenly counterpart of the terrestrial Ganges, and the goddess Ganga is the divine personification of the earthly Ganges. She is the daughter of the Himalayas, where the Ganges originates. The Milky Way is said eventually to merge with the Ganges and with its underworld counterpart at the holy city of Benares. Because they are all the same river, they link the gods and the dead with the living. Pilgrimages on behalf of ancestors are made to the river. Through funeral ritual, the Ganges assists souls on their way to the world of the dead. Regarded as pure and cleansing, the waters themselves are the nectar of immortality. The Ganges is known as the River of Heaven, that is, the Milky Way. It is a river that transcends worlds, and it delivers to the dead the bliss of the beyond.

Certainly in California, the Milky Way had an esoteric and spiritual meaning. In fact, throughout California, many Indians made a corridor to the afterlife out of the Milky Way.[16] The Chemehuevi of the Mojave Desert called it the "Ghost (or Spirit) Trail" and believed that the spirits of the dead journey far to the north to the Spirit Land.[17] Even in the far northwest part of California, we encounter the same theme—a husband's pursuit of the soul of his dead wife—among the Shasta Indians. They said the trail she walked to the other world was the Milky Way. They told a story about a man who tried to follow his dead wife to that realm, and he failed to retrieve her from death's grasp.[18] Maidu Indians, who lived near Sacramento, believed that a soul found its way to the next world by climbing into the sky with the Sun. At noon, the soul reached the highest point it could go in the company of the Sun, and from there it embarked on its own for the Milky Way. That path carried it to its heavenly home.[19]

In the northeastern part of California, Floyd Buckskin, a member of the Pit River Indians Tribal Council, has reported Ajumawi beliefs about the journey to the land of the dead. Departing from the body at death, the shadow, or soul, migrates southwest. It leaves the Fall River Valley, and at the Pit River, it turns west and continues to the Pacific Ocean. Before picking up the trail to the west, the shadow must first go everywhere it had ever visited while it was still alive. Arriving at the coast, the shadow heads north and soars to the summit of Mount Shasta. From the mountain top, the shadow transfers to the Milky Way. The Ajumawi call the Milky Way "the pathway of spirits." When the Milky Way arcs over Mount Shasta, the shadow is able to travel east and join Hewisi the Creator at sunrise. This itinerary has a seasonal aspect, for the Milky Way climbs out of the northeast before dawn at summer solstice. The Ajumawi say the Milky Way is aligned at this time with the trail followed on the Earth by the dead and aligned with the Sun as well. Because these celestial and terrestrial routes are all so congruent, it is easier for those who die at this time of year to travel to the Creator.[20]

Graphic representations of the Milky Way appear in ground displays prepared for the coming-of-age ceremonies for Kumeyaay youth. The Kumeyaay, who occupied territory in what is now San

Diego County, prepared a ground drawing for the adolescent boys that included a white horizontal band in the middle of a ring, and the Kumeyaay confirmed that the band stands for the Milky Way.[21] Another group of Kumeyaay, sometimes known as the Tipai, incorporated celestial symbols into a ground display with a different format. In this one, the white cord stretches diagonally above several dots known to represent stars and stands for the Milky Way, the "backbone of the night."[22]

Constance Goddard Du Bois' 1908 study of the religion of the Luiseño confirms their belief that the Milky Way is a spirit, and the place where their spirits go at death. The Milky Way appears in the Luiseño story of Creation and figures prominently in Luiseño spiritual life. Key ceremonies included coming-of-age initiatory rites for the youth, organized and conducted by shamans, and funeral rituals connected with the destiny of the dead, and both incorporated Milky Way imagery.[23]

A sacred down cord used in Luiseño ritual is specifically linked with the Milky Way, and the Milky Way is frequently mentioned in the mourning songs. Its name is Luiseño is *Piiwish Ahuutax*. *Piiwish* means "whitish" and "headband,"[24] while the word *Ahuutax* means "raised up" or "exalted one," and is used only with the Milky Way.[25]

In the Luiseño Creation myth, the cosmos starts empty and quiet.[26] The only thing that existed was *Kivish Atakvish*, or Alone-and-empty. In time, another mysterious being arrived. This was Pale White, and Pale White created two round things. At this point, Pale White left and was not seen again. Although Pale White's esoteric meaning is not known with certainty, another version of this story implies that Pale White is a mystical, primordial, abstract personification of the Milky Way. In three days, the two round things came to life. They were male and female. They recognized each other and argued about who was older and who had seniority in this universe. She identified herself as Alone-and-empty. He claimed affinity with the sky. After they mated, he departed and became the sky. As Mother Earth, she gave birth to all of the First People and sent these children to cardinal directions and the center, which establish the order of the Luiseño cosmos. The design of ground displays used in Luiseño boys' initiation rituals was based on this concept of cardinality and was said to symbolize the world.[27]

Mother Earth and Father Sky eventually realized that this universe they had populated with their children was still completely in the dark. The children traveled around a bit and via San Bernardino and Lake Elsinore finally wound up in Temecula. All the while they kept bumping into each other because it was so dark. In Temecula, the First People decided it was better to light a candle than curse the darkness, and so they made Temet the Sun. They got everybody together to launch him into the sky with a milkweed fiber net. At first he went north, but because that wasn't right, they put him back in the net and tried again. That time he went south and came back. So they catapulted the Sun into the west. He traveled a little bit that way but then came back once more. Finally, they tossed him toward the east, and he continued on his present course. Then, through further ritual action, they put the Sun on an annual itinerary between its northern and southern limits.[28]

We know from Du Bois that the Luiseño symbolized the Milky Way with a net known as the *wanawat*.[29] This net was placed in a trench, dug roughly in the shape of a human body. It was part of the boys' initiation ceremony, which was associated with the Chingichngish religion practiced by the Luiseño and many other southern California Indians at the time Boscana encountered them. Three flat stones were spaced along the length of the net. The boys had to enter the trench and hop from stone to stone. A misstep was regarded as an omen of a short life for any boy who lost his balance.

This rather explicit report regarding instruction of the youth may help to explain some of the rock art in Luiseño territory. The ceiling of a rock shelter in Mockingbird Canyon, near Riverside, California, is painted with a white, net-like design. At both ends of it, and to the side in the middle, are painted red disks, also textured with a net-like design. John Rafter and Vernon Hunter have plausibly interpreted this painting as a representation of the Sun at its two solstice-crossings of the Milky Way, and at the equinox, when it stands apart from the Milky Way.[30] The three disks may also stand for the three stones placed in the *wanawut* in the initiation ceremony. Through analogy, the young boys are launched into adulthood and the proper course in life, just as the young Sun was launched into its proper course in heaven. Rafter has found the Sun/Net motif repeated at several other rock art sites in Luiseño and neighboring territory, including a shelter at the Motte-Rimrock Reserve (Penney Ranch), near Perris.[31] The Milky Way also showed up in the girls' initiation ceremony as an element in a ground display (or sand painting). Most of these designs included a set of three concentric rings, all broken on the north side. They were colored white, black, and red, and stood, respectively, for the Milky Way, the night sky, and the "root" of existence, or spirit.[32] These Milky Way connections with Luiseño rites of passage underscore the theme of transcendental transformation. A passage like this is like the passage from life to death, for the child dies as the adult is born. The soul, guided in part by the Milky Way, simply takes up a new residence.

Harrington, as cited in Boscana,[33] demonstrates through linguistic arguments that the ceremonial string and eagle-down headband, the Milky Way (in Spanish they called it "that band or belt in the sky"), gray hair, and spirit (of life, like the breath of life, rather than of the body, which is the substance within, the heart, the center) are all analogous. Du Bois quotes quite specifically how this impersonal spirit of life we each possess ascends to the Milky Way at death. It is said to rise with Antares. According to Du Bois,

> Wanawut is the symbol of the Milky Way, the Spirit to whom our spirits go when they die. Since the spirit cannot be seen, some symbol of it is required for the instruction of the candidates. The figure is shown to them and explained. Piiwish, the Milky Way, was put up where he is a sign that we are only going to live here for a little while. Death came from Ouiot (Wiyot); but when we die our spirit will be sent to Piwish Ahuta.[34]

Songs for the spirits of the dead are sung to liberate them from the earth and to "tie" them to heaven, via the Milky Way.[35]

Natural landmarks and ritual sites animated the landscape through their mythological power, power that was often linked with Luiseño astronomical conceptions. In this regard, an entry I discovered in

Harrington's unpublished field notes is particularly interesting.[36] On July 31, 1932, he drove with José Albanos, his primary Luiseño consultant, and Albanos pointed out the Wanawut Rock on the old Pala-Temecula road. "The rock is between the new (present) road, which is to the west, and the old road (which is to the east)." His consultant confirmed that the rock was named *Wanawat* and that the white band on the rock was the *Wanawat*. "The *Wanawut* looks like a long streak in the rock." Another consultant says the *Wanawut* is "a thing like a *piwic* worn like a belt around the waist."

Harrington's description of the location of this landmark and his mileages, presumably from Pala, prompted me to ask colleagues who sometimes frequented the area to look around a little for the rock. Four days after I told archaeologist Dr. Bruce Love about it, I received a telephone call from him confirming he had found it. It is located right where Harrington said it was. We visited the rock on July 7, 1993 with two Luiseño singers, Raymond Basquez and Mark Macarro.

The *wanawut* is a natural seam of white quartz, itself a symbolically important substance, in a large and upward-looming granite boulder (fig. 6). The white band looks as if it were drawn with engineering precision. Like the Milky Way when it traverses the zenith, the band in the rock rises from one side of the huge boulder, climbs over the top, and descends to the ground on the other side. It appears to emerge from the earth on both sides of the rock, and Mark Macarro observed that in the songs, the Milky Way is said to be "rooted" in the earth. On the south side of the boulder, the white band branches in two, a feature which corresponds nicely with the branching of the Milky Way in the Cygnus rift.

Dark interstellar dust between us and the more distant stars of the Milky Way in the direction of Cygnus block the starlight and make it look as if the Milky Way splits into two branches there. This split is called the Cygnus rift. The Luiseño spiritual associations of the Milky Way are closely congruent with the potentially sacred character of the site, for the split in the white band on the Wanawut Rock corresponds to the summer Milky Way, which is what is implied by the reference to the spirit rising to it with Antares.

The oldest Greek reference to celestial immortality is a comment by

Ion of Chios, a fifth-century B.C.E. Pythagorean poet who wrote: "when someone dies he becomes like the stars in the air."[37] Plato developed the idea with extensive detail in the *Timaeus*, where he informs us that the Demiurge fashions the immortal component of every human soul from leftovers remaining from the preparation of the World Soul.[38] These ingredients were divided into the same number as the stars in the sky, and each soul was assigned to its own star. Souls relinquish their celestial sanctuaries to animate human lives on earth, and when they die, they return to the stars from which they came. Plato's student Heraclides Ponticus composed the *Empedotimus* in the fourth century B.C.E. and in it affirmed that the final refuge of disincarnated souls is the Milky Way.[39] It was also the route by which souls made their way to and from the Earth. An epitaph from Athens in the fourth century B.C.E. tells us these ideas were more than the ruminations of an astronomically-oriented philosopher. It singles out the Milky Way as the ultimate destination of the deceased: "I, a godlike man, leave my body to Earth my Mother. He's gone to the Band of the Blest, the circle of Aither."[40] The inscription puts eschatological theory to work in the ritual of the funeral.

Despite these specific references, other celestial stations were targeted by the dead, including the moon and various stars and constellations. The dead were even thought to become stars. Even though late in the fifth century B.C.E. the Greek atomist philosopher Democritus of Abdera had correctly speculated that the Milky Way is really the "shining of innumerable stars too faint and close together" to be distinguished individually,[41] it was still possible in pagan Rome to laminate this understanding with the concept of celestial souls and conclude that the stars were really innumerable spirits which had left the world and which were particularly populous in the Milky Way, a territory congested with the souls of the dead.[42] This doctrine of the astral destiny of the soul may have originated in the fifth or sixth century B.C.E. in Mesopotamia. Much later, in the second century C.E., the Greek travel writer Pausanias did credit the belief in the immortality of the soul to the Chaldaeans and "the Magi of India," and in time, the Mesopotamian notion of celestial divinity became linked with concept of the immortal soul.[43] The astral basis of Roman belief

Figure 6.

A boulder with a natural vein of quartz, near Pala, California, was known to the Luiseño as the Milky Way rock. The white band of quartz grows out of the base on the north side, loops over the top, and drops down to the south, splitting on the way. It is, in fact, a remarkable natural simulation of the Milky Way in its summer configuration. Photograph by E. C. Krupp.

certainly emerged from these trends. The Roman poet Virgil (first century B.C.E.), author of the *Aeneid*, informs us that great men and legendary heroes are *catasterized*—transformed into celestial beings. Augustus Caesar, Heracles, Romulus, and others acquired astral immortality and took posts in heaven where they acted as go-betweens with the gods.[44] Ovid, another poet of the same era, describes the celestial apotheosis of Julius Caesar in the *Metamorphoses* (15.838–42).[45] Caesar's soul is seized from his "murdered corpse" and made a "bright star,"

> So that great Julius, a god divine
> From his high throne in heaven may ever shine
> Upon the Forum and our Capitol.

This habit of launching the souls of heroic figures into heaven prompted the Latin writer Manilius, who composed his *Astronomica* in the first century C.E., to find a place for Augustus Caesar even higher than the Milky Way. His poem is the earliest surviving treatise on astrology, and in it (1.754ff),[46] he also suggests that the Milky Way may be a "host of stars" that "has woven its fires in a dense circlet and glows with a concentrated light." These stars, perhaps, are the souls of heroes, "men deemed worthy of heaven" (but not quite as worthy as Augustus Caesar) who, freed from their bodies and released from the Earth, migrate to the Milky Way, where they dwell "in a heaven that is their own" and "live the infinite years of paradise, and enjoy celestial bliss."

The realm of the dead, then, was generally believed to be located in the stars, especially in the Milky Way, which was often equated with the Elysian Fields.[47] The notion is a natural consequence of celestial gods. The Milky Way was already associated with the gods, for Ovid described it as a road lined with the palaces of the gods (*Metamorphoses* 1.169–78).[48] Much earlier, in the fifth century B.C.E., the Greek poet Pindar paved the way for a milky highway to heaven for the divine by calling the Milky Way the road of the gods. The soul, in this scheme, has an affinity with the gods and wants to rejoin them. Because they reside in the sky, the soul must return to the sky. If the Milky Way is the road of the gods, it is also an Interstate on the itinerary of the soul. Cicero, the Roman statesman and orator, had, in the first century B.C.E., already explored these themes in his *Dream of Scipio*, following Plato's lead in the *Republic* (the vision of Er).[49] In this visionary narrative, Scipio the Younger dreams himself into the sky, where he finds his father and Scipio Africanus, his adoptive grandfather (and the Roman general who defeated Hannibal). They meet in "the radiant circle of dazzling whiteness,"[50] which the Romans have learned from the Greeks to call the Milky Way. Those who practice virtue for its own sake return to the stars, according to Cicero,[51] for that is where their souls originated. The stars are the "true home of the soul."[52]

By late antiquity, these ideas were even more astronomically formalized. In *The Cave of the Nymphs*, the Greek philosopher Porphyry contrived a celestial mechanism for populating the earth with souls and returning them at death to heaven. He identified the intersections that the Milky Way makes with the ecliptic—in the signs of Cancer and Capricorn—as *termini* on the heaven-to-Earth-and-back-again railroad.[53] The summer and winter solstices reside in these two signs of the zodiac. At these junctions, significant seasonal stations of the Sun amplified the meaning of the Milky Way. Entry-level souls, like those of heroes and gods, are associated with the Sun. They depart from heaven through the northern solstice gate, in Cancer, and arrive back in the sky through the Capricorn gate in the south. The portal of the soul's descent was called the Gate of Men, and the Gate of Gods was its route for return. The ancient concept that the Milky Way is the old path of the Sun further endorsed this picture.[54]

Porphyry also tells us that Pythagoras said that the Land of Dreams "is composed of souls, which are gathered into the Milky Way; and the Milky Way is named from the milk with which these are nourished when they have fallen into genesis."[55] This is the old story of Heracles and Zeus pressed into service on behalf of the world's myriad souls. The newly-born soul must be nurtured spiritually as the newly-born child is nursed physically. Mother's milk sustains the infant. Celestial milk transports the soul.

The astral themes in Hellenistic and Roman religion eventually operated in the context of the salvation of the soul. Mithraic tradition,

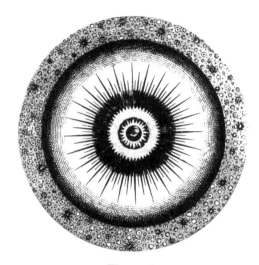

Figure 7.
The transcendental character of the Milky Way persisted in the eighteenth century's metaphysical speculations of Thomas Wright, who at
times imagined the milky band as our perception of a spherical shell of
stars which housed a supernatural and divine Agent who acted there on
behalf of the eternal Being that presides over the entire cosmos and
occupies its center. Wright represented the Agent as an eye that watches
over everything under the Milky Way.

like earlier Christianity, was rooted in that motif, and Porphyry
reports that Mithras presided over the destiny of souls and the
mechanisms of their travel. The Milky Way and its solstitial gates were
under his control. It was in the soul's interest to become a dedicated
companion of Mithras.[56]

Macrobius, a Latin commentator in the first half of the fifth century
C.E., emphasized the transcendental importance of the intersections
of the Milky Way with the path of the Sun and so verifies that these
ideas persisted into late antiquity.[57] The Neoplatonist commentaries
of Philopon of Alexandria confirm that the Milky Way was still said to
be a road of souls and a road traveled by the dead in the sixth century
C.E.

Dante Alighieri, Italy's pivotal poet, standing at the shore of the
European Renaissance, wrote in Italian rather than Latin, and incor-

porated the entire medieval world-view into a world treasure of epic allegory, *The Divine Comedy*. It details a thirteenth-century "cosmovision" that embraces everything from astronomical phenomena to the desire and destiny of the soul. It reaches from the throne of God to the inner circle of Hell. It is a masterpiece of the art and philosophy of its time. Dante's astronomical references are numerous and include reflections on the metaphysical character of the Milky Way.[58] He compares the star-like spirits of Heaven, which wheel through Paradise in homage to Aristotelian uniform circular motion, to celestial objects, which behave according to the same rules.[59] The spirits of the fifth heaven are, he says, like the Milky Way (14.97–101).[60] In another work (*Convivio* 2.15.44–86), Dante uses the Milky Way to demonstrate the metaphysical dimension of the physical universe:

> Since the Galaxy is an effect of those stars
> which cannot be perceived except so far as
> we apprehend these things by their effect,
> and since Metaphysics treats of primal substance
> which in the same way we cannot apprehend
> except by their effects, it is plain that there is
> a close resemblance between the starry heaven
> and Metaphysics.[61]

There, for now, is where we must leave the soul—locked in the caress of the metaphysics of the Milky Way. In time, all this will change, but even after Galileo, in 1610, resolves the milky highway of heaven into "nothing but a congeries of innumerable stars grouped together in clusters,"[62] others would lodge the eye of God in the middle of the Milky Way. In the eighteenth century, Thomas Wright called this divine, supernatural presence the "primary Agent of omnipotent and eternal Being" who presides over the cosmos from the center of the universe and observes and sustains each galaxy (fig. 7).[63]

Modern astrophysics sanctions neither souls nor a primary Agent of omnipotent and eternal Being in the center of the Milky Way or in any other galaxy, but the physical and the transcendental may yet meet in the galaxies' cores. That is where popular culture and imagination try to come to terms with massive black holes like that known to haunt the heart of M87 in the Virgo cluster. If souls are at all responsive to gravity, they must go boldly where all have gone before.

Notes

1. E. C. Krupp, "Cosmos on Parade: A Year, More-or-less, of Sky Jinks and Earth Tremors, Part One: Eclipses and Earthquakes," *Griffith Observer* 58 (December 1994), 1–17 ff.; 6.

2. E. C. Krupp, *Beyond the Blue Horizon: Myths and Legends of the Sun, Moon, Stars, and Planets* (New York: HarperCollins, 1991), 256.

3. Stephen Herbert Langdon, *The Mythology of All Races, Volume 5: Semitic* (New York: Cooper Square Publishers, 1931; reprint 1964), 175; Stephanie Dalley, *Myths from Mesopotamia* (Oxford: Oxford University Press, 1989), 182.

4. E. C. Krupp, "Celestial Analogy and Cyclical Renewal," paper presented at the American Anthropological Association 92nd Annual Meeting, Washington, D.C., November 19, 1993.

5. Uno Holmberg, *The Mythology of All Races, Volume 4: Finno-Ugric/ Siberian* (New York: Cooper Square Publishers, undated; reprint 1964), 434–36.

6. V. V. Napolskikh, "Proto-Uralic World Picture: A Reconstruction," in *Northern Religions and Shamanism*, Ethnologica Uralica 3, ed. Mihály Hoppál and Juha Pentikäinen (Budapest and Helsinki: Akadémiai Kiadó and Finnish Literature Society, 1992), 4–10; Géza Roheim, *Hungarian and Vogul Mythology*, Monographs of the American Ethnological Society 23 (Locust Valley, New York: J. J. Augustin, 1954), 20–22.

7. Johan Turi, *Turi's Book of Lappland* (New York and London: Harper & Brothers, 1910), 289; Holmberg, *The Mythology of All Races*, 434.

8. E. C. Krupp, "Migrating Birds and the Milky Way," *Sky & Telescope* 86 (October 1993), 58–59.

9. Natalia Belting, *The Moon Is a Crystal Ball* (Indianapolis: Bobbs-Merrill, 1952), 33–38.

10. Carla Corradi-Musi, *Uralic Mythology and Folklore*, Ethnologica Uralica 1, ed. Mihály Hoppál and Juha Pentikäinen (Budapest and Helsinki: Ethnographic Institute of the Hungarian Academy of Sciences and Finnish Literature Society, 1989), 243.

11. Richard Hinckley Allen, *Star-Names and Their Meanings* (New York: G. E. Stechert, 1899), 476.

12. Allen, *Star-Names and Their Meanings*, 474.

13. Theony Condos, *Eratosthenes' Katasterismoi*, Ph.D. thesis: translation and commentary (Los Angeles: University of Southern California, 1970). Now published in an expanded edition: Theony Condos, *Star Myths of the Greeks and Romans: A Sourcebook, Containing* The Constellations *of Pseudo-Eratosthenes and* The Poetic Astronomy *of Hyginus* (Grand Rapids: Phanes Press, 1997).

14. Translated in Condos, *Star Myths of the Greeks and Romans: A Sourcebook*, 109–110.

15. Kali Nath Mukherji, *Popular Hindu Astronomy* (Calcutta: Nirmal Mukherjea, 1905; reprint 1969), 7–26.

16. Travis Hudson, "California's First Astronomers," in *Archaeoastronomy and the Roots of Science*, ed. E. C. Krupp (Boulder, CO and Washington, D.C.: Westview Press and American Association for the Advancement of Science, 1984), 45, 48.

17. Carobeth Laird, *The Chemehuevis* (Banning, California: Malki Museum Press, 1976), 92.

18. Edward W. Gifford and Gwendoline Harris Block, *California Indian Nights Entertainments* (Glendale, California: Arthur H. Clark, 1930), 189; Rosemary Holsinger, *Shasta Indian Tales* (Happy Camp, California: Naturegraph, 1982), 35–36.

19. Alfred Kroeber, *Handbook of the Indians of California*, Bulletin of the Bureau of American Ethnology 78 (Washington, D.C.: Smithsonian Institution, 1925), 441.

20. Krupp, *Beyond the Blue Horizon*, 273.

21. Kroeber, *Handbook of the Indians*, 662.

22. Leslie Spier, *Southern Diegueño Customs*, University of California Publications in American Archaeology and Ethnology 20 (Phoebe Apperson Hearst Memorial Volume) (Berkeley: University Press, 1923), 319–20.

23. Constance Goddard Du Bois, *The Religion of the Luiseño Indians of Southern California*, University of California Publications in American Archaeology and Ethnology 8.3 (Berkeley: University of California Press, 1908), 86, 88, 162–63.

24. John Peabody Harrington, *Luiseño Linguistic and Ethnographic Notes: Papers of John P. Harrington*, Part 3, Southern California Basin (Washington, D.C.: United States Anthropological Archives, Smithsonian Institution, no date, *c.* 1930), spool pages 115, 149, 400.

25. Fray Geronimo Boscana, *Chinigchinich*, annot. John Peabody Harrington (Banning, California: Malki Museum Press, 1933; reprint 1978), 197.

26. Du Bois, *Religion of the Luiseño Indians*, 129; Kroeber, *Handbook of the Indians*, 667–78.

27. Du Bois, *Religion of the Luiseño Indians*, 179.

28. Du Bois, *Religion of the Luiseño Indians*, 143–45.

29. Du Bois, *Religion of the Luiseño Indians*, 85–86.

30. Vernon Hunter and John Rafter, "Solar and Stellar Observations at Mockingbird Canyon," in *Earth and Sky*, ed. Arlene Benson and Tom Hoskinson (Thousand Oaks, California: Slo'w Press, 1985), 151–62; John Rafter, "Primitive Solar and Stellar Observations in Riverside County," *La Pintura* 8 (Newsletter of the American Rock Art Research Association, 1982), 4; John Rafter, "Mockingbird Canyon's Milky Way," in *Rock Art Papers* 1, ed. Ken Hedges (San Diego: San Diego Museum of Man, 1983), 75–80; John Rafter, "Mockingbird Canyon Study Expanded," in *Rock Art Papers* 2, ed. Ken Hedges (San Diego: San Diego Museum of Man, 1985), 33–46.

31. John Rafter, "Searching for More Sun and Net Designs," in *Rock Art Papers* 9, ed. Ken Hedges (San Diego: San Diego Museum of Man, 1992), 135–42.

32. Du Bois, *Religion of the Luiseño Indians*, 88.

33. Boscana, *Chinigchinich*, 197.

34. Du Bois, *Religion of the Luiseño Indians*, 86.

35. Du Bois, *Religion of the Luiseño Indians*, 86.

36. Harrington, *Luiseño Linguistic*, spool 117; 50–51.

37. Franz Cumont, *After Life in Roman Paganism* (New York: Dover Publications, 1922; reprint 1952), 95.

38. F. M. Cornford, *Plato's Cosmology* (London: Routledge & Kegan Paul, 1937), 142.

39. George Sarton, *A History of Science*, vol. 1 (New York: Norton, 1952), 507.

40. Jack Lindsay, *Origins of Astrology* (New York: Barnes & Noble, 1971), 248.

41. M. A. Orr, *Dante and the Early Astronomers* (London: Gall and Inglis, 1913), 61.

42. Franz Cumont, *Astrology and Religion among the Greeks and Romans* (New York: Dover Publications, 1912; reprint 1960), 94.

43. Cumont, *Astrology and Religion*, 94.

44. Lindsay, *Origins of Astrology*, 248.

45. Ovid, *Metamorphoses*, trans. A. D. Melville (Oxford: Oxford University Press, 1987), 377.

46. Manilius, *Astronomica*, trans. G. P. Goold (Cambridge: Harvard University Press, 1977), 65.

47. Cumont, *Astrology and Religion*, 104.

48. Ovid, *Metamorphoses*, 6.

49. Orr, *Dante*, 168.

50. Orr, *Dante*, 168.

51. Orr, *Dante*, 168.

52. Orr, *Dante*, 168.

53. David Ulansey, *The Origins of the Mithraic Mysteries* (New York: Oxford University Press, 1989), 61–62.

54. Cumont, *After Life*, 152.

55. Ulansey, *Origins*, 61.

56. Ulansey, *Origins*, 61.

57. Lindsay, *Origins of Astrology*, 360.

58. Orr, *Dante*, 303–306.

59. Orr, *Dante*, 301–302.

60. Dante Alighieri, *The Paradiso*, trans. John Ciardi (New York: New American Library, 1970), 165.

61. Orr, *Dante*, 305.

62. Charles A. Whitney, *The Discovery of Our Galaxy* (New York: Knopf, 1971), 35.

63. Stanley Jaki, *The Milky Way: An Elusive Road for Science* (New York: Science History Publications, 1972), 192.

Nature and Nature's God: Modern Cosmology and the Rebirth of Natural Philosophy

THEODORE ROSZAK

> "Hydrogen is a light, odorless gas, which, given enough time, turns into people."
>
> —The new cosmology, abridged version

IN THE FALL OF 1992, a major cosmological conference took place at the University of California at Berkeley. In attendance were many of the most notable astronomers and astrophysicists in the world. In the course of the meeting, a public symposium was held that drew an overflow crowd to the campus auditorium. Three well-known scientists (Paul Davies, John Barrow, and Roger Penrose) joined two theologians in discussing "Cosmos and Culture." Word had gotten around in the audience that the original title for the event—"God and Cosmos"—had been vetoed by the conference organizers as sounding too sensational. Whether or not the rumor was true, the symposium succeeded in being professionally cautious to the point of boredom. That was clearly not what its audience had expected. Judging by the searching philosophical and religious questions sent forward at the end of the evening, there were a good many on hand who would have relished hearing what the scientists had to say about God.

If that is why they came, they might have done better to loiter in the foyer. There they would have found God much under discussion as part of an intellectual confrontation that never gained admittance to the auditorium. Before the symposium began, an indignant member of the San Francisco Bay Area Skeptics' Society could be found patrolling the lobby, busily collaring people and distributing a self-published tract. The skeptic's case was a thoughtful and well-documented warning: all cosmology based upon the Big Bang is a treacherous compromise of scientific godlessness:

> We've all heard about creationism of the Biblical variety trying to force its way into the public schools under the guise of "creation science." Yet how many of us are aware of a similar, yet not so clearly (at first sight) erroneous type of creationism that has succeeded not only in getting into school textbooks, but is believed by most holders of astronomy and physics degrees as well? I'm referring to the religion of cosmology known as the Big Bang theory, a modern variant of Biblical creationism taught as the gospel by most scientists.

"Real science," the uncompromising skeptic concluded, "deals with what is knowable. Real scientists do not write books ostensibly about astronomical/cosmological science with titles such as *The Mind of God*—the new book by Professor Paul Davies."

To appreciate the full irony of the skeptic's defense of "real science" against *"most* holders of astronomy and physics degrees," one need only observe the agitated maneuvers taking place in what he would surely regard as the enemy camp. Quite by accident one day, I tuned in on a local evangelical radio station where an astronomer, a Biblical fundamentalist from a religious campus in the Middle West, was railing against the new cosmology. He too was admonishing his listeners not to be taken in. Though the man's scientific reading was remarkably up to date, his theology dated back to the Scopes Trial: true believers have only one source of reliable information about the universe—the Bible. They must scrupulously avoid looking to science to learn God's truth. If for no other reason, the new cosmology must be rejected because it violates the chronology of Genesis. The Bible clearly states that the world was created in six days some six thousand years ago. Since the Big Bang dates back rather farther (at least 15 billion years), this proves that nothing discovered by scientific instruments can ever be the true moment of creation. How then to account for the red shift and cosmic background radiation—the basic evidence for cosmic expansion? The fundamentalist astronomer raised exactly the same objections as the atheist skeptic. These must be observational artifacts—distortions produced by the apparatus.

The skeptic and the fundamentalist could be right. The new cosmology may one day be overthrown by just such a finding. Even in mainstream astronomy, there are critics who still reject the Big Bang in favor of other models. There is, for example, a school of plasma cosmology that believes the universe is infinitely ancient, continuing to evolve without beginning and without end.[1] A few holdouts have gone so far as to denounce Big Bang cosmology as a conspiratorial plot against sound science.[2] What such objections overlook is the fact that, as cosmologies go, Big Bang theory has more evidence going for it than any rival system has ever been able to muster. No cosmological system of the past—including the pre-expansionist universe that was the official worldview of science down to the 1920s—has had a solid observational foundation. This was why cosmology held such a marginal status in science until the twentieth century. There seemed to be no way to prove anything about the universe at large; one could simply speculate and spin out hypotheses. The infinity and the eternity of the pre-Big Bang cosmos were simply assumed by default. An eternal universe conveniently avoided the need to account for an origin, a line of thought that might lead dangerously close to a creative moment. That way lay theology. Even more important, the eternity of the universe provided the time necessary for everything to fall into place by accident. *Sub specie aeternitatis* even the most improbable things become possible.

By now the general public must be reasonably aware that the universe is not what it once was—even as recently as a generation ago. There has been abundant coverage of such spectacular new astronomical ideas as black holes, quasars, pulsars, dark matter, and cosmic background radiation. For the first time in history, as we see farther into the deep void and take ever finer readings, cosmology is making news. Reports of dramatic new findings and ideas appear steadily in the media. What has yet to be clearly registered even by the educated public is the philosophical crisis that results when one weaves these findings together into a coherent picture. With each new discovery, the fears of the Bay Area skeptic grow more justified. The long-standing compact between natural science and agnosticism is coming undone. All the latest cosmological findings are balancing out in a way that makes it more and more difficult for nonreligious intellect to feel at home in the universe.

In its December 1992 edition, *Time* magazine ran a special Christmas feature that filled its cover with the question "What Does Science Tell Us About God?" After interviewing a number of scientists, the magazine reached a predictably cautious conclusion: "The theological possibility is still certainly alive." Even that much of a concession is remarkable. At the beginning of this century, the same question would have produced an all but unanimous answer: "God? He doesn't exist . . . or if He does, there's no way we can know."

Now references to the deity abound in the popular literature of science. In his introduction to Stephen Hawking's *A Brief History of Time*, Carl Sagan observes that "the word God fills these pages." Hawking, for example, finishes his book by describing "the ultimate triumph of human reason" as "knowing the mind of God." Similarly, Richard Feynman, observing that the universe has the look of a curiously well-constructed hierarchical order, once dropped the remark that we cannot be certain which end of that hierarchy—the simplicity of the subatomic or the intricacy of the human mind—"is nearer to God—if I may use a religious metaphor." Of course he may—but the frequency with which that metaphor is surfacing these days in science writing is striking.

Steven Weinberg is surely correct in believing that scientific references to God are often casual, sometimes almost flippant. But he is exactly wrong when he concludes that "scientists and others sometimes use the word 'God' to mean something so abstract and unengaged that He is hardly to be distinguished from the laws of nature."[3] On the contrary. In most cases "God" is the word scientists invoke when they are confronted by something so deucedly clever that it seems worrisomely incompatible with "the laws of nature," or at least eludes a smooth reduction to basic physical principles. In the presence of more and more smart phenomena, even hard-headed scientists begin to wonder if perhaps "somebody has been monkeying around" with the universe—to use the words of astronomer Fred Hoyle. Calling that somebody or something "God" is a way of granting the nature of things an intricacy that approaches the work of intelligence. In Hawking's phrase, the reference to "mind" is as much a sign that the intellectual weather is changing as is the reference to "God." The physicist Freeman Dyson puts it more directly: "I do not claim that the architecture of the universe proves the existence of God. I claim only that the architecture of the universe is consistent with the hypothesis that mind plays an essential role in its functioning."[4]

If by "God" we mean anything that leads us to suspect that intelligent design rather than blind chance offers a better explanation for the order of nature, then God is fitfully emerging as a respectable scientific idea in our time.

Deism and the Politics of Godlessness

Or rather *re*-emerging. Over the last century, the alliance between natural science and agnosticism has come to seem so unshakable that we easily forget how pious the founding fathers of science were. Among them, it was simply taken for granted that the vocation of the scientist was "to read God's mind in the works of nature." The infinite void of space was understood to be God's "sensorium," a vital matrix in which divine will kept everything functioning and in its place within the great chain of being. Deism, the religious style that prevailed among scientists and the educated public during the seventeenth and eighteenth centuries, was often called "natural religion"—meaning religion grounded in "the laws of Nature and of Nature's God."

Modern science might never have managed to bootstrap itself into existence without the Judeo-Christian image of a law-giver God to Whom the laws of nature could be referenced. Even so, by the beginning of the nineteenth century natural religion was all but defunct. Where Newtonian piety had once ruled, now the agnosticism of Laplace or the outright atheism of Baron d'Holbach increasingly enlisted the best minds of the age. Why? This shift in the philosophical consensus had nothing to do with empirical fact; nothing had been discovered in nature that disproved Deism or validated godlessness. Irreligion was imported from *outside* science. Its source was ethical, not scientific. It derives from the turbulent political ethos of the late-eighteenth century. Science had become the ally of revolutionary politics. Determined to see "the last king strangled in the guts of the last priest," rebellious spirits set about obliterating every trace of ecclesiastical as well as aristocratic privilege. Theirs was an intellectual scorched earth strategy, resolved to level anything that might shelter priestly authority. At their hands, Deism was destined to die an ironic death. Devoted as they were to strict logic and empirical evidence, the Deists proved vulnerable to the crusading atheism that swept the intellectual elite of the Western world in the time of the American and French Revolutions. By the end of the nineteenth century, science, which was once meant to hymn the praises of the Creator, had come to be universally regarded as religion's deadliest enemy. It had sub-scribed to a politics of godlessness that seemed the only way toward what Kant called "mankind's coming of age."

Deism foundered on two philosophical weaknesses. The first was its uneasy historical association with the Judeo-Christian tradition. No God was ever less like the God of Abraham, Isaac, and Jacob than Newton's Great Watchmaker, yet everything Deists said about the deity inevitably called to mind the wrathful Jehovah that walks and talks through the Book of Genesis and who figures in the enigmas of Christian trinitarian theology. The Deists dearly wanted a more abstract and universal deity; but try as they would, they could never disentangle the Author of Nature's Laws from the sectarian, anthro-pomorphic God of Moses and Jesus. In the eyes of crusading skeptics, that association implicated all religious thinkers, even the hyper-rational Deists, in the intolerance and obfuscation of clerical author-ity.

Second, the Deists made the mistake of assuming that the laws of nature could be accounted for only by invoking a divine legislator. But as scientists became more accustomed to explaining natural phenom-ena by a limited number of mathematical rules, the less need they had for divine intervention. Increasingly they felt free to eliminate all reference to external supervision in the universe. The "argument from design" for the existence of God seemed all but liquidated by classic debunking exercises like Tom Paine's *The Age of Reason* and David Hume's *Dialogues on Natural Religion.*

In the Newtonian universe, "physical explanation" came to mean reduction to matter in motion. Matter meant atoms—hypothetical entities that were intended to be as wholly other as possible from life and mind. The mathematically measurable behavior of these indestructible, invariant balls of stuff—their velocity, density, elasticity, their bounding and rebounding—would eventually answer all questions about nature. Everything was "nothing but" a mechanical process mindlessly driven by blind force. Probability became the religious skeptic's trump card. Given *enough time,* it was confidently assumed that randomly wandering matter moving in obedience to a few simple laws of motion would produce the universe as we know it—including ourselves in body and mind.

How much time? The nineteenth-century physicist Ludwig Boltzmann once sought to calculate how long it would take for everything in the universe as we know it to drift accidentally into place. His answer—not quite sensibly expressed in terms of "years"—was $10^{10^{80}}$. This may be the largest number ever computed as part of a serious explanatory exercise in the physical sciences. It is so large that all the scientists there have ever been—even if they all lived to the age of Methuselah—could not set down all the zeroes it would require to express it. This posed no difficulty for Boltzmann. He assumed that the cosmos made available an infinite amount of time as well as an infinite amount of space. The world was after all eternal; it had always been there, a great thermodynamic wilderness inhabited by bouncing atoms. "In such a universe," Boltzmann reasoned, "which is in thermal equilibrium as a whole and therefore dead, relatively small regions of the size of our galaxy will be found here and there; regions (which we may call 'worlds') that deviate significantly from thermal equilibrium for relatively short stretches of these aeons of time." In fact, in such a universe, the existing, highly improbable arrangement of things we are pleased to regard as "*the*" universe today might not only fall into place fortuitously, it might do so an infinite number of times. As late as the 1950s, the Nobel laureate in biology, George Wald, was still convinced that chance combinations over some two billion years could account even for so complex a phenomenon as the origin of life. "Given so much time, the impossible becomes possible, the possible probable, and the probable virtually certain. One has only to wait: time itself performs the miracles."[5]

Looking back now, one is astonished at the crude, totally nonempirical simplicity of this worldview. Though few scientists will acknowledge the fact, for the better part of its history, Western physics was undergirded by a conception of matter for which empirical evidence was never produced. There are no hard balls of ultimate stuff any more than there were, as was once supposed, crystalline spheres holding up the heavenly bodies. Moreover, if such atoms did exist, how could they, by purely fortuitous aggregation, take on the permanence of form and behavior that is so obviously characteristic of nature? Today, physicists still purport to offer us "physical" explanations of the universe; but now their focus is upon a burgeoning population of elusive "particles" rather than atoms as the irreducible stuff of nature. The difference between atoms and particles is all the difference between one scientific paradigm and another; but it is a safe bet that most people—even the well-educated—interpret what they hear about high energy physics by picturing particles as a smaller kind of atom: hard, durable, invisible *somethings* that stick together and make the word "physical" mean pretty much what it meant in Newton's day. This allows scientists to continue pretending that they have never been seriously wrong about anything as basic as what the universe is made of. Today, one comes across mainstream scientists who blithely recount "the death of materialism" and dismiss "the matter myth" as patently absurd. By "matter myth" they mean "the belief that the physical universe is nothing but a collection of material particles in interaction, a gigantic purposeless machine." But whose myth was this in the first place?[6]

In the course of the nineteenth century, even as scientific intellectuals became more and more ideologically wedded to godlessness, the actual physical foundations of agnostic orthodoxy were being steadily eroded. The crisis arose within science itself, indeed within the hardest of the hard sciences—physics. At least since Michael Faraday's time, most of what was being discovered about nature could not be gracefully accommodated within the framework of Newtonian physics. The study of electricity was producing speculation about embarrassingly nonmaterial phenomena called "fields." So successful was field theory to become that many scientists would now regard fields as more fundamental than the things—atoms or particles—that fill them. Yet the fact that action within a field can be expressed mathematically should not distract us from recognizing how very ethereal a concept this is. All efforts to assign fields a material consistency (whether as effluvia or ethers) have failed. A field is, at last, a piece of the empty void—but the void given rational shape. By what? "Forces" within it. This makes the field very like the Deists' old notion that space is God's sensorium. But the sensorium is the mind of God extended through space—knowing all, controlling all. In Newton's formulation, in His sensorium, God perceives things the way we perceive ideas. God *thinks* the universe; and that is what gives it order. Like so many scientific ideas, the field hides a wealth of old metaphysics.

So exotic was the field as a concept that William Crookes, inventor of the cathode ray tube, was actually taken off into explanations that borrowed from spiritualism. Wondering if ectoplasm might be a form of radiant energy, Crookes eventually drifted into psychical research. His tougher-minded colleagues might have lamented such woolliness, but before the century was out, thinkers as weighty as Jules Poincaré and Ernst Mach had demonstrated that, by way of mechanical atoms and combining laws alone, one could not make physics work. And all the while, matter, that which once made materialism "material," was continuing to diffuse into strange vibrations and spectral waves. As Karl Popper once put it, "materialism has transcended itself." But in doing so, it was becoming as elusively impalpable as mentality or spirituality.

It is one of the triumphs of science that quantum theory has found a way to continue offering "physical" explanations for phenomena as subtle and elusive as the proliferating "particle zoo." But all that really survives of physicality Old Style is the conviction that, whatever physical things may be, their behavior can be expressed mathematically. It is abstract mathematical relations—ideas in the minds of scientists—that continue to make physics "physical." And this, in turn, has allowed science to shore up its commitment to godless explanations. Quanta are radically probabilistic, the dice that supposedly make the universe a baffling game of chance fully predictable only on the macrocosmic level. Along these lines, quantum mechanics has paid a neat philosophical dividend for agnostic thought. One of the chief goals of agnosticism has been to undermine the delusions of grandeur that once placed the Earth at the hub of the universe. In a godless universe, human existence has to be nothing special. As a mode of explanation—supposedly the most "fundamental" of all—quantum mechanics achieves just that. It has served to make human life and thought seem even more cosmically irrelevant. "As we have discovered more and more fundamental physical principles," Steven Weinberg observes, "they seem to have less and less to do with us. . . . Our species has had to learn in growing up that we are not playing a starring role in any sort of grand cosmic drama."[7]

As vast and cold as the old Newtonian universe may have been, it could at least be regarded as a structure that was accessible to common sense. Adrift in the infinite void, human reason nevertheless mirrored the reason of Nature's God. Not so in the quantum universe. It brings with it a boundless store of mathematical paradox that has served to make our place in nature as thinking beings all the more anomalous. The physicist Richard Feynman once began a lecture series on the arcane subject of Quantum Electrodynamics with the wry observation that "nobody who comes to a science lecture expects to understand anything." That included his students . . . and himself. But not to worry. All he wished to do was to show his audience "nature as She really is. Absurd."

Feynman may not have intended the connection, but "absurdity" is

among the central categories of existentialist philosophy, where it is
hardly meant to amuse. Rather it is meant to concentrate our attention
on the paramount fact that we live in a universe that makes no human
sense. As a character in one of Dostoyevsky's tales puts it, "Nature does
not consult you; it does not care a damn for your desires or whether
its laws please or don't please. You have to accept it as it is." Facing up
unflinchingly to the absurdity of the human condition is a testing of
character: its purpose is to sweep away childish illusions about God
and immortality. In this way it cures us of the "bad faith" that comes
of basing our lives on religious fantasy and moral authority. Feynman
probably never realized it, but his abstruse lecture on one of the most
paradoxical theories in modern physics undergirds that very sense of
cosmic pathos that leads along other lines to the angst of Samuel
Beckett's *Waiting for Godot*. For some, like the Nobel laureate Jacques
Monod, the central human value of modern science is hygienic
disenchantment. It purges the mind of all pretension, all pride, all
vainglory:

> By a single stroke [science] has claimed to sweep away the tradition of a
> hundred thousand years, which had become one with human nature
> itself. It has written an end to the ancient animist covenant between man
> and nature, leaving nothing in place of that precious bond but an anxious
> quest in a frozen universe of solitude.

No philosophy has gone farther than atheist existentialism in
bravely facing up to man's fate in a godless universe. When I was an
undergraduate in college, the cheerless credo of postwar thinkers like
Sartre, Heidegger, and Camus seemed like the last word in the last
chapter of the history of philosophy. These were men exploring the
extreme boundary of the human condition: the radical disconnection
between consciousness and the alien cosmos. That boundary was an
objective fact established by science. In a universe that belonged to
science, this was where philosophy ended—in this courageous act of
stoical resignation. But at the very moment that the existentialists
were drawing their bleak conclusions, a new cosmology was emerging

that would soon call their despairing atheism into question.

The change was taking place on two fronts: *complexity* and *time*.

Complexity and Coincidence

At the beginning of the scientific era, the great intellectual promise of science was that it would simplify our understanding of nature. The simplicity that scientists sought for was understood to be really *there*, an empirical property of the world—indeed, its most basic property. The principle of parsimony corresponded to that simplicity and would one day reduce everything to a few succinct laws of force governing the behavior of a uniform atomic stuff.

That is not how things have turned out. While theory continues to seek simplicity, the ongoing empirical investigation of nature in ever more fine-grained detail by telescopes that see farther, microscopes that look deeper, and particle accelerators that squeeze more bits and pieces out of the material foundations of nature has uncovered a universe of overwhelming complexity—with more findings reporting in every day: more kinds of subatomic particles, more kinds of celestial bodies, more kinds of biological structures, ever trickier chemistry, more and stranger states of matter. The scientific use of the word "simplicity" has become weasely indeed. Now, at best, the formulations of scientists may be simple; but not what they refer to.

Suppose one is presented with a physical or chemical formula that explains how something happens—for example the way in which segmentation genes regulate the organization of body parts in the embryo of a fruit fly. In what sense does the discovery of master genes like these "simplify" our understanding of genetics? Granted, the operation of the master gene can be diagrammed and its chemical action stated by a few formulas. To that degree, things have been "simplified." But in another sense, what we have learned about developmental genetics has become much less "simple" precisely because the actual phenomenon, as it plays out in time and as it must have evolved into existence, has revealed more complexity than we knew before. The master gene helps us understand why other genes do what they do; but now we have the master genes to account for, and not just chemically, but historically. How could such an elegantly coordinated system have arisen from what came before? How can we account for that without introducing any hint of goals, purposes, or intentions? To the degree that scientists keep finding out more about the way things work—and that is what science is all about—they are steadily working away from simplicity and toward complexity. Even if they produce a Theory of Everything that can be expressed in a few neat formulas, the "everything" they are explaining will be confoundingly complex—thanks to their own conscientious research and experimentation.

These days "sciences of complexity"—like chaos theory—come in for a great deal of attention in the popular press. There even exists a world-renowned center wholly dedicated to their pursuit: Murray Gell-Mann's Santa Fe Institute in New Mexico. The goal of the work done at the Institute is to discover special, "higher level" laws that may govern complex systems. Are there, for example, forms of spontaneous self-organization that simply "fall" into an ordered state upon reaching a certain level of complexity? Is evolution governed by such laws—as much so as by natural selection? Might life itself have arisen in that way? Stuart Kauffman, a member of the Institute, is among those who believe that such laws are the "origins of order" in the universe; his hypothesis that self-organizing systems may arise spontaneously from inherent properties of matter that has reached the "edge of chaos" has been described as "heretical." Kauffman himself pleads guilty to the accusation. "The origin of life," he states, "rather than having been vastly improbable, is instead an expected collective property of complex systems of catalytic polymers and the molecules on which they act. Life, in a deep sense, *crystallized* as a collective self-reproducing metabolism in a space of possible organic reactions. This view is indeed heretical."[8]

Perhaps even more cutting is the criticism that complexity theories like Kauffman's are a mere fad that will soon pass from the scene. The charge of faddishness seems to arise from the ornate computer simulations Kauffman and other complexity theorists have created to explore their ideas. The field is indeed crowded with ingenious computerized models for analyzing everything from finance to the human genome. (The spread is not all that great; the Santa Fe Institute shelters a Citicorp program for the study of that peculiarly man-made chaos called the stock market.) On a video terminal the simulations can be so dazzlingly graphic one might almost conclude that the phenomena are a kind of Nintendo gimmickry that inheres in the computer programs that manipulate the models. The objection reminds one of the seventeenth-century clergy who believed Galileo's telescope was itself responsible for creating the moons of Jupiter. Computer models may or may not help us discover the hidden sources of cosmic order; but what complexity theory studies is ultimately *not* in the computers. Complexity is in nature. It is really there; it has been found to be there by solid empirical science. Moreover, it has *always* been there whether scientists have perceived it or not. And there is still more to be found. For even the most advanced computer simulations cannot match the complex systems that have somehow evolved out of the history of time. Nor have we any law that explains the overall hierarchical form that all these systems assume. The universe is no longer a void randomly filled with things and forces; it is stacked from top to bottom with systems, resilient patterns that bind things and forces together in increasingly intricate ways.

A century ago complexity was almost wholly limited to the messy, jumbled world of biology. In contrast to the austere mathematical elegance of physics, the study of organic forms took science into realms of astonishing intricacy: the life-cycle of the metamorphosing caterpillar, the convolutions of the human nervous system. Biologists confronted by the overwhelming detail and messiness of their field suffered a sort of "physics envy," hoping one day to reduce their ornate systems to the rigorous, geometrical purity of physical models. Though Darwin himself was a pious Victorian gentleman, his more tough-minded peers hoped that the theory of natural selection he left behind would one day offer a sound, mechanistic—and godless—explanation for the wonders of evolution. But even among the biologists, there has always been a fringe of dissenters who regard those explanations with suspicion, seeing them as too much like speculative rabbits pulled out of a hat. Many who accept evolution as proven beyond question still find natural selection an insufficient mechanism for the process. In order to make the theory work for every biological structure and behavior, one has to credit selection with omniscient qualities of judgment and foresight. Can the step by step evolution of "organs of extreme perfection" (as Darwin once called the eye, the stomach, the heart) really be explained as the result of genetic roulette and blind selection? Can organs that have developed far beyond selective advantage—most importantly the human mind that discovered evolution—be accounted for by a mechanism whose only operative principle is selective advantage?

Science keeps undermining its own search for simplicity. Especially in biology, things that once seemed dismissively simple constantly blossom into stunningly intricate structures. When I was a schoolboy, biology textbooks were just beginning to depict the cell as more than a featureless blob of something called "protoplasm." The microscopic stuff of life was being differentiated into "globules" and "granules" and still-mysterious threads called "mitochondria." Encompassing all this was a membrane that was still being depicted as nothing more than a thin line holding the oozy organic jelly together. Now, not only has protoplasm long-since bubbled away in the rich chemical stew that makes up the living cell, but the once one-dimensional membrane has thickened into a structure of inexhaustible complexity that requires a special field of study in its own right.

From time to time scientists have hazarded estimates for the probability that complex structures like the living cell might have appeared by the interaction of chance and selection. In the late 1970s Fred Hoyle and Chandra Wickramasinghe calculated the odds that life could have arisen by blind chance from some sort of primordial soup. Rather than trying to compute the probability for an entire organism evolving into existence, they limited the problem to twenty or thirty key amino acids in the enzymes of a hypothetical cell. The number they came up with was one chance in $10^{40,000}$.[9] It is unlikely magnitudes of this kind that led Hoyle to conclude:

I do not believe that any scientist who examined the evidence would fail to draw the inference that the laws of nuclear physics have been deliberately designed with regard to the consequences they produce inside the stars. If this is so, then my apparently random quirks have become part of a deep-laid scheme. If not, then we are back again at a monstrous sequence of accidents.[10]

Orthodox Darwinists remain committed to the "monstrous sequence of accidents." But even if they should be right about the science of life, we now know that the complexity we once attributed only to living things extends well beyond biology. Fundamental matter—the "building blocks" of the universe as it is still called—is itself radically complex. Alfred North Whitehead was not so wrong when he spoke of physics as the study of "the smaller organisms." Every atom conceals a magnificent internal architecture of finely balanced forces. And like everything else in nature, that architecture is an evolving, historical creation. On the largest scale, the galaxies are intricate structures that must have formed at an unexpectedly early stage of cosmic evolution—as if formative tendencies yet unknown to science were there from the beginning waiting to turn mere clumps of primitive matter into blazing cathedrals of light. In these pre- and non-biotic realms, there is not even as slender a reed as selection to lean upon to explain how form is impressed upon chaos. Ironically, the complexity of biology is far more characteristic of nature than the simplicity of classical physics. Biological complexity, we now realize, is only a special case of the complexity of physical systems throughout nature. And all the systems relate to one another hierarchically and historically in a way that looks very much like a "deep-laid scheme."

The first scientist to take note of the evolving and hierarchical character of the universe was the astronomer Harlow Shapley. In 1930 Shapley, who shares credit with Edward Hubble for elaborating our understanding of the expanding universe, floated an idea whose significance went unnoticed in his own day. In his book prophetically titled *Flights from Chaos: A Survey of Material Systems from Atoms to Galaxies*, Shapley described the universe as a system composed of subsystems building up from some basic "cosmoplasma" toward organic structures here on Earth. Even atoms, Shapley observed, are no longer the "little, hard, ultimate chunks of matter" postulated by "scientific dogma." The overall picture of nature is one of "progress toward order"—a conclusion that directly challenged the prevailing assumption that the cosmos is winding down toward entropic doom. Where in this progression do we find the human mind? At the farthest edge of complexification, Shapley supposed . . . but then added a jarring conjecture. "If mind appears at all, might it not possibly enter every class and subclass" in this hierarchy of systems?

That same year James Jeans, writing on "the mysterious universe," concluded that "the universe begins to look more like a great thought than like a great machine":

> Mind no longer appears as an accidental intruder into the realm of matter; we are beginning to suspect that we ought rather to hail it as the creator and governor of the realm of matter.

Which is as close as one can come to the Deist's God without naming names.

With each passing year we are learning more about the uncanny balance of forces and circumstances that underlie Shapley's "progress toward order." Hubert Reeves, Director of Research at the *Centre Nationale de la Recherche Scientifique* in Paris, commenting on the "apparently fortuitous events that appear to have been indispensable to the appearance of human beings," lists a few of the "cosmic coincidences" on which the grand cosmic hierarchy depends:

> A quite extraordinary coincidence involving certain nuclear parameters made possible the birth of carbon in red giant stars. The relative populations of photons and nucleons happened to give the universe the longevity needed for the appearance of life, and at the same time permitted the formation of stars and galaxies. The list of these "miraculous coincidences" is long. . . . humans are part of a lengthy history that involves the entire universe from the time of its birth. Our nucleons were

born in the great original fire; they were assembled into nuclei in the fiery hearts of stars. These nuclei have clothed themselves with electrons to make atoms and simple molecules in interstellar space. In the primitive ocean and on the continents, the combinations continued tirelessly. At each stage, new levels of complexity have appeared.[11]

Since ancient times, people have tried to understand the cosmos by telling stories about it. Their tales invoked gods and heroes: anthropomorphic figures who once strew the sky with stars or summoned the beasts from the bowels of the Earth. We can no longer believe in such personal agents; but we can once again tell a story about the universe and all that fills it. It turns out to be an eventful evolutionary adventure in which the elements and forces of nature organize themselves, confront and overcome obstacles, and steadily rise to Reeves' "new levels of complexity." The physicist Brian Swimme, collaborating with the ecological philosopher Thomas Berry, has sought to tell that tale in a popularized cosmological narrative they call "the universe story."[12] The approach taken by Swimme and Berry may have too much undisguised teleology about it to pass muster in the scientific mainstream—it features highly personified natural forces that plan and seek and do—but the general outline of what they have to tell is not so very different from similar works by established scientists. Lynn Margulis' *Microcosmos: Four Billion Years of Microbial Evolution* or even Steven Weinberg's *The First Three Minutes*[13] are both presented as historical accounts of great cosmic changes in which things and forces appear as actors in a drama fashioning the world into the intricate structure it has become. Margulis tells us, for example, that "bacterial confederacies . . . cooperated and centralized, and in doing so formed a new kind of cellular government." Weinberg prefers to narrate the early history of the cosmos as a movie that passes frame by frame in which the fundamental particles must struggle through obstacles like "the deuterium bottleneck." The urge to translate what was once a lifeless collection of physical and chemical formulae into a narrative of evolving complexity is becoming irresistible.

Time in Short Supply

In the year his book *A Brief History of Time* was published (1988), Stephen Hawking had an interview with Pope John Paul. They discussed the theological implications of the new cosmology. Unlike Hawking's boneheaded fundamentalist critics, the Pope saw nothing to object to in the Big Bang. He did, however, caution that scientists should resist trying to probe beyond the Big Bang; that was the moment of creation and it belonged to God.

The Pope need hardly have worried. Hawking's theories allow for no probing because they do not allow for a moment of creation. Hawking has likened the question "What came before the Big Bang?" to the question "What lies north of the north pole?" In the Big Bang, everything including time itself was created; there was no "before." In that sense, there is no "place" for God in Hawking's universe. The new cosmology all but eliminates the familiar First Cause on which a great deal of theology has been built. But in granting the universe a story-like character, it raises a second dilemma for godless intellect. *Time.* Time may not have a beginning, but it does have a duration. There is only so much of it. And with the advent of Big Bang theory in modern cosmology, science has suddenly found time to be in short supply. Hawking's cute little phrase "the *history* of time" marks a torturous twist in scientific thought. The grand vistas of eternity that once made any remote improbability possible have vanished. The universe is now understood to have an age. It is a ripe old age—15 to 20 billion years—but hardly as much time as we need for randomness to work all its wonders of natural complexity.

Odds like those computed above by Fred Hoyle become even more striking when we realize that physical theory no longer has "world enough and time" at its disposal to account for what chance alone can do. F. B. Salisbury is among those who have attempted to include the age of the universe in calculating biological probabilities. He set about estimating the probability for the haphazard assemblage of the thousand nucleotides necessary to constitute a single small enzyme containing a mere three hundred amino acids. His conclusion was that there would be not even a fraction of the time needed in the entire history of the universe. This left Salisbury to observe that *chance* itself may be the factor that has to be eliminated if the evolutionary explanation of life is to retain its cogency. An ironic proposal. Chance, previously so powerful an explanatory device, now becomes the obstacle to coherent explanation.[14]

Admittedly, there is a problematic character to calculations like those above. One might object that the odds are always against any particular thing happening in the real world. Think of how people often marvel at the unlikely train of events that led to meeting the person they married. In the course of time, *something* is always "turning up." Yet after the fact, retrodicting the likelihood that whatever *has* happened ever *could* have happened will always yield immense improbabilities. That is why, even when the odds are very, very long, chance can never be ruled out. There is always some minute probability that the highly improbable will happen. If the universe now seems to provide too little time for multiple trial and error repetitions, there is no way to prove that things could not have turned out as they did on the first roll-out of the cosmic dice.

But can we really *believe* that? Statistics may be objective; but belief is a state of mind. Scientists overlook the fact that chance is not a purely mathematical category; it borders on the subjective. For one thing, we have no way to begin the calculation of any probability—especially about the whole course of cosmic time—without choosing a starting point and selecting initial conditions. These are matters of choice and discrimination. Finally, just like the gambler who must decide if the odds are good enough to bet on, once the calculation is done, we must assume an attitude toward the number that results. Having calculated any set of odds, one must then make a judgment: "do I find such a probability believable?" We make such commonsense calculations every day of our lives; they are no less relevant to great cosmological questions.

There is a factor at work here that might be called the Credulity Index: *how much do you believe chance can accomplish all by itself?* Some— those who rank high on the Credulity Index—will still say they find it totally believable that chance can produce a coherent universe. They may even feel a certain righteous pride in saying so: they are being tough, rigorous, orthodox. But this does invert the nature of blind faith. Until our own day, believing in anything other than randomness as the basis for all that exists in the universe required an act of faith that defied rationality. Now, believing that the universe came into existence by random physical processes requires an even more heroic leap of faith.

Ours is no longer that simple mechanistic universe in which something like guiding intelligence can be blithely ruled out as a way of accounting for self-organization and self-regulation. Our historical universe, filled with finely articulated and evolving structures, brings back into prominence one of the oldest perceptions in our relations with nature: the appearance of design.

Design in Modern Dress

In the Western world, design has always been associated with God—the old gentleman with the long white beard who resides beyond the clouds. That is precisely the God that anticlerical revolutionaries set out to exterminate in the Age of Reason. Yet, in the last decade of the twentieth century, following the greatest wave of new empirical findings in its history, scientific thought is finding even more design of the natural world than it did in the age of Newton. As the philosopher of science Errol Harris observes, "The argument from design in modern dress" is not "a resort to God as a cloak to cover our ignorance, but is the logical consequence of the very nature of our knowledge and of the structure of the universe as discovered by empirical science."[15]

Few scientists would care to embrace the theological backlog that clings to the argument from design as it was originally formulated by the Deists; nevertheless, something much like Deism is reappearing. It arises from a wealth of scientific discoveries that spontaneously inspire intimations of teleology. We are seeing science rediscover its role as natural philosophy, that broad, humanistic style of thought that characterized the study of nature until the great agnostic onslaught of the early nineteenth century. Up to that point, scientists regarded themselves as philosophers participating in a general cultural enterprise that was as much in touch with human need as with natural fact. In that enterprise the most important contribution natural philosophy had to make was the explication of the world's orderly design.

Now, as our appreciation of deep structures in the cosmos increases, our sense of design in nature is being stood on its head. An older generation of natural philosophy was struck by the seeming simplicity of the universe. A few laws of motion and the invariant properties of the atoms were enough to make nature intelligible. "Nature is pleased with simplicity," Newton proclaimed, "and affects not the pomp of superfluous causes." God was deduced from that very simplicity; in it the Deists saw the ingenuity of a divine intelligence. There seemed no other explanation for how so much came from so little. In the new natural philosophy it is complexity, not simplicity, that betokens design. The deeper we look into nature, the more nested hierarchies we find—and all of them building up and up into the laddered progression of subsystems and supersystems Mario Bunge depicts in the following chart (fig. 1). What else besides some form of purposeful intelligence could hold all this together?[16]

In biological theory there has long been a maverick school of thought called "emergent evolution." Emergence is grounded in a sense of amazement at how organized much has come out of how (seemingly) disorganized little. Can this thrust toward complexity really be boiled down to chance and blind selection? Traditionally, emergence was limited to the realm of life, where it has tended to shade off into Vitalism, a school of thought that mainstream biology regards as heretical. But with the coming of the new cosmology, the whole history of the universe stretches before us as an emergent phenomenon. This gives us a new way of defining our human place in nature. It yields a curious new kind of centrality—not in space but in time. Rather than seeing the Earth and the life it bears as being the physical center of the universe, we can now see ourselves as standing on the frontier of time. As far as we know, there is no complexity in all the complexifying universe that surpasses that of the human imagination.

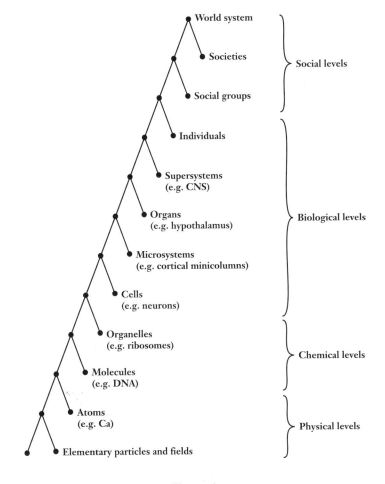

Figure 1.
The supersystems and subsystems of a human being.

The measure of our significance (which need not be read as "superiority") might be calculated in terms of *surprise*.

Imagine an interlocking sequence of emergent systems spread out from the beginning of time until now. Then ask: starting from the sizzling photon soup of the Big Bang, how unpredictable is the evolution of the first subatomic particle, the first galaxy, the first star, the first molecule, the first living cell, the first articulately intelligent brain, and at last the mathematical formulation of the evolution of the first subatomic particle? At every step along the way, the unpredictability increases, the experience of surprise mounts—until one may reach the point of needing to postulate an intelligence which was there at the beginning to account for the narrative unfolding that we call the history of time.

But where does this experience of surprise lodge? Obviously, in our own observing and wondering minds here at the still extending frontier of the process. Can it be that the process, in search of appropriate appreciation, unfolds toward that experience of surprise as its point of closure, only by way of such reflexivity becoming "real"?

More and more frequently in popular presentations of the new cosmology we come upon graphics like the two below which include the human frontier with its backward-looking and wondering eye as an integral part of the narrative. For example, the illustration for the 1992 COBE (Cosmic Background-radiation Explorer) expedition (fig. 2) shows the satellite looking back through time to the origin of the universe, which has finally evolved the scientific intelligence to invent the satellite and read its own history. Similarly, the giant "U" in figure 3 illustrates John Wheeler's conception of a "participatory universe." It depicts "a self-excited circuit" that closes with the advent of the conscious observer. Wheeler's main point of reference is the need of quantum mechanical phenomena to be read out before an event can "take place." But does not the same "observer-participancy" apply to the entire cosmos that builds up from the quanta?

"Observers," John Wheeler has conjectured, "may be necessary to bring the universe into being." His participant-observer—the eye that closes the loop between substance and sentience—is required in order to actualize physical reality. At this point, Wheeler approximates one of the most hotly-debated ideas in modern cosmology: the Anthropic Principle. In its most extreme interpretation, the Anthropic Principle regards the emergence of intelligence as the inevitable goal of cosmic evolution. The so-called "cosmic coincidences" that account for life are not coincidences at all. They are the grammar of destiny articulating the arrival of the human mind. The universe is delicately arranged

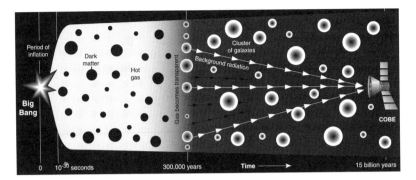

Figure 2.

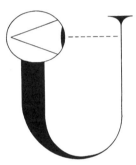

Figure 3.

to support life because that was its purpose from the start. The physicist Frank Tipler believes the purpose goes further. It includes not simply the appearance of intelligence but its migration across the universe—perhaps in some computerized form—until it ingests all matter into thought.

Theories like this sound more like prophecy than science; they surely jar modern scientific orthodoxy. But as extravagant as the Anthropic Principle may seem, it has been matched by those who wish to counter any claim life and mind may have upon special status. There is, for example, the "many universes" model. It asks us to imagine endless and infinite repetitions of cosmogenesis; eventually the repetitions exhaust every physical possibility, along the way producing numberless dead universes where the observing eye never emerges. Thus, in some undiscovered portion of space or in the course of innumerable Big Bang–Big Crunch oscillations, the extraordinary structure of the universe we see about us can be accounted for by mere chance: we have happened because everything has happened. The universe is . . . nothing special.

The many universes theory reads like a last ditch attempt to salvage the explanatory power of chance. Ironically, it does so by violating one of the classic tenets of modern science: the famous rule called "Occam's razor," which bids us never to multiply entities beyond necessity. In its frantic attempt to explain away the wonder of things, the many universes model would multiply whole universes to infinity. Once again, it is an example of skeptics being willing to believe anything.

At some point in an essay like this it becomes imperative to declare an interest. Otherwise, some may suspect there is a secret agenda at work. Is there a religious subtext hidden beneath the criticisms I raise here? Given the fact that I can no longer see the validity of dichotomized categories like "spiritual" and "physical," "mind" and "matter" that have traditionally structured the debate between religion and science, I am not sure what anybody would understand me to be saying if I declared that I was or was not "religious." If I am religious, it is with no rejection of the physical; if I am scientific, it is with no rejection of the spiritual. This certainly does not make me religious in any conventional church-going sense. I cannot think of any established religious community that would claim me as a member.

When I was a child, I thought as a child. In both my catechism classes and my science classes I was left with no doubt where the material world left off and the spiritual world began. At a later stage of my life— about the time I completed my first college course in Logical Positivism—I elected to be an atheist and materialist, again with no doubt what these words meant. Now all the categories that once governed the long historical debate between true believers and atheists seem to be as antiquated as the terms that once agitated the minds of the medieval schoolmen. They are remnants of an ideology of godlessness that belongs to a bygone era. Just as many scientists cannot disassociate religion from persecuting intolerance, so I find myself unable to separate that ideology from a brutally debunking program that seeks to discourage the sense of honest wonder. There is a kind of science—smugly committed to radical disenchantment—that I find as anti-scientific as evangelical Christianity.

In any case, my main purpose in writing this essay relates to science more than to religion. I accept science as my society's main approach to understanding the cosmos. My concern is that, as it comes down to us freighted with an outmoded commitment to godlessness, science has denied itself access to useful philosophical categories like inten-tionality and teleology. This has severely crippled it as a mode of inquiry. Out of its historical hostility to theology, science has censored its capacity to introduce purpose and design into its understanding of nature; its commitment to debunking reductionism has blinded it to the full appreciation of natural systems; its adoption of a one-dimen-sional objectivity has wounded its capacity to read human nature into the greater nature around us.

These are grave intellectual and moral failings; worse still, they are tinged with exactly the sort of fanaticism from which science once promised to free us. These days one finds the word "dogma" more frequently attached to scientific ideas—like the non-inheritability of acquired characteristics—than to religious teachings; so too the word "heresy" turns up with worrisome frequency in scientific discourse. And in almost all cases the anathema attaches to ideas about nature that suggest design and intention. One of the heretics of modern science, James Lovelock, who discovered the controversial Gaia hypothesis, laments the fact "now that science has moved into the niche partially vacated by religion, there are respected scientists who preach a kind of atheistic materialism that asserts that science can explain everything. It can never do this, not even to the limits of human understanding. There is no place for certainty in science."[17]

The intolerance Lovelock bemoans remains deeply rooted in the history of science. It stems from an ideological commitment that was intended to cast science as the prime defender of reason in our society.

But the "reason" science is defending is the narrow nihilistic skepticism of the eighteenth-century village atheist. One almost despairs to see science in danger of betraying its own highest principles of open inquiry.

Almost, but not quite. Because there exist among the scientists men and women of great conscience and even greater curiosity who genuinely seek to know the truth. And the truth is there to be found. It is making itself known by fits and starts in the new cosmology and in the sciences of complexity. Watch and listen to the scientists who are reporting the new cosmology to us as all the pieces slip into place. Note the thrill of unexpected discovery in their voices, the glimmer of amazement in their eye. They know that something profoundly important is beginning in our time. A new worldview of intoxicating depth and richness is being born and with it a new appreciation for what Aristotle once called "final causes"—the ends toward which natural forces seem to tend as if they were operating under the guidance of designing intelligence.

In 1992 the COBE satellite sent back messages that have been called the most important finding in the history of science: "the Holy Grail" of cosmology, as Michael Turner of the University of Chicago termed it. Another member of the COBE team, George Smoot, remarked, "If you're religious, it's like seeing God." COBE was launched to make minute measurements of the cosmic background radiation that is the vibrant relic of the Big Bang. The discovery of that radiation in 1964 by Robert Wilson and Arlo Penzias was epoch-making; to all but a few skeptics background radiation proves the explosive origin of the universe. But the finding presented a problem. The radiation seemed to be absolutely uniform in all directions and therefore unable to account for the galactic structure of the cosmos. Where did the galaxies come from in a universe that was formlessly smooth in all directions? COBE discovered that there are irregularities or lumps in the background radiation, probably the result of early cosmic turbulence. From the turbulence came "topological defects" in space; and from the defects clumps formed that might have produced the gravitational clustering that transformed primordial matter into galaxies.

Notice the language used to describe the finding. "Lumps," "clumps," "defects," "turbulence." These are curiously understated terms to describe the "Holy Grail of cosmology." They also become highly misleading when one realizes that not just any old "irregularity" will do to build a galaxy. There must be the "right kind" of irregularity. No doubt when the process is fully understood, it will have to be added to the lengthening list of cosmic coincidences that make the universe a fit home for living, thinking beings. "Lumps" and "clumps" are left over from agnostic science; they are the sort of casual and evasive phrases that are meant to avoid the implication of design. Clumps and irregularities would seem to be merely accidental accumulations of stuff: no big deal. But one can see the matter more teleologically. The clumps might be viewed as gravitational "seeds" from which the galaxies have sprouted like flowers of fire. In any case, when the COBE findings were reported to the world, members of the research team called the discovery "the handwriting of God."

When scientists invoke God in this way, they may not do so out of any deep religious impulse. It is their way of celebrating the extraordinary fact that there is something rather than nothing in the universe—and an ordered and magnificent something at that. And even more astounding: they are here to study it. They may not literally mean that the universe is the product of divine reason, but they are crediting it with qualities that elicit the same emotional response. When others who are more religiously inclined credit the world's magnificence to God, they are offering up that same celebration. And what they are celebrating is what scientists have themselves shown us to be the world's harmony. When skeptics rush forward to trounce on that celebration, they are undoing the best efforts of science for the sake of voicing a narrow ideological orthodoxy.

I too have been using the word "God" in this essay in the way scientists themselves frequently do: for aspects of nature so wondrously contrived that it is difficult to avoid speaking of them as the results of intelligent design. I realize, as many religious thinkers would be quick to point out, that the God I speak of is not much of a God. In this respect, the new natural philosophy suffers from the same defect as the old: its "deity" is little more than an explanatory principle. Abstract mentality of this order has nothing to do with personality; it does not speak to our longing for moral purpose or immortality. This is not the God to whom one calls out through the dark night of the soul. We find here no consolation in time of grief, no forgiveness of sin, no mothering warmth or fathering security. For all this one must continue to look to faith.

Children of the Universe

Nevertheless, the new natural philosophy is not without religious significance. It offers us something that neither the mainstream religion nor the science of the Western world have offered before: a vital realization of our ecological implication in nature.

In times past both science and Christianity—though each for different reasons—taught that between humanity and nature there is a great gulf fixed. Neither granted human consciousness a "natural" place in nature. The Judeo-Christian tradition elevated both God and the human soul above the physical world, defining each as "spiritual" in a sense that set spirit at odds with matter. As we have seen, such a division no longer makes sense in light of what modern science tells us about the inexhaustible potentiality of matter. Science, on the other hand, with its alienated stance and debunking habits, left human consciousness as an unaccountable accident in the void. Seeking to displace the Earth from the special place that it had held in traditional cosmology, modern science set out to make life and mind ever more marginal: mere epiphenomena in a vast, impersonal universe. Neither scientist nor theologian integrated the human and the natural in a way that yielded a sense of our kinship with the universe and of our ethical obligation to the living planet. There is in fact a deep psychological continuity between the Christian hostility to paganism and the rise of modern science. Both are committed to the desacralization of the natural world.

That we are "strangers and afraid in a world we never made" has been one of the central tenets of agnostic humanism in the modern world. Scientists going honestly about their task of explicating nature over the past three centuries have progressively eaten away at all the metaphysical structures that once lent human existence cosmic importance. The most effective way they went about that task was by emphasizing the factor of size. The universe of modern science is so unimaginably big that the Earth seems to fade into insignificance within it. Julian Huxley once said we live in "a universe of appalling vastness, appalling age, appalling meaninglessness."

But within the new cosmology, size—traditionally the most oppressive measure of mankind's unimportance in the order of things—takes on a radically different character. We now know that the universe is exactly the "right" size to support life on our planet; a smaller universe would not do for that purpose. In an historical universe, time, space, and matter are linked in more than a purely mathematical way; they unfold together through the process of expansion that creates all three. That process of expansion is at every point laying down the conditions that make life possible. Life could not have come into existence until the universe had time to cool by way of expansion. The cooling is required for particles and the first stable elements to evolve. That same process of expansion permits the formation of galaxies and stars. In turn, it is the life and death cycle of stars that makes stellar nucleosynthesis possible, without which the heavier elements that go into the making of a solid planet, and the life upon it, could not appear. This tightly coordinated historical sequence is the only route to life as we know it. The age and size of the universe, far from being oppressively alien, are intimately related to the appearance of life and mind on at least one planet.

In my school days, every science classroom I can remember used to display Mendeleyev's famous periodic table of the elements on the wall, one of the great achievements of modern thought. Here were all the building blocks of the universe from hydrogen to the latest discovery among the heavy elements, and all of them beautifully spread out in an orderly mathematical sequence. But why should that be? Why did the elements have this family resemblance to one another? The question was the same that biologists had once asked about the anatomy of living creatures. Why did they seem related to one another? In both cases, the answer has turned out to be the same. All these things are related—historically. *They evolved from one another.* Matter also has an evolutionary development. In one cosmologer's terse formulation: "hydrogen is a light odorless gas which, given enough time, turns into people."

Hubert Reeves, who marvels at the "astonishing fertility of matter," is among the few scientists who has been willing to immerse himself in the full philosophical significance of this remarkable cosmological fact. He believes there is an "ultimate hypothetical principle" yet to be found that has "contained from the beginning the recipe for intelligence and consciousness."[18] In a 1992 television documentary, he spells out the full implications of that vision:

> There was this old attitude that . . . people do not belong here, that we
> are an impossible chance, . . . that we're foreign to this universe. I think
> what cosmology shows is that this is not true. We are a product of the
> evolution of the universe. And we are in the same history, in the same
> evolution as the stars and the frogs. We are all part of the same universe
> and all part of the evolution which has led to different objects, aspects,
> beings and in this sense we belong to this universe, we are the child of this
> universe, we are made out of stardust.[19]

Skeptics may still find it possible to shrug off Reeves' enraptured rhetoric. Advocates of chance will always have the option of countering, "that's simply the way things turned out as a matter of chance. If they hadn't, we would not be here to marvel at the result." But what does it cost to invoke that response? Discounting wonder surely demands a terrible form of emotional self-censorship—and in any case makes for a poor kind of science. Are we to believe that intellectual rigor requires us to suppress the experience of amazement that scientific curiosity has brought us?

The new cosmology is having a difficult time spelling out its deeper philosophical implications. It is still struggling against a backlog of skeptical resistance. This makes for an instructive contrast with earlier periods in the history of science. Once scientists and scientific intellectuals were eager not simply to explain science to their society but to fathom its human meaning. In the eighteenth century, within Isaac Newton's own lifetime, writers as important as Voltaire were already turning the new worldview into philosophy, poetry, and theology. Their efforts succeeded in making science the centerpiece of the Age of Reason and the handmaiden of egalitarian politics during the revolutionary era that followed. Similarly, in the late nineteenth century, leading intellectuals were busy retailing the meaning of evolution while Darwin was still alive. The Social Darwinists transformed the science of their day into a powerful ally of capitalist industrialism. Though the New Physics of the early twentieth century proved far less easy to communicate in all its advanced mathematical subtlety, intellectuals were busy integrating what they understood of relativity and the uncertainty principle into the popular culture soon after the Copenhagen School made itself known. In a period of cultural dislocation when more and more absolute values were being called into question, the science of that period seemed to reflect the rootless relativism, ambiguity, and paradox of all things.

The new cosmology has its own special relevance to the needs of our time. Our runaway industrial society needs nothing so much as a renewed sense of sympathetic reciprocity with the natural world that has for so long been our long-suffering victim. That is precisely what our new picture of the universe offers. Yet few ranking scientists are willing to take up the assignment. I suspect this is because the new worldview deviates so radically from the godlessness that remains axiomatic in professional science. The scientific community and many intellectuals who look to it as a basis for their values are loathe to face the strenuous revisions that attend the new natural philosophy. It has been so very convenient to brush aside the religious traditions of the world and to treat the universe as "nothing but" a vast, spontaneous accident. Our secular humanist culture lacks the basic vocabulary necessary for taking up the metaphysical and theological questions that the discovery of intelligent design in the universe must inevitably evoke. Godlessness has become such a comfortable point of view: simple, neat, absolute. Few scientists welcome having to rethink it. But what we now understand of the Big Bang and all that follows from it in the "brief history of time" quite simply changes everything. If we are to take science seriously on its own terms, the new cosmology it has visited upon us necessitates the greatest cultural revision since the demise of the Ptolemaic worldview.

Notes

1. See, for example, Anthony L. Peratt, "Not With A Bang," in *The Sciences*, January/February, 1990. Also see Paul Marmet, "The Deceptive Illusion of the Big Bang Cosmology," *Physics in Canada* (September 1990), 97–109.

2. Eric J. Lerner, *The Big Bang Never Happened: A Startling Refutation of the Dominant Theory of the Origin of the Universe* (New York: Times Books, 1991).

3. Steven Weinberg, *Dreams of a Final Theory* (New York: Pantheon Books, 1992), 244.

4. Freeman Dyson, *Disturbing the Universe* (New York: Harper & Row, 1979), 146.

5. George Wald, quoted in Stuart Kauffman, *The Origins of Order: Self-Organization and Selection in Evolution* (New York: Oxford University Press, 1993), 21.

6. See, for example, Paul Davies and John Gribbin, *The Matter Myth* (New York: Viking, 1992).

7. Steven Weinberg, *Dreams of a Final Theory* (New York: Pantheon Books, 1992), 255, 260.

8. Stuart A. Kauffman, *The Origins of Order: Self-Organization and Selection in Evolution* (New York: Oxford University Press, 1993). On the Santa Fe Institute, see the report by M. Mitchell Waldrop, *Complexity: The Emerging Science at the Edge of Order and Chaos* (New York: Simon and Schuster, 1992).

9. Fred Hoyle and N. C. Wickramasinghe, *Lifecloud: The Origin of Life in the Universe* (London: J. M. Dent, 1978). For a critical response to Hoyle, see the article by H. N. V. Temperley in *New Scientist* (August 19, 1982), 505–6, where it is objected that Darwinians do not believe the entire enzyme system was generated all at once, but that it evolved from "simpler systems." This would simply seem to spread the improbabilities out over time.

10. Hoyle quoted in John Barrow and Frank Tipler, *The Anthropic Cosmological Principle* (New York: Oxford University Press, 1986), 22.

11. Hubert Reeves, *Atoms of Silence* (Cambridge: MIT Press, 1984), 144–45.

12. Brian Swimme and Thomas Berry, *The Universe Story: A Celebration of the Unfolding of the Cosmos* (San Francisco: HarperSanFrancisco, 1992).

13. Lynn Margulis and Dorian Sagan, *Microcosmos* (New York: Summit

Books, 1986); Steven Weinberg, *The First Three Minutes* (New York: Basic Books, 1977).

14. F. B. Salisbury, "Natural Selection and the Complexity of the Gene," *Nature* 224 (1970), 342.

15. Errol Harris, *Cosmos and Anthropos* (Atlantic Highlands: Humanities Press International, 1991), 172.

16. Mario Bunge, "From Neuron to Mind," *News in Physiological Sciences* (October 1989), 206–9.

17. James Lovelock, "Gaia: Science or Myth?" *The New Statesman*, 1992.

18. Hubert Reeves, *The Hour of Our Delight* (New York: Freeman, 1993), 132.

19. "The Unexpected Universe," part three of *The Space Age*, PBS series, broadcast November 1992. Also see Hubert Reeves' most recent work, *The Hour of Our Delight*.

Creativity:
The Meeting of Apollo and Dionysus

F. DAVID PEAT

IN THIS TALK I want to say something about creativity and why it is so important for our modern world. In particular, I am going to touch on the idea of creativity as something that bubbles up out of the matter of the cosmos and how it can be found within the very substance of our bodies. Although my background is that of a physicist, over the last years I have been talking to artists and composers and I will be drawing upon examples of the way in which their particular creativity emerges out of the body. Another influence has been my contact with Native Americans—particularly the Blackfoot who live just east of the Rocky Mountains and the Mohawk who live south of the St. Lawrence river.

Through dialogue circles they taught me a different way of seeing the world so that I have been able to look at our European or Western ways of thinking in a fresh light. I suppose that is an example of creativity!

Healing

In part, my talk is going to be about the importance of healing. There is certainly a great need for healing in a world torn apart by war and conflict, violence in society, the breakdown of inner cities and the pollution of our natural environment.

Healing, I believe, requires a new way of being in the world, a transformation of human consciousness and a new sense of shared meaning.

It seems to me that we sense a lack of shared meaning in our world

This talk was given at the Institute International de Psychanalyse et de Psychotherapie Charles Baudoin, in Brussels.

and grounding to the earth and human society in general. This leads people to explore alternative religions, shamanism, and all manner of experiences in their agonized search for an answer, a ground to their life. Yet when people seek the transcendental out of a sense of desperation they leave themselves open to all manner of forces. For Native Americans this phenomenon of "soul loss" can be very real.

If you happen to be a Blackfoot then you are part of a profound shared meaning. Many Natives speak of having "A Map in the Head." This is something learned in childhood as you sit around the fire at night and listen to the songs and stories of the elders; you learn it by watching the animals, by coming to know the land in which you live, by talking to rocks and trees, by participating in ceremonies, and by entering into a wider reality within dreams. This Map in the Head is a connection to the time of creation, a guide to the world of powers and energies, and also a protection.

But what do we, in our modern world, have to contain the powers and forces the psyche may encounter? We are like those chemists and physicists in the first decades of this century who played around with radioactive materials without using any protection. Or like someone who wanders into a high voltage laboratory and begins to touch the apparatus. Moreover, the danger is not just to individuals, but to our whole society, which is in danger of losing its collective soul.

Connected to this is the danger of inflation. Economic inflation is bad enough, but psychic is even worse! Our psychic inflation is expressed in our desire to escape from the body, from the world of matter, from human society, from nature, and into the world of the spirit.

Our world also has great difficulties in dealing with what Jungians call the shadow, that dark area within ourselves which we try to deny by projecting it onto others. The events of our century has been so terrible that we cannot face what our species is capable of doing. The British composer Michael Tippett's answer to the holocaust is contained in his opera "A Child of our Time" and the words "I must know my shadow and my light and then I will become whole." Resolution comes in the Oratorio though the use of Negro spirituals that express the aching soul.

We cannot afford to continue this destructive cycle of denial of the Earth and our bodies though inflation of the psyche. We can no longer deny our collective shadow. We have to face ourselves and this requires a new form of action which is essentially creative.

Aspects of Creativity

When I use that word "creativity" I am thinking of four main areas, areas which I will explore a little later in my talk. These are creativity as:

1) An act of renewal
2) A state of openness, active listening, and willingness to change.
3) In the conventional sense, of making something new, original and unexpected.
4) The art of healing, which, I believe, combines the other three forms of creativity.

It is an enormously creative act to watch and listen, to stay with something, to suspend action. It is enormously creative even to allow our children to grow up. It is creative because the natural reaction of our Western minds is to exert control. We want to analyze, to reduce things to problems, and then immediately to seek a solution—some way of predicting, manipulating, and controlling the world. This can work quite well when it comes to practical issues, but in other cases it may be more important to suspend action, to look, to listen, and then to attempt some act which flows harmoniously out of the whole meaning, movement, and essence of the situation.

Think of a doctor who arrives at the scene of a traffic accident and does nothing. First the doctor simply looks at the injured person. Only after making a primary assessment does he touch the patient in order to make a physical examination and then, finally, attempt some medical intervention.

We are constantly striving, constantly making an effort, constantly trying to anticipate the future and control its outcome, constantly asking how we can become more creative. But what if creativity is as inevitable as breathing and what we are really doing most of the time is blocking this natural force?

I say that this force is perfectly natural because it is an essential part of nature. If we don't see this immediately then maybe it is because our vision is still blocked by what could be called the Newtonian paradigm. This was of a world of independent objects in motion. Change only took place though the application of force and the transfer of energy. Leibniz criticized Newton on the grounds that Newton's God wound his watch at the moment of creation and then left the stage. It was a mechanical universe with no room for the spirit of creativity. And before the Darwinian revolution even plant and animal species were fixed and eternal, as was society with its particular levels for the rich and the poor.

All that has changed. Physicists have a new vision of the world—but the problem is that it has yet to change our everyday thinking. Ilya Prigogine speaks of the transformation of our vision from that of Being to that of Becoming. No longer do we see fixed objects but rather emergent structures, new forms not anticipated from the levels below. Systems are open to their environments; they are aware of changing contexts and strike a balance between internal stability and openness to transformation. Creativity is ubiquitous. It streams through the firmament.

The physicist David Bohm pictured the electron, as well as other elementary particles, not as an object but as a process, an action that is constantly collapsing inward from the entire universe and then scattering outward again. Or as an unfolding out of a ground of ceaseless movement—the implicate order—and then enfolding again. For Bohm matter is in a constant state of coming into manifestation and then unmanifesting. Matter in its very essence is therefore creative. Creativity is inherent in each star and in each particle of dust. Creativity is the essence of our physical bodies. My own vision is of each piece of matter as an inexhaustible inscape, an inner song of authenticity, an endless process of renewal.

How close all this is to the Vedic image of the universe as a constant breathing, a coming into existence followed by an exhalation into the ground of all being. All this is repeated over and over again.

Likewise, for the Blackfoot, everything that is not creatively renewed will be swallowed up by the eternal flux. Even the cosmos would not exist were it not for a continuous creative act of renewal—an act that involves all of life, from the spirits, powers, and keepers of the animals, to the ceremonies of the Blackfoot society and the singing of the birds. Maybe even rocks participate in the song of creation. This creativity is like a spring of water bubbling out of a rock; it is not ego-bound—there is no striving, no effort in it. We are part of this; our very essence of being is unconditioned creativity.

Now what do we mean by creativity? Not simply producing something new. Creativity goes far deeper than that. I am thinking of it as Renewal, Openness, Novelty, and Healing. Let's begin with renewal.

I once knew a baker with mystical leanings! Each morning I would buy a fresh, warm loaf of bread. Day after day, month after month, the bread looked the same, it weighed the same, it contained the same ingredients, yet it was created afresh. It was made new. The baker once told me he made the bread with love and with all the creativity he had.

When parents tell the same bedtime story night after night they are also giving birth to something new. A pianist performs the same concerto in different cities. Many times it is "assez bien" but there are those occasions when, with the help of the active participation of the audience, something totally fresh is created—exactly the same notes are played but they are heard as if for the very first time. The icon painter is confined to use formal gestures and a preordained color scheme yet he is creating something new, a container for the spiritual. Creativity is the activity of listening on the part of the therapist.

The ceremonies of Native Americans are done for the whole of creation. The goal of Islamic alchemy was not so much to produce gold, or even a personal transformation, but to enter into relationship with the original moment of creation, the naming of all things by Allah, and in this way to assist in the renewal of all creation.

The second area, aspect, or side of creativity is openness, unconditioned listening. Life seeks stability, but it must also remain open and flexible to the world outside. This requires enormous creativity.

The world is flux, things pass away, contexts change, people grow and age, organizations flourish or atrophy. To remain healthy means being able to accept change. It means supporting change in others—one's children, a partner, the profession in which one is engaged. It means facing the fear inside, coming to terms with the shadow. Not clinging to the past. It is a harmony between the need to renew and foster what is important and be open to that which must die and be replaced. Creativity is a willingness to accept endings, to discard, to sacrifice. It is the goddess Kali who must destroy in order to create.

Native American metaphysics sees society as a living thing, an expression of the consciousness of the people and the original compacts made by the ancestors with the spirits of the world. But societies only live on because they are actively renewed. They tell me that the great vanished civilizations of the past—the Olmec, Mayan, Anasazi—were not destroyed by natural forces, nor by external invasion. Rather the people decided that contexts had changed and it was no longer appropriate to perform acts of renewal. The people stayed where they were. It was the civilization, a particular order, that had vanished.

The third area, novelty, reflects the American poet Ezra Pound's dictum, "Make it New." Creativity as making things that are different, original, like nothing seen before. The paradigm is Picasso, who seemed to produce something new and different every day of his life. Or Mozart, whose creativity was a pure, unconditioned outpouring of spirit.

There is a time for creative renewal and a time for creative change, for destruction of what already exists and replacement by the new. Byzantine art, which enjoyed renewal for so long, was no longer fulfilling to a painter like Giotto, or Ciambue, and so new, more humanistic modes of expression were developed. Enormous energy is needed to break apart the old paradigm. Ways of thinking are held on to deeply and unconsciously.

Here is the creativity of a Picasso and a Mozart, but also that of an Einstein and a Cézanne who both sought radical changes to the existing order. Cézanne spent his whole life struggling to "realize his sensations" before nature and to create a new order of painting. Einstein spent his time reading the philosophers Kant and Hume, but had to reach down deeply into his own thought processes in order to produce a revolution in our concepts of space and time.

Finally there is creativity as the synthesis of the previous three overall types—renewal, openness, and radical change. I think of this form of creativity as healing, making whole, bringing back into balance, restoring harmony. It is the natural creativity of the human body which at every moment is assaulted by radiation, bacteria, viruses, poisons, and other trauma, yet constantly repairs and sustains itself. Creativity is healing of the body, society, and, indeed, the entire planet.

Healing is also an act of sacrifice, for the healer must support inner tensions and paradoxes within the body, tensions which can often make a person ill. I believe that our present society is placing enormous demands upon the healer. Healers are not necessarily doctors and therapists, for composers, artists, writers, actors, and filmstars are also called upon to perform the role of shamans. They are often made physically ill by the internal tensions they must hold. Some societies are wiser, so that the act of healing is undertaken by the entire society. For the !Kung of the Kalahari, the healer dances in order to invoke and raise the temperature of the sacred Num that can burn and destroy. Once filled with the Num, the healer is able to see within and to heal. It is the responsibility of the society to protect the healer by removing some of the Num when it gets too hot, and cooling down the healer.

The Mystery of Matter

I have suggested that creativity is perfectly natural and present in each one of us, in the very matter of our bodies. Now I want to look a little closer at matter. To the Sufi mystic, every tree, flower, and grain of dust sings the glory of Allah. In the West, and despite centuries of science, the inner essence of matter remains a mystery. To the contemporary physicist, matter has been transformed from an object to a process.

The physicist David Bohm argued that quantum reality is so very

different from our everyday large-scale experience that it requires a
new language for its discussion. Our Indo-European languages are
strongly noun-based and subject-object structured. For Bohm they
represent a barrier to deeper understanding. The essence of the
quantum world is flux, movement, transformation, symmetry, and
relationship, rather than individual objects in interaction. For Bohm
the essence of such a reality requires a verb-based, process-based
language—probably one very close to that still spoken by the Blackfoot.

The physicist Wolfgang Pauli, who was involved in many scientific
discussions and a collaborator with Carl Jung, pictured atomic reality
as a battle between symmetry and antisymmetry. Pauli had consulted
Jung during a crisis in his life and his long series of dreams are
discussed in Jung's *Psychology and Alchemy*. They also collaborated on
The Nature and Structure of the Psyche, which includes Jung's exploration of the phenomenon of synchronicity.

Pauli argued that just as Jung had discovered the objective side to the
unconscious—that is the collective consciousness which transcends
the individual, personal history of repressed experiences—so too
physics must uncover the "subjective in matter." In particular he felt
that science must come to terms with what he termed "the irrational
in matter." To take an example, quantum theory can offer no account
for the disintegration of a radioactive nucleus or predict when this will
occur. For Pauli it was an irrational act. Another example would be the
way in which, when a quantum measurement is made, a large number
of different potentialities collapse into a single actuality. The process
is totally discontinuous and lies outside the power of quantum theory
to explain.

Jung was concerned with synchronicity—what he termed an "acausal
connecting principle." Pauli for his part believed that abstract mathematical symmetries were the key to the cosmos. He even pictured the
duality between symmetry and antisymmetry as a battle between God
and the Devil. Now symmetries do not appear to be tangible things;
they are not objects that can be grasped or directly observed. They
come very close to what Jung called archetypes. Yet it is the guiding
role of antisymmetry, for example, that gives structure to the material

world. Without antisymmetry, also called Pauli's exclusion principle, all the electrons in an atom could collapse into the same state and the chemical elements would lose their distinct properties.

In terms of electrons this means that there is an ordering principle, a connecting principle, that has nothing to do with interactions or forces or causality. At the level of quantum physics it is a true "acausal connecting principle," a true synchronicity between the material level and something non-material.

Pauli, from the perspective of physics, and Jung from that of depth psychology, were both approaching the "psychoid," that deep level where the unconscious merges into matter. The psychoid is variously described as "neither matter nor mind, and both"—or by the metaphor of the speculum that reflects one world into an other while, at the same time, transcending them. In one way of looking, the psychoid is material and it is also mental. In another, it transcends these categories which, after all, are only the distinctions created by thought.

We have already seen that as we approach the atomic level the ordinary world of causality and of independent physical objects in interaction with each other dissolves away and leaves a world of abstract symmetries, processes, transformations, flux, and Pauli's "the irrational." It is a world in which matter is constantly coming into being and fading away. This subatomic level is one of pure creativity, and this must also the nature of the psychoid, which lies beyond the distinctions of matter and spirit. Creativity is to be found at the level of the psychoid. It bubbles up into the manifest world where it expresses itself mentally and physically.

In this sense creativity is synchronistic since its origins lie in the deep ground beyond matter and mind. Its metaphor is that of the artist who requires both the mental image or intention and the material substrate. These are then brought together in the creative act which leaves both matter and consciousness transformed and renewed.

Creativity is deeply connected to this mystery of matter. It is the meeting of Apollo and Dionysus—the world of Platonic order and abstraction incarnating into the flux and chaos of the world. In this divine encounter Apollo is forced to acknowledge the contingency that lies within the grain of the world. Likewise, the drunken ecstasy of Dionysus is bound by the chains of harmony and abstraction. Apollo and Dionysus, spirit and matter—each is transformed by the other.

A continuous act of sustained creation is present within each one of us. We contain within us the primordial ocean out of which all life evolved. The atoms of our bodies were created in nuclear syntheses within the hearts of the stars. The elementary particles out of which these atoms are composed were formed out of the Big Bang. And if physicists like Bohm are to believed, our body is a constant process of renewal, each elementary particle being a process that unfolds out of the entire universe and folds back again.

It is also a fact of physics that each of us literally stands at the very center of the universe. The cosmos was created in a singularity of space-time, a point that began to expand in an explosive fashion. Today each point in space is a fossil of that primordial explosion. Each point is that point at which creation began.

The Middle Ages saw the human body as a microcosm of the macrocosm—"as above so below." This was also the conviction of David Bohm, who felt that because his body contained the same matter out of which the universe is created, then within him could also be found the deepest understanding of the nature of matter, its order and laws. Something very similar was said by the philosopher Henri Bergson, who argued that reality is ultimately unknowable through the mind yet, since this same reality is the stuff of our bodies, it can be known within the body.

In Bohm's case, he was aware of certain interior sensations, muscular dispositions, and acts of proprioception. On one occasion when thinking about physics he had a particular sensation. This was joined by a second sensation. Then the two combined to produce something quite different. This was directly related to a mathematical result about quantum theory, one that turns out to be very counter-intuitive.

Einstein told Bohm that he too "thought" by means of subtle muscular tensions. His work on non-linear field equations of space-time was helped by the movements he sensed within his arm as he squeezed a rubber ball.

What is curious in Bohm's case is that mathematical results came to him out of the body—without the various logical and deductive steps needed to derive a result. Conscious work was something that came later—having to sit down and work out a proof for what had unfolded out of his body in a very different way.

What we take as the experience of mind and consciousness is only a small part of something much larger that is distributed within the entire body. It takes place at the muscular, visceral, and biochemical levels. It is at this material level that much of our natural creativity is to be found.

To give one example, there is evidence from brain scans that during performance a professional musician suppresses the active listening region of the brain. What is being produced in performance appears to emerge out of an orchestrated vocabulary of inner muscular gestures, each of which seems to be specifically related to feelings and emotions. In this sense the music is emerging out of the very physicality of the body. Of course conscious study of the musical score has been involved earlier, but the act of performance may be quite different. There is a wonderful anecdote about the Canadian pianist, Glenn Gould, who was practicing a particular piece by Bach but could not produce what he felt inside because the sound he was making on the piano had become too distracting. In the end, he put two radios on top of the piano, turned them up to full volume and went on practicing!

The pianist Alan Rowlands told me that despite intense study and practice he had difficulty understanding a particular passage in one of Beethoven's late piano sonatas. As he put it, the passage was musically ungrammatical; it was as if something had been left out. It did not seem to make sense. Then, on one occasion, he had a very strong sense of the presence of the audience, breathing with him and supporting him. As he approached it, the passage simply played itself. Only later, on reflection, was he able to come to terms with what he had played and to realize the inevitability of its inner logic. In this case creativity transcended the boundaries of the individual and became a ritual of the entire group—audience and performer.

The significance of the body and its role in creativity is the subject of several contemporary artists such as the sculptors Anthony Gormley and Anish Kapoor as well as the performance artist, Maria Abramovich. In making his work, which is based upon his own body, Gormley speaks of entering the dark space within the body. It is a place rarely visited in our own age, the place in which the body has its existence: a place beyond ego, beyond history, beyond space and time. As Gormley puts it, this space is beyond good and evil, although it may contain both good and evil. This is the space of pure potentiality and creativity. As far as Anish Kapoor is concerned, a pure act of creativity which transcends the personal and biographical can induce in his material—in the stone and pigment—what he terms an alchemical transformation. Again, this is something that lies beyond mere causality and the action of one object upon another.

Creativity and Healing

When art brings us to a dark internal space it exercises a healing function. The idea of the artist or musician as a shamanic figure is an ancient one. Orpheus tamed the wild beasts with his music. Within many indigenous cultures songs have healing properties. Indeed, songs are considered to be living beings in their own right. What is important is not so much the act of the healer who sings, as the song that sings itself, which makes itself manifest through the medium of the singer's body. In so doing, the song heals the sickness within person. The sickness itself may have a spiritual origin and the song restores wholeness to the body and meaning to a life.

The function of the shamanic singer/healer is very much in evidence with the British composer Sir Michael Tippett. Tippett has spoken to me about being possessed during the act of composition—enthused and possessed by a god. His task was to hold within his body, over an extended period of composition that lasted several years, the tensions and forces that would later emerge in the music. The result made him profoundly ill. In this he could identify with other composers such as Berlioz when composing the opera "Les Troyens," or Beethoven of the last works. Again, by sitting with the inner tensions of the body, by containing them to the point of sickness, the shaman is able to create an act of healing for others.

But here let me add a note of caution. Shamanic figures can also be disruptive, self-destructive, antisocial, and sometimes violent. In the case of artists I wonder if it is because they are allowing themselves to remain open to what Pauli called "the irrational in matter." There are times when the artist may help to renew meaning within a society and times when he must break that meaning apart in his search for new forms. It is interesting to note the degree to which art can still shock and offend.

Although they don't seem all that eager to talk about it, I get the sense from Native American friends that there are healers one would be happy to see and others who are best avoided except at times of severe crisis when their special powers are required.

In our own culture the bubbling creativity of Picasso did not preclude his callous and brutal attitude toward women. Cézanne's creativity did not preclude his extreme rudeness and defensiveness. And think of the outstanding writers of the United States and try to list those who were not alcoholic. There is always a price to pay and the brighter the light burns the darker the shadow is.

Cézanne and Time

The creativity which emerges out of the body demands its own time. This is not the psychological time of anticipation and expectation, but something more organic and material. It is the time needed for a seed to germinate, for fruit to ripen, for food to digest, for the alchemical workings within the athanor. It is time that must be accepted and lived with. It is the time of listening as the therapist sits with a patient. For Tippett, although the process made him ill, he knew intuitively this was the time demanded by his very organism. As the Native Americans insist, a ceremony can only be performed when "the time is right."

To be creative one must allow this organic, visceral experience to "take its time." Parents provide a safe and secure environment for a child's growth. They listen and watch without attempting to hang on to what is passing away or to reach forward to what may be.

This essence of creativity is contained with a remark the poet Rilke relates about the painter Cézanne. Cézanne sat before the motif "like a dog, just looking, without any nervousness, without any ulterior motive." At the time Cézanne was doing something radical; he was discovering an entirely new order for painting. But the only way he could do this was by containing the inner sensations of his body and allowing them to manifest on the canvas in their own time. His portrait of Vollard took over 140 sittings and was left incomplete. The best Cézanne could say was that parts of the waistcoat were not bad. He was still painting a still life long after the fruit had rotted in the bowl. Again and again he returned to Mount St. Victor. He once said he could spend his life in front of the motif—now sitting a little to the left and now to the right.

Cézanne would sit and eventually he would make a mark—small parallel brush strokes of orange in this place, and over there another cluster of orange marks. Days later he may cool the orange with blue—pushing it farther back into the landscape. Here he makes a mark of green. It is deliberately ambiguous. It could be part of the foliage of a tree in the foreground, or the green of bushes in the middle ground. But, as Rilke said, the miracle is that "it is as if every place knew about all the others." Another painter observed "here is something he knew and now he's saying it; right next to it there's an empty space, because that was something he did not know yet."

The act of painting for Cézanne was pure physicality, the realization of sensations within his body. Toward the end of his life Cézanne felt that all he had were his "little sensations." But they took him into a world that lies beyond conscious thought and emotion. Rilke realized that it lay even beyond love: "While it may be natural to love each one of those things in the landscape if one shows this, one makes it less well; one judges it instead of saying it."

In Cézanne's own words, "le paysage se reflète, s'humanise, se pense en moi. Je l'objective, le projette, le fixe sur ma toile . . . je serait la conscience subjective de ce paysage, comme ma toile en serait la conscience objective."

I find that passage quite remarkable because it sums up so much of what I have been trying to understand about creativity. And here I'd like to interject something purely personal. I have struggled for a long time with Cézanne, more than with any other painter. I spent a long time in front of his paintings. I can't say that I like or dislike them. That simply does not come into it. It is more that he engages me in a way that goes beyond analysis or reason. And so I would read what art critics say about Cézanne and then go back to look at a painting. Yes, I could see the way he created a new perspective out of color. Yes, I could see how he analyzed the picture into a variety of planes. Yes, I could go on and on with this. Yet, in the end, none of that seemed to be to the point. Then, earlier this year, the big Cézanne exhibition opened at the Tate gallery in London and I visited day after day, each time seeing something new. Finally, one day, I stood in front of a particular painting and asked myself "what is really going on?"

Finally an answer came. I had always been aware of sensations within my body when I looked at Cézanne—inner movements, tensions, sensations of orientation, and so on. Now I paid more attention to these inner sensations and the way they seemed to be orchestrated. It wasn't about looking any more but about feelings and experiencing. I was hit with an intuition, a firm conviction, that these were the sensations Cézanne himself had experienced as he sat before the same motif. I rushed to the library and sure enough I discovered that quotation above—"je serait la conscience subjective de ce paysage, comme ma toile en serait la conscience objective."

The new order Cézanne created for painting involved simultaneously an order of gestures and colors upon the flat canvas and, at the same time, a reading of these gestures in terms of depth, movement, and so on. As a counterpoint to the order of flatness, there is the order of a multiplicity of planes, areas, and regions in perceptual space that form a dramatic counterpoint with what we expect to see. Thus the foreground should be closer than the trunk of a pine, yet it is simultaneously farther away, and a patch of green shares in both the immediate foreground as well as the distant plane in the background. What I now saw was the way in which this is informed by, and recreates, such an intense symphony of internal sensations and movements.

Again, as with the composer Tippett, there is such tension in this, this holding onto the feelings. I quote Cézanne again—"always with me the realization of my sensations is always painful. I cannot attain the intensity that is unfolded before my senses." This recalls a letter I had from the English painter, David Andrew. He felt that nature "looked him," that is, looks at itself through him, so that "art is nature in action." The art of painting for him was an act of dreaming where, in a series of paintings, forms emerge, shift, transform, and crystalize. The environment "knows" him and paints itself though him. And here I should add this work is not purely representational since he is not so much responding to an external object but to "the vibration of related bodily sensations."

Projective Identification

Likewise nature thought itself through Cézanne and his painting became the objective expression of the "sensations" he experienced. I, in turn, standing before his painting, experience those sensations, the same sense of the motif becoming conscious and thinking itself.

This invites me to explore what psychotherapists call "projective identification" or transference. Mental projections are normally spoken of as taking place onto a blank screen. Something within the therapist triggers a projection in which the supposedly objective therapist is now perceived as the patient's father or some other figure from childhood. The perceptive therapist must contain the transference and use its energy in the patient's process of healing.

Over recent years I have talked to therapists about their experiences of projective identification. Often they will tell me about that one case which stuck them deeply and possessed some numinous, troubling, or inexplicable element. The accounts they gave me suggested the actual projection of certain contents of consciousness, an aspect of the self with all its memories, feelings, intentions, and so on, from one mind to the other. In such instances they had direct access to bizarre feelings, memories, knowledge, and attitudes—either in dreams or during a therapeutic session. On later reflection they realize these lay beyond their own experience and could only have come from the patient.

Probably "projection" is not the correct word for what is happening in such cases. It does appear as if, for a short period of time, consciousness is shared and that the duality between matter and mind is transcended. Although its origins may lie in neurosis, I wonder if it is a profoundly creative act. Let me give you a metaphor. In chemistry there are certain reactions—such as the combination of oxygen and hydrogen to form water—that cannot take place at room temperature. The reason is that a barrier of energy must be first overcome in order for the molecules to rearrange their geometry before they can react. This energy barrier can be overcome if a catalyst is used. Molecules adsorb on the surface of a catalyst, such as platinum, where they temporarily borrow a little energy, rearranging themselves until they interact. When they leave the catalyst they pay this energy back. Another role played by the surface of the catalyst is to slow things down and give the molecules time to meet and interact.

Suppose something has become fixed in a person's life; they are unable to move, unable to increase the dimension of their life. They are closed and stunted in their growth. By themselves they do not have sufficient energy to bring about a restructuring of the psyche. But suppose that such contents can be projected onto or shared with the mind of the therapist. The therapist is temporarily possessed by this sub-personality, but in such a contained way that it can, for the first time, be observed in a dispassionate manner by the patient. In this manner the patient and therapist generate the energy necessary to bring about a transformation of the psychic material to the point where it can be reabsorbed by the patient and structured in a new and more flexible way.

I speculate that this process is far more universal than we may believe. It happens not only at the level of pure psyche but also with matter. It is what is present in Cézanne's paintings and in what Anish Kapoor felt as an actual physical, alchemical transformation of pigment and stone in truly successful work. It is as if mind, sensation, consciousness—call it what you will—enters the material realm and causes it to transform.

I think here of alchemy in the Sufi tradition, at least as conveyed to me by the Islamic scholar William Chittick. The great work of renewal takes place within the womb of matter. It moves though the long processes of purification, separation, distillation, and so on. It involves the use of fire and the containment within the athanor. As Carl Jung realized, the operations of alchemy have a metaphorical relationship with psychological individuation. Islamic mystics speak of polishing the mirror, that organ of perception within the heart that must be cleansed until it perfectly reflects the light of creation. Thus the goal of alchemy is not so much to produce gold but to bring about an inner transformation in which the mirror is finally cleansed and the world is seen for what it truly is—pure gold. Carl Jung stopped at this point but the alchemical mystics went further. They realized that at the deepest level matter and spirit, body and soul, can never be separated. Thus, if the inner world transforms, then so must the outer. The external, physical transformation of base metal into gold becomes as real, as actual, as the inner transformation of the psyche.

Now I am aware that all this may sound a little crazy. Producing actual gold. Paintings that contain consciousness. The matter of the world changing spirit. Have I fallen victim to inflation? Have I been spending too much time in that mountain top village in Italy? Is my mind filled with fairy stories?

It is perfectly possible to explain all this without ever leaving the world of Cartesian duality. One could talk about the connection between inner muscular tensions and emotional states, and their representation in terms of gestures on a canvas. In this sense, states of consciousness could indeed be encoded within a painting and available for others to "read." Now I happen to think that this is quite true, that complex internal states can indeed be encoded within art and music as gestures, forms, and so on. But that may not be the total story. After all, if a dream, in Freudian theory, is overdetermined and capable of many different readings, all of them in a sense valid, then why not reality itself?

As the Spanish playwright Calderón put it, "life is a dream." The symbolist Albert Aurier asked, "Isn't a literature of a dream a literature of true life?" Or as the philosopher Hippolyte Taine wrote, "Our external perception is an internal dream which is found in harmony with external things. . . . instead of saying that hallucination is false external perception, it is necessary to say that external perception is *true hallucination.*" For David Andrew, an aspect of this hallucination-that-is-reality is the act of painting, an active dreaming in which nature comes to know him, "my loves, my fears, my joys, my sorrows," and to express its essence through him. Art, for him, is nature in action.

Shakespeare dumped them all together—"the lunatic, the lover and the poet"—all slightly mad yet all operating with a heightened perception that can be curiously infectious, enabling us to see the world, reality, in new ways. The painter Patrick Heron argues that the function of painting is to enable us to see the world, and that someone like Cézanne allows us to see the world in a new way. "The actual 'objective' appearance of things is something that does not exist—or rather, it exists as data that is literally infinite in its complexity and subtlety, in the variety and multiplicity of its configurations." He goes on to say that the mind injects order into that amorphous cloud of visual stimuli and that the origin of this order lies in painting. I would go further. All the arts—and this goes back to societies in which there was no distinction between religion and ritual and theater, song, dance, and decoration—all create the order in which we can live, the sense of meaning that we can all share. At times the artist must renew this order, at other times transform it. This order, I believe, funda-mentally exists in a realm that transcends our distinctions between matter and mind, body and spirit.

And so I will allow painting, music, and all such acts of creation and renewal to be overdetermined and contain within themselves a mul-tiplicity of levels of meaning and being. Nature perceives itself, it comes to know the artist, and the artist manifests this act of feeling though the transformation of matter. Creativity is the marriage of matter and spirit, a mutual inner transformation in which the indi-vidual, society, nature, and matter at times become renewed and at times take on new meanings and structures.

I am sure that if a hard nosed physicist were listening he would reject what I am saying. But he would also be forced to acknowledge that the germs of such ideas are already in the air—and germs he would certainly think they are! The biologist Rupert Sheldrake has long been offending orthodoxy with his notion of morphogenetic fields that guide everything from the growth of crystals to the instincts of animals to the structure of human languages. While I may have some problems with the specifics of Sheldrake's proposal, I do think that there is something very interesting in what he says—particularly in that these fields transcend the traditional divisions between what is considered to be matter and what is considered to be mind, memory, and behavior.

There was also the physicist David Bohm who proposed the notion of what he termed "Active Information." According to Bohm the electron, or any other elementary particle, is guided by a field of information. It is guided in the sense that an ocean liner, powered by great engines, will change its direction under the influence of the tiny amount of energy inherent in a radar signal. For Bohm, information is not simply a passive record of facts but a physical activity within nature. It is a field of information about the structure and configuration of the universe. In turn the activity of this information gives form to—literally "in-forms"—the processes and movements of matter. Bohm developed such ideas at the quantum level but believed that the concept extended to all levels. It is as if a new principle has been added to physics. Once there was matter and energy. Now there is matter, energy, and information. There is a field of information, or meaning, for the healthy human body. There is even a field of information for human society.

Other researchers have proposed related ideas. As far as I am concerned, as scientific notions they remain only half formed. A great deal more thought and investigation is needed before a really significant breakthrough can be attained. But I do believe that this cloud of ideas probably contains a significant insight. It suggests that science is about to enter a new region in which it must learn to face Pauli's "subjective side to matter."

At all events, such ideas are in the air, and if the Native Americans are to be believed, then ideas are beings—beings just waiting for someone to make them incarnate. Or, as they said in the Middle Ages, "the angels love to sing to us. We simply have to learn to be silent in order to hear their song." For me, the angel's song can be found both within the world of spirit and deep within the inscape of the natural world.

Mithras with Stars Beneath His Cape.

Detail of fresco from Mithraeum at Marino, Italy. Second century C.E.

Mithras, the Hypercosmic Sun, and the Rockbirth

DAVID ULANSEY

ONE OF THE MOST PERPLEXING aspects of the Mithraic mysteries consists in the fact that Mithraic iconography always portrays Mithras and the sun god as *separate* beings, while—in stark contradiction to this absolutely consistent iconographical distinction between Mithras and the sun—in Mithraic inscriptions Mithras is often *identified* with the sun by being called "sol invictus," the "unconquered sun." It thus appears that the Mithraists somehow believed in the existence of two suns: one represented by the figure of the sun god, and the other by Mithras himself as the "unconquered sun." It is thus of great interest to note that the Mithraists were not alone in believing in the existence of two suns, for we find in Platonic circles the concept of the existence of two suns, one being the normal astronomical sun and the other being a so-called "hypercosmic" sun located beyond the sphere of the fixed stars.

In my book *The Origins of the Mithraic Mysteries*, I have argued that the god Mithras originated as the personification of the force responsible for the newly discovered cosmic phenomenon of the precession of the equinoxes. Since, from the geocentric perspective, the precession appears to be a movement of the entire cosmic sphere, the force responsible for it most likely would have been understood as being "hypercosmic," beyond or outside of the cosmos. It will be my argument here that Mithras, as a result of his being imagined as a hypercosmic entity, became identified with the Platonic "hypercosmic sun," thus opening up the way for the puzzling existence of two "suns" in Mithraic ideology.

The most important source for our knowledge of the Platonic tradition of the existence of two suns is the *Chaldaean Oracles*, the collection of enigmatic sayings generated late in the second century C.E. by a father and son both named Julian. These oracular sayings were, as is well known, seized upon by Porphyry and later Neoplatonists as constituting a divine revelation. For our purposes, the most important element in the Chaldaean teachings is that of the existence of two suns. As Hans Lewy says:

> The Chaldaeans distinguished between two fiery bodies: one possessed of a noetic nature and the visible sun. The former was said to conduct the latter. According to Proclus, the Chaldaeans call the "solar world" situated in the supramundane region "entire light." In another passage, this philosopher states that the supramundane sun was known to them as "time of time. . . ."[1]

As Lewy showed definitively in his study, the *Chaldaean Oracles* were the product of a Middle Platonic milieu, since they are permeated by concepts and images known from Platonizing thinkers ranging from Philo to Numenius. It is thus likely that the Chaldaean concept of a hypercosmic sun is at least partly derived from the famous solar allegories of Plato's *Republic*, in which the sun is used as a symbol for the highest of Plato's Ideal Forms, that of the Good. In Book 6 of the *Republic* (508A ff.) Plato compares the sun to the Good, saying that as the sun is the source of all illumination and understanding in the visible world (the *horatos topos*), the Good is the supreme source of being and understanding in the world of the Forms (the *noetos topos* or "intelligible world"). Plato then amplifies this image in his famous allegory of the cave at the beginning of Book 7 of the *Republic*. In this famous passage, Plato symbolizes normal human life as life in a cave, and then describes the ascent of one of the cave-dwellers up out of the cave where he sees for the first time the dazzling light of the sun outside the cave.

Thus in Book 6 of the *Republic* we see the image of the sun used as a metaphor for the Form of the Good—the source of all being which exists in the "intelligible world" beyond the ordinary "visible world" of human experience—and then in Book 7, in the allegory of the cave, this same image of the sun is used even more concretely to symbolize that which exists outside of the normal human world represented by the cave.

In addition, as has often been noted, there seems to have been a connection in Plato's imagination between his allegory in Book 7 of the *Republic* of the ascent of the cave dweller to the sunlit world outside the cave and his myth in the *Phaedrus* of the ascent of the soul to the realm outside of the cosmos where "True Being" dwells. The account in the *Phaedrus* reads:

> For the souls that are called immortal, so soon as they are at the summit [of the heavens], come forth and stand upon the back of the world: and straightway the revolving heaven carries them round, and they look upon the regions without. Of that place beyond the heavens none of our earthly poets has yet sung, and none shall sing worthily. But this is the manner of it, for assuredly we must be bold to speak what is true, above all when our discourse is upon truth. It is there that true being dwells, without colour or shape, that cannot be touched; reason alone, the soul's pilot, can behold it, and all true knowledge is knowledge thereof.[2]

As R. Hackforth says,

> No earlier myth has told of a *hyperouranios topos* [place beyond the heavens], but this is not the first occasion on which true Being, the *ousia ontos ousa*, has been given a local habitation. In the passage of *Rep.* 6 which introduces the famous comparison of the Form of the Good to the sun we have a *noetos topos* contrasted with a *horatos* (508C): but a spatial metaphor is hardly felt there. . . . A truer approximation to the *hyperouranios topos* occurs in the simile of the cave in *Rep.* 7, where we are plainly told that the prisoners' ascent into the light of day symbolises *ten eis ton noeton tes psyches anodon* (517B); in fact, the *noetos topos* of the first simile has in the second developed into a real spatial symbol.[3]

Paul Friedländer agrees with Hackforth completely in seeing a connection in Plato's mind between the ascent from the cave in the

Republic and the ascent to the "hypercosmic place" in the *Phaedrus*:

> The movement "upward" . . . had found its fullest expression in the allegory of the cave in the *Republic*. [Now in the *Phaedrus*] . . . the dimension of the "above" is stated according to the new cosmic coordinates. For the "intelligible place" (*topos noetos*) in the Republic (509D, 517B) now becomes "the place beyond the heavens" (*topos hyperouranios*) . . . [4]

What is, of course, important to see here is that there exists already in Plato the obvious raw material for the emergence of the idea of the "hypercosmic sun": when the prisoners escape the cave in the *Republic* what they find outside it is the sun, but if Hackforth and Friedländer are correct the vision of what is outside the *cave* in the *Republic* is linked in Plato's mind with the vision of what is outside the *cosmos* in the myth recounted in the *Phaedrus*. It would therefore be a natural and obvious step for a Platonist to imagine that what is outside the cosmic cave of the *Republic*—namely, the sun, the visible symbol of the highest of the Forms and of the source of all being—is also what is to be found outside the cosmos in the "hypercosmic place" described in the *Phaedrus*.

An intermediate stage in the development of the concept of the "hypercosmic sun" between Plato and the *Chaldaean Oracles* can be glimpsed in Philo's writings, for example in the following passage from *De Opificio Mundi*:

> The intelligible as far surpasses the visible in the brilliancy of its radiance, as sunlight assuredly surpasses darkness. . . . Now that invisible light perceptible only by mind . . . is a supercelestial constellation [*hyperouranios aster*], fount of the constellations obvious to sense. It would not be amiss to term it "all-brightness," to signify that from which sun and moon as well as fixed stars and planets draw, in proportion to their several capacity, the light befitting each of them . . . [5]

Here we see Philo referring to the existence in the intelligible sphere of a "hypercosmic star" (*hyperouranios aster*) which he links with the image of sunlight, and which he sees as the ultimate source of the light in the visible heavens.[6] Philo's formulation here is, of course, strikingly similar to the Chaldaean concept of the hypercosmic sun, the description of which by Lewy we should recall here: "The Chaldaeans distinguished between two fiery bodies: one possessed of a noetic nature and the visible sun. The former was said to conduct the latter. According to Proclus, the Chaldaeans call the 'solar world' situated in the supramundane region 'entire light.'"[7]

The trajectory we have been tracing from Plato through Middle Platonism to the *Chaldaean Oracles* continues beyond the time of the *Chaldaean Oracles* into early Neoplatonism, for we find the concept of the existence of two suns clearly spelled out in the writings of Plotinus, in a context that makes it clear that for Plotinus one of these suns was "hypercosmic." In chapter 3, paragraph 11 of his fourth *Ennead*, Plotinus speaks of two suns, one being the normal visible sun and the other being an "intelligible sun." According to Plotinus,

> that sun in the divine realm is Intellect—let this serve as an example for our discourse—and next after it is soul, dependent upon it and abiding while Intellect abides. This soul gives the edge of itself which borders on this [visible] sun to this sun, and makes a connection of it to the divine realm through the medium of itself, and acts as an interpreter of what comes from this sun to the intelligible sun and from the intelligible sun to this sun . . .[8]

What is especially interesting for us is that in the same third chapter of the fourth *Ennead*, a mere six paragraphs after the passage just quoted, Plotinus explicitly locates the intelligible realm—which he has just told us is the location of a second sun—in the space beyond the heavens. The passage reads:

> One could deduce from considerations like the following that the souls when they leave the intelligible first enter the space of heaven. For if heaven is the better part of the region perceived by the senses, it borders

on the last and lowest parts of the intelligible.[9]

As A. H. Armstong says of this passage, "There is here a certain 'creeping spatiality'... [Plotinus'] language is influenced, perhaps not only by the 'cosmic religiosity' of his time, but by his favorite myth in Plato's *Phaedrus* (246D6–247E6)."[10] In any event, we here find Plotinus in the third chapter of the fourth *Ennead* first positing the existence of an "intelligible sun" besides the normal visible sun, and then locating the intelligible realm spatially in the region beyond the outermost boundary of the heavens.

Finally, to return to the *Chaldaean Oracles*, the fact that the Chaldaean concept of the "hypercosmic sun" was at least sometimes taken in a completely literal and spatial sense is shown by a passage from the Platonizing Emperor Julian's *Hymn to Helios*. According to Julian, in certain unnamed mysteries it is taught that "the sun travels in the starless heavens far above the region of the fixed stars."[11] Given the fact that Julian's thinking was steeped in the Neoplatonic philosophy of Iamblichus who was deeply committed to the *Chaldaean Oracles* as a source of divinely inspired knowledge, and given the fact that the doctrine of the "hypercosmic sun" is an established teaching of the *Chaldaean Oracles*, it is virtually certain, as Robert Turcan points out in his remarks about this passage, that Julian is referring here to the teaching of the *Chaldaean Oracles*.[12] The passage from Julian, therefore, shows that the "hypercosmic sun" of the *Chaldaean Oracles* was understood as being "hypercosmic" not in a merely symbolic or metaphysical sense, but rather in the literal sense of being located physically and spatially in the region beyond the outermost boundary of the cosmos defined by the sphere of the fixed stars.

Our discussion thus far has shown that in the late second century C.E. there is found in the *Chaldaean Oracles* the doctrine of the existence of two suns: one the normal, visible sun, and the other a "hypercosmic" sun. The evidence from Julian shows that the "hypercosmic" nature of this second sun was understood as meaning that it was literally located beyond the outermost sphere of the fixed stars. The fact that the *Chaldaean Oracles* emerged out of the milieu of Middle Platonism suggests that the doctrine of the "hypercosmic sun" found in the *Oracles* did not develop overnight, but that it has roots in the Platonic tradition, most likely, as we have seen, going back ultimately to Plato himself: specifically, to the allegory in the *Republic* of the ascent beyond the world-cave to the sunlit realm outside, and the related myth of the *Phaedrus* describing the ascent of the soul towards its ultimate vision of the *hyperouranios topos*, the "hypercosmic place" beyond the heavens. An intermediate stage between Plato and the *Chaldaean Oracles* is found in Philo's reference to the "hypercosmic star" which is the source of the light of the visible heavenly bodies, and slightly later than the *Chaldaean Oracles* we find Plotinus making reference to two suns, one of them being in the intelligible realm which he places spatially beyond the heavens.

We may say, therefore, that it is likely that there existed in Middle Platonic circles during the second century C.E. (and probably much earlier as well) speculations about the existence of a second sun besides the normal, visible sun: a "hypercosmic" sun located in that "place beyond the heavens" (*hyperouranios topos*) described in Plato's *Phaedrus*.

We see here, of course, a striking parallel with the Mithraic evidence in which we also find two suns, one being Helios the sun-god (who is always distinguished from Mithras in the iconography) and the other being Mithras in his role as the "unconquered sun." On the basis of my explanation of Mithras as the personification of the force responsible for the precession of the equinoxes, this striking parallel becomes readily explicable. For as we have seen, the "hypercosmic sun" of the Platonists is located beyond the sphere of the fixed stars, in Plato's *hyperouranios topos*. But if my theory about Mithras is correct (namely, that he was the personification of the force responsible for the precession of the equinoxes) it follows that Mithras—as an entity capable of moving the entire cosmic sphere and therefore of necessity being outside that sphere—must have been understood as a being whose proper location was in precisely that same "hypercosmic realm" where the Platonists imagined their "hypercosmic sun" to exist. A Platonizing Mithraist (of whom there must have been many—witness Numenius, Cronius, and Celsus), therefore, would almost automatically have been led to identify Mithras with the Platonic "hypercosmic sun," in which case Mithras would become a second sun besides the normal, visible sun. Therefore, the puzzling presence in Mithraic ideology of two suns (one being Helios the sun-god and the other Mithras as the "unconquered sun") becomes immediately understandable on the basis of my theory about the nature of Mithras.

Finally, the line of investigation I have pursued here can also allow me to provide a simple and convincing interpretation for two further puzzling elements of Mithraic iconography. First, all the various astronomical explanations of the tauroctony which scholars are currently advancing (including my own) agree that the bull in the tauroctony is meant to represent the constellation Taurus. However, the constellation Taurus as seen in the night sky faces to the *left* while the bull in the tauroctony always faces to the *right*. How can this apparent discrepancy be explained? On the basis of my theory this question has an obvious answer. For although it is the case that the constellation Taurus as seen from the earth (i.e., from *inside* the cosmos) faces to the left, it is also the case that on ancient (and modern) star-globes which depict the cosmic sphere as it would be seen from the *outside*, the orientation of the constellations is naturally reversed, with the result that on such globes (like the famous ancient "Atlas Farnese" globe) Taurus is always depicted facing to the right exactly like the bull in the tauroctony. This shows that the Mithraic bull is meant to represent the constellation Taurus as seen from outside the cosmos, i.e. from the "hypercosmic" perspective, which is, of course, precisely the perspective we should expect to find associated with Mithras if my argument in this paper is correct.[13]

Second, the line of investigation I have pursued here can also provide a simple and convincing interpretation of the iconographical motif known as the "rock-birth" of Mithras, in which Mithras is shown emerging out of a rock. As is well known, Porphyry, quoting Eubulus, explains in the *Cave of the Nymphs* that the Mithraic cave in which Mithras kills the bull, and which the Mithraic temple imitates, was meant to be an image of the cosmos (*De Antro.* 6). Of course, the hollow Mithraic cave would have to be an image of the cosmos as seen from the *inside*. But caves are precisely hollows within the rocky earth, which suggests the possibility that the rock out of which Mithras is born is meant to represent the cosmos as seen from the *outside*. Confirmation of this interpretation is provided by the fact that the rock out of which Mithras is born is often shown entwined by a snake, a detail which unmistakably evokes the famous Orphic motif of the snake-entwined cosmic egg out of which the cosmos was formed when the god Phanes emerged from it at the beginning of time.[14] It thus seems reasonable to conclude that the rock in the Mithraic scenes of the "rock-birth" of Mithras is a symbol for the cosmos as seen from the outside, just as the cave (the hollow within the rock) is a symbol for the cosmos as seen from the inside.

I would argue, therefore, that the "rock-birth" of Mithras is a symbolic representation of his "hypercosmic" nature. Capable of moving the entire universe, Mithras is essentially greater than the cosmos, and cannot be contained within the cosmic sphere. He is therefore pictured as bursting out of the rock that symbolizes the cosmos (not unlike the prisoner emerging from the cosmic cave described by Plato in *Republic* 7), breaking through the boundary of the universe represented by the rock's surface and establishing his presence in the "hypercosmic place" indicated by the space into which he emerges *outside of the rock*.

And, to conclude, in this context it is no accident that in the "rock-birth" scenes Mithras is almost always shown holding a torch; for having established that his proper place is outside of the cosmos, Mithras has become identified with the "hypercosmic sun": that light-giving being which dwells, as Proclus says,

> in the supermundane (worlds) [*en tois hyperkosmiois*]; for there exists the "solar world (and the) whole light . . ." as the *Chaldaean Oracles* say and which I believe.[15]

Notes

1. Hans Lewy, *Chaldaean Oracles and Theurgy* (Paris: Études Augustiniennes, 1978), 151–52.

2. 247B–C; trans. R. Hackforth, *Plato's Phaedrus* (Cambridge: Cambridge University Press, 1952), 71, 78.

3. Ibid., 80–81.

4. Paul Friedländer, *Plato I: An Introduction* (New York: Pantheon Books, 1958), 194.

5. 8.31; trans. F. H. Colson, *Philo* (London: William Heinemann, 1929) vol. 1, 25.

6. Philo often speaks of God using expressions such as the "intelligible sun" (*noetos helios* [*Quaest. in Gen.* 4.1; see Ralph Marcus, trans., *Philo Supplement 1: Questions and Answers on Genesis* (Cambridge: Harvard University Press, 1953), 269, n. 1]) or similar expressions involving light and illumination located in the intelligible realm. For references see Pierre Boyancé, *Études sur le songe de Scipion* (Paris: E. de Boccard, 1936), 73–74; Lewy, *Chaldaean Oracles*, 151, n. 312; David Runia, *Philo of Alexandria and the Timaeus of Plato* (Leiden: E. J. Brill, 1986), 435 and n. 143. Boyancé (pp. 73–74) quite reasonably argues that such expressions were identical in Philo's mind with the *hyperouranios aster* ("hypercosmic star") of *De Opificio Mundi* 8.31.

7. For a superb discussion of the broader context in which the development of the concept of the "hypercosmic sun" most likely occured, see Boyancé, *Études*, 65–77. Recently A. P. Bos has argued that the story of the ascent to the sunlit world outside of the cave in Plato's *Republic* was explicitly connected by Aristotle with Plato's image in the *Phaedrus* of the ascent of the soul to the "place beyond the heavens," and that this connection played a central role in one of Aristotle's lost dialogues whose major elements were then preserved and utilized by Plutarch in his *De Facie*. See A. P. Bos, *Cosmic and Meta-Cosmic Theology in Aristotle's Lost Dialogues* (Leiden: E. J. Brill, 1989): the argument is complex and the book should be read as a whole, but see especially pp. 67–68, 182. The development of the concept of the "hypercosmic sun" also must, of course, be seen in the context of the evolution of the "solar theology" described by Franz Cumont in his *La théologie solaire du paganisme romain* (Paris: Librairie Kliensieck, 1909). A very important and intriguing argument is made for the presence of a tradition of a "hypercosmic sun" in Orphic circles by Hans Leisegang, "The Mystery of the Serpent," in Joseph Campbell, ed.,

The Mysteries (Princeton: Princeton University Press, 1955), 194–261. The Greek magical papyri and the Hermetic corpus provide numerous examples of solar imagery in which the sun is in various ways symbolically elevated to at least the summit of the cosmos, if not explicitly to a "hypercosmic" level. Finally, Hermetic, Gnostic, and Neoplatonic texts all betray an almost obsessive concern with enumerating and distinguishing the various cosmic spheres and levels, and especially with establishing where the boundary lies between the cosmic and the hypercosmic realms (the hypercosmic realm being identified by the Hermetists and Neoplatonists with the "intelligible world" and by the Gnostics with the "Pleroma"). This concern with establishing the boundary between the cosmic and the hypercosmic must have fed into speculations about the "hypercosmic sun," and—intriguingly—one of the clearest symbolic formulations of this boundary between the cosmic and the hypercosmic is found in the religious system of the *Chaldaean Oracles* (exactly, that is, in the system in which we find explicitly formulated the image of the "hypercosmic sun"), where the figure of Hecate is understood as the symbolic embodiment of precisely this boundary (on the image of Hecate in the *Chaldaean Oracles* see now Sarah Iles Johnston, *Hekate Soteira* [Atlanta: Scholars Press, 1990]).

8. 4.3.11.14–22; trans. A. H. Armstrong, *Plotinus* (Cambridge: Harvard University Press, 1984), vol. 4, 71–73.

9. 4.3.17.1–6; ibid, pp. 87–89.

10. Ibid., p. 88, n. 1.

11. *Hymn to Helios* 4.148A; trans. W. C. Wright, *Julian* (Cambridge: Harvard University Press, 1962), 405.

12. Robert Turcan, *Mithras Platonicus* (Leiden: E . J. Brill, 1975), 124. Julian was well acquainted with the *Chaldaean Oracles*: see Polymnia Athanassiadi-Fowden, *Julian and Hellenism* (Oxford: Oxford University Press, 1981), 143–53. Roger Beck has recently suggested that Julian is referring here to the Iranian cosmology in which the sun and moon are located beyond the stars (*Planetary Gods and Planetary Orders in the Mysteries of Mithras* [Leiden: E.J. Brill, 1988], 2–3, n. 2). However, Julian's intimate association with Iamblichus and the *Chaldaean Oracles*, in which the doctrine of the "hypercosmic sun" is well established, renders the possibility that Julian is referring to the Iranian tradition highly unlikely. As Hans Lewy says, "There seems to be no connection between [Julian's teaching] and Zoroaster's doctrine according to

which the sun is situated above the fixed stars" (*Chaldaean Oracles*, 153, n. 317). However, it is certainly true that the existence of the Iranian cosmology placing the sun beyond the stars could easily have provided some additional motivation for the emergence of the identification between the "Persian" Mithras and the Platonic "hypercosmic sun" for which I have argued here. On the Iranian cosmology, see M. L. West, *Early Greek Philosophy and the Orient* (Oxford: Oxford University Press, 1971), 89–91; Walter Burkert, "Iranisches bei Anaximandros," *Rheinisches Museum* 106 (1963), 97–134.

13. It should be noted that the fact that the bull in the tauroctony faces to the right renders untenable Roger Beck's suggestion that the tauroctony is a picture of the night sky as seen by an observer on earth at the time of the setting of the constellation Taurus ("Cautes and Cautopates: Some Astronomical Considerations," *Journal of Mithraic Studies* 2.1 [1977], 10; *Planetary Gods and Planetary Orders in the Mysteries of Mithras* [Leiden: E. J. Brill, 1988], 20), since such an observer would see Taurus facing to the *left*. The fact that the bull in the tauroctony faces *right* is explicable only if we understand the tauroctony as the creation of someone who had in mind an astronomical star-globe showing the cosmic sphere as seen from the outside, and not—as Beck argues—an image of the sky as seen from the earth.

14. That the rock from which Mithras is born was identified with the Orphic cosmic egg is in fact proven beyond doubt, as is well known, by the striking similarity between the Mithraic Housesteads monument (Maarten Vermaseren, *Corpus Inscriptionum et Monumentorum Religionis Mithriacae* [The Hagure: Martinus Nijhoff, 1966/1960], 860), which shows Mithras being born out of an egg (which is thus identified with the rock from which he is usually born), and the famous Orphic Modena relief showing Phanes breaking out of the cosmic egg (*Corpus Inscriptionum et Monumentorum Religionis Mithriacae*, 695). In connection with this Orphic–Mithraic syncretism, Hans Leisegang, "Mystery of the Serpent" (above, n. 8), especially pp. 201–15, has collected a fascinating body of material—including among other things the Modena relief and the passage from Julian which I have discussed above—supporting the contention that the breaking of the Orphic cosmic egg is linked directly with the concept of the "hypercosmic." Leisegang's discussion as a whole provides strong support for my general argument in this

paper.

15. *Chaldaean Oracles* Frag. 59 (= Proclus, *In Tim.* 3.83.13–16); trans. Ruth Majercik, *The Chaldaean Oracles* (Leiden: E. J. Brill, 1989), 73. The sun was often imagined in antiquity as a torchbearer, as for example in a fragment from the Stoic Cleanthes: "Cleanthes . . . used to say . . . that the sun is a torchbearer" (cited in Jean Pépin, "Cosmic Piety," in *Classical Mediterranean Spirituality* [New York: Crossroad, 1986], 425); a fragment from Porphyry: "In the mysteries of Eleusis, the hierophant is dressed as demiurge, the torchbearer as the sun . . ." (cited in Pepin, "Piety," p. 429); and of course Lucius in Apuleius' *Golden Ass* 11.24: "In my right hand I carried a lighted torch . . . thus I was adorned like unto the sun. . . ." (trans. W. Adlington, Apuleius, *The Golden Ass* [London: William Heinemann, 1928], 583).

Love, a Musician *is profest,*
And, of all Musicke, is the best.

ILLVSTR. XX.

Book.2

I F to his thoughts my *Comments* have assented,
By whom the following *Emblem* was *invented,*
I'le hereby teach you (*Ladies*) to discover
A true-bred *Cupid,* from a fained *Lover*;
And, shew (if you have Wooers) which be they,
That worth'est are to beare your *Hearts* away.
    As is the *Boy,* which, here, you pictured see,
Let them be *young,* or let them, rather, be
Of *suiting yeares* (which is instead of *youth*)
And, wooe you in the *nakednesse,* of *Truth*;
Not in the common and disguised *Clothes,*
Of *Mimick-gestures, Complements,* and *Oathes.*
Let them be *winged* with a swift *Desire*;
And, not with *slow-affections,* that will tyre.
But, looke to this, as to the principall,
That, *Love* doe make them truly *Musicall:*
For, *Love's* a good *Musician*; and, will show
How, every faithfull *Lover* may be so.
    Each *word* he speakes, will presently appeare
To be melodious *Raptures* in your eare:
Each *gesture* of his body, when he moves,
Will seeme to *play,* or *sing,* a *Song of Loves:*
The very *lookes,* and *motions* of his eyes,
Will touch your *Heart-strings,* with sweet *Harmonies*;
And, if the *Name* of him, be but exprest,
T'will cause a thousand *quaverings* in your breast.
Nay, ev'n those *Discords,* which occasion'd are,
Will make your *Musicke,* much the sweeter, farre.
    And, such a mooving *Diapason* strike,
As none but *Love,* can ever play the like.

Musical Emblems in the Renaissance: A Survey

CHRISTINA LINSENMEYER-VAN SCHALKWYK

THE WORD EMBLEMATA comes from the Greek *emballo*, "to put in," as in inlaid work. From this is derived *emblem*, meaning that which is a "symbolical figure or composition, which conceals an allegory."[1] By the definition "to insert," the process of the emblematist is better understood. The poet or artist, when creating emblematically, was inserting

> decorative elements to be arranged on the surface of a manuscript or printed page, aiming at a eurythmic interplay between the three elements—motto—picture—epigram—which at the same time, served to express deep-seated philosophical convictions about life and religion.[2]

An emblem was thus described as "*opus quod rebus insertis constat*," a work consisting of inserted elements.[3]

The term *emblema* was coined by Andreas Alciati (author of the first emblem book) *circa* 1522 and is believed to have already indicated the combination of pictorial and verbal insertions.[4] Many terms have been used synonymously with "emblem," and there is controversy about what differentiates these substitute terms from each other. Writers and researchers often use these other expressions ambiguously and incorrectly in generalizations. Terms used as a substitute for "emblem" are: *impresa, bigarreures, entretiens, marqueture, pegma, Sinnbild, symbolum, theatrum,* and *devises,* and they are relatives to the emblem in some form or manner, whether they are predecessors of it or

A version of this paper was presented at the American Musical Instrument Society's twenty-fifth International Meeting at The Shrine to Music Museum in Vermillion, South Dakota in 1996.

contemporary variations.

The emblem, as developed in the sixteenth century and used for the next two hundred years, is comprised of three elements: 1) a picture, typically an engraved or woodcut illustration of some object or scene; 2) an epigram which is a poem, verse, or quotation typically borrowed from another writer; and 3) a motto, most often a couplet or word, whose purpose is to present the idea behind the emblem concisely by clarifying the relationship between the picture and epigram. The three elements then function together as a graphic expression of thought. The form of the emblem can also be viewed as dyadic in its juxtaposition of picture and text, where the motto and epigram combine as one ingredient by reason of their common source in literature. This two-part structure, of picture and text, creates a trinity, where the third element is the meaning of the emblem's symbolism extracted by the interpreter. This trinity has been compared to the three constituents of personality: the spirit or vivifying force, the memory, and the source of action or will:[5]

Emblem	Personality
Picture	Spirit
Text	Will
Meaning	Memory

The emblem's structure, an overall effect created by the union of its parts, is significant because it exists as an organic whole.

Origins and Sources

The emblem books of the Renaissance draw their origins from many sources. The most significant influences upon these writers were classical and pagan images, Egyptian hieroglyphs, and, inevitably, the medieval allegorical tradition. The first and most influential emblem book, by Alciati in 1542, is a typical compendium of these pre-Renaissance sources. Alciati found his images and text in classical myth and allegory; Christian and biblical tradition; medieval nature lore; Horapollo and other sources of Egyptian hieroglyphs; heraldry and devices; and literary conceits.[6] The Renaissance taste for allegory, along with a veneration for past knowledge, seems to have made the emblem book an inevitable phenomenon.

As regards the classical influence, the emblematists were drawn to the images found in Greek epigrams, medals, coins, literature, and pagan mythology. The inscriptions found on medals and other ancient artefacts are analogous to the emblem. The conceit elaborates upon an object, such as a statue or bas-relief, while emblems are comprised of both a visual object and text which function together. Medals and coins similarly depict representations of some object or person, which is intended to have significance. Classical literature, especially that of Horace, Ovid, and Homer, was quoted by the emblematists, often without reference, to be juxtaposed with pictures also borrowed from classical mythology. Taken together, they become an allegory, carrying mythical implications that go beyond appearance. The emblematist Otto Van Veen's *Horatii Emblemata* (1612) is an emblem book which employs themes and ingredients from classical history and theology, and is based upon quotations from Horace.[7]

Nilous Horapollo, a late antique writer, provided the link between ancient Egypt and the European Renaissance with his Greek interpretation of the ancient hieroglyphs.[8] The first edition of Horapollo's *Hieroglyphs* was printed in Venice in 1505 by Aldus Manutius, and was a readily available source during the Renaissance. The Renaissance Humanist thought that the hieroglyphs embodied and communicated hidden truth and wisdom.[9] The interest in hieroglyphs later inspired Piero Valeriano's *Hieroglyphica, sive de sacris Aegyptorum aliarumque gentium literis* (Basel, 1556). This book is a kind of encyclopedia of hieroglyphics, as interpreted by the Renaissance, and an exposition of medieval nature symbolism. The kind of expression carried by these symbols also influenced the production of Cesare Ripa's *Iconologia* (Rome, 1593), another type of symbol dictionary. It used *"imagini"* to depict human forms showing the virtues and vices of man, and became a "recipe-book for designers and engravers."[10] The work of Ripa and Valeriano were typical Renaissance creations, enhancing and communicating ancient ideas. Later emblem books drew on these works as well as on Alciati.

Medieval literature and thought also affected the emblematists, contributing bestiaries, lapidaries full of nature lore, allegorical interpretations of the Bible, and illustrated fables. In relation to the medieval models, the emblem books were described as being "a predictable outgrowth of illuminated manuscript folios."[11] The traditions of heraldry and tournament device were also involved in this tradition of images that carry a meaning, which here will be named *visual signifiers*. The heraldic device related to the emblem in a way described by Mario Praz:

> Since the rules of the device were rigidly fixed by academics in Italy, whereas the emblem developed comparatively free from precepts on the other side of the Alps, it may be said that the device is to the emblem what the classical is to the romantic, or as the closed form is to the open form.[12]

Other forms that were a product of the medieval and Renaissance fondness of signifiers include illustrated broadsheets, dance-of-death sequences, *Biblia Pauperum*, and ornamented title pages. All of these means of expression furthered the interest and interchange of symbolic and iconographic thought between authors, artists, and society. The emblem literature was a significant product of the Renaissance iconographical movement, and its theory incorporates both the poetic and pictorial arts.

Functional Relation Between the Components

The source of the emblem's symbolic power lies in the functional relation between its parts. The emblem combines the mute picture of the image with the talking picture of the literary text; the resulting picture of signification is understood in terms of moral or mystical significance.[13] The mind's eye is used to complete the true meaning that the symbolic picture reveals when juxtaposed with a particular text. Paolo Giovo had in mind a two-part structure: he saw the relation of the image to the motto as being comparable to the body and soul of the emblem respectively. He also believed that their relation to each other was an interdependent one in order to further understand the meaning intended by the emblem.[14] If the text or picture changed, the meaning was changed. Moreover, the perspective of one interpreter may lead to a different understanding from that of an interpreter of different perspective. "For just as the cube, having been thrown, stands firmly on any of its six faces, so the emblems—a game too—is capable of being seen and of making sense from several different angles."[15] The idea of *polysemy*—one signifier carrying several meanings—is accepted and respected by the emblematists.[16] The functional relation between the components of the emblem is made possible by the function of the symbols used.

From a Neoplatonic perspective, designing icons was one of the "most serious tasks for the philosopher, as it was by means of the image that one approached the ineffable Reality which was the Divine Oneness."[17] The signifier was the medium, which expressed the deepest truths and wisdom concisely; the intuitive icon, then, had an expression not available to discursive language. The emblem can be seen as expressing its symbols in two ways: first, as a mode of Hermetic expression or esoteric language, modeled on the hieroglyphs, which only a few will understand; and second, a way of portraying ethical and religious truths even to the children and illiterate.[18] Both levels of understanding provide a lesson of wisdom and knowledge to the intellect and the eyes.

Purpose of the Emblem Book: *Utile dulci*

The emblem books make it possible to recreate the mentality of society during the Renaissance. The books covered subjects of symbolism, natural sciences, philosophy, politics and statecraft, religion, morals, pedagogy, history, and astrology.[19] Daily life could be seen through these allegorical creations of society, and the popular "emblem game" was played by all classes. As Rosemary Freeman says concerning George Wither's *Collection of Emblemes Ancient and Moderne*:

> Wither's book is essentially social, and all those who joined in reading it took part consciously in a psychological exercise. Surprise and ignorance were jointly involved, and it is very easy to re-create the kind of society—puritanical and amused—in which the game was played.[20]

The emblem was both a teaching aid and an artistic model. It was a way of portraying ethical and religious truths, as well as the chivalric tradition, for the emblem contained the information everyone needed to know in order to become a proper gentleman or lady of the time. Titles of the emblem books advertised them as "chapbooks of wisdom,"[21] and they can be understood as having the same function as society books such as Castiglione's *Book of the Courtier* and others of its type. The emblem was also a visual education, compared to "experience" as a guide or teacher for acquiring knowledge.[22] The emblems not only taught ideas, but also were "vehicles by which neoclassic metaphor was brought to the thousands of Europeans" who did not have access to the painting or literature of their time.[23] Fabricii da Teramo, an emblematist who, in his *Allusioni, imprese, et emblemi*, claimed to be "campaigning through his emblemata to expel 'the monstrous sphinx of ignorance unleashed in this century,'"[24] considered the literature he created as a contribution to learning and wisdom.

Since emblems were useful for all classes, their poetry was of both a popular and a scholarly tradition.[25] The teaching method of the emblem books upheld the Horatian concept of *utile dulci*: the "pleasing" paving the way to the "useful." The emblem was a memorable teaching that made the popular "emblem game" an easy way to become cultured. The emblems were a pleasant way to learn something that would not be so enjoyable if learned another way, and perhaps not as well-learned or memorable. As Bacon wrote, "Emblems reduce intellectual conceptions to sensible images, and that strikes the memory and is more easily interpreted on it than that which is intellectual."[26]

Emblem books and other Renaissance tabletop books also had significance as artistic models—not only as representations of artistic forms, but also as a source of ideas for the artist. Perrière's *Le Theatre des Bons Engins* (1539) was described as "one of the loveliest books on the market, at a time when printing had reached an excellence not surpassed. Moreover, unusually fine borders frame pictures and texts alike."[27] These samples of Renaissance design served as "pattern-books" for artists, craftsmen, engravers, lacemakers, jewelers, and embroiderers whose artwork comprised the houses, clothes, furniture, and other examples of the time. The books were, for this end, literally cut into patterns for use by the artist. This practice explains why many editions are scarce today, even though publishing records show that there were hundreds of emblem books printed.

The trend of these books "affected virtually every mode of communication—and, necessarily, perception—in the sixteenth and seventeenth centuries."[28] In addition, the novelty and developing art of printing encouraged the creativity and elaborations of the emblematist and artist, and made the circulation of emblem books possible. The concurrence of the development of printing and the popularity of emblem books is no coincidence.

Humanist Significance of the Emblem

The earliest phase of *ars emblematica* was *c.* 1522—*c.* 1575,[29] and the central period of emblem book popularity was from about 1550–1650. The fashion for emblems did not suddenly disappear,[30] but remained present until the latter half of the nineteenth century.[31] Appropriately, the "Golden Age" of the emblem has been considered as being concurrent with the "Golden Age of metaphor."[32]

In addition to the creative function already discussed, emblem books possessed an intellectual function. The emblematists, who intentionally constructed their books to reflect the wisdom, philosophy, ethics, and religion of the time, called their books "lookingglasses."[33] Their beliefs about literature, literary theory, and aesthetics "reveal broad based opinion and prejudice which supported and contemplated the neoclassical contents of the Renaissance *artes poetica* and *artes pictoriae*."[34] Thus the Renaissance emblem books were not only outlets for creative literature, but expressions of humanistic thought. The Humanists were attracted to the emblems and interpreted their pictorial symbolism and text in the same way they did the hieroglyphs and the classical sources: "the humanist had an emblematic turn of mind, which sought significance in all things."[35]

To fully understand the emblems, it is necessary to consider Renaissance thought. The Neoplatonic tradition's theory of symbolism understood the signifier as the medium which not only expressed the deepest truths concisely, but in some sense *embodied* them. According to this theory, the icon could express an essential truth in a way that went deeper than discursive language.[36] Christoforo Giarda (1595–1649), a teacher of rhetoric in Milan, exemplified Neoplatonic theory in his *Bibliothecae Alexandrina Icones Symbolicae* (Milan, 1626 and 1628). Through the medium of the emblem, he explains

> that the mind which has been banished from heaven into this dark cave of a body, its actions held in bondage by the senses, can behold the beauty and form of the Virtues and Sciences, divorced from all matter and yet adumbrated if not perfectly expressed, in colours, and is thus roused to an even more fervent love and desire for them.[37]

As Gombrich notes, from a Neoplatonic perspective,

> if the visual symbol is not a conventional sign but linked through the network of correspondences and sympathies with the supra-celestial essence which it embodies, it is only consistent to expect it to partake not only in the "meaning" and "effect" of what it represents but to become interchangeable with it.[38]

Drawing on the doctrine of correspondences and theories of magical sympathy as developed in the writings of Marsilio Ficino, Pico della Mirandola, Cornelius Agrippa and others, emblems were capable of embodying higher knowledge. They could thus aid in the "intellectual intuition of ideas and essences."[39] This higher degree of knowledge is something above human reason because it is more akin to inspiration from the divine. The Renaissance idea of *ekstasis* through divine frenzy was one common to all creators who incanted the proper Muse for inspiration.

The impression made by an emblem, understood as a flash of idea, is the same as the impact of music: both the emblem and the music transform us. Marsilio Ficino, then considered the modern Orpheus, must have agreed on the relation between symbols and music as to their power to affect.[40] He expressed his belief that the right image engraved upon the right stone could have an effect upon one's state of health, as could musical performances. Ficino also compares images and music as both having power beyond their signification:

> Just as one lyre resounds by itself when the strings of another are plucked, the likeness between the heavenly bodies and the image on the amulet may make the image absorb the rays from the stars to which it is thus attuned.[41]

Ut pictura poesis

The Horatian phrase, *ut pictura poesis*,[42] grew into a complicated way of regarding literature, and was especially relevant for the emblematists because of their emphasis on the graphic arts.[43] This catch phrase of the Renaissance led painting and poetry, which both imitate Nature, to become twin sisters,[44] and was fuel for the emblematists to create a higher expression of symbolism, through the juxtaposition and interchangeability of the arts. The Renaissance made every possible connection between the poetic and pictorial arts: painting was considered mute poetry, and poetry a speaking picture.[45] In J. B. Boudard's *Iconologie* (Vienna, 1766), his allegory of *Peinture* represents painting as a gagged figure of mute poetry. The humanistic period created a code of clichés in its creative literature that were the vehicle of seventeenth-century neoclassicism; and the emblem combined the iconography of painting and poetry into a purposeful medium that reawakened clichés that had lost their vividness by overuse.[46] Logically, it seems inevitable that the parallel between poetry and painting existed because there was justification for it, and "nowhere does one find . . . a more harmonious marriage of artistic and literary metaphor than in the innumerable and popular emblem books of the Renaissance."[47]

The Arts as an Expressive Vehicle

The emblematists practiced this interchangeability of the arts to achieve a higher expression of symbolism. The idea that they have a common source in Nature, leads to mimesis: a kind of imitation of ideas taken from Nature and ancient and contemporary artists. The emblematists were not alone in copying, but were followed by armorers, bell casters, clothiers, cabinet makers, jewelers, weavers, and other trades,[48] who used it as an inspiration for the decorative and expressive in their work. The greatest painters and poets of the time sought inspiration from the emblem books and vice versa such as: Hans Holbein, Jr., Giulio Bonasone, Raphael, Hans Baldung Grien, Jerome Bosch, Michaelangelo,[49] Shakespeare,[50] and Johnson.[51] "In general, it may be said that all observations on imitation encountered in the poetic and pictorial arts of the Renaissance found vivid echo in the emblem books."[52]

This sharing between the arts led to a recycling of ideas, which in turn inspired fresh ideas. The artists justified their borrowing by the belief that everything initially derived from the images visible in Nature: this ancient opinion was called the "System of Universal Emblematics."[53] This system also understood ideas as existing independently of their linguistic expression, because they constituted a universal language: a kind of sign language comprehensible to all of Europe.[54] A system of symbolic signs clarified meanings which medieval and Renaissance language made ambiguous. There was a belief that before the Tower of Babel and the confusion of tongues, the Adamic language had actually represented the inner nature of things.[55] The emblem's implication of signifiers, as well as its tradition of using more than one language within a given emblem, heightens its expressive capability.

The vocabulary of the arts was also interchangeable. Titian called his most accomplished paintings "*poesie*."[56] The idea of emblematists imitating others to create their own works can be associated with the idea that the emblem itself is a mosaic composition: smaller pieces put together to create the whole. Giarda states that in order for poetry to reach its "natural goal of imitation all the instruments of all the Muses should be assembled and placed at the disposal of the poetic faculty."[57]

Poesia and Music as Allegorical Figures

The association of music and poetry in the Renaissance meant that the seven Liberal Arts needed to be regrouped because neither music nor poetry had a place in the Trivium as communicative arts. Music belonged to the Quadrivium—the four arts based on number (also including arithmetic, geometry, and astronomy). In the later Middle Ages, music became more of a member of the Trivium (grammar, rhetoric, and logic), and joined the verbal arts. Coluccio Salutati's redefinition was to the same effect. To the Trivium he added the ornaments of rhythm from arithmetic; quantity from geometry; melody from music; and proportion from astronomy. From these ornaments and his reorganization of the verbal arts came poetry.[58] His definition gave poetry and music a place in both the Quadrivium and the Trivium. This combination recalls ancient Greece and the unity of the poet-musician.[59]

The allegorical figure *Poesia* finds her origin in this consideration of the poetic arts. Raphael's *Poesia*—represented in the *Stanze* of the Vatican (1509–1511) as having laurel, wings, lyre, a clasped folio volume, and a posy reading *"Numen afflatus"* (divine inspiration or breath)—anticipated the emblematist generation. Giarda's version of *Poesia* (1628) has the poet's laurel and she holds three instruments representing the three popular poetic forms of the time:

Heroic poetry: trumpet
Lyric poetry: lyre or *viola da braccio*
Pastoral poetry: flageolet or flute[60]

Ripa's *Poesie* is imaged holding a trumpet, viol, and quills, and Davenant's, in the *Temple of Love*, is holding a trumpet, flageolet, and lyre. Davenant also describes her as attractive to every man because of her "visage inflamed and pensive" and turned towards Heaven, the source of her *furor poeticus*. She also wears an evergreen laurel, for she makes men immortal and "ensures them against the blows of time."[61] Her heavenly origin is reflected in her starred garment—as is Boudard's *Poésie*. In the case of lyric poetry, there is some inconsistency in which stringed instrument is chosen to represent it. It seems not so important which stringed instrument is used, but that it should be stringed rather than brass, wind, or percussion. Since the *viola da braccio* was also known as the *"lira,"* it is this instrument that typically represents lyric poetry. There are instances, for example, where the text may say lyre, yet a *viola da braccio* is shown. Giarda's *Poesia* has a *viola da braccio* to signify lyric poetry, but Boudard's *Poème lyrique* holds a lyre.[62]

Boudard also represents the allegory of *Musique*. She is seen with the anvil and hammer of Pythagoras' harmonic proportions, and the text speaks of the balance of the lyre, music's divine proportion, and performance theory. Music as a symbol is also commonly used to represent harmony or concord—particularly political agreement and friendship. In Henry Peacham's *Minerva Brittana* (or *A Garden of Heroical Devises*, London, 1612),[63] music—as a force harmonizing discord in life—is represented here not by instruments, but by a notated musical example of counterpoint.[64]

There is an iconographic hierarchy among the classes of instruments evident in the emblems. Stringed instruments are at the top of the chain. It is not a coincidence that harps, lutes, viols—the instruments most resembling the human voice—are held in the highest regard. The fact that they are strung with gut is also significant because of the lore of the Greek use of sun-baked tortoises for lyres. The tortoise also represented the marriage of Heaven and Earth,[65] and the instrument created from the tortoise was a vehicle for the marriage of heavenly harmonies and human emotions.[66]

In the example of Boudard's depiction of *Poésie*, she is seen only with a lyre; the intention is not to separate the forms of poetry, but to signify a highly regarded form of art. A hierarchy of art is seen in Giarda's *Poesia*, who is presented with the three instruments of poetry, yet discards the lower instruments of dance at her feet: the violin, less majestic horn, and tambourine. The idea of a hierarchy of instruments is reflected not only in the higher and lower art forms, but also in the ranks of mythological figures: their powers, the influence and source of their instrument's power, and their degree of virtue versus vice.

Paganism, Myth, and Musical Imagery

The music and musical instruments of the mythical figures represented in the emblems comprise two instances of duality: 1) the stringed versus the wind and percussion, representing the Apollonian versus the Dionysian, and 2) the representation of music by instruments according to whether it serves virtue or vice.[67] In antiquity, music formed a substantial part of Apollonian and Dionysian worship.

The instruments used by the cults, as well as their use of particular musical modes, produced certain effects upon the listener, depending on the cult.[68] In the emblems, Apollo and Dionysus are depicted as a unity in duality; they are both from the same source (as children of Zeus), yet they have opposing temperaments. Their dualistic characteristics—introversion and extroversion, rational and emotional, verbal and wordless, contemplative and sensual, spiritual and earthly— are reflected in their music and their instruments.[69] In the emblems, the two signify eternal youth and balance in opposition for a happy, healthy life: Dionysus keeping away the cares of life with wine, and Apollo keeping away illness with food.

Apollo's characteristics of eternal youth, wisdom, and a high moral character; his domain of medicine, music, and prophecy; and his likening to the Sun, the central source of light, and metaphor for enlightenment; allow for extensive use of his figure in emblem allegory. In the emblems he is holding a lyre or a *viola da braccio*, and pictured slaying a serpent, chasing Daphne who turned into a laurel tree, and at his temple in Delphi. The Delphic oracle, which became the supreme authority on matters of religion and statecraft, was also a theme that combined the qualities of Apollo: a juxtaposition of musical harmony, religious or political wisdom, and the *furor propheticas* of the entranced Pythoness. Apollo is pictured not only with his instrument, but also with bow and arrows; these two aspects—music and warfare—were the ideal skills of the Renaissance courtier.

Apollo is a signifier of ordered musical harmony, control, and the intellectual. The seven strings of the lyre that he received from Hermes signify the seven planetary spheres.[70] The symbolic number seven also relates to Apollo's association with music, perfect order, transformation and unification of all hierarchical orders, grace, the seven virtues, wisdom, intellect, philosophy, and health. In one emblem his lyre has five strings; five represented with Apollo can symbolize health and love, good judgment, understanding, and the five Christian talents.[71] Musically, five corresponds to the five sacred notes—sol, fa, re, mi, do.[72] Apollo's figure and his music, which affects the living world, represent the ordering and harmony of the spheres. Giarda mentions Apollo as the source of poetic fury: "poets are

UNFORESEEN FEAR

The forest god Pan sounds his horn so loudly that
he disperses his enemies, the giants, whom he
would not have otherwise overcome, nor
harrassed. Similarly at times an army is frightened
by nothing but the horn so that the god Pan
rightly says, "My horn fights with these people."

Figure 1.

Pan, the bringer of panic, shown with his horn, from Hunger, *Emblemata*
(Paris, 1542).

warmed by the agitation of Apollo, enlightened by the sight of him, shining in his brilliance."[73]

Apollo's counterparts are the nine Muses, daughters of Zeus and Mnemosyne, and personifications of the highest inspirations of artistic and intellectual minds: Calliope, epic poetry; Erato, lyric poetry and hymns; Urania, astronomy; Clio, history; Melpomene, tragedy; Euterpe, instrumental music; Terpsichore, dance; Thalia, comedy; and Polyhymnia, singing. They are often pictured with Apollo and seen with their identifying symbols.[74]

The superiority of stringed over wind instruments is enhanced by the emblems that refer to the competition between Apollo and Marsyas, who is depicted as a satyr. Apollo playing his lyre or *viola da braccio* was clearly the winner before the match had begun, and Marsyas' flute was no challenge. The significance of stringed instruments lies not only in their voice-like tone, but also that they could accompany the player's poetry simultaneously as did the Greek instruments of poetry—the lyre and the cithara. Music combined with poetry was the vehicle of religious worship and moral education—an attribute of human rationality. The half-beast Marsyas, on the other hand, was without verbal poetry.[75] The power of music combined with poetry, a juxtaposition of arts, is a prominent theme in the emblems.

Dionysus or Bacchus, the god of nature and fertility, represents the growing force of life in animals and plants. The Dionysiac frenzy and Bacchanal are the disorderly passions of earthly pleasures embodying instinct rather than intellect. Bacchus is depicted playing a "vile" drum (tambourín), speaking the sounds of intoxication leading to insanity and intercourse, and with horns on his head.[76] Dionysus is red-skinned because his liver is scorched from drinking and he did not do as the wise, who dilute their wine with water (by a fourth, third, or half depending on the emblematist; in one text, moderation is prescribed as not more than half a litre). Drinking must be watered down and taken in moderation for maintaining health and avoiding the punishment of over-indulgence. The emblems all agree that pleasures do not come easily.

Bacchus' followers are the satyrs: half-beast, with earthly desires and disorderly behavior, whose instruments are of the wind family.[77] Impure satyr-horns are given to those who do not observe moderation in life and become older, arrogant, mad, and "shake effeminate rattles."

The satyr-like god Pan represents the force of Nature and the nature of things; his name means "the All." His top half is human, encompassing the heart and head of reason; his bottom, animal half encompasses the loins of instinct, sexuality, and procreation. He created his instrument the syrinx, a seven-reed panpipe signifying, as Apollo's strings, the harmony of the seven planets. Seven, a symbol of indefinite number, is associated with Pan and the idea of indefinite "many."[78] Like Apollo, Pan is represented in one emblem as having only five reeds constituting his pipe. The symbolic number five, when associated with Pan, symbolizes growth, organic fullness of life, fertility, the erotic, the powers of Nature,[79] and musically, it produces the ancient pentatonic scale.

Pan is shown with Apollo in their competition between stringed and wind instruments. King Midas is the judge, and he is given asses' ears because he did not declare Apollo the winner. Pan is also shown blowing his pipe, or a large horn that causes panic: sudden fear and disorder afflicting humans and animals because of cowardice, a lack of virtue (fig. 1).

Orpheus is also represented in the emblems and can be identified with both Apollonian and Dionysian traits. This ambiguity is present in the two versions of his history: one myth has him a Thracian and follower of Dionysus, and the other as the son of Calliope, a Muse of Apollo. Orpheus, the force of eloquence, is shown charming and ordering wildness with his music as does Apollo.[80] In the underworld, his voice of music is a mediator between this world and the next, life and death. His wisdom and intellect, however, do not yield him success in the underworld,[81] but with his voice of music, he becomes a shamanic figure—a mediator between this world and the next, death and life.[82]

When voyaging with Jason and the Argonauts, Orpheus encounters the luring song of the sirens. The sirens are pictured with plucked and bowed string instruments as well as wind instruments, and all with sweet pleasure on their faces. Their music, however, is not a vehicle for virtue as that of Orpheus and Apollo, but is rather a test of it and has no intrinsic value except for the external senses. As in the story of Ulysses, his wisdom is not fooled by their appearance and in the emblem text, scholars are said to have nothing to do with the temptations of superficially attractive harlots. The music of the sirens is a contradiction of Nature, just as their appearance is.

The power of poetry to enchant animals and inanimate nature is also a characteristic of Arion. The story of his encounter with the dolphin is pictured in all of Arion's emblems (fig. 2). His music enchants the dolphin to save him when the sailors force him out of the boat. The music of his harp or *lira da braccio* makes the beasts more virtuous than the treacherous humans. His musical power represents the harmony and ordering of the universe, the prevalence of virtue over avarice, and the relation between faith and innocence.[83] Amphion, another character similar to Orpheus and Arion, is pictured building the wall of Thebes with the power of his lyre's music.

Musical Instruments: Their Associations and Significance

The stringed instruments used in the emblems—harp, lyre, cithara, *lira da braccio*, and guitar, all have the same general symbolism by their common factor of strings. They represent the relationship between Heaven and Earth, the harmonious union of cosmic forces, profane and divine love, contemplation, scholarliness, poetry, song, and political concord.

The poetic lyre has five strings—possibly representing the five senses with which we perceive art—and is pictured with the scroll of the verbal arts. The two are surrounded by garlands of ivy in the form of a circle—symbolizing eternity. Ivy represents the enduring fame of the poet because it never withers, and its pale center is like the poet's skin, pale from studying. There is a connection here between the immortal poet and the lyre, and Apollo with his lyre representing eternal youth.

In the emblems, the idea of using music for fame is considered a "great abuse," and leads to further "vanities." This relates to a theme in Dutch and Flemish painting of the seventeenth century, the *vanitas* picture. These paintings delivered a moral to the viewer that worldly knowledge, pleasures, wealth, power, and over-indulgence in the arts were transient, and the single-minded pursuit of them was foolish.[84]

The emblems depict vanity versus the valuable use of time; the pursuit of music can be for pleasure, or more noble purposes. An emblem picturing King David and his harp, expresses that music's purpose has always been intended for the worship of God, and the Ten Commandments are spoken of as a ten-stringed instrument, a vehicle for serving God, and a bridge from earth to heaven. The Divine harp not played also represents vanity, and is compared to man's reason abandoned. Another emblem describes a guitar abandoned as being useless, and only worth what artful hands can make of its sound. A talking lute case is even depicted; it says it has no value because it has no voice, and compares itself to a leader who is not followed by his kingdom. Profane love is also represented, usually by Cupid as a lute player, who inspires love and knows how to play on the heartstrings. Cupid's love is declared the best musician of all, and love and virtuous devotion are inspired by music's power.

The idea of music as vanity is also discussed in relation to virtue. Instruments are abandoned on a table in favor of more noble endeavors, because life is too short and should not be wasted in such pleasures. There are references in the emblem text to Telemachus, who did not waste his time as did the suitors, but pursued nobler adventures. The vanities are also capable of stealing the heart of a fickle woman who can be tempted with song. This type of woman is rendered as a fool, in opposition to the virtuous woman who is steadfast and can endure such temptation.[85]

Instrument Tuning as Metaphor

A lute's tuning is a metaphor for concord between nations or differently governed groups, and a string out-of-tune is compared to a party not agreeing with the common good. A leader, just as a player, must have a skilled hand to create harmony. To be effective, the music must be in tune, just as a leader must promote concord to be successful. A well-tuned instrument is a sign of peace and political or friendly

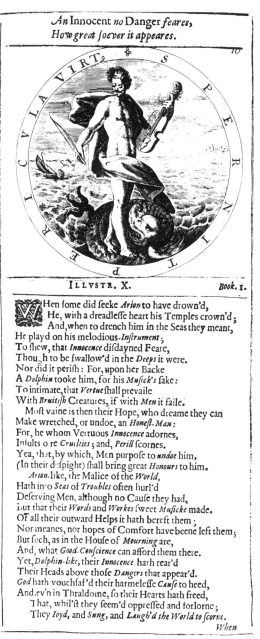

An Innocent *no* Danger *feares,*
How great *foever it appeares.*

ILLVSTR. X. *Book.* I.

When fome did feeke *Arion* to have drown'd,
He, with a dreadleſſe heart his Temples crown'd;
And, when to drench him in the Seas they meant,
He play'd on his melodious-*Inſtrument*;
To ſhew, that *Innocence* diſdayned Feare,
Though to be ſwallow'd in the *Deeps* it were.
Nor did it periſh: For, upon her Backe
A *Dolphin* tooke him, for his *Muſick's* fake:
To intimate, that *Vertue* ſhall prevaile
With *Bruitiſh* Creatures, if with *Men* it faile.
Moſt vaine is then their Hope, who dreame they can
Make wretched, or undoe, an *Honeſt-Man*:
For, he whom Vertuous *Innocence* adornes,
Inſults o re *Crueltics*; and, *Perill* ſcornes.
Yea, that, by which, Men purpoſe to *undoe* him,
(In their deſpight) ſhall bring great *Honours* to him.
Arion-like, the Malice of the *World,*
Hath in o *Seas* of *Troubles* often hurl'd
Deſerving Men, although no Cauſe they had,
But that their *Words* and *Workes* ſweet *Muſicke* made.
Of all their outward Helps it hath bereft them;
Nor meanes, nor hopes of Comfort have beene left them;
But ſuch, as in the Houſe of *Mourning* are,
And, what *Good-Conſcience* can afford them there.
Yet, *Dolphin-like,* their *Innocence* hath rear'd
Their Heads above thoſe *Dangers* that appear'd.
God hath vouchſaf'd their harmeleſſe *Cauſe* to heed,
And, ev'n in Thraldome, ſo their Hearts hath freed,
That, whil'ſt they ſeem'd oppreſſed and forlorne;
They *Ioyd,* and *Sung,* and *Laugh'd the World to ſcorne.*
When

Figure 2. Arion, shown atop his dolphin rescuer, with viol in hand.
George Wither, *A Collection of Emblemes, Ancient and Moderne* (1635).

concord, which extinguishes fear. The lack of fear—innocence—is related to the sweet harmony of Arion and his resulting lack of fear turned into faith. Fear and lack of faith render man unable to hear the sweet harmonies of music. Love as a sympathetic vibration is represented by two lutes tuned together; the second one vibrates when the first is plucked (fig. 3). A high-tuned lute is a warning against too much devotion to study and music playing. One emblem pictures a fool who is useless for the common good because he cannot tune his lute; also useless is the musician who plays only for himself to hear, which represents selfish friendship.

A lute with a broken string is a symbol of discord, and the cicada or cricket is a signifier of mended harmony from the story of Eunomus of Locrus. Eunomus broke a string during a contest against Aristo and a chirping cicada sat in place of the broken string and sang with a perfect voice. Eunomus beat his rival, and to thank Apollo and the Muses for their assistance, he cast the cicada in bronze as an offering. This cicada signifies music, his victory, and showed that music was pleasing to the gods.

Wind and Brass Instruments

The flute is represented, as were the satyrs, as a lascivious and phallic symbol used to portray ideas of dance, delight, lust, fertility, and deception. Fortuna is often pictured with a flute, blindfolded and standing on a sphere, playing her instrument to incite dance. The flute is also played by the bird-catcher in one emblem, to make sweet music that will bring the birds into unhappiness. This contradiction of sweet singing to bring misfortune upon someone is the same for the music of the sirens.

One emblem describes a flute being made out of an ass's bones; this relates to the idea that an instrument can possess a certain power derived from the material of which it is made, as Pan's flute out of Syrinx, who gains new life from her transformation. This empowering effect takes place also with instruments possessing a symbolic number of strings: the power of the signified is activated by its form and source.

The trumpet is symbolic of the call to action to start the day, and in the role of the battle-trumpeter. It also represents the voice of glory,

QVID NON SENTIT AMOR!   85
XLII.

Figure 3. Love as a Sympathetic Vibration.
An emblem from Jacob Cats' *Silenus Alcibiadis* (1618) shows two lutes
tuned together in concord. The second one vibrates when the first one
is plucked.

announcement in a fanfare, and a joyous, happy voice. Clio, Euterpe
and Calliope are some of the allegorical figures shown with a trumpet.

The allegory of Fame can be identified by her trumpet: an attention-
getting, heralding voice who announces the representation of worthy
figures.[86] She is shown interacting with a poet who is happy with his
sincere conscience that separates him like a wall from the vices and
troubles of the world, yet he is responsive to her.[87] Fame announces
and distinguishes the honorable poet who is guided by her and Time—
both winged for the journey—to Elysium where Apollo with his lyre
and the nine Muses and are portrayed. Fame, however, as well as other

Honors and Dignities are shown bowing down to, and being subject to wealth and riches. The trumpet is lower on the hierarchical ladder and also has a less profound significance for the emblem.[88]

Percussion Instruments

The only percussion instrument pictured in the emblem is the drum. In addition to it identifying Dionysus' attributes, it is represented in battle and concerns death and fear. In one emblem, a leader is mentioned who desired a drum to be made out of his skin after he died in order to instill fear in his people after his life was over. In this instance, the instrument's design is again a source of power.

Accepting this system of hierarchies does not belittle instruments of a lower class in terms of significance; the picture would indeed be much different if considered from an Eastern perspective. Just as in the duality of Apollo and Dionysus, all parts of the whole are necessary for completion, and within these sections, all aspects of the parts, each with their particular role, have significance for the harmony of the spheres.

The Emblematic Characteristics of Musical Drama

The Florentine *intermezzi* of 1589, performed at the wedding of the Grand Duke Ferdinand I and Christine of Lorraine, is an illustration of the emblematic characteristics of musical drama. Many of the subjects of the six *intermezzi* are the same as found in the emblems, concerning the harmony of the spheres, Apollo, the Muses, Arion, and Bacchus. The presentation of the *intermezzi* can be seen as a performance version of the emblem concept, concerning the same subjects, with signifying costumes and props, and having the same function of lyric and moralizing poetry. Both the emblems and the *intermezzi* juxtapose the visual and verbal to make an impression upon the minds of their audience.

The idea of a hierarchy of instruments within the emblems is reflected in the practical and symbolic musical practices of the time. The emblems' division of the instruments is similar to the classification in early instrumental music. *Haut* and *bas* ("high" and "low") refer to the loud and soft qualities of the instruments. Loud instruments such as shawms, trumpets, and drums were appropriately for outdoor performances; soft instruments, such as lutes, viols, and harps were for the intimate and reserved indoor performances. The emblems considered the more refined, quiet, and orderly instruments as higher in status and expressivity.

The notion that a certain instrument holds implications of social status is also conveyed. The allegorical figures related to the divine, such as Apollo and King David, are identified by their lyre and harp. The lower figures of earthliness and pleasure, such as Bacchus and Pan, are identified by their reed pipe and drum—the lesser wind and percussion classes. In one emblem, a beggarly old figure is represented by his hurdy gurdy, an instrument used in dance music, along with the shawm and violin, and regarded as a lower-class instrument. The *intermezzi*, similarly, use particular instruments to identify certain characters or classes of people: for instance a pipe for a shepherd, or a *viola da braccio* for Arion. The degree of expressivity in relation to the hierarchy of instruments is significant in the emblems and in the contemporary musical practice. The emblems represent the most expressive musicians—Orpheus, Apollo, King David, Arion, and Amphion—with their respective, highly-regarded instruments.

Orféo's *Possente spirto*

The idea of a hierarchy of expressivity is exemplified in the climax of Monteverdi's *Orféo* (first produced in Mantua, 1607). *Possente spirto*, Orféo's attempt to charm Caronte with his music to gain entrance into the Underworld, is in the form of a strophic song—using the same harmonic progression with each verse. Strophic form relates the music to literary form, and the *intermezzi* combine music, image, and poetry, just as in the emblems considered.

Orféo's hymn is a repeated monodic line interspersed with different ritornellos, and the significance of each of the four verses lies in its instrumental accompaniment. First, the accompaniment is by two violins (instruments of dance), second by two cornetti (representing the lower, Dionysian classifications), and the third by double-harp (signifying the higher, Apollonian class of instruments). A bowed string trio accompanies the fourth and final verse; this verse also has no ornamentation, but lets the simple tone of the instruments sing, and only now does Orféo gain entrance into the Underworld. The simplicity of the last verse and its effect upon Caronte are significant in relation to the humanism of the Florentine Camerata and their interest in the powers of Greek music and the Orphic hymns.

The symbolism used in *Orféo* and the *intermezzi* is brought to new light when considered as part of an emblematic era. It is important to consider emblematic concepts in relation to musical drama, in order to better understand the symbolic meanings and relationships that were most likely clear to a Renaissance audience.

Iconography and Organology

It is interesting to see what conclusions can be drawn from the emblems by their presentation, definition, sources, function, and implications. Their iconography combines the symbols and allegories of literature with those of music, humanistic music philosophy, and artistic inspiration, to form the art of emblematics—an art with form, content, and purpose. The abundance of musical ideas and images shows the function of music as a symbol and allegory, as well as its role as a significant art-form for society. Many perspectives of the Renaissance mind are presented, including images of performers, listeners, instruments, and social and moral implications. The performers and listeners portrayed provide information about the ideas of performance and music's *effect* upon the listener as understood by the Humanists. Some of the instruments also function to identify a character or define a social status.

The visual representation of the instruments makes clear that their function as part of the emblem is not to communicate performance technique. In the majority of the emblems, the instruments shown are held away from the body, similar to ancient art, or are not in a playing position at all. The artwork of the emblem is, for the most part, not of great skill in perspective or realism, but its significance is rather in the easily recognizable scenes and signifiers.

Concerning organological significance, it seems that the emblematists were concerned primarily with making the family or type of instrument discernible. The inconsistencies between text and picture about names of instruments in the same family—for example, lyre versus harp—further show that the authors were not as concerned with the detail of each instrument. The degree of specificity identifies a particular family of musical instruments, rather than an organologically exact depiction. It is reasonable to ask whether the instruments are depicted proportionally, correctly, or even whether they are imaginary designs. It seems unlikely, given that the text is often inconsistent in naming the instrument shown, that the emblematists were very concerned with proper organology.

Conclusion

The emblem books are a window into the thought and practices of the Renaissance. By using music and musical instruments as a focus and guide, many more topics and ideas are unveiled. The use of music and instruments as signifiers leads to the consideration of other subjects: the creative mind and artist, literature, art, printing, the musician and performance philosophy, musical theory and practice, the movements of Humanism, ancient revivals, Platonism, Christianity, education, and politics; the list could extend into an indefinite chain of associations. Overall, the topics in the emblems surveyed here have the qualities of ordering ideas and creating associations, just as the thinkers of the Renaissance did. The nature of their history, inspiration, purpose, and social and moral justifications offers a lens through which to study this abundantly diverse period in the history of music and otherwise.

Notes

1. J. W. Mollet, *An Illustrated Dictionary of Words Used in Art and Archaeology*, 124.

2. William S. Heckscher, *The Princeton Alciati Companion*, 28.

3. Heckscher, *The Princeton Alciati Companion*, 29.

4. Heckscher, *The Princeton Alciati Companion*, 29.

5. Hans Meier, Richard Newald, and Edgar Wind, *Kulturwissenschaftliche Bibliographie zum Nachleben der Antike*, 10.

6. Peter M. Daly, *Literature in the Light of the Emblem*, 8.

7. See Otto Van Veen, or Vaenius, *Horatii Emblemata* (Antwerp, 1612).

8. Meier, *Kulturwissenschaftliche Bibliographie zum Nachleben der Antike*, 6.

9. Daly, *Literature in the Light of the Emblem*, 20–21.

10. Elbert N. S. Thompson, *Literary Bypaths of the Renaissance*, 37–38.

11. Robert J. Clements, *Picta Poesis*, 19.

12. Mario Praz, *Studies in Seventeenth-Century Imagery*, 81.

13. Praz, *Studies in Seventeenth-Century Imagery*, 171.

14. Clements, *Picta Poesis*, 24.

15. Meier, *Kulturwissenschaftliche Bibliographie zum Nachleben der Antike*, 3.

16. It is interesting to note the etymological source of "polysemy" (a word having many meanings): *poly-* + Gk *sema* (sign), thus equating "meaning" and "sign."

17. Jennifer Speake, ed., *Encyclopedia of the Renaissance*, 219–20.

18. The *Biblia Pauperum* and the artwork of medieval cathedrals also functioned as an education for the young and illiterate. See Praz, *Studies in Seventeenth-Century Imagery*, 169.

19. Clements, *Picta Poesis*, 231.

20. Wither, *A Collection of Emblemes Ancient and Moderne* (1635), intro. Rosemary Freeman, xi. Published in 1635, Wither's work was the first emblem book to appear in England.

21. Clements, *Picta Poesis*, 230.

22. Mollet, *An Illustrated Dictionary of Words Used in Art and Archaeology*, 2.

23. Clements, *Picta Poesis*, 28.

24. Clements, *Picta Poesis*, 230.

25. Clements, *Picta Poesis*, 13.

26. Clements, *Picta Poesis*, 230.

27. Guillaume de la Perrière, *Le Theatre des Bons Engins*, vii–viii.

28. Meier, *Kulturwissenschaftliche Bibliographie zum Nachleben der Antike*, 1.

29. Hecksher, *The Princeton Alciati Companion*, 30.

30. Meier, *Kulturwissenschaftliche Bibliographie zum Nachleben der Antike*, 1.

31. Praz, *Studies in Seventeenth-Century Imagery*, 201.

32. Clements, *Picta Poesis*, 27.

33. Clements, *Picta Poesis*, 233.

34. Clements, *Picta Poesis*, 13.

35. Daly, *Literature in the Light of the Emblem*, 21.

36. Speake, ed., *Encyclopedia of the Renaissance*, 219.

37. From the introduction of Giarda's *Bibliothecae Alexandrina Icones Symbolicae* (Milan, 1626); trans. from E. H. Gombrich, "Icones Symbolicae: The Visual Image in Neo-Platonic Thought," 164.

38. Gombrich, "Icones Symbolicae," 176. "Warburg described as *Denkraumverlust* this tendency of the human mind to confuse the sign with the thing signified, the name and its bearer, the literal and the metaphorical, the image and its prototype" (165).

39. Gombrich, "Icones Symbolicae," 170.

40. "*Affectus*" (or "*affetti*") in *The Princeton Alciati Companion* correlates with other subjects: man's passions, the four temperaments, and the rhetorical tradition of music in the Renaissance.

41. Gombrich, "Icones Symbolicae," 176. Ficino discusses at length the astrological practice of amulets in his *De vita coelitus comparanda*.

42. The phrase is from Horace's *De arte poetica*; cited in Clements, *Picta Poesis*, 173–74.

43. Clements, *Picta Poesis*, 225.

44. This exploitation of the relationship between the two arts led Lessing to write his counter-argument in *Laokoön*.

45. A statement of Plutarch discussed in Clements, *Picta Poesis*, 174.

46. Clements, *Picta Poesis*, 27–28.

47. Clements, *Picta Poesis*, 28.

48. Clements, *Picta Poesis*, 226.

49. Heckscher, *The Princeton Alciati Companion*, 31.

50. Clements, *Picta Poesis*, 228–29.

51. Clements, *Picta Poesis*, 10.

52. Clements, *Picta Poesis*, 227.

53. Praz, *Studies in Seventeenth-Century Imagery*, 18.

54. Daly, *Literature in the Light of the Emblem*, 16.

55. Meier, *Kulturwissenschaftliche Bibliographie zum Nachleben der Antike*, 6.

56. Meier, *Kulturwissenschaftliche Bibliographie zum Nachleben der Antike*, 9.

57. Clements, *Picta Poesis*, 179.

58. Claude V. Palisca, *Humanism in Italian Renaissance Musical Thought*, 333.

59. Cf. the title page of *Horatii Emblemati*; the image of van Veen is portrayed with a lyre representing his role as a poet.

60. An instrumentless satyr represents the not very popular fourth form of poetry—satirical.

61. Clements, *Picta Poesis*, 34.

62. Baïf's *musique mesurée* movement and the Florentine Camerata limited themselves to setting verse to dramatic and lyric poetry, which was considered by Aristotle as inseparable from music. See D. P. Walker, "Musical Humanism in the Sixteenth and Early Seventeenth Centuries," 7.

63. Cf. Rosemary Freeman, *English Emblem Books*.

64. John Hollander, *The Untuning of the Sky: Ideas of Music in English Poetry 1500–1700*, illustration following p. 242.

65. Steven Olderr, *Symbolism: A Comprehensive Dictionary*, 142.

66. Apollo's instrument is associated with the tortoise-shell lyre and the myths concerning the birth of music. See Herbert Whone, *The Hidden Face of Music*, 68.

67. A possible relation may be made between the Apollonian versus the Dionysian approach, and "Optimist Gnosis"—knowledge of Divine through sensual world—versus "Pessimist Gnosis"—return to the Divine by denial of the sensual world—as discussed in Anthony Rooley's "*I Saw My Lady Weepe*: The First Five Songs of John Dowland's Second Book of Songs," 213.

68. Lynn Frier Kaufmann, *The Noble Savage: Satyrs and Satyr Families in Renaissance Art*, 21.

69. These dualities are found in Michael Maier's *Atalanta Fugiens: An Edition of the Emblems, Fugues and Epigrams*, 20.

70. Accepting creation as resting on the principles of math and music, it follows that instruments imitating these forms can be a better vehicle for expression, as well as an aesthetic or symbolic sign.

71. Olderr, *Symbolism: A Comprehensive Dictionary*, 50.

72. Kathi Meyer-Baer, *Music of the Spheres and the Dance of Death: Studies in Musical Iconology*, 357.

73. Clements, *Picta Poesis*, 55.

74. Note the numerological similarity of the pagan Apollo and his nine Muses, and God with his nine choirs of angels.

75. One emblem depicts Apollo's revenge on the defeated Marsyas; he tied him to a tree and flayed him alive.

76. Animal horns in relation to Bacchus relate to fertility, the phallus, immortality, and madness. See Olderr, *Symbolism: A Comprehensive Dictionary*, 68.

77. The instrument hierarchy is seen in satyr practices. Even though they were associated with wind instruments, in Greek vase paintings some play the lyre because of their role in the dithyramb, the poetry sung in honor of Dionysus. Satyr-priests played lyres and satyr-rapists the flute. See Lynn Frier Kaufmann, *The Noble Savage: Satyrs and Satyr Families in Renaissance Art*, 23; 26–7.

78. Olderr, *Symbolism: A Comprehensive Dictionary*, 120.

79. Olderr, *Symbolism: A Comprehensive Dictionary*, 50.

80. Boudard's *Iconologie* (Vienna, 1766) images *Eloquence* holding a lyre.

81. The theorist John of Grocheo (*c.* 1300) interpreted the Orpheus–Eurydice myth in a different light: Orpheus did not know the theory of music, for if he had he would have been able to deal with the cosmic powers he faced; he was therefore only a cithara player (a *cantor* not versed in musical theory) and not a *musicus* educated in theory and therefore more highly esteemed at the time. See Kathi Meyer-Baer, *Music of the Spheres and the Dance of Death*, 76–77.

82. John Warden, ed., *Orpheus: The Metamorphoses of a Myth*, 7.

83. Lack of faith is shown one emblem to make the effects of music unheard because of fear.

84. Thomas Noblitt, "Johann Georg Plazer: Music and Visual Allegory," 212.

85. In Boudard's *Iconologie*, *Plaisir* is pictured with a lyre.

86. See Tom L. Naylor, *The Trumpet and Trombone In Graphic Arts 1500–1800*, 5–6.

87. The Muse Clio is shown in Boudard's *Iconologie* with a trumpet; she can be related to Fame as she is the Muse of History.

88. Boudard pictures trumpets in his *Iconologie* in the allegories of *Louange*, *Prophétie*, *Renommée*, *Réprimand*, *Triton*, *Vaine Gloire*, and *Terreur*. The personification of Terror, or panic, is also portrayed in the emblems containing the Satyrs and Pan as discussed above.

Bibliography

Alciatus, Andreas. *The Latin Emblems: Indexes (Index Emblematicus) and Lists*; and *Emblems in Translation (Index Emblematicus)*. Edited by Peter M. Daly, Virginia W. Callahan and Simon Cuttler. 2 vols. Toronto: University of Toronto Press, 1985.

Bachmann, Werner. *The Origins of Bowing*. Translated by Norma Deane. London: Oxford University Press, 1969.

Chan, Mary. *Music in the Theater of Ben Johnson*. Oxford: Clarendon Press, 1980.

Clements, Robert J. *Picta Poesis: Literary and Humanistic Theory in Renaissance Emblem Books*. Rome: Edizioni di Storia e Letteratura, 1960.

Coates, Kevin. *Geometry, Proportion and the Art of Lutherie*. Oxford: Clarendon Press, 1985.

Colonna, Francesco. *Hypnerotomachia Poliphili*. Reprint of 1499 ed. New York: Garland, 1976.

Corbett, Margery, and Ronald Lightbown. *The Comely Frontespiece: The Emblematic Title-Page in England 1550–1660*. London: Routledge and Kegan Paul, 1979.

Daly, Peter M., ed. *The European Emblem: Towards an Index Emblematicus*. Waterloo: Wilfrid Laurier University Press, 1980.

——————. *Literature in the Light of the Emblem: Structural Parallels between the Emblem and Literature in the Sixteenth and Seventeenth Centuries*. Toronto: University of Toronto Press, 1979.

Fischer, Henry G. "Organology and Iconography of Ancient Egypt and the Renaissance." *Metropolitan Museum Journal* 24 (1989), 47–52.

Freeman, Rosemary. *English Emblem Books*. London: Chatto and Windus, 1948.

Friedman, John Block. *Orpheus in the Middle Ages*. Cambridge: Harvard University Press, 1970.

Godwin, Joscelyn. *Athanasius Kircher: A Renaissance Man and the Quest for Lost Knowledge*. London: Thames and Hudson, 1979.

——————. *Robert Fludd: Hermetic Philosopher and Surveyor of Two Worlds*. Grand Rapids: Phanes Press, 1991.

——————, ed. *The Harmony of the Spheres: A Sourcebook of the Pythagorean Tradition in Music*. Rochester: Inner Traditions, 1993.

Gombrich, E. H. "Icones Symbolicae: The Visual Image in Neo-Platonic Thought." *Journal of the Warburg and Courtland Institutes* 11 (1948), 163–88.

Graves, Robert. *The Greek Myths*. New York: Penguin Books, 1955.

Hecksher, William S. *The Princeton Alciati Companion*. New York: Garland, 1989.

Henkel, Arthur. *Emblemata: Handbuch zur Sinnbildkunst des XVI und XVII Jahrhunderts*. Stuttgart: J. B. Metzler, 1967. An index that represents over six hundred emblem books by many different authors.

Henry, Elisabeth. *Orpheus with His Lute: Poetry and the Renewal of Life*. Carbondale: Southern Illinois University Press, 1992.

Hollander, John. *The Untuning of the Sky: Ideas of Music in English Poetry 1500–1700*. Princeton: Princeton University Press, 1961.

Kaufmann, Lynn Frier. *The Noble Savage: Satyrs and Satyr Families in Renaissance Art*. Ann Arbor: UMI Research Press, 1984.

Lindley, Mark. *Lutes, Viols and Temperaments*. Cambridge: Cambridge University Press, 1984.

Lyons, Bridget Gellert. *Voices of Melancholy: Studies in Literary Treatments of Melancholy in Renaissance England*. New York: Barnes and Noble, 1971.

Maier, Michael. *Atalanta Fugiens: An Edition of the Emblems, Fugues and Epigrams*. Translated by Joscelyn Godwin. Grand Rapids: Phanes Press, 1989.

Meier, Hans, Richard Newald, and Edgar Wind. *Kulturwissenschaftliche Bibliographie zum Nachleben der Antike*. London: Cassell and Company, 1934.

Meyer-Baer, Kathi. *Music of the Spheres and the Dance of Death: Studies in Musical Iconology*. Princeton: Princeton University Press, 1970.

Mollet, J. W. *An Illustrated Dictionary of Words Used in Art and Archaeology*. London: Sampson, Low, Marston, Searle, and Rivington, 1883.

Mosely, Charles. *A Century of Emblems: An Introductory Anthology*. Aldershot: Scolar Press, 1989.

Munrow, David. *Instruments of the Middle Ages and Renaissance*. Oxford: Oxford University Press, 1976.

Naylor, Tom L. *The Trumpet and Trombone in Graphic Arts 1500–1800*. Nashville: The Brass Press, 1979.

Noblitt, Thomas. "Johann Georg Plazer: Music and Visual Allegory." In Thomas Noblitt, ed., *Music East and West: Essays in Honor of Walter Kaufman* (New York: Pendragon Press, 1981), 209–24.

Olderr, Steven. *Symbolism: A Comprehensive Dictionary* (Jefferson: McFarland, 1986).

Palisca, Claude V. *Humanism in Italian Renaissance Musical Thought*. New

Haven: Yale University Press, 1985.

Praz, Mario. *Studies in Seventeenth-Century Imagery*. Rome: Edizioni di Storia e Letteratura, 1964.

Rachum, Ilar. *The Renaissance: An Illustrated Encyclopedia*. New York: Mayflower Books, 1937.

Rooley, Anthony. *"I Saw My Lady Weepe*: The First Five Songs of John Dowland's Second Book of Songs." *Temenos* 2 (1982), 197–216.

Schullian, Dorothy M. and Max Schoen, eds. *Music and Medicine*. New York: Henry Schuman, 1948.

Speake, Jennifer, ed. *Encyclopedia of the Renaissance*. New York: Market House Books, 1987.

Stapleton, Michael. *The Concise Dictionary of Greek and Roman Mythology*. New York: Peter Bedrick, 1982.

Thompson, Elbert N. S. *Literary Bypaths of the Renaissance*. New Haven: Yale University Press, 1924.

Walker, D. P. "Musical Humanism in the Sixteenth and Early Seventeenth Centuries." *Music Review* 2 (1941), 1–13.

Warden, John, ed. *Orpheus: The Metamorphoses of a Myth*. Toronto: University of Toronto Press, 1982.

Whone, Herbert. *The Hidden Face of Music*. London: Victor Gollancz, 1974.

Wind, Edgar. *Pagan Mysteries in the Renaissance*. New Haven: Yale University Press, 1958.

Winternitz, Emanuel. *Musical Instruments and Their Symbolism in Western Art: Studies in Musical Iconology*. New Haven: Yale University Press, 1979.

Yates, Frances A. *The Art of Memory*. Chicago: University of Chicago Press, 1966.

——————. *The Valois Tapestries*. London: Warburg Institute, 1959.

Young, Alan R. *The English Tournament Imprese*. New York: AMS Press, 1988.

Emblem Books

Alciatus, Andreas. *Emblematum Libellus*. Reprint of 1542 ed. Darmstadt: Wissenschaftliche Buchgesellschaft, 1975.

Bocchi, Achille. *Symbolicarum Quaestionum de Universo Genere*. Reprint of 1574 ed. New York: Garland, 1979.

Boudard, J. B. *Iconologie*. Reprint of 1766 ed. New York: Garland, 1976.

Giarda, Christophoro. *Bibliothecae Alexandrina Icones Symbolicae.* Reprint of 1628 ed. New York: Garland, 1979.

Palmer, Thomas, Sir. *The Emblems of Thomas Palmer: Two Hundred Poosees.* Reprint of Sloane MS 3794. Edited by John Manning. New York: AMS Press, 1988.

de la Perrière, Guillaume. *Le Theatre des Bons Engins: Auquel sont contenuz cent Emblems moraulx.* Facsimile reproduction of 1539 ed. Delmar: Scholars' Facsimiles and Reprints, 1964.

Philostratus, Flavius. *Les images.* Reprint of 1614 ed. New York: Garland, 1976).

Ripa, Cesare. *Iconologia.* Reprint of 1644 ed. Translated by Jean Baudouin. New York: Garland, 1976.

van Veen (or Vaenius), Otto. *Horatii Emblemata.* Reprint of 1612 ed. in *The Philosophy of Images: A Garland Series* with an introduction by Stephen Orgel. New York: Garland, 1979.

Wither, George. *A Collection of Emblemes Ancient and Moderne.* Reprint of 1635 ed. with an introduction by Rosemary Freeman. Columbia: University of South Carolina Press, 1975.

PHILOSOPHORVM.

feipfis fecundum æqualitatē infpiffentur. Solus
enim calor tēperatus eft humiditatis infpiffatiuus
et mixtionis perfectiuus, et non fuper excedens.
Nā generatiōes et procreationes rerū naturaliū
habent folū fieri per tēperatifsimū calorē et æqua
lē, vti eft folus fimus equinus humidus et calidus.

Illustration from the *Rosarium Philosophorum*

On the scrolls, Sol is saying, "O Luna, let me be thy husband"; Luna
says, "O Sol, I must submit to thee"; and the dove says, "The spirit
is what unifies."

Jung and the Alchemical Imagination

JEFFREY RAFF

WHEN I WAS A STUDENT at the C. G. Jung Institute in Zurich in the early 1970s, I had the good fortune of studying with Marie-Louse von Franz and of working with analysts who had been greatly influenced by her. Today there are divergent schools of Jungian thought. Those who follow the tenets held by von Franz are now a minority. But when I was in Zurich she and her teachings were considered the quintessential interpretation of Jung's thought. It was a great privilege to study with her and particularly to hear her lectures on alchemy.

For von Franz, Jung's writings presented more than a psychological system, or a mode of analyzing others. For her, and for those of us studying with her, "living with the unconscious" was a way of life, and, in fact, a spiritual practice. We consulted our dreams and performed active imagination to learn to be "in Tao" and to unite with the center of the psyche, the divine core that Jung named the self. Living with the self was a religious experience for us.

Seen from this perspective, Jung presented a spiritual teaching that is related to the tradition we know today as "esoteric." Gerhard Wehr demonstrated Jung's affiliation with the esoteric tradition that includes alchemy when he wrote:

> The experience of depth psychology, the process of individuation that must be undergone, is itself an esoteric event which changes people to the depth of their being, extends their consciousness, and brings their personality to the maturity of the whole person.[1]

In this paper I will present what I consider the essential features of the Jungian spiritual system. I will also relate that system to alchemy. Jung discovered that many alchemical ideas were similar to his own, and his lifelong interest in alchemy stemmed from his recognition that those images and motifs amplified his own theories. Of course Jung looked at alchemy from the perspective of the psyche, rather than as a physical or chemical discipline. His interpretations were based on the hypothesis that alchemy was a symbolic system created, in large part, by the projection of unconscious images onto matter. In alchemy he discovered the psyche's description of itself and of its own transformation. Moreover, he discovered a Western path towards enlightenment.

My presentation of Jung's spiritual model is essentially true to his work and to the teachings of von Franz. I am, however, interpreting them according to my own understanding. In addition, I hope to expand Jung's understanding of the self and individuation to include experiences that derive not from the unconscious but from a transpsychic realm I have termed the psychoid. Jung used the term *psychoid* to refer to a level of reality in which matter and psyche are indistinguishable, and discussed it in relationship to synchronistic phenomena as well as to the interconnection between instinct and psychic image. I use the term to cover experiences of energies and entities that subjectively feel alive, independent, and not part of the psyche. More objectively, such experiences have greater impact on the individual and often produce physical changes or profound transformations of consciousness. They are often coupled with acausal phenomena, such as spontaneous healing. To the person who has them, experiences of the psychoid do not resemble psychic experiences. Before discussing these occurrences further, however, I wish to present the main features of the Jungian spiritual model.

* * *

Jung believed that the goal of life was the process he termed individuation. There are many ways to understand this process, but from almost any perspective it concerns the creation of the self. The experience of the self and the processes through which it is manifested form the core of Jungian spirituality. For Jung, the self was almost impossible to distinguish from "what has always been referred to as

'God.'"[2] As a living center of the psyche the self functions as the *spiritus rector* of daily life.[3] It is a guide and director and, more, a partner to the ego, or conscious personality. Partnership with the self forms the essence of Jung's view of spirituality.

Jung described religious attitude as a "careful and scrupulous observation of . . . a dynamic existence or effect not caused by an arbitrary act of will."[4] Since in Jung's model the self is the composite of these effects, I could describe the religious attitude as paying attention to the self or as making it into an inner partner. The ego scrupulously observes the manifestations of the self and harmonizes with them. Von Franz summed up this concept when she wrote in *Man and his Symbols*:

> Some profound inner experience of the Self does occur to most people at least once in a lifetime. From the psychological standpoint, a genuinely religious attitude consists of an effort to discover the unique experience and gradually to keep in tune with it . . . so that the Self becomes an inner partner towards whom one's attention is continually turned.[5]

The self is the center of the psyche, but it is not a static center. It possesses a dynamic existence that is experienced by the ego in the form of dreams, impulses, and imaginal happenings of all kinds. The self is not only the center of the psyche; it is the archetype of wholeness and as such carries a sense of the complete personality. The self is the personality as it could be if it were developed to its fullest. For Jung, wholeness referred to the union of the conscious and unconscious parts of the personality or the union of the ego and the unconscious. The self is therefore the union of the conscious ego with the unconscious.

The unconscious consists of two main components, the personal and the collective. The former contains the complexes and other materials that could belong to conscious life and in fact are part of the ego's personality. The latter holds the archetypes, which are impersonal and universal forces that belong to humankind as a whole. While the ego may integrate complex material as part of its growth, it cannot do so with the archetypes, which do not belong to any one person. However, the self, as center of the psyche, is capable of organizing and harmonizing the archetypal forces. Before the process of individuation, the psyche is a chaotic place in which archetypal forces and complexes compete with both the ego and the self for dominance. Though the self exists at this point, it is weak and unable to harmonize the archetypes effectively. As the process of individuation unfolds, the self becomes more and more powerful and is accordingly more effective in creating order within the psyche. The self before individuation I name the latent self, while the self after individuation I term the manifest self.

In order to understand this harmonizing quality of the self, it is necessary to discuss Jung's definition of "spirit." In his article "The Phenomenology of the Spirit in Fairytales," Jung came to the conclusion that there were three major attributes of spirit. The first is spontaneous movement and activity. The spirit is free to do and create as it will and is not under the control of the ego. The second attribute of spirit is the capacity to spontaneously produce images, and the third is the "sovereign manipulation of these images."[6] The spirit is that which gives rise to images within the psyche and creates experiences of these images. It is the spirit that creates the images that form the substance of the dream life. In this sense the ego does not make up dreams; rather, it encounters them as they unfold through the spontaneous manifestation of the spirit.

The freedom of the spirit to create images and imaginal events is significant not only for dreams, but also for any encounter with the unconscious. It seems as if every content of the unconscious, whether complex or archetype, possesses the capacity to represent itself in imaginal form. In this sense, every content has a spiritual aspect through which it gives rise to imaginal experience. This should come as no surprise to those who have been possessed by the inner voice of an anima or animus figure, or those who have been seized by the affect of a complex. We might imagine the psyche as a chaotic place, in which every part is capable of generating its own image. With every aspect of the inner world able to personify itself, the result is a conflicting chorus of voices, each singing its own melody, with no regard for the others. This chaos is evident in severely-disturbed and psychotic individuals who are unable to protect themselves from the cacophony of their inner spirits.

Balancing this disorder, however, is the self, the principle of order and harmony. The self is the center of the psyche around which all the other parts orient themselves. It brings order to and harmonizes all aspects of the psyche to create an orchestrated whole. Seen in this way, the self is the center around which the archetypes are grouped in their respective order. The mandala is the symbol for the self when it functions in this way. Jung wrote:

> [The] basic motif is the premonition of a center of personality, a kind of central point within the psyche, to which everything is related, by which everything is arranged, and which is itself a source of energy. The energy of the central point is manifested in the almost irresistible compulsion and urge to *become what one is* . . . Although the center is represented by an innermost point, it is surrounded by a periphery containing everything that belongs to the self . . . This totality comprises consciousness first of all, then the personal unconscious, and finally an indefinitely large segment of the collective unconscious whose archetypes are common to all mankind.[7]

Jung called the mandala, with its emphasis on order and balance, a premonition of the self. It is a premonition, because the self, which is capable of organizing all the archetypes, is the manifest rather than the latent self. While the latent self orders dream experiences, it does not possess the power to coordinate the psyche. Only when the latent self has been transmuted into the manifest self through a variety of psychological experiences is true harmony established.

Before the creation of the manifest self, the ego may believe itself strong and in control of its own life and psychic processes, but complexes manifest at almost any time, disrupting the order which the ego struggles to maintain. A successful businessman who is very much "on top of things" at work may experience uncontrollable rages at home. A career woman may weep inconsolably for no known reason. The ego's order is a charade a complex can easily puncture. In addition, if an individual comes under the power of an archetype, the fragile sense of identity conferred by the ego may easily be swept away.

Individuals in the grip of archetypal forces and emotions will perform acts they normally would abhor, and, with almost no sense of control or responsibility, may murder, rape, and destroy. Witness, for example, what previously ordinary men did under the influence of such an archetypal image as "ethnic cleansing."

Jung also noted that the energy of the self creates the almost irresistible urge to be oneself. The self manifests itself as images and experiences that reflect who one could be if one dared to individuate. The self pushes one to experience and express one's own uniqueness; and to this end, it must order the archetypal world. The archetypes are collective forces, and the images that they produce are universal, so an individual might simply follow these images, and, thereby, have numinous experiences. Yet he or she would never create the manifest self, which is unique and individual.

Although Jung did not conceptualize the process in this way, I imagine an ordering of the psychic chaos through the action of the self. As the self brings the archetypes into harmony, it effects the patterned order of the mandala structure with each archetype in a complementary relationship to the whole. In this process, the archetypes lose their universal and collective qualities and actually contribute to the uniqueness that is the self.

In summary, for Jung, a religious attitude consists of attending to the self or of living with the self as an inner partner. Because the self creates dream images, visions, and active imagination, one can maintain relationship with the self by engaging those images. In the normal, latent condition, however, the self competes with complexes and archetypes, which also manifest as images. Spiritual practice then consists not only of paying attention to the self, but also of working with it in such a way that it becomes powerful and dominant within the psyche. This work, the spiritual work *par excellence*, transforms the self from its latent to its manifest state. In so doing it transforms the whole personality, including the ego and the unconscious.

The manifest self must be created; it rarely emerges from the latent self spontaneously. Jung often speaks of redemption when referring to the need to transform the self. Transformation and redemption relate to self-creation as they also relate to the work of the alchemist.

Jung found in alchemy the tradition that most resembled his own system. Just as the Jungian seeks to manifest the self, the alchemist seeks to create the philosopher's stone. Just as the psyche moves from chaos to harmony, the alchemist works with chaos to create harmony. Let us now examine in more detail the alchemical images that amplify Jung's notion of the self and its manifestation.

The first and indispensable conclusion that guided Jung throughout his work with alchemy was that the philosopher's stone symbolized the self. Without this correlation, none of his writings on alchemy make sense. Just as the stone was the mysterious goal of the alchemical *opus*, the self was the goal of the individuation process. Both the self and the stone were formed from the union of opposites and both related to the divine presence and energy within the psyche, as well as within matter. Just as the self is the potential wholeness of the human being, the stone is the inner man possessed of a body, soul, and spirit. In sum, "the lapis represents the idea of a transcendent totality which coincides with what analytical psychology calls the self."[8]

The creation of the stone, like that of the self, begins with chaos. One of the names for the *prima materia*, the arcane first matter from which the stone is created, is *chaos*. Eirentheus Philalethes, for example, wrote that the spirit with which the work began "is nothing else but a Chaos, the Wonder of Wonders of God, which every man almost hath, and knows it not, because as it appears to the World it is compact in a vile, despised form . . ."[9] Another alchemist wrote that the first matter "represents, in a fairly complete way, the original Chaos, which contained all that was required for the original creation, that is, universal matter and universal form."[10] Like the latent self, the *prima materia* contains within itself all things, or at least the potential for all things:

> And this prime matter is found in a mountain containing an immense collection of created things. In this mountain is every sort of knowledge that is found in the world. There does not exist knowledge or understanding or dream or thought or sagacity or opinion or deliberation

> or wisdom or philosophy or geometry . . . that is not present there. And
> there does not exist hatred or malevolence or fraud or villainy or deceit
> or tyranny . . . that is not present there.[11]

The self amplified by the image of the *prima materia* contains within
itself all possible psychic life and experience, yet only as potential. As
the latent self is transmuted into the manifest self, these possibilities
are achieved.

Many alchemists also portray the movement from the primal matter
to the realized stone as a movement from chaos to harmony. In the
alchemy of Jabir, the method is that of balance, creating the perfect
equilibrium which produces the stone. Zosimos wrote that the primal
substance is slain and dismembered according "to the rule of harmony."[12] Finally, Eirenaeus Philalethes wrote that the alchemist must
create the proper proportions, inner and outer, in order to produce
"Harmony that is good Musick."[13] The movement from chaos to order
corresponds to the way in which "the contradictoriness of the unconscious is resolved by the archetype of the nuptial coniunctio, by which
the chaos becomes ordered."[14] In the coniunctio the opposites are
united, harmony replaces chaos, and the manifest self is formed.

Just as in alchemy the union of opposites is a prevalent and powerful
motif, so too in the Jungian spiritual model, for it is through the union
of the opposites that the self is made manifest. In his paper on the
transcendent function, Jung presented a paradigm for the process
which transforms the latent into the manifest self.[15] Before discussing
this paradigm, I would like to remind the reader that the self as union
of opposites is not just a theoretical notion, but something that the
individuating ego experiences. It is difficult to imagine what the union
of opposites feels like, but there are two primary ways that it may be
understood.

In the first place, the opposites may be joined sequentially. In this
case, the individual is kind when kindness is appropriate, and severe
when severity is required. She is not afraid of her own dark side, nor
is she dominated by it, but expresses it in a suitable manner. Such a
person expresses all of the parts of her personality, each in its
appropriate place. As Zen Buddhism says, she eats when she is hungry

and sleeps when she is tired. She is also angry and sad, happy and kind, depending on the circumstances she faces.

There is another way in which the opposites are united, and this might be thought of as a simultaneous union. Though the sequential process just described still operates, the state of consciousness associated with the self can no longer be defined in terms of the opposites. The ego, as part of the manifest self, does not experience itself in terms of masculinity or femininity, nor in terms of good and evil, but rather its locus of identification stands outside all of these attributes. Since such a state of being eludes verbal description, the most one can say is that it defies definition in normal categories. As an experience, however, it feels absolutely unique and complete unto itself. Such a self can only be understood as one of a kind. That it can be defined only in terms of itself does not mean it lacks relationship to others and to the outer world. Relationship is essential to life experience, and the outer world is part of the union of opposites that manifests the self. The self, though, is not defined either by relationship or the outer world, but by its own particular being and consciousness. Among the most important of the psychological processes which form the unique self is the transcendent function.

The transcendent function is the psychological mechanism that unites the opposites and helps bring the self to manifestation. In the Jungian model, the psyche includes the conscious mind with the ego at its center, and the unconscious. To effect a union of opposites, the contents of the unconscious must be joined with the ego so as to create a third position that unites both of them. Since the transcendent function "arises from the union of conscious and unconscious contents,"[16] it creates the third position.

There are several ways in which one may attempt to unite the opposites. In analysis, the analyst presents the client with the messages of the latter's dreams, and if the client takes them seriously he or she begins to include ideas and experiences normally outside his or her range of psychic life. For example, a very intellectual man will have to consider the role of feelings and begin to make choices based on what he feels, and not just on what he thinks. A timid woman will have to find the courage to deal with her domineering husband, and so on.

Paying attention to dreams sooner or later brings up the opposite to our normal and comfortable points of view. Analysis requires an openness and willingness on the part of the client to consider other ways of living.

Though the transcendent function may be evoked in analysis, or by paying attention to dreams, Jung felt that there was one technique above all others that would trigger it into activity. This technique, termed *active imagination*, forms an indispensable part of Jung's spiritual model.

As a first step to engage the transcendent function the ego turns to the unconscious with an open and receptive attitude. Given this attitude, the next step is to find a way to give voice to the unconscious, so that the ego may experience its messages. Earlier I mentioned that the spiritual aspect of the psyche is the capacity to produce and manipulate images. Archetypes or complexes, through this spiritual capacity, manifest as images, what Jung called "personifications."[17] Dreams provide examples of this process for they are inhabited by inner figures of all kinds. Yet dreams, according to Jung, are not always useful in facilitating the transcendent function. During dreaming, the conscious ego is asleep and, therefore, cannot interact on an equal level with the unconscious. For the transcendent function to operate successfully, the two opposites must be differentiated and have sufficient tension between them. The ego needs to be fully awake and aware and capable of holding its position while interacting with the image from the unconscious.

During active imagination, the ego, while completely awake, experiences unconscious contents or products, which may take the form of an image, a voice, a feeling, or even a bodily sensation. The ego, having focused its attention on the unconscious, must give up all critical thinking and simply open itself to what the unconscious presents. In this state of receptivity, it must wait for the unconscious to manifest in some way. Once it has seen, heard, or felt something, the ego then makes a response. It then waits for the unconscious to respond to its response. For example, a woman may wish to contact an animal she has seen in a dream. Meditating and stilling her mind, she either imagines the animal and holds that image until it comes alive and acts in some way, or she remains in emptiness and requests that the animal come to her. Once the animal appears to her inner vision, she can begin to engage with it in some fashion. In the form of active imagination that I favor, the ego dialogues with the inner figure. Such a dialogue consists not only of words, but may include an exchange of feelings, or simply a sudden knowing about the inner figure. In any case, the unconscious content, whether it is a complex or an archetype, manifests and personifies as an inner figure. In this form, it communicates its information to the ego.

Engaging inner figures can be an amazing experience. Such an endeavor gives a voice to the others within us, and though they must not be trusted blindly, they need to be considered if a person hopes to be whole. By dialoguing with an inner woman, a man may learn much about his own feminine nature and about the feminine in general. A woman may cultivate the masculine strength she has previously lacked, or engage with the personification of feminine wisdom.

Not only does active imagination create an exchange of information and attitudes between the ego and the unconscious, it can trigger the transcendent function. Suppose, for example, a man dialogues with his inner feminine figure, who tells him that he is much too heady and contemptuous of feelings. He resists and tells her he feels as much as he wants to. She replies that without feeling he is an empty shell. There is so much more to him than his mind, she insists. As this and further exchanges take place, there is a growing tension within the psyche. If the ego is fluid enough not to repress the voice of the feminine, and strong enough to resist giving in to it, a third position evolves which includes the points of view of both the ego and the inner figure.

The transcendent function is not a rational operation. One does not simply choose a third position and decide to follow it. Rather, the transcendent function is an experience in which the psyche is transformed. Normally this transformation occurs when a symbol or experience arises from the tension generated by holding the opposites together. In our example, the man, in a dream or active imagination, might experience the power of feeling and a range of emotions quite new to him. Having had this experience, he is altered by it forever. However, the transcendent function changes both the ego and the inner figure. Both take on some of the attributes of the other. But more than this, the self is formed which integrates both ego and inner figure in a unity previously unknown. In our example, the man who previously ignored feelings is so affected by the transcendent function that he now feels without even trying. His feelings are accessible and part of his life in a way he would never have previously imagined possible. At the same time, the feminine inner figure, or anima, has changed as well. She is no longer concerned with feelings alone, but serves as guide to the deeper parts of the unconscious. Moreover, where previously she would intrude as moodiness or irritability, she now serves the self on its quest for completeness. Previously remote or intrusive, she now finds her proper place within the mandala form of the self.

The self is formed of the union of opposites. The transcendent function unites the opposites into a third whole that is the self. Active imagination creates the contact between the ego and the inner figure necessary to produce sufficient tension to stimulate the transcendent function. Thus, the three pillars of Jungian spirituality are all interconnected and related. The self is formed when the ego is willing to engage in active imagination work, and the transcendent function is the means by which the self comes into being.

So interrelated are the self and active imagination that von Franz believed that as the self came into being the ego actually began to live in the world of active imagination:

> this is the plane on which active imagination takes control. With the inner nucleus of consciousness you stay in the middle place . . . you stay within your active imagination, so to speak, and you have the feeling that this is where your life process goes on . . . *You keep your consciousness turned towards the events which happen on the middle plane, on the events which evolve within your active imagination.*[18]

Living on the central plane, keeping one's focus on the inner world and its activity, corresponds to the religious attitude of paying attention to the self. In the state described by von Franz, the religious attitude has become a natural way of life.

In this regard Jung also found ideas similar to his own in the writings of the alchemists. He was one of the first to recognize the powerful role imagination played in the alchemical world. I have found in my own research many examples of the power of imagination in the formation of the stone. To the alchemists imagination was anything but unreal. They did not confuse it with fantasy, or the efforts of the ego to titillate itself. They saw in imagination a means to encounter wise teachers, angels, and spirits, as well as the means by which spiritual power could be invested in the philosopher's stone.

Ruland, who compiled his lexicon of alchemical terms in the sixteenth century, defined meditation as the "name of an Internal Talk of one person with another who is invisible, as in the invocation of the Deity, or communion with one's self, or with one's good angel."[19] His definition might easily serve to define active imagination. Through the interaction with what I have been calling inner figures, the alchemists learned the secrets of their mysterious operations. Theodore Kirkringius, in his commentary to Basil Valentine, argued that the alchemists discovered much arcane information through revelation from an inner figure. He wrote of the power of such revelations when he stated "how often those things which he [the alchemist] long sought and could not find, have been imparted to him in a moment, and as it were infused from above, or dictated by some good Genius." Paracelsus wrote that when a man imagines within himself his "imagination is united with heaven, and heaven operates with him that more is discovered than would seem possible by merely human methods."[20]

Imagination was a source of revelation, a means of dialoguing with inner guides and even one's good angel. It was furthermore the means by which the alchemists could fashion the stone. Through the imagination, heaven "operates with him" to create elixirs and even the stone itself. Oswald Croll, a disciple of Paracelsus, perhaps put it best:

> By the help of Imagination all magical operations and all wonderful things are done through the natural in born faith, by which we are at peace with the very spirits themselves. The Imagination worketh in Man like the sun, for as the bodily sun worketh without an instrument upon the subject, burning it to coals and ashes, so the incorporeal cogitation

of man worketh on the subject, by the spirit only as with a visible instrument; what the visible body doth that also doth the invisible body . . . [21]

In this remarkable passage, Croll argued that imagination, like the sun, is capable of action at a distance; though no visible means are apparent, imagination can transmute the subject, or prime material. I could adduce other writers to demonstrate that Croll was not alone in this belief, but these few quotes should suffice to demonstrate the power attributed to imagination by many alchemists.

Just as the imagination is pivotal in the creation of the philosopher's stone, it is the essential ingredient in the formation of the manifest self. Though writers like James Hillman have emphasized the power of imagination in recent years, active imagination itself has been neglected. In active imagination the image is not a metaphor, but a living embodiment or personification of unconscious content. Moreover, the imaginal processes impact the human practitioner on body and soul, and create the inner transmutations that define individuation. Jung realized the power of imaginal interaction with inner figures when he wrote, "instead of deriving these figures from our psychic condition, we must derive our psychic condition from these figures."[22] In other words, our psychic condition is profoundly affected by inner figures, and active imagination with them can go far toward altering that condition. I have seen people in the midst of depression dialogue with an inner figure whose words altered the person's mood dramatically. I have even witnessed one case of physical healing through the intervention of an inner figure.

In any event, Jung found in the alchemical notion of the imagination confirmation for many of his own ideas about active imagination. Every instance of active imagination carried out successfully stimulates the transcendent function, which, by uniting the opposites, creates the self.

The alchemical process most related to the transcendent function is the *coniunctio*. Just as the transcendent function binds together two opposites—one emanating from the unconscious, one belonging to the ego and consciousness, and creates a third transcendent whole—

so too the *coniunctio* unites two opposites to form a third. This third, at the highest level, is the stone which, through the *coniunctio*, comes into being with all of its magical properties.

As with so many of the major alchemical symbols and motifs, the *coniunctio* has a variety of meanings. It can be a union of mercury and sulphur in the alchemical vessel; it can refer to the union of body and soul, or soul and spirit, or even the union of the whole man with the transcendent unity of life. It need not occur at the end of the work, but at almost any time from the beginning. Typically death and rebirth follow the conjunction, save at the final moments of the alchemical work, when the stone which never dies is created. When describing these later stages the alchemists give voice to ecstatic utterances in their attempt to capture the inexplicable nature of the stone. Figulus, who gathered writings from earlier alchemists and combined them with writings of his own in his compendium *A Golden and Blessed Casket of Nature's Marvels*, wrote of the *coniunctio*:

> This is the Resurrection from the Dead, in which Soul, Body, and Spirit, after Purification, come together again; and—on our philosophical Last Day—will arise as a new glorified body and a new spiritual man without blemish and sin.[23]

Paracelsus, too, enters the realm of mysticism and spiritual mysteries when he writes of the *coniunctio*:

> Thereupon follows the greatest arcanum, that is to say, the Supercelestial Marriage of the Soul, consummately prepared and washed by the blood of the lamb with its own splendid, shining and purified body. This is the true supercelestial marriage by which life is prolonged to the last and predestined day. In this way, then, the soul and spirit of the Vitriol, which are its blood, are joined with its purified body, that they may be for eternity inseparable.[24]

There are, to be sure, less rhapsodic descriptions of the conjunction, but these two quotes should convey the sense that for many of the alchemists the *coniunctio* was a profound mystery leading to eternal life and unity of the personality. The transcendent function, and its parallel motif, the *coniunctio*, is indeed one of the great arcana of alchemical and psychological work. Jung dedicated his masterly work, *Mysterium Coniunctionis*, to the study of the conjunction as it related to the creation of the self. In this work, as in no other, he struggled to formulate the basis of a new model for Western spirituality.

I cannot of course discuss all that in this article, or even all that it has to say of the conjunction. Rather, I will focus on Jung's discussion of the theory of Gerhard Dorn.

Dorn, a spiritual alchemist and a disciple of Paracelus, whose exact birth and death remain unknown, began writing sometime around 1565. He presented a theory of the conjunction that Jung found fascinating. In Dorn's theory, there are three levels of the conjunction. They are the *unio mentalis*, or mental union; the *unio corporalis*, or union of the body; and the union with the *unus mundus*, the one divine world that stands behind the world of phenomenal existence. Dorn outlines the three stages in the following fashion:

> We conclude that meditative philosophy consists in the overcoming of the body by mental union. This first union does not as yet make the wise man, but only the mental disciple of wisdom. The second union of the mind with the body shows forth the wise man, hoping for and expecting the blessed third union with the first unity [the *unus mundus*].[25]

Each stage of union would correspond to a stage in the development of the self as the individuation process proceeds. I shall present and elaborate on Jung's ideas regarding the first two levels, and offer my own theory of the nature of the third.

According to Dorn, the first conjunction occurs when the soul has been "removed" from the body and is thereby freed from its contaminating influences and passions. The mental union would correspond in Jung's model to the confrontation with the unconscious. The ego, casting off its illusion of psychic dominance, comes to terms with the reality of the unconscious and begins to work with dream messages and inner figures of the imagination. Jung observed that the ego has a special power, the power of focus and attention. This power is transformative, for the ego's attention has a strong impact. When the ego turns its focus to the inner world the unconscious is activated. According to Jung, the "attention given to the unconscious has the effect of incubation, a brooding over the slow fire needed in the initial stages of the work."[26] The attention of the ego stimulates the unconscious into increased activity and serves to break down the barriers existing between them. The mental union begins when the ego knowingly and deliberately pays attention to the unconscious, thereby stirring it into increased activity.

It should be clear by now that the self cannot exist if the ego is lost or in any way impeded. It is for this reason that the Jungian spiritual model differs from almost all other models in the value and dignity it affords to the ego. An ego obscured by complexes, possessed by an archetype, or identified with the material world, is not capable of creating union with the unconscious. But an ego that pays attention to the unconscious is the *sine qua non* of self-formation. Unlike other models, which do their best to rid themselves of the ego, the Jungian paradigm ennobles it. As Jung pointed out, God could never be known "unless the futile and ridiculous ego offers a modest vessel in which to catch the effluence of the Most High and name it with his name."[27] It is equally hard to imagine the philosopher's stone coming into being if there were no alchemists to perform the operations required for its creation.

One could compare the mental union to the beginning of analysis when an individual learns to respect his or her dream life. During this period, however, the respect given to the unconscious is only mental. For example, a man might have dreamt about his inner feminine nature; by paying attention to these dreams, he might have begun to consider the qualities of the feminine and what it might be like to express them. But he has not yet begun to live out his feminine nature in his outer life. There is a very long period in analysis and in any spiritual work in which the undertaking remains an ideal, but not a lived reality. A client may come into analysis and discuss the need to change her style of life for months before actually beginning to alter the way in which she lives. The first period is one of reflection and consideration and is very important, for without proper preparation one could never enter the next stage, the union with the body.

In the second level *coniunctio*, the mind, purified and transformed, is reunited to the body. Psychologically, this would correspond to two transformations. In the first place, all the knowledge gained in the first stage is now put into practice and lived out in daily life. In analysis, this stage is termed integration. It is the final stage of any analysis, and one of the most difficult to achieve. It occurs when analysis has actually stopped, and the client, now on his or her own, must find a way to bring all that was learned in analysis into practical application.

To give a very simple example of this stage, imagine that a woman has worked with a contrasexual figure, the animus. The woman's ego has engaged in a great deal of work with the inner masculine voice, which has repeatedly told her she must find the courage to assert herself in the world. She has considered this dilemma from every angle, and though she wishes to be brave she finds it very difficult to put into practice. She attempts several times to put forth her own ideas at work and finally succeeds in being heard and taken seriously. Following this she finds it increasingly less difficult to speak her mind to others. The courage previously found only in the unconscious has been integrated into her conscious life. When the image or message presented by the unconscious and accepted by the ego is applied in daily life, the individual has reached the second stage of union. At this level, the messages of our dreams and our active imaginations are put into practice with often transformative effects. Individuals at this stage may make all types of life-changing decisions. For some people, the changes do not affect the structure of their outer life, but the way in which they experience life. For example, an individual may not have to change jobs or relationships, but finds himself feeling the events of his daily life much more profoundly.

I have often heard Jungians criticized for being too mental, too heady, and impractical. But a successful analysis creates the second *coniunctio* in which the individual puts into practical application all the messages of the dream world. If one does not integrate the unconscious into the everyday world, the union with the unconscious remains stunted.

The bodily union signifies the integration of the inner voices into ordinary life. But there is another, even more profound meaning to this level. Though the first level culminates in an idea or an image of the self, the second level occurs when the self becomes a living reality. Moving from a construct or possibility, the self becomes a real fact of daily life. Once this new center begins to function, it harmonizes and organizes the inner world, gradually arranging the archetypes and complexes about a common center. Experientially, the new center produces a feeling of inner strength and solidity. The manifest self feels powerful and eternal, as if nothing could shake it or move it off its moorings. An individual within whom the manifest self lives feels confident and self-contained. The center was once fixed on the ego— a small, frail craft—and now has shifted to the self, a giant and unsinkable vessel that weathers any storm. But the ego is not destroyed. Just as the unconscious is transformed by the production of the manifest self, the ego too is radically altered. The consciousness of the personality now identifies less with the ego, and more with the manifest self, of which the ego is a part. The ego's locus of identification has shifted to include the whole self, and the consciousness of which it was previously the center is now focused on the self. Such a consciousness is deeper, wider, more extensive and more stable. Moreover, the ego's repertoire of conscious states has grown considerably, and altered states of consciousness are not infrequent phenomena. It is most difficult to describe the state of being and of consciousness that accompanies the creation of the manifest self. In fact one would never be prepared to experience them had not the first level union provided moments of connection with the self that become durable in the second level.

The new center continues the work of attending to those parts of the unconscious and of life experience that have not yet been integrated into the manifest self. Its power of attention is greater than that of the ego's, and so it works with the unconscious and outer life situations at an accelerated speed. The manifest self continues to individuate as it integrates previously unexplored material. This process never ceases, for the self is capable of infinite growth and transformation, whether it finds its material for growth within or without. Emerging from the second *coniunctio*, the manifest self continues to multiply its own power, depth, wisdom, and solidity. In this sense, the processes following the attainment of the second level union correspond to the alchemical *multiplicatio* through which the power of the stone is multiplied infinitely. This multiplication continues even after the attainment of the third level.

Jung described the emergence of the new center as a surrender of the conscious man to the self, "to the new center of personality which replaces the former ego."[28] As Jung pointed out, the self replaces the former ego; or one could also say the transformed ego is the new center. The ego is now a self, and the second *coniunctio* has been attained.

With the formation of the self at the second level, the work might seem to have reached its culminating point. The self is alive and functioning and the ego and the unconscious have united in its formation. Dorn, however, believed that the formation of the stone was incomplete until joined with the mysterious level of existence he termed the *unus mundus*. According to Dorn, God first created one world, the *unus mundus*, which he next divided into two—heaven and earth. But the *unus mundus* remains as a third realm that unites heaven and earth:

> Beneath this spiritual and corporeal binarius lieth hid a third thing, which is the bond of holy matrimony. This same is the medium enduring until now in all things, partaking of both their extremes, without which it cannot be at all, nor they without this medium be what they are, one thing out of three.[29]

Dorn meant by the third union that the individual who has succeeded in the mental and bodily unions now marries the self with the world of the infinite, the "real" world that God first created. This world of ultimate reality is neither physical nor spiritual, but is the medium by which these opposites are united. The world in which psyche and matter and body and spirit are unified is the world I have called psychoid.

The *unus mundus* is worthy of far greater study, but I shall confine myself to explaining my understanding of the third *coniunctio*. For once

Jung fails to do full justice to an alchemical concept. A close reading of his explanation of the third level union fails to differentiate it from his definition of the second. In both cases, he depicts the union as a joining of the ego and the unconscious and the subsequent formation of the self. He falters at this point, I suspect, because of his reluctance to posit transpsychic experience. In my years of working with visionary material, alchemical symbols, and my own experiences, I have come to believe that there does in fact exist a transpsychic world that may be experienced. Using and altering Jung's concept of the psychoid, I postulate the actuality of a psychoid realm that is neither psychic nor physical, but an intermediate third realm in which the normal concept of opposites fails to apply.

The psychoid is a difficult notion to explain, but unless we are ready to argue that the psyche is the only reality other than the physical world, there is need for such an idea. Dorn is not the only thinker who posits such a realm. The Sufi mystics argue that there was a world existing between the Divine world and the world of ordinary reality, which they termed an imaginal reality.[30] To be sure, their notion of imagination is not the same as ours. A close study of Ibn 'Arabi's life and work, for example, reveals that he experienced spirits, guides, and Divine Names appearing in the outside world, though they themselves were not physical.[31] Imagine for a moment the difference between closing your eyes and evoking an image of a spirit guide and actually meeting that spirit guide on the street outside your house. Are these the same experiences? One consists of an inner image which clearly belongs to the unconscious, while the other appears as a living entity with its own life and being. Experiencing a spirit or even a ghost that exists outside the psyche is not common, but neither is it unheard of. Such occurrences, and many others like them, require an explanation. One such would be that there exists a transpsychic reality in which spirit takes on form and body, and body itself is profoundly altered to include spirit.

There are many motifs and images within alchemy itself that point to such a realm, or at least a belief in one. For example, a Sufi alchemist wrote that to understand the power of the philosopher's stone, one had to realize that it was a body that functioned like a spirit. Even so, the operation of the stone would be inconceivable if carried out on ordinary physical matter, but becomes possible when the nature of spirits is correctly understood. For the physical component of the stone is like the "spiritual body of those who live in Paradise."[32] In other words, alchemy works because it deals not with the ordinary physical substances, but with substances that are both corporeal *and* spiritual.

Interestingly, Robert Fludd, a well-known Hermeticist, presented a very similar idea when he argued that the stone was the equivalent of the body of Christ after the resurrection. He argued that the stone consisted "of a divine and plusquamperfect spirit and a *body exalted from corporeality unto a pure and spiritual existence*, from mortality into immortality, and being the patterne of Christ risen again, it must needs have the power to multiply infinitely . . . "[33] [My italics] I could cite many more such images, but perhaps it is enough to mention the pervasive alchemical theme of making body spirit and spirit body.

If alchemical images could serve Jung in his conception of the self, they may serve us as well in trying to comprehend the psychoid realm. In any event, it seems necessary to conceptualize a transpsychic world in order to understand some of the deepest images of alchemy. Moreover, there are experiences that defy explanation through resorting to the idea of the unconscious alone. For example, von Franz and her co-workers argue that some dreams of the dead actually involve encounters with the spirits of the departed and are not explicable in terms of inner contents. Dreams of this nature have a different feel than normal dreams. The deceased who appear in the dreams appear to be real and not at all like inner figures. Emmanuel Kennedy-Xipolitas calls such dreams "metapsychic" and notes that they "have an intense emotional impact on the dreamer and are characterized furthermore by a unique, indescribable feeling . . ."[34]

Experiences of the psychoid may also occur in visionary and meditative states as well as in dreams, and are differentiated from active imagination experiences due to the level of reality they possess. If I may cite a personal example, I once woke in the middle of the night. As I lay in bed completely awake and aware of my surroundings, I found myself transported to the top of a mountain. I was in a precarious position and my fear of heights asserted itself so that I at once fell to my knees. A figure in a hooded robe walked over to me and said, "are you afraid, even here?" He touched my chest and I found myself back in bed in an ecstatic state. While on the mountain I was quite aware of the cold, the feel of the rocks, and my fear of heights, and though I knew I was not in the ordinary world, my senses told me I was in a completely real world that was not within my psyche. The being in the hooded robe I knew to be a spirit, yet one whose touch I could feel on my body, which was certainly not my ordinary body. The physical nature of the spirit and its touch and the complete reality of the scene are characteristics of psychoidal experiences, as too is the ecstasy that followed.

Let us now return to the third *coniunctio*. Since the second level has resulted in the formation of the manifest self, I would argue that the third is the union formed between the manifest self and the psychoid world. This union may be effected in a number of different ways, but just as the psyche has its center—the self—the psychoid seems to have its center. Just as the self personifies in images, so the center of the psychoid may appear as a living divine being. Just as the self is created by interaction with inner figures, union with the *unus mundus* is obtained by relationship with a psychoidal figure. I have argued elsewhere that there is a twin to the self that exists in the psychoid that I have termed the ally.[35] The notion of such a twin is not new, for it may be found in the Zoroastrian and Sufi traditions. The Sufis have a theory that the inner man is a being of light. This inner light being would correspond to the self. But they also believed that there is a divine twin to this man of light who is also a being of light. The second man of light would correspond to what I have called the *ally*. The ally would be a twin to the self that has its own existence and autonomy apart from the psyche. The psychoid twin is divine, and embodies all the powers of the divine in the intermediate world.

Union between the self and its twin completes the process of individuation by uniting the psyche and the psychoid. For the third level to occur, the individual human being must unite with the one world of spirit that at the same time is the intermediate world that fosters union between the human and divine. The third *coniunctio* would be the union of individuated human with the divine world through union with his ally.[36] Jung was himself aware that the third union was of a very profound nature, and when he let go of his theoretical position and grew poetic, he offered this musing about it:

> We could compare this [union] only with the ineffable mystery of the *unio mystica*, or *tao*, or the content of *Samadhi*, or the experience of *satori* in Zen, which would bring us to the realm of the ineffable and of extreme subjectivity where all the criteria of reason fail. . . . It is and remains a secret of the world of psychic experience and can be understood only as a numinous event, whose actuality, nevertheless, cannot be doubted.[37]

Jung does not hesitate to compare the experience of the third *coniunctio* to enlightenment experiences of other traditions. It is, in essence, the Jungian form of enlightenment.

* * *

I have tried in this paper to show that Jung's model of spirituality is rooted in the existence of the self, active imagination experiences through which the self may be experienced, and the transcendent function which unites the opposites and brings the manifest self into being. In addition, I argue that the self and its experience leads one to the psychoid world, in which the self may find its spirit twin and unite with the divine reality. Alchemy remains an invaluable source of symbols and images that reveal the self and its processes. Alchemy may now also become a font of information about the psychoid world, and the third *coniunctio*. Through the individuation process and the eventual union of self and divinity, the contemporary individual discovers a new and uniquely Western form of enlightenment.

Notes

1. Gerhard Wehr, "C. G. Jung in the Context of Christian Esotericism and Cultural History," in *Modern Esoteric Spirituality*, ed. Antoine Faivre and Jacob Needleman (New York: Crossroad, 1995), 382.

2. C. G. Jung, *Mysterium Coniunctionis* (Princeton: Princeton University Press, 1970), par. 778.

3. Jung, *Mysterium Coniunctionis*, par. 777.

4. C. G. Jung, *Psychology and Religion* (New Haven: Yale University Press, 1938), 4.

5. Marie-Louise von Franz, "The Process of Individuation" in C. G. Jung [and others], *Man and His Symbols* (Garden City: Doubleday, 1964), 210.

6. C. G. Jung, *The Archetypes and the Collective Unconscious* (Princeton: Princeton University Press, 1969), par. 393.

7. Jung, *The Archetypes and the Collective Unconscious*, par. 634.

8. C. G. Jung, *Alchemical Studies* (Princeton: Princeton University Press, 1970), par. 134.

9. Eirenaeus Philalethes, "An Exposition upon Sir George Ripley's Preface," in *Alchemical Works: Eirenaeus Philalethes Compiled*, ed. S. Merrow Broddle (Boulder: Cinnabar, 1994), 160.

10. Paracelsus, "A Short Catechism of Alchemy," in *The Hermetic and Alchemical Writings of "Paracelsus" the Great*, ed. A. E. Waite (Kila, Montana: Kessinger, n.d.), I, 301.

11. Al-Iraqi, *The Book of Knowledge Acquired Concerning the Cultivation of Gold* (Edmonds: The Alchemical Press, 1991), 18.

12. Jung, *Alchemical Studies*, par. 86.

13. Philalethes, "An Exposition upon Ripley's Compound of Alchymie" in *Alchemical Works: Eirenaeus Philalethes Compiled*, 214.

14. Jung, *Mysterium Coniunctionis*, par. 88.

15. C. G. Jung, *The Structure and Dynamics of the Psyche* (Princeton: Princeton University Press, 1969).

16. Jung, *The Structure and Dynamics of the Psyche*, par. 131.

17. C. G. Jung, *Analytical Psychology: Its Theory and Practice* (New York: Pantheon Books, 1968), 80–81.

18. Marie-Louise von Franz, "The Inferior Function," in James Hillman and Marie-Louise von Franz, *Lectures on Jung's Typology* (Dallas: Spring Publications, 1984), 69.

19. Martinus Rulandus, *A Lexicon of Alchemy or Alchemical Dictionary* (Kila,

Montana: Kessinger, n.d.), 226.

20. Paracelsus, "Hermetic Astronomy," in *The Hermetic and Alchemical Writings of "Paracelsus" the Great*, II, 313.

21. Oswald Croll, *Philosophy Reformed and Improved in Four Profound Tractates*, trans. H. Prinnell (London, 1657), 71.

22. Jung, *Alchemical Studies*, par. 299.

23. Benedictus Figulus, *A Golden and Blessed Casket of Nature's Marvels* (Kila: Kessinger, n.d.), 227.

24. Paracelsus, "The Aurora of the Philosophers," in *The Hermetic and Alchemical Writings of "Paracelsus" the Great*, I, 61–62.

25. Dorn, cited in Jung, *Mysterium Coniunctionis*, par. 663.

26. Jung, *Mysterium Coniunctionis*, par. 180.

27. Jung, *Mysterium Coniunctionis*, par. 284.

28. Jung, *Mysterium Coniunctionis*, par. 704.

29. Cited in Jung, *Mysterium Coniunctionis*, par. 659.

30. Cf. Henry Corbin, *Creative Imagination in the Sufism of Ibn 'Arabi* (Princeton: Princeton University Press, 1981).

31. Cf. Claude Addas, *The Quest for the Red Sulphur: The Life of Ibn 'Arabi*, trans. Peter Kingsley (Cambridge: The Islamic Texts Society, 1993).

32. Shaikh Ahmad Ahsa'I, "Physiology of the Resurrection Body," in Henry Corbin, *Spiritual Body and Celestial Earth*, trans. Nancy Pearson (Princeton: Princeton University Press, 1989), 209.

33. Robert Fludd, *Truth's Golden Harrow*, in C. H. Josten, "Truth's Golden Harrow: An Unpublished Alchemical Treatise of Robert Fludd in the Bodleian Library," *Ambix: The Journal of the Society for the Study of Alchemy and Early Chemistry* 3 (April 1949), 110.

34. Emmanuel Kennedy-Xipolitas, foreword to Marie-Louise von Franz, *On Dreams and Death*, ix.

35. Jeffrey Raff, "The Ally," in *The Sacred Heritage: The Influence of Shamanism on Analytical Psychology*, ed. Donald F. Sandner and Steven H. Wong (New York: Routledge, 1997).

36. For further discussion of the third *coniunctio*, see Jeffrey Raff, *Jung and the Alchemical Imagination* (York Beach: Nicolas-Hays, 2000).

37. Jung, *Mysterium Coniunctionis*, par. 771.

Two Platonic Voices in America:
Ralph Waldo Emerson and Thomas M. Johnson

David Fideler

In the late 1800s Hellenic Neoplatonism constituted a vital, grassroots philosophical movement in America, during the time that philosophy was becoming an academic and technical discipline. The New England transcendentalists such as Emerson, Alcott, and Thoreau were avid readers of Plato and the late Neoplatonists in the translations of Thomas Taylor (1758–1835), the British Platonist who made the first complete English translation of Plato's dialogues, but interpreted them from the perspective of late Neoplatonic metaphysics and theology. It was the dual influence of the transcendentalists and Thomas Taylor's legendary status that helped to inspire the formation of several Plato societies in the Midwest and the translating and publishing efforts of Thomas M. Johnson, founder and editor of two journals, *The Platonist* and *Bibliotheca Platonica*.

In this paper I discuss how Ralph Waldo Emerson (1803–1882) and Thomas M. Johnson (1851–1919) represent two distinctly different Platonic voices in America, despite their common admiration of Thomas Taylor. But before discussing Johnson and Emerson, perhaps a few words should be said about Thomas Taylor.

Thomas Taylor the Platonist

Born in London in 1758, Taylor's first study was mathematics, before turning to Greek and Latin. At a young age, while working at a bank, he took up the study of Aristotle, which led to Plato, Plotinus, and Proclus. Taylor offered twelve lectures on Platonic philosophy at

This paper was given at the conference on "Platonism and Neoplatonism in American Thought and Scholarship," Vanderbilt University, May 20–24, 1999.

the home of John Flaxman, the sculptor, and after that devoted his life to translating texts of Greek philosophy. His first published translation was Plotinus' "On the Beautiful" (*Enneads* 1.6), with *The Hymns of Orpheus* appearing in the same year (1787). This was followed by his translation of the *Commentaries of Proclus on the First Book of Euclid's Elements*, after which scarcely a year passed without the publication of some new translation or original work of his own. Taylor's contemporary Floyer Sydenham had undertaken a complete translation of Plato's works late in his life, but his health failed and he died at the age of seventy-seven in a debtor's prison. Taylor took over the project and published the first complete translation of Plato's works in English.[1] He also published the first complete translation of Aristotle and a veritable host of Neoplatonic works: *The Orations of the Emperor Julian*; Sallustius' *On the Gods and the World*; *Select Works of Plotinus*; Iamblichus's *Life of Pythagoras*; Proclus' massive *Commentaries on the Timaeus of Plato*; Proclus' *Platonic Theology*; Iamblichus *On the Mysteries*—the list goes on and on.[2] In short, laboring in poverty and obscurity, Thomas Taylor came as close to translating the entire Platonic and Neoplatonic corpus as anyone ever has, or probably as any individual ever will.

Taylor's translating program, however, was not that of modern, academic scholarship—a perspective that was just emerging—rather his aim was "to diffuse the salutary light of genuine philosophy."[3] As Kathleen Raine notes, "his learning was inspired by a zealous wish to combat the mentality of his age"—the mechanistic materialism that was increasingly coloring the English spirit, and was later denounced by Blake, Coleridge, and Shelley—who were all influenced by Taylor's translations. As Taylor himself lamented,

> in our times, the voice of wisdom is no longer heard in the silence of sacred solitude; but *folly*, usurping her place, has filled every quarter with the deafening clamours of despicable sectaries, while the brutal hand of commerce has blinded the liberal eye of divine contemplation.[4]

Taylor dedicated his translation of Proclus' *Commentaries on the*

Timaeus "To the Sacred Majesty of Truth," and sought to combat the materialism of his time by restoring "that sublime theology that was first obscurely promulgated by Orpheus, Pythagoras, and Plato."[5] At other times, however, his prose could be more militant. In his introduction to Plotinus' *Concerning the Beautiful* (1787), Taylor wrote that

> impetuous ignorance is thundering at the bulwarks of philosophy, and her sacred retreats are in danger of being demolished, through our feeble resistance. . . . the foe is indeed numerous, but, at the same time, feeble: and the weapons of truth, in the hands of vigorous union, descend with irresistible force, and are fatal wherever they fall.

While his translations inspired the English Romantic poets and his acquaintances included William Blake, Mary Wollstonecraft, Isaac Disraeli, and Thomas Love Peacock, Taylor's work, if not being attacked, otherwise languished in obscurity—that is, until his work came to America.

Thomas Taylor Comes to America

Thomas Taylor was the favorite Platonist of the American transcendentalists. Emerson began his lifelong study of Plato at the age of twenty, and discovered Taylor's *Works of Plato* three years later in 1826. Similarly, when Bronson Alcott discovered Plato in Taylor's translation in the summer of 1833, it marked a turning point in his life. To underscore its importance he inscribed the precise date on his calendar in red ink—a color he reserved only for his marriage, the births of his daughters, the opening of the Civil War, and the assassination of Lincoln.[6] Taylor's translations and writings became widely sought after by the transcendentalists, and when Alcott traveled to England he made it a special point to bring back to America as many works by Taylor as he could find.[7] During his second trip to England, Ralph Waldo Emerson eagerly sought out information about Taylor. The most significant report of Taylor's importance in America appears in Emerson's account of his conversation with

William Wordsworth. Meeting with Wordsworth in 1848, Emerson told him that "it was not credible that no one in all of the country knew anything of Thomas Taylor, the Platonist, whilst in every American library his translations are found."[8]

Thomas Taylor's greatest American disciple would turn out to be Thomas Moore Johnson, a lawyer from Osceola, Missouri, a small town of a thousand located on the banks of the Osage River. Johnson, later known as "the Sage of the Osage," studied Greek and Latin at Notre Dame. One day Johnson was thumbing through a classical journal at the university when he discovered Taylor's translation of the *Chaldean Oracles*, which inspired him to take up the study of Neoplatonism.[9] Like Alcott's discovery of Taylor, it was an event that would change his life. Only a few years later, at the age of twenty-three, Johnson found himself writing to Alcott, explaining that he was planning a book that would

> give a systematic account of the Philosophy of Plato as expounded by the Neo-Plato-icians—so called. After a diligent study of Plotinus, Proclus, Julian, Taylor, etc., etc., I consider myself qualified to explain the dogmas of Plato and his disciples.[10]

Johnson went on to ask Alcott for his "opinion as to the probable success of such a work." Alcott told his young correspondent that "students of Plato and of the Alexandrians are rare," but went on to note that "a reaction ... appears to be setting in against the materialism of the scientists, and idealism may have its day presently."[11] Alcott would remain a lifelong correspondent of Johnson's, and when Johnson decided to publish his journal *The Platonist*, the first issue was planned to coincide with the opening of Alcott's Concord Summer School of Philosophy in 1879.[12]

Johnson's work can be fully understood only in terms of the larger Platonic movement that flowered in the Midwest in the late 1800s, a movement intimately linked with the transcendentalists and the Concord School of Philosophy, which is documented in Paul Anderson's study *Platonism in the Midwest*. My task today is not to explore that particular movement, but to offer a portrait of "representative men," to borrow a phrase of Emerson's. Both Emerson and Johnson have much in common, but in other ways their approaches are worlds apart. By exploring their respective approaches and character, we discover two different visions of the role that philosophy has to play in American life. In essence, we discover two different Platonic voices.

Thomas M. Johnson: The Sage of the Osage

Of all the Midwestern Platonists, Thomas Johnson was the greatest scholar. He was a competent though somewhat stiff translator, bringing out works of Damascius, Iamblichus, Porphyry, Proclus, and Synesius, some for the first time in English.[13]

Ever since the conversion to Taylor and the Neoplatonists in his youth, Johnson seems to have lived a secluded existence. From that point on, his inner life revolved around the study of Neoplatonism, outwardly reflected in a bibliophilia that later threatened to engulf his home. Over the years he acquired a library of 8,000 volumes, a large percentage of which were rare Platonic texts imported from Europe. In 1899 he was forced to construct a separate structure behind his home, affectionately called his "book house." This four-room stone building overlooked the Osage River, complete with fireplace, couch, and shelves reaching from floor to ceiling. According to an obituary published in the *St. Clair County Democrat*, Johnson "literally lived with his books, he slept with them and ate in their company."[14] He would spend about an hour with his wife each day, and make two trips to the post office—one in the morning, and one in the afternoon—to pick up the latest titles arriving from Europe. Johnson's library was the single greatest collection of Platonic texts in America at the time, and probably still represents the greatest collection of works by Thomas Taylor ever assembled on this continent.[15]

Johnson was not an original thinker, nor did he strive to be; Johnson was an American disciple of Thomas Taylor, whom he emulated. He was a devoted Platonist, and like Taylor believed that Plato was best understood from the perspective of the Neoplatonists, whom they saw as his genuine interpreters. In this sense, Plato's work was akin to a sacred canon. Philosophy was not progressive, but was ultimately a study which consisted of finding a proper way to understand the canon. As Paul Anderson notes, for Johnson "Platonism was an authoritative body of truth, Plato its prophetic genius, the Neoplatonists the high priests, and anyone who believed the essence of the canon a member of its sacred order. . . . The function of the scholar, and also of the thinker, according to Johnson, was to take a body of recognized truth, make it available through translation and commentaries, and interpret it, for each new generation."[16] In this sense, like Taylor, Johnson was an enthusiastic proponent rather than a critical academic.

Another way in which Johnson emulated Taylor was through what Jay Bregman describes as his "flair for condescending Olympian rhetoric."[17] In the first issue of *The Platonist*, Johnson explained the mission of the journal:

> In this degenerated age, when the senses are apotheosized, materialism absurdly considered philosophy, folly and ignorance popularized, and the dictum, "get money, eat, drink and be merry, for to-morrow we die," exemplifies the actions of millions of mankind, there certainly is a necessity for a journal which shall be a candid, bold, and fearless exponent of the Platonic Philosophy—a philosophy totally subversive of sensualism, materialism, folly, and ignorance. This philosophy recognizes the essential immortality and divinity of the human soul, and posits its highest happiness as an approximation to, and union with, the Absolute One. Its mission is to release the soul from the bonds of matter, to lead it to the vision of true being—from images to realities,—and, in short, to elevate it from a sensible to an intellectual life.[18]

Elsewhere in the same issue Johnson wrote that

> The genuine lovers of Wisdom are very few. The fact is, that about nine-tenths of human beings are adverse to the acquisition of intellectual knowledge, and delight to revel in the mire of ignorance. They can perceive the necessity (?) for laboring for years like slaves to accumulate

money in order to gratify desires of the senses, but they appear utterly incapable of apprehending the essential superiority of the mind to the body, the transcendent excellence of Wisdom, and the real object of this sensuous, material life, which is to purify and perfect the soul, so that it may be enabled to return to the intelligible world whence it came, or was sent. To these human earth-worms this [material] existence is a finality . . .[19]

Johnson's *Platonist* was one of the first philosophical journals published in America, and enjoyed an international circulation. Despite the journal's failure on the financial level,[20] it represents an important though little-known chapter in the history of Platonism and American philosophy. Both the *Platonist* and *Bibliotheca Platonica* made important contributions to Platonic scholarship; and in addition to his twenty translations, Johnson was cofounder of the Western Philosophical Association, which later developed into the American Philosophical Association.

Ralph Waldo Emerson's Spiritual Empiricism

Like Johnson, Ralph Waldo Emerson was a Neoplatonic thinker who treasured the works of Thomas Taylor. But the difference is Emerson's engagement with the world and his emphasis on spiritual empiricism. Already in 1833, after resigning his post at the Second Church in Boston, Emerson noted in his journal that "all necessary truth is its own evidence: no doctrine of God need appeal to a book; that Christianity is wrongly received by all such as take it for a system of doctrines . . . it is a rule of life not a rule of faith."[21] Similarly, while Emerson would exalt the Neoplatonists in both his private journals and public writings, the necessity and integrity of direct experience remained primary for him.

Emerson's *Nature*, his first published work, is a Stoic and Neoplatonic manifesto. The first published edition opens with an epigraph from Plotinus: "Nature is but an image or imitation of wisdom, the last thing of the soul; nature being a thing which doth only do, but not know."[22] As Emerson writes, "Every natural fact is a symbol of some spiritual fact."[23] "Man is conscious of a universal soul within his individual life" and "this universal soul he calls Reason: it is not mine, or thine, or his, but we are its; we are its property and men."[24] Emerson explains, "The visible creation is the terminus of the circumference of the invisible world," yet "the universe becomes transparent" when "the light of higher laws than its own shines through it."[25] As Plotinus had taught, Nature is the image of Soul, Soul is the image of Intellect, and Intellect is an image of the ineffable One. But for Emerson, *Nature* is not a call to embrace a particular philosophical tradition; it is a call to embrace the world of direct experience.

As he would later write in *The Over-Soul*, one class of men speaks "*from within*, or from experience, as parties and possessors of the fact, and the other class, *from without*, as spectators merely . . ."[26] Emerson notes that "among the multitude of scholars and authors, we feel no hallowing presence; we are sensible of a knack and skill rather than inspiration."[27] Yet "the faith that stands on authority is not faith. The reliance on authority measures the decline of religion, the withdrawal of the soul."[28]

Emerson does not reject the value of tradition *per se*, but he does reject tradition should it become a conceptualization, a substitute for genuine experience, or a worship of dead forms. Thus his famous complaint and proposal at the beginning of *Nature*:

> Our age is retrospective. It builds the sepulchres of the fathers. It writes biographies, histories, criticism. The foregoing generations beheld God and nature face to face; we, through their eyes. Why should not we also enjoy an original relation to the universe? . . . The sun shines to-day also . . .[29]

Like so much of Emerson's work, *Nature* is a call for direct experience on the part of the individual. And while Emerson's idealism is rooted more in Neoplatonism than any other tradition,[30] the essay is not a call to a specific philosophical tradition. The Greeks saw the universe as a *kosmos*, a theophany, a manifestation of divine beauty and reason. Yet, if our own eyes are purified, we too can have the original experience, and express it in our own way, in a way appropriate for our own time. *Nature*, in the words of Robert Richardson, "is intended to be self-validating. We are not asked to take it on faith, or on authority, or in a historical context. It is not argued or defended, just presented."[31]

The Scholar vs. the Academic

Thomas Moore Johnson surrounded himself with 8,000 books, and Emerson, for his part, seems to have read everything. He was constantly reading, taking notes, and indexing his notebooks. By the time of his death, Emerson's notebooks had reached 230 volumes.[32] But in Emerson's philosophy of reading, the study of books was the means to an end, and not an end in itself.

Despite his insatiable reading, there were certain types of books he would not read:

> He would not read theological or academic controversy . . . He disliked books intended to comment on other books. In a blunt moment he called them "books by the dead for the dead." He wanted original firsthand accounts—travel books, memoirs, testaments, statements of faith or discovery, poems. He would read your poem or your novel but not your opinion on other people's poems or novels.[33]

Emerson's philosophy of reading comes out most clearly in his Harvard address, *The American Scholar*. By *scholar* Emerson means a *writer*, and perhaps a public speaker—a public intellectual rather than a professional academic. Emerson explains that humanity's natural state is one of wholeness, but "in the divided or social state" the various functions of humanity are "parceled out to individuals":

> In this distribution of functions, the scholar is the delegated intellect. In the right state, he is, *Man Thinking*. In the degenerate state, when the victim of society, he tends to become a mere thinker, or, still worse, the parrot of other men's thinking.[34]

Emerson identifies three primary influences on the mind. These are the world of nature, the world of the past (best reflected in books), and the world of action. Emerson refers disparagingly to "the book learned-class, who value books, as such . . . Hence, the restorers of readings, the emendators, the bibliomaniacs of all degrees."[35] He admits that "books are the best of things, well used," but if "abused, among the worst."[36] The one thing of value in the world is the active soul, and the ultimate end of books is "for nothing but to inspire."[37] Once again in *The American Scholar*, Emerson calls for an original relationship to the universe that goes beyond the worship of dead forms:

> The book, the college, the school of art, the institution of any kind, stop with some past utterance of genius. This is good, say they—let us hold by this. They pin me down. They look backward and not forward. But genius looks forward: the eyes of man are set in his forehead, not in his hindhead: man hopes: genius creates.[38]

While this statement must have irritated some of those present, Emerson tempered his remarks by saying that he would do nothing "to underrate the Book."[39] Nonetheless, he insisted that "books are for the scholar's idle times" and that "Man Thinking must not be subdued by his instruments."[40] Moreover, Emerson proposed that there is an art of "creative reading":

> The discerning will read, in his Plato or Shakspeare, only that least part— only the authentic utterances of the oracle—all the rest he rejects, were it never so many times Plato's and Shakspeare's.[41]

Or, as he put it elsewhere, "Shakespeare will never be made by the study of Shakespeare."[42] The problem is that "man is timid and apologetic; he is no longer upright; he dares not say 'I think,' 'I am,' but quotes some saint or sage."[43] Yet contrary to this intellectual timidity, Emerson holds that

> There is one mind common to all individual men. . . . What Plato has thought, he may think; what a saint has felt, he may feel; what at any time has befallen any man, he can understand. . . . Of the universal mind each individual man is one more incarnation.[44]

For Emerson, in the work of the true scholar, the world of nature, the world of the past, and the world of action are all integrated in the living present. In this way, Emerson's vision and epistemology is participatory: "Only so much do I know, as I have lived. Instantly we know whose words are loaded with life, and whose not."[45] Yet by going into his own mind, the scholar and the poet sees into *all* minds. "The scholar is that man who must take up into himself all the ability of the time, all the contributions of the past, all the hopes of the future."[46] In this way, the scholar's role in society is active and formative. He performs a public function by reminding individuals of their integrity, human promise, and essential relatedness to the animating fire of the Divine Mind. "The office of the scholar is to cheer, to raise, and to guide men by showing them facts amidst appearances."[47]

Two Platonic Voices

Like Thomas Johnson, Ralph Waldo Emerson found in Neoplatonic idealism a spiritual counterbalance to the materialism of his time. In raising the question "What is the end of human life?," Emerson responded that

> It is not, believe me, the chief end of man that he should make a fortune and beget children whose end is likewise to make a fortune, but it is, in few words, that he should explore himself.[48]

Yet Emerson's critique of materialism—and the mere utilitarianism he saw dominating American culture—was more subtle, measured, and less dualistic than Johnson's wholesale condemnation of the "human earth-worms" who comprise the bulk of society. Emerson duly noted the predominance of "the material interest" in America, and suggested that we hear "too much of the results of machinery, commerce, and the useful arts."[49] Greed, hesitation, and following are "our diseases," and he maintained that "the rapid wealth which hundreds in the community acquire in trade, or by the incessant expansions of our population and arts, enchants the eyes of all the rest." Nonetheless, Emerson chose not "to look with sour aspect at the industrious manufacturing village, or the mart of commerce." Thus he wrote,

> I love the music of the water-wheel; I value the railway; I feel the pride which the sight of a ship inspires; I look on trade and every mechanical craft as education also. But let me discriminate what is precious herein. There is in each of these works an act of invention, an intellectual step, or short series of steps taken; that act or step is the spiritual act; all the rest is mere repetition of the same a thousand times. And I will not be deceived into admiring the routine of handicrafts and mechanics, how splendid soever the result, any more than I admire the routine of the scholars or clerical class. That splendid results ensue from the labors of stupid men, is the fruit of higher laws than their will, and the routine is not to be praised for it.[50]

Tragedy, he maintained, occurs when "the laborer is sacrificed to the result" of commerce and mechanical routine.

Ralph Waldo Emerson and Thomas Johnson have much in common. Both were Platonists and admirers of Thomas Taylor. Like Taylor, both were critical of the materialism of their time, and both found in Neoplatonic idealism a viable alternative to the materialistic and mechanistic worldview. Finally, both Emerson and Johnson were clearly interested in social reform. But despite these essential similarities, no two Platonic voices could be further apart.

Ralph Waldo Emerson was a public intellectual who, with rhapsodic lyricism, championed the idea that philosophical reflection can play a vital role in human society. His *Nature*, while deeply rooted in Platonic ideas, presents a philosophical vision that is contemporary and participatory, completely lacking any antiquarian focus; thus, while criticizing the fact that "our age is retrospective," Emerson suggests that it is not only possible but also imperative "to enjoy an original relation to the universe," to discover a living "poetry and philosophy of insight and not of tradition."

By contrast to Emerson, Thomas Johnson was essentially a dogmatic and backward-looking thinker—a revivalist who believed that the Neoplatonic philosophy could spark a spiritual reformation in reaction to "the materialism of the age"—at least among the few capable of appreciating it. For Johnson, Platonism was an authoritative body of truth that could counteract the decadence of the modern world, and he saw his task as making Platonism's truth available to his own generation through translations, reprints, and commentaries.

In this sense we can see that Emerson, rather than Johnson, was closer to the spirit of Plato himself—the Plato who envisioned philosophy as a living dialogue, who declined to set forth elaborate doctrines in writing, and who formed the Academy not as a seminary to disseminate a dogma or ideology, but as a forum for ongoing discussion and critical thinking. In this way, too, we can see how the Later Neoplatonists like Proclus departed from the spirit of Plato and were in many ways an anticipation of medieval Scholasticism. This is reflected not only in their production of laboriously-detailed commentaries, but more specifically in their overriding attention to Aristotelian system-building—namely in their transformation of Platonism into a highly sophisticated, metaphysical and logico-deductive scaffolding for late pagan theology.[51]

Ultimately, the orientations of Emerson and Johnson are of more than academic interest, for we can see the tendencies they embody more widely reflected in human nature—not only throughout history, but in our own time. In this way, their orientations invite us to consider the role that philosophy has to play in public life today.

Emerson has sometimes been criticized as not being a systematic or analytical philosopher, but that is to miss the point.[52] There are different styles of philosophizing, yet Emerson remains one of the few philosophers who was truly active in American life. While Emerson's essays do contain critical arguments, his primary aim was to awaken self-reflection, critical thinking, and an authentic, living vision of the world's radiance in the minds of his audience. In this sense, Emerson's goal was recollection or *anamnêsis*—a reawakening of vision to that which is essential and integral in human life. Along these lines Plotinus had written that "there is another way of seeing which everyone has but few people use."[53] But in the end, perhaps Emerson put it the best:

> The problem of restoring to the world original and eternal beauty, is solved by the redemption of the soul. The ruin or the blank, that we see when we look at nature, is in our own eye. The axis of vision is not coincident with the axis of things, and so they appear not transparent but opake. The reason why the world lacks unity, and lies broken and in heaps, is because man is disunited with himself.[54]

Notes

1. Of the fifty-five dialogues, Syndenham had translated nine; Taylor translated the remaining.

2. For a complete bibliography of his published works, see Kathleen Raine and George Mills Harper, editors, *Thomas Taylor the Platonist: Selected Writings* (Princeton: Princeton University Press, 1969), 523–33. This volume also contains two valuable introductions by Raine and Harper respectively, "Thomas Taylor in England" and "Thomas Taylor in America," which I have drawn upon in this account.

3. Quoted by Raine, *Thomas Taylor the Platonist*, 11.

4. Thomas Taylor, trans., *The Philosophical and Mathematical Commentaries of Proclus on the First Book of Euclid's Elements* (London, 1792), II, 317.

5. Thomas Taylor, *Miscellanies in Prose and Verse* (London, 1787), viii.

6. Odell Shepard, *Pedlar's Progress: The Life of Bronson Alcott* (Boston, 1937), 160.

7. When Bronson returned to America with books collected for the library of the Fruitlands utopian community, sixteen of the 214 titles were by Thomas Taylor.

8. *The Journals of Ralph Waldo Emerson*, edited by E. W. Emerson and W. E. Forbes (Boston and New York, 1909–1914), V, 295.

9. Another influence that aroused Johnson's interest at this age was the list of Neoplatonic authors that Emerson cites at the end of his essay on *Intellect*.

10. Letter dated March 8, 1874, in the Free Public Library, Concord, Massachusetts. Quoted in *Thomas Taylor the Platonist*, 74.

11. Unpublished letter in the possession of Franklin P. Johnson, quoted in *Thomas Taylor the Platonist*, 75.

12. In fact, the first issue of *The Platonist* did not appear until February 1881.

13. For a bibliography of Johnson's translations and his own writings, see Paul Anderson, *Platonism in the Midwest* (New York: Temple University Publications/Columbia University Press, 1963), 205–207. While some of the works are quite short, Johnson translated approximately twenty different texts.

14. Quoted in an unpublished paper by Robert A. Shaddy, "Thomas Moore Johnson, the 'Sage of the Osage': Neoplatonic Thought from Osceola,

Missouri." The complete quotation from the 1919 newspaper reads: "The Sage of the Osage literally lived with his books, he slept with them and ate in their company. He would spend, so it is stated, about an hour each day with his wife, descending to pots and pans, and furniture, newspapers and the like, and perhaps a change of linen. Two little trips he would make each day to the express office—one in the morning, one in the afternoon—to get books for which he had no shelves in the library. Perhaps he would deposit the books under the table or bed and forget where he had put them."

15. His son, Francis P. Johnson, a professor of art at the University of Chicago, donated the philosophical part of the collection to the University of Missouri in Columbia, September 25, 1947. This collection contains 1,600 volumes. Johnson's papers and correspondence are held by the family. His collection of Taylor's works was nearly complete—about eighty volumes.

16. Anderson, *Platonism in the Midwest*, 178–79.

17. Jay Bregman, "Thomas M. Johnson the Platonist," *Dionysius* 15 (December 1991), 93–112; p. 93.

18. *The Platonist* 1.1 (1881), 1.

19. Johnson, "The Nature and Destiny of the Human Soul," *The Platonist* 1.1 (1881), 3.

20. The final issue was published in June, 1888, with the sixth issue of volume four. Johnson later started another journal, *Bibliotheca Platonica*, with four issues being published between 1888–1889.

21. Quoted in Robert Richardson, Jr., *Emerson: The Mind on Fire* (Berkeley: University of California Press, 1995), 151.

22. The last part of this line may have been taken from Ralph Cudworth.

23. *Nature*, 19. I am quoting from *The Works of Ralph Waldo Emerson*, 4 vols. (New York: Charles C. Bigelow, n.d.).

24. *Nature*, 19.

25. *Nature*, 24. Or as he would write in a later essay, *The Method of Nature*, "In the divine order, intellect is primary; nature, secondary; it is the memory of the mind. That which once existed in intellect as pure law, now taken body as nature" (134).

26. *The Over-Soul*, 185.

27. *The Over-Soul*, 185.

28. *The Over-Soul*, 190.

29. *Nature*, 8.

30. On Emerson's Neoplatonism, see Russell B. Goodman, "Emerson's Mysical Empiricism," in John J. Cleary, editor, *The Perennial Tradition of Neoplatonism* (Leuven: Leuven University Press, 1997), 519–35. See also Gay W. Allen, *Waldo Emerson* (New York: Viking, 1981), chapters 13 and 17.

31. Richardson, *Emerson: The Mind on Fire*, 234.

32. Richardson, *Emerson: The Mind on Fire*, 43.

33. Richardson, *Emerson: The Mind on Fire*, 220.

34. *The American Scholar*, 61.

35. *The American Scholar*, 65.

36. *The American Scholar*, 65.

37. *The American Scholar*, 65.

38. *The American Scholar*, 65

39. *The American Scholar*, 67.

40. *The American Scholar*, 66.

41. *The American Scholar*, 67. Punctuation modernized.

42. *Self-Reliance*, 56

43. *Self-Reliance*, 45.

44. *History*, 3–4.

45. *The American Scholar*, 68.

46. *The American Scholar*, 81.

47. *The American Scholar*, 72.

48. *The American Scholar*, quoted in Richardson, *Emerson: The Mind on Fire*, 261.

49. *The Method of Nature*, 130.

50. *The Method of Nature*, 131.

51. I am thinking especially of such works as Proclus' *Platonic Theology* and *The Elements of Theology*. Despite the fact that Proclus' system rests upon an apophatic foundation (the One, after all, is beyond both Being and Intellect), these works owe as much to an Aristotelian desire for systemic, logico-deductive "closure" as they do to any Platonic influence.

52. Like Pierre Bayle, Emerson believed that philosophy is a corrosive, "proper at first to confront error, but if she be not stopped there, she attacks truth itself" (Richardson, *Emerson: The Mind on Fire*, 68).

53. Plotinus, *Enneads* 1.6.8.

54. *Nature*, 53.

A. Bronson Alcott

Alcott's Transcendental Neoplatonism and the Concord Summer School

JAY BREGMAN

IN HIS transcendentalist manifesto *Nature*, Emerson takes into account the *Enneads* of Plotinus. He is aware of the "beyond-being" of the intelligible Sun, "the One" or "the Good," the interpenetrating nature of things, unified by sympathy and correspondence, conveniently expressed by Proclus in the *Elements of Theology*, proposition 103: All things in all things, but appropriate to their ontological level.[1]

The One's image, Nous or Intellect (one/many), contains in "undivided-division" the Platonic Forms, whereas Intellect's product, the Over-Soul—Plotinus's Soul (one *and* many)—has all the forms as One Being. But as it moves away from Nous (by *tolma* or "self-assertion"), it flows into Nature and animates the world as a multiplicity; it also pours out into the individual human soul which thereby knows by instinct or intuition the noetic world of the spirit. Like Porphyry who "telescopes" the hypostases, and Plotinus who sometimes "fudges" them,[2] Emerson also calls the Over-Soul "that Unity . . . that One." And, as in Plotinus, each of us is an intelligible realm having within the individual psyche a reflection of the One, Nous, and Soul, "psychically."

The transcendentalists' unorthodox emphasis on "the god within man" led to accusations of spiritual humanist idolatry. Self-Reliance is reliance on the Over-Soul, contiguous with the Self—thus it is mystical and Plotinian. But, as Copleston says, "the Over-Soul incarnates itself in a particular way in each individual";[3] thus the individualistic American turn: be yourself, don't conform, never imitate—"an original relation to the universe."

Emerson's friend, Amos Bronson Alcott, had discovered and read the Romantic "pagan" Neoplatonist Thomas Taylor's translations of

Plato by the 1830s; soon after that, his Proclus and Plotinus. Following a visit to England in the 1840s, he returned to America with several of Taylor's translations. Alcott was an enthusiastic convert to Neoplatonic Idealism and religious syncretism. He was absolutely convinced that this world is only an image of the real spiritual world. His words were often oracular and vague; his conviction was fundamental. For Emerson in his moments of doubt, Alcott could, as a native of it, make the "Platonic cloud-land as solid as Massachusetts."[4]

Alcott aimed at the creation of a universal religion combining the best of Oriental, Greek, and Christian thought, and the idea of the "lapse" of the soul through a Plotinian descent from the *noetic* realm. His inspiring presence, lectures, and writings attracted a wide audience, as well as some criticism, often from more rigorous Idealists.

Emerson was himself sharply critical at times: "I am afraid A. can as little as any man separate his driveling from his divining . . . There are three degrees in Philosophy. Plato came with geometry; that was one degree. Plotinus came with mythology, Zoroastrian or Magian illumination & C., an exalted or stilted Plato: that was the second degree. But now comes my friend with palmistry, phrenology, mesmerism, and davisan revelation; this is third degree; and bearing the same relation to Plotinism which that bore to Platonism." Nevertheless, "my friend Alcott has magnificent views. His natural attitude explains Plato."

Though he followed Emerson's *Nature* in its main outlines, Alcott was the most spiritually radical transcendentalist: revelation is perennial and progressive; God is within and without. Material things are symbols of spiritual things; matter is a revelation of mind. Revelation can come to us directly from the divine, through nature. Yet the material world is the result of a cosmic "lapse" (*tolma*) and therefore imperfect. The human soul is in need of regeneration and salvation. Originating in the *noetic* realm, an incarnate divinity, it could find salvation within itself.

Alcott's *Philosophemes*, which he published in the *Journal of Speculative Philosophy* as late as the 1860s and 1870s, elaborate his Neoplatonic concerns. The original human being is the eldest of creatures (a type of *Logos*), progenitor of all below him. All debased forms in Nature are consequent on man's degeneracy prior to their genesis (compare the "fallen" Cosmic Anthropos of the *Hermetica*).[5] The original human essence is impaired,[6] and the division of the sexes occurs. The primal man, Prometheus, is the image of god in the soul; of the cosmos in the body ("Prometheus imago dei in animo; mundi in corpore"). Man is a theometer, *connexus*, the spirit's acme, mediator of mind and matter.[7] He aids in creation[8] and is able to understand and work with the spermatic embryos through which the divine mind implants its archetypes by charging matter with form and transmitting life into things. The way to redemption is through realization of the One personal Sprit, understood first and best by the Greek philosophers, Parmenides, Pythagoras, Plato, and Plotinus.[9] The divine Instinct, Love, which supersedes knowledge, connects us with the world of the spirit.

The Greek gods are interpreted as powers of Mind, of which the world is a symbol. A good example is Hermes, the ideal Reason that generates the visible world—in short, the Logos of the Over-Soul. Creation itself is a descent of the spirit. The human mind, inherently connected with the *Logos*, can employ a "new calculus"—a dialogic for resolving things into thoughts, matter into mind, man into God, many into One.[10] Alcott alludes to Plato's Cave: at present, the thinker views men as Troglodytes, like Plato's groundlings unconscious of the sun shining overhead; they in turn pronounce him the "dreamer." But ultimately "the few" Platonic philosophers will lead "the many" in the work of redemption.

Alcott's revived later-Hellenistic syncretism is apparent in a section on the descent of the soul, where he quotes from a *Hymn* of Synesius, Hierocles' *Comments on Pythagoras*, and the *Hermetica*. Following the latter, he explains that Nature is "reason immersed . . . and plunged into matter . . . it doth not know but do" (the *Hermetica* and cf. *Enneads* 3.8.3). The ancients obscurely signified this in the mysteries by representing Hermes as the generative *Logos*. Nature is the *orbus pictus* of Spirit and mind, as Plotinus says, "the exemplary cause of the world." The Idealist, contrasted by Proclus to the materialist who believes in matter's primacy, understands this. As the *Chaldaean*

Oracles say (known to Alcott as the *Oracles of Zoroaster*): "The Paternal Mind hath sowed in symbols in all souls." These, then, may aid the lapsed man as he "strives throughout matter to recover his lost self." Symbols in the soul are a key to salvation in Iamblichean theurgy— they were implanted by the gods and through them the theurgist seeks reunification with the gods. So too with Alcott's "Divination": spiritual hunches, close to Intuition/Instinct, allow us to discern the most important things in connection with the soul and Noetic reality. (An "American original take" on theurgy.)

One can see how influential the theurgic Neoplatonists were to a part of Alcott's thought process; he sometimes quotes them without acknowledgment or quotation marks. The autarkic soul seeks nothing external: "It were better to live lying on the grass, confiding in divinity and yourself, than to lie on a golden bed with perturbation," from Iamblichus's *On the Pythagoric Life*, was a text basic to transcendentalism. This passage was also a favorite of Henry David Thoreau.[11]

Alcott's conception of prayer is essentially theurgic—like corresponds to like as Image to Archetype, and nature is unified through "cosmic sympathy of the whole," originally a Stoic conception, similar to Thoreau's favorite "Solar *seira*" (i.e., chain or series) down from: Invisible Sun, "the Good"; Intellectual Sun (i.e., Helios, Immediate Creator of the visible Cosmos); Visible Sun; Solar Daimons; Heroes; Humans; the Lion; the Cock; the Heliotrope; the Sunstone—all levels of being. Such is prayer's efficacy that it unites all inferior with superior powers, and all pray but the First—this last phrase is a famous line from Proclus.[12]

"Divination" is based on unerring Instinct—"the sole *undepraved* power . . . in man." Thus the "power" needed for salvation is already "in the soul"—implanted "theurgically," "as if" by "the gods." This, of course, is in direct opposition to old-time New England Orthodox Calvinism.

K. W. Cameron's straightforward introduction to the transcendentalists' view of Nature clarifies the religious dimension of Alcott's thought: "Nature is a kind of mediator between the Over-Soul and Mankind. It takes the place of TORAH in Jewish thought and CHRIST in Christian theology."[13]

Through spiritual Instinct, then, comes the realization that the One of Nature is also the One in the Self. The "lapse" is overcome, as the descent is followed by reascent. In developing his arguments, Alcott quotes Plato, the *Hermetica*, Ficino, Zoroaster (the *Chaldaean Oracles*), Plotinus, Empedocles, Henry More, Cudworth, Thomas Taylor, and Bishop Berkeley, on such diverse topics as man, the soul, cosmology and the "great chain of being," metaphysics, memory, and sense perception.

In syncretistic mode, Alcott attempts a "Lichtheologie": Zoroastrian, Johannine, Hebrew, and Philosophical Greek: "The magi said of God, that 'he had light for his body and truth for his soul.' 'God,' said St. John, 'is light and in him is no darkness at all.' And David, 'Thou art clothed with light as with a garment.' And according to Plutarch, Empedocles thought 'ether, or heat, to be Jupiter.'"

"Transcendentally," the Johannine light is Creative Reason, or the vitalizing *Logos* in which the worlds are conceived and brought forth. "Nature is but the cloud that hides the face of the Godhead." Here Alcott anticipates R. Friedman's contemporary idea of the Cosmos conceived of as "the hidden face of God."[14]

The St. Louis Hegelians considered Alcott a Neoplatonist born out of his time,[15] an American original, yet an archaic mentality, who preached from the timeless perspective of one who saw Becoming as the "working image" of Being and who believed in metempsychosis— to whom the pre-existence of the soul was as certain as the present existence.

The Concord Summer School of Philosophy

As early as 1842, Alcott had proposed the idea of a Concord Summer School: a place where "spiritual philosophy" would flourish, as a corrective to the rise of Lockean empiricism and other "materialistic" ideas. By the 1880s, when Alcott's idea was realized, the nineteenth-century crisis of secularization had already entered its post-Darwin phase. Agnosticism and Atheism were on the rise, not merely in a few narrow "enlightened" circles, but more generally among the educated public.

Originally, transcendentalism had been as much a reaction to denatured and rationalized religion as it was to empiricism and materialism. Its enthusiastic spirit and communal experimentation was the Harvard dissident's answer to contemporary evangelical revivalism. Then, materialism and impoverishment of spirit were the perceived problems. But in the second half of the century, as industrialism expanded and the bourgeois revolution was realized, materialism in science and philosophy became the central issue. In the eighteenth century, Locke, who accepted some form of the design argument, was not a threat to tolerant religion or deism per se, and Hume's more devastating arguments were largely ignored. Romantic rebels like Blake, opposed, at bottom, the Enlightenment's "Geometer God," more than the atheism of the still relatively obscure neo-Epicureans and anti-clerical materialist Lucretians. Even Laplace's quip to Napoleon, "God, sire, is not a necessary hypothesis," had the import of a clever *bon mot* rather than a serious challenge to religion.

Early nineteenth-century Idealist philosophy was seen as a potent antidote to the more excessive Enlightenment trends. But Darwin was another matter. Evolution was now, by no means, obviously teleological, as had been thought. It seemed the rise of life was a random affair. Physical scientists began to suspect, along with Epicurus, that the cosmos had come into being *to automaton*, by accident. The transcendentalists and Hegelians had a sophisticated (i.e., "nonliteral") understanding of Genesis. For them, this was not the problem, but rather the larger question of the "spiritual origin" and destiny of humanity.

The argument from comparative religion, as we shall see, was employed against the Great Reductionisms of Darwinists and others. The degree and kinds of secularization that had enabled the transcendentalists to affirm higher truth in non-Christian religious traditions, was based on forms of tolerance for the most part associated with the Renaissance as well as the Enlightenment: the genial, reformed spirit of tolerance in Erasmus; Montaigne's classical skepticism and caution in respect of dogmatism; the religious universalism of Cusanus and the Florentine Neoplatonists, whose influence on the Cambridge Platonists was an important Platonic source of transcendentalism.

But the secularism of the radical materialists was another matter. It was anti-religious and anti-Idealist. Even the most tolerant form of religion was still a quaint anachronism. Religion could and should be explained away to make room for a scientific and progressive world-view. The Enlightenment Fundamentalists had arrived. Yet in philosophy, Idealism, both Platonic and Hegelian, still seemed to many to be viable and as yet unrefuted. The Concord School would attempt to uphold the Idealist viewpoint in the face of the new challenges.

Summer Session

The school opened in 1879 and met until 1888, the year of Alcott's death. There was no specific core set of beliefs, and there were certainly wide areas of philosophical disagreement. But "the lecturers generally agree in an utter repudiation of materialism and in maintaining the existence of a personal, self-conscious, spiritual cause above the material universe."[16] Professors, ministers, and men and women of letters presented lectures on divers topics, as well as occasional poems.

Alcott himself opened the first session of 1882, the year of Emerson's death, where he presented his Neopythagorean views of the lapse of the soul and its atonement, in the background of an emanated chain of Being. At other sessions, in addition to his own ideas, he discussed historical forms of mysticism, including that of Plotinus. Mrs. Ednah D. Cheney spoke on the history of art; Hiram K. Jones, at this and other sessions, on the Platonic themes of "remembrance," immortality, the pre-existence of the soul, education, mythology, and the Forms. He viewed Plato's thought as perennial and applicable to his own time. The St. Louis Hegelian, W. T. Harris, lectured on the history of philosophy and attempted to subsume all thought, including Neoplatonic, under an Hegelian umbrella. Other lectures were delivered on literature, German philosophy, history, and modern society. Emerson himself contributed poems to the first three sessions. Among the lecturers were F. H. Hedge, the post-Kantian transcendentalist minister; Harvard professor Benjamin Peirce, the father of the seminal American "Pragmaticist" C. S. Peirce; other St. Louis Hegelians;

later transcendentalists such as Cyrus Bartol; as well as the Presidents of Harvard and Yale colleges.[17]

Harper's Weekly covered the conference favorably. The August 19th, 1882 edition characterized the objective of the school: "to prevent our drifting blindly—to prevent, that is, not by obstructive conservatism, but by progressive comprehension." To "seek through philosophy the one central principle on which the world, the universe, rests."[18] In this era, Germany was for Americans the center of academic life. So the *Harper's* editors meant to make an impression when they said "at a time when Germany itself is overpowered by the influence of Mill, Spencer and Darwin, and the genius of materialism is getting a strong hold everywhere, it is interesting to find that the Concord School reasserts with breadth and penetration the supremacy of mind . . ." Science *is* affirmed, but it is ultimately "tributary to the highest ends of existence."[19]

Nevertheless, the next decades would see major challenges to Absolute Idealism, at which point the Neoplatonism and the Hegelianism of the later transcendentalist thinkers—at least in its current form—would become anachronistic and archaic. Those thinkers who tried to maintain such positions into the twentieth century— for example, Thomas M. Johnson, the American Thomas Taylor— became for the most part rather more dogmatic and somewhat reactionary.

The Emerson commemoration was held on the sixth day of the school's twenty-four day session; it was reminiscent of a National Endowment for the Humanities Summer Institute with divers lectures. Among the eulogists, Cyrus Bartol took up the cause of theism, now being seriously challenged. Indeed, the arguments *among* philosophical and religious Idealists were now secondary; a united front against materialist atheism was the order of the day. Such allowances had been made before, for example, the seventeenth-century Cambridge Platonist, Ralph Cudworth, was happy to enlist the support of non-Orthodox and even non-Christian forms of "soft monotheism" in opposition to the "mechanick atheism." But the challenge of modern science was more persistent, more cogent, and certainly far more *socially* powerful, and far less dangerous to adhere to than in previous centuries. Thus, said Bartol, Emerson understood the priority of "the unapparent, invisible, eternal power and Godhead (as much as did the Apostle Paul); he was an artist, always seeing the One who makes the unity and the universe."[20]

The nontrivial issue of 1882 was "whether we come of the unconscious, unalive and unaware, or of the Living One."[21] The challenge of the contemporary agnostic, "that most refined specimen materialism gives birth to,—the 'know nothing' in the intellectual world,—considers impertinent all curiosity beyond phenomena and their laws."[22] Today, if God is to appear again, it won't be through some common confession, or church. Thus Emerson, in his last days, went to regular meetings—a tacit admission that his earlier radicalism had led to "excesses." In the contemporary religious crisis, it was no longer possible to effectively be a religious universal syncretist with the nation at large for a pulpit. Or so thought Bartol.

Alcott's poem "Ion" equates Emerson with the Greek rhapsode through a profusion of classical imagery. A Neoplatonic seer who

> For endless Being's myriad-minded race
> Had in his thought their registry and place,—[23]

And according to Joel Benton, Emerson the poet, who is "related to Hafiz and Firdusi, and the Oriental muse, reports the correspondence between the soul and material things."[24]

The Hegelian W. T. Harris thought Emerson's prose was at times elevated above dialectical unity. He spoke from the higher unity of absolute identity where Absolute Reason and the Unity of the "Over-Soul" coincided:

> There is nowhere in all literature such sustained flight toward the sun— "a flight," as Plotinus calls it, "of the alone to the Alone"—as that in "The Over-Soul."[25]

Perhaps the most interesting tribute, from a Neoplatonic perspective, is the "theurgist" Alexander Wilder's portrait, that of a mystagogue, who embodied the Old Wisdom, or Philosophy: Emerson never wholly left the pre-existent noetic realm. Like Plotinus, only a little of him was fixed to the body, or even his famous countenance; his "transcendent self" was unlapsed and "back beyond genesis and the changeable."[26] Like his own "Plato," he embodied all the former wisdom of the world East and West; Emerson gave us Platonic lessons in our own language. His essays, like Plato's *Dialogues*, are like a "dithyramb . . . a sacred chant with mystic import, such as worshippers employed at the Mysteries."[27] "We need not stumble over the . . . un-Anglican (sic) books of Thomas Taylor, whose language often obscures what he would say, now that we have the eloquent utterances of Emerson . . . *This Plato of America* was the most original of our authors."[28]

Alcott, the Dean of the school, opened and closed the proceedings, and spoke himself on various topics, in addition to his poetic dedication to Emerson. In his Salutatory Address on July 17, 1882, delivered in his usual oracular style, he likened Philosophy to the divine source of the True, the Beautiful, and the Good. He also quotes the Neoplatonist/Pythagorean Hierocles on philosophy as the purification from matter and the perfection of human nature in its purified likening to God. Two days later, July 19th, he discoursed on "Personality," which unifies, as opposed to "individuality" which separates. Personality is triune: intellect thinks truth; soul, in living, seeks the good; and will, willing, seeks the right. Our three-stranded personality "dropped down from the Godhead into matter." Thus it is immanent Godhead. "Perhaps the *daimon* of Socrates was the Spirit in the conscience, forbidding him to do certain things."[29] Though many have been tempted to ridicule this "New England Sage," it must be acknowledged that in some ways Alcott really *did* sound like a late antique Philosophical Oracle!

Memory is at least, in part, the Platonic *anamnesis* of a pre-incarnate state. As Alcott explained in his talk on the "Ascending Scale of Powers" given July 29: "As we ascend from sense experience, through fantasy, which gives sense impressions meaning, to discursive reason, which generalizes and deduces truths" we reach imagination which deals with *ideas*, the visible *and* invisible forms of things. Finally, through Spiritual Conscience, we ascend Platonically to the "Beautiful, the True and the Good."[30]

As a Persian poet shows, "individuality" separates, personality unifies. Thus the lover at the Beloved's door as "I" is *not* admitted, but as "thyself" *is* admitted.[31] In Egyptian mythology Osiris represents personality, the aim to assimilate, to will the divine Will; his evil brother Typhos represents the "path of separation from the divine Will."[32] Thus "fallen souls" are free to choose one of these paths. Unfallen soul has only one will; we can draw ourselves upward again— to the unfallen state—by seizing hold of the Platonic trinity.[33] The soul is pre-existent and eternal and able to choose the good;[34] souls never came into time, but universal soul manifests itself in objects which are in time. In that sense that which *sub*-sists in God, *ex*-ists, or "comes out" from divinity in time. This is strikingly like Plotinus' notion of "we," i.e., the "unconscious" part of the soul that never leaves the noetic realm.

In his closing remarks of August 12, Alcott alludes to Emerson, who "at Concord had been one of saintly life"—who saw the universal truth of Plato and Aristotle, and spoke in the name of Jesus, "if I know what Jesus taught."[35]

Alcott's contribution at Concord was, as expected, that of the Pythagorean-Christian syncretist, whose archaic formulations seem naive, Romantic, and rather too literally Neoplatonic in an age of increasing philosophical and scientific sophistication. Nevertheless, though he must have seemed a bit preposterous, Alcott was the originator of the idea of the Concord Summer School and remained an important presence there.

Among the lecturers, perhaps the most in tune with non-Christian forms of Neoplatonism and syncretism was Alexander Wilder, M.D. He was a contributor to Thomas M. Johnson's journals, *The Platonist* and *Bibliotheca Platonica*, as well as translator of Iamblichus' *On the Mysteries*. Wilder rehearses the late antique Porphyrian anti-Christian Neoplatonic line that Ammonius Sakkas, the teacher of Plotinus, *abandoned* the Christianity of his youth, and sought the remains of the *true wisdom religion of the ancients*, among the current multiplicity of religions and doctrines. Following Pythagoras and the Eleusinian Hierophant Eumolpus, he initiated his disciples by a secret rite and taught esoteric doctrines, not to be divulged.[36] Secrecy was soon broken; implied by Porphyry and Iamblichus to be connected with contemporary Hellenic, Mithraic, Persian, and Egyptian mysteries. The ancient wisdom was also the source of philosophy. Further, the mysteries influenced Gnosticism.

"As the widowed Isis searched everywhere for the mutilated fragments of her husband's body, so did Ammonius Sakkas, in his quest for truth, explore the various faiths which found expression at Alexandria." His greatest disciple was the great Plotinus. Plotinus is described in a sketch largely borrowed from Porphyry's *Life* and the remarks of Augustine on the philosopher as the Great Teacher resuscitated. But Wilder presents Porphyry in Emersonian fashion, "in many respects . . . the representative man" of the Neoplatonic school. Iamblichus, "his successor," is accurately represented as one who "took a new departure . . . to identify philosophy with the theurgy of the Egyptian worship and the angelology of Assyria . . . a priest and hierophant rather than a sage, or student of the higher wisdom."[37] For Iamblichus, who had an exact and detailed knowledge of spiritual traditions, "worship stood at the foundation and philosophy was the superstructure."[38]

All Alexandrian "polytheists" acknowledge the One *prior* to the first God (Mithras), the *Alone*, abiding in Eternity. Mithraism and Neoplatonism both teach the descent of the soul and its ascent to the Divine. The One has been the Egyptian "Concealed God" (*Hermetica*), the Babylonian One adored in silence (the *sigê* of the *Chaldean Oracles*), his eternal repose ever-inspiring incessant Energy. Perhaps anticipating Afrocentric ideas, Mithras, Wilder claims, was first Ethiopian or Kushite and later became the divinity in the Disk in Assyrian symbology—that is, Persian. (The *Chaldean Oracles*, replete with fire imagery were still confused with the oracles of Zoroaster, elevated fire, "the Divinity in the Disk, the One.")[39]

All of this is completely consistent with Plato's conception of Real Being, experienced as the soul's approach to the Idea of the Good, the "sun" of the noetic realm. Contemporary rationalists who cannot perceive this, are akin to Paul's "psychic men," who are without the ability to discern spiritual truths.[40]

Neither are such people attuned to mystics' experiences, as Paul's being caught up in the "third heaven" to hear ineffable things, or the *Union* (with the One) of Plotinus and Porphyry, a "superior exaltation . . . evidently identical with the *yoga* and *nirvana* of the Buddhists and Brahmins." That the ecstatic condition is a "psychical fact, and in some sense a function of human existence, cannot be candidly denied."[41] Every religion has been founded on numerous phenomena of this kind. "Plotinus seems, however, to have explained it. 'You can apprehend the Infinite only through the faculty superior to the understanding by entering into a condition in which you are your finite self no longer, in which the Divine Essence is communicated to you.'"[42] The Neoplatonists, then, have also contributed to our knowledge of the varieties of religious experience. They professed, concludes Wilder, "to bring down the Divinity to men; but, in candor, it must be understood that they meant the elevating of men to Divinity."[43]

Wilder appears to be a modern, nineteenth-century equivalent of a late antique tolerant Hellenic syncretist, more akin to the third-century Roman emperor Severus Alexander, reputed to own busts of Abraham, Orpheus, Apollonius, and Jesus, than to the Iamblichean theurgist and Hellene intolerant of Christianity, the fourth-century emperor Julian.

F. B. Sanborn sprinkles his piece, "Oracles of New England," with classical and biblical syncretistic allusions, in which he claims that Plato "does not surpass the Oracular wisdom of Emerson," whose poem *The Sphinx* is "the best epitome of philosophy."[44] The transcendentalist's Sphinx is neither "the Boeotian monster" nor the huge Egyptian goddess, whose image remains in the sands; rather she is the compassionate *mundane soul*—a sort of Demiurge, referring to the world-making craftsman of Plato's *Timaeus*—who acknowledges that the wise poet has unlocked her "riddle of the painful earth."

Oedipus becomes a Neoplatonist who sees into the *anima mundi!*[145] Alcott considered the poem as worthy of an academic chair for its interpretation as Plato's *Timaeus* and Aristotle's *de Anima.*

Neoplatonically-toned transcendentalist syncretism created the basic conditions for the modern American reception of Comparative Religion.[46] Thus, for example, Mircea Eliade's chair at the University of Chicago and the popularity of Joseph Campbell may also be connected to transcendentalist foundations. Eliade, who wrote his M.A. thesis on the Florentine Renaissance Neoplatonists, said at a 1973 conference in his honor that Ficino, Pico, and the Florentines not only rediscovered and translated forgotten texts, but discovered a *new religious horizon.* In his introduction to the Penguin edition of Bulfinch's *Myths of the Greeks and Romans,* Joseph Campbell attributes to the Renaissance revival of Neoplatonic mysteries in art and thought and "pro-cosmic" Hermetic writings the beginning of the modern post-Orthodox Christian appreciation of myth.[47] However one-sided this judgment—after all, some important *Hermetica* represent late antique "gnostic devaluation of the cosmos"—it nevertheless conveys the *feeling* of a transcendentalist, who is willing to elevate the "pagan" or "heretical" above traditional Christian doctrine, as Emerson did in "Intellect," when he called early Christians *parvenus and popular,* compared to the older and wiser largely Neoplatonic philosophical religion.

Though by the 1890s the old metaphysics began to appear no longer viable, thinkers like William James emphasized the significance of religious experience. His modern idealist Harvard colleague, Josiah Royce, issued a paradoxical challenge to rising "scientism" when he asserted that the mystics were the *only pure empiricists* in the history of thought. Some more or less Platonic systems of metaphysics have been able to find a framework within the parameters of modern science. A. N. Whitehead's Process Philosophy, for example, is in part based on relativity and quantum theory. Some modern cosmologists and authors working from their discoveries see, in the emerging view of reality, room for the reinstatement of an almost Neoplatonic worldview.[48] But the intellectual world remains divided at best on these issues.

Today, then, Idealist and other metaphysical arguments remain unconvincing to many, and the claims of "perennialists" seem to imply an almost reverse positivist "counter science." On the other hand, mystical experiences and thought systems have been well documented and thoroughly discussed. It is fair to say that only the myopic, the "tone deaf," and the ideologically-committed reductionists still dismiss them as "pathological" nonsense, or some such thing. A new philosophy of science, through austere and careful arguments, may, in the spirit of Kepler, yet suggest a "logos" that reflects in objective thought the laws of nature as the best explanation for the intelligibility of the world.[49] But until such developments occur, unlike the transcendentalists, whose thought, *as philosophy*, has not held up, our task is to present cogently the ideas of the great mystics, including Plotinus, without avoiding or seriously distorting the scientific world-view.

Notes

1. Proclus, *The Elements of Theology*, E. R. Dodds, trans. (Oxford: Oxford University Press, 1965).

2. See A. C. Lloyd, ch. 18 B, "The Monistic Tendency of Porphyry," in A. H. Armstrong, ed., *The Cambridge History of Later Greek and Early Medieval Philosophy* (Cambridge: Cambridge University Press, 1970), 277–88 ff.

3. Frederick Copelston, *A History of Philosophy* (New York: Image Books, 1967), vol. 8, 20.

4. Quoted by G. M. Harper in *Thomas Taylor the Platonist: Selected Writings*, ed. G. M. Harper and K. Raine (Princeton: Princeton University Press, 1969), 59.

5. *Journal of Speculative Philosophy* 1 (St. Louis, 1867), 165.

6. *Journal of Speculative Philosophy* 1, 166.

7. *Journal of Speculative Philosophy* 1, 167.

8. *Journal of Speculative Philosophy* 1, 168.

9. *Journal of Speculative Philosophy* 2 (1868), 49.

10. *Journal of Speculative Philosophy* 1, 168.

11. See Thoreau's journal entry of April 13, 1841, in *Thoreau's Literary Notebook*, ed. Kenneth W. Cameron (Hartford: Transcendental Books, 1964), 40.

12. See Kenneth W. Cameron, *Transcendental Apprenticeship: Notes on Young Henry Thoreau's Reading* (Hartford: Transcendental Books, 1976), 168.

13. See Kenneth W. Cameron, *Young Emerson's Transcendental Vision* (Hartford: Transcendental Books, 1971), 48; 406–8.

14. See R. E. Friedman, *The Disappearance of God* (Boston: Little, Brown, 1995). This is a similar but independent conclusion to that of Daniel Matt, who points out the uncanny closeness of the Kabbalah's largely Neoplatonic *Genesis* cosmology and the theory of the "Big Bang." See Daniel Matt, *God and the Big Bang* (Woodstock, VT: Jewish Lights, 1998).

15. See F. B. Sanborn and W. T. Harris, eds., *A. Bronson Alcott: His Life and Philosophy*, 2 vols. (reprint, New York: Biblo & Tannen, 1965), vol. 2, 602–5.

16. *Concord Lectures on Philosophy: Comprising Outlines of all the Lectures at the Concord Summer School of Philosophy in 1882*, ed. Raymond L. Bridgeman (Cambridge: Moses King, 1883), 10.

17. *Concord Lectures on Philosophy*, 5–13.

18. *Concord Lectures on Philosophy*, 12.

19. *Concord Lectures on Philosophy*, 12.

20. *Concord Lectures on Philosophy*, 55.

21. *Concord Lectures on Philosophy*, 56.

22. *Concord Lectures on Philosophy*, 55.

23. Verse II, *Concord Lectures on Philosophy*, 57.

24. *Concord Lectures on Philosophy*, 61.

25. *Concord Lectures on Philosophy*, 65.

26. *Concord Lectures on Philosophy*, 71

27. *Concord Lectures on Philosophy*, 72.

28. *Concord Lectures on Philosophy*, 72.

29. *Concord Lectures on Philosophy*, 32.

30. *Concord Lectures on Philosophy*, 109.

31. *Concord Lectures on Philosophy*, 129.

32. Emerson considered Synesius' work *On Providence* as "one of the majestic remains of literature" and a sequel to Plutarch's *On Isis and Osiris*. It is likely that Alcott was influenced here. See J. Bregman, "The Neoplatonic Revival in North America," *Hermathena* 149 (Winter 1990), 99–119; 102.

33. *Concord Lectures on Philosophy*, 129.

34. *Concord Lectures on Philosophy*, 149.

35. *Concord Lectures on Philosophy*, 168.

36. *Concord Lectures on Philosophy*, 141.

37. *Concord Lectures on Philosophy*, 142.

38. *Concord Lectures on Philosophy*, 143.

39. *Concord Lectures on Philosophy*, 143.

40. *Concord Lectures on Philosophy*, 143.

41. *Concord Lectures on Philosophy*, 144.

42. *Concord Lectures on Philosophy*, 144.

43. *Concord Lectures on Philosophy*, 144.

44. *Concord Lectures on Philosophy*, 128.

45. *Concord Lectures on Philosophy*, 128.

46. On this topic, the best, most accurate guide is A. Versluis, *American Transcendentalism and Asian Religions* (New York: Oxford University Press, 1993).

47. See Thomas Bulfinch, *Bulfinch's Mythology*, compiled by Bryan Holme,

intro. J. Campbell (New York: Penguin, 1979), 6.

48. See above, n. 14.

49. A carefully argued study moving in this direction, while avoiding hasty "mystical" conclusions based on insufficient evidence, is Roland Omnès, *Quantum Philosophy: Understanding and Interpreting Contemporary Science* (Princeton: Princeton University Press, 1999).

Chaos and the Millennium

RALPH ABRAHAM

1. Introduction

In this short lecture I want to discuss three things: The first is *Chaos*, secondly, the *Millennium*, and finally and most importantly, *Chaos and the Millennium*, and how they go together in an essential way.

2. The Mathematics of Chaos and Bifurcations

Chaos means the chaos of everyday life, but also, it means *chaos theory*, a new branch of mathematics also known as *dynamical systems theory*. The question naturally arises as to whether there is a connection between the mathematical model of chaos and the chaos of everyday life. For a long time I rejected this connection, but now I feel it is justified.

Mathematics has the branches which are standard in history books: arithmetic, geometry, dynamics, and so on. These branches are more or less old. Algebra and geometry are very old subjects, coming to us from ancient city-states like Sumer, Babylon, Indus, and Egypt. Dynamics is newer, only three or four hundred years old. A new branch of mathematics would be a tremendous novelty, and pose a challenge to the orthodoxy of mathematics at universities, because for a long time there has not been a new branch of mathematics. But now there are new branches. Chaos theory is a new branch of mathematics, one which has evolved into a mass movement and major social transformation called the *chaos revolution*.

Now I would like to introduce briefly the five most essential concepts from chaos theory: *states, trajectories, attractors, basins,* and *bifurcations*.

This talk was given for the National Collegiate Honors Council, San Francisco, October 31, 1996.

2.1. *States*

The most fundamental and important of the basic notions of chaos theory is the *state space*. This is at the basis of everything and goes back to geometry. It is an imaginary geometrical model for a system. Let's say you have a restaurant. The groceries come in the back door, and the satisfied customers go out the front door leaving money behind. Now you count up the supplies and the money left behind; these counts represent the state of the restaurant (as an economic system) at a given instant. But they may also be regarded as the coordinates of a point in a geometric space, a model for the system. This geometrical model is the state space of this example.

2.2. *Trajectories*

Now here enter the *dynamics* of the dynamical system: the system changes. Every minute it has a slightly different state. So its representative in the model is a point wandering around in the state space. It is a moving point which draws a curve called a *trajectory*. And this is where mathematicians put a simple restriction. It is imagined that at every point (state) in this state space there is a single *vector*, which gives the direction and speed of any trajectory which will ever pass though that state.

2.3. *Attractors*

Suppose we have such a model and we are interested in the long-term behavior of the system. This means that we only want to know, twenty years from now, for example, if there will be a fortune to pass down to the next generation or not. In other words: what is the long-term expectation of a trajectory in the model? We have to start from one point and follow the instructions, drawing the trajectory of the system for a long time. And when we do that, we come to what is called an *attractor*. There are three kinds of attractors:

- A point attractor, otherwise known as a static attractor, a good model for death,
- A periodic attractor, or oscillation, a model for simple life, and
- A chaotic attractor, a model for more complex life.

The third sort, amazingly, was discovered only recently and unexpectedly, thanks to computer graphics.

Attractors are models for the long-term behavior of an idealized mathematical model for practically any kind of a dynamical system subject to this very rigid restriction that the rules of evolution don't change in time, a so-called *autonomous dynamical system*.

2.4. *Basins*

It is important to know that a typical dynamical system has more than one attractor. Suppose, for example, that there were two. Then some trajectories would evolve toward one, while other trajectories would wind toward the other attractor. And if one attractor models death and the other life, it may be very important to know which final state is in your future! The *basin* of an attractor is the piece of the state space filled by trajectories tending to that attractor. If there are two attractors, then the state space falls naturally into two pieces: the basin of death and the basin of life. Each attractor has a basin, and each basin contains a single attractor.

2.5. *Bifurcations*

Now suppose the rules *do* change in time. Then the attractors and their basins might change. One kind of attractor can change into another kind. An attractor (along with its entire basin) might disappear into the blue, or a new one appear out of the blue. A basin might suddenly explode or implode, radically changing in size. These significant changes in the picture of the state space determined by the attractors and basins are called *bifurcations*. There are three kinds of bifurcations:

- Subtle bifurcations, in which an attractor changes type,
- Catastrophic bifurcations, attractors appear out of (or disappear into) the blue, and
- Explosive bifurcations, in which attractors drastically change size.

It is this aspect of chaos theory which has been of the utmost importance in the applications to the sciences, and to history.

3. The Mathematics of History
So now let us look at history from the perspective of chaos theory.

3.1. *Interesting Times*
In the preface of *The Age of Bifurcation*, subtitled "Interesting Times," futurist and systems philosopher Ervin Laszlo writes:

> There is an old Chinese curse that says "May you live in interesting times." I don't believe anyone would dispute that we do indeed live in interesting times. Most interesting. But whether these times are accursed or blessed is probably less clear to many people. My own orientation is that neither is the case. We are under no dark cloud. Nor do the heavens smile upon us. What the world will be like for us and our progeny is very much up to us. This belief constitutes the basic underlying premise upon which our work is predicated. This century has seen the advent of an era in which the range of possibilities for life, for the quality of life, and perhaps even for the persistence of life on our planet, is very much if not entirely to be determined by what we, the human inhabitants of the planet, do. And what we do, we assert, will be a direct consequence of what we believe and know—of how we approach problems and situations.

Some people are pessimistic and others optimistic, but Laszlo says that he is neither. According to studies made by the World Future Society, and published in its monthly magazine, *The Future*, the predictions of futurists are right about two times out of three. So we must take Laszlo seriously. The World Future Society also surveys to see what other people think about the future. They surveyed thousands of people, and found that two-thirds were more optimistic than pessimistic.

Sociologist Paul Ray has studied three subcultures in the United States. These he calls:

- The *Heartlanders* (*Traditional Stream*, dating from about 1870)
- The *Modernists* (*Modern Stream*, from 1920), and
- The *Cultural Creatives* (*Transmodern Stream*, 1970)

He defines these groups according to three different world views. Heartlanders favor a return to the past. Modernists champion the secular, economic, and scientific paradigm of the twentieth century. Cultural Creatives are bearers of a new world view, currently evolving in reaction to the shadow side of the Modern Stream. In a social research survey in 1994, Ray sampled about two thousand people in the United States. He found the proportions of these three subcultures to be:

- Traditional, 29%, equivalent to 56 million adults of today's United States population
- Modern, 47%, or 88 million adults, and
- Transmodern, 24%, or 44 million adults

He concludes that we are now at a Great Divide between the Modern Stream and its Transmodern sequel, the latter yet to be determined.

In this talk we are going to take sides with Ervin Laszlo, the World Future Society, Paul Ray, and the 44 million Transmoderns. And we are going to bring the Chaos Revolution into the picture.

3.2. *Bifurcations in History*

At one time people thought that history was continuous and gradually changing, that nothing ever happened suddenly. This was the opinion of Leibniz, who contributed ideas of evolution and linear progression to history. Leibniz is the coinventor with Newton of the calculus, and was also a futurist and historian. Applying the new mathematical ideas of his time to history, he came up with his *principle of continuity*. He was a *gradualist*.

The idea of *bifurcation* (or *catastrophe*) is a different idea—an idea of discontinuity, of punctuated or saltatory change, sudden or miraculous transformation.

Laszlo concludes his preface:

The issues are burning, the stakes enormous, the options impressive.

These truly are interesting times. This stands to reason. We stand in humankind's greatest age of bifurcation.

For him, bifurcation is an important new word and mathematical concept. He uses it in place of the equivalent general terms, *major social transformation*, or *Great Divide*. He sees history as consisting of flat spots punctuated by major social transformations or bifurcations. This is like the evolution of species in the Darwinian sense where long flat spots are followed by the sudden emergence of new species, which may be triggered by collisions with comets. Laszlo is a *bifurcationist*. Even more: he says that this current transformation, our own bifurcation, is the biggest one in human history. Quite an idea!

3.3. *Histomaps*

Historiography is the study of structure in history. And now that mathematics has been redefined as the study of space-time patterns, we could say that historiography is the mathematics of history.

Jacob Burkhardt of Switzerland was an early bifurcationist. He analyzed the Italian Renaissance as a catastrophic bifurcation, and made his reputation with this theory. It was the first of the saltatory or discontinuous theories of history, coming shortly after Leibniz and his principle of historical continuity.

A controversy developed over this interpretation: was the Renaissance a sudden, catastrophic bifurcation, or just a gradual change? The conservatives in this controversy believed in the continuity of history. They noted that, a century earlier, Petrarch, Bocaccio, and others had introduced new ideas in literature which were more or less characteristic of what was later called Renaissance Humanist thought. They said that history was continuous, while Burckhardt and his followers said that it was discontinuous. This controversy, still ongoing today, led to a whole school of the philosophy of history, which came to be known as historiography.

My idea of historiography consists of the space-time pattern of world cultural history, the history movie, superimposed over the space-time pattern of our biosphere, the biogeographical movie. But the simplest representation of this combined space-time pattern is a *histomap*. In a histomap, geography, which really lives on the two-dimensional sphere of the earth, is reduced to one dimension for convenience, so that geographical space plus time comprise a two-dimensional display in which to locate space-time events.

A histomap by Edward Hull, from around 1900, may be the best histomap ever made. In it, the map of the world is a one-dimensional, vertical interval about eighteen inches high. The time span is a horizontal line several feet long. It starts in 2,500 B.C.E. and ends more or less now, with approximately two inches corresponding to a century. A later histomap, published by John Sparks in 1931, was the first to actually use the word *histomap*.[1]

A small piece of Hull's histomap is shown in figure 1. The colored streams denote cultures. They suddenly get wider when there are more people or more territory. There are thin ones and thick ones and they change in their relative sizes as we go down the river of time. Between and around them are icons from archaeological and historical records.

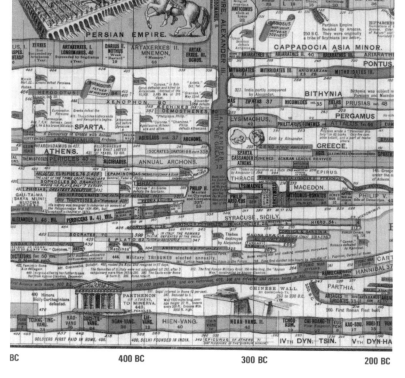

Figure 1.
A Section of Hull's Histomap.

3.4. *Bifurcations in a Histomap*

A bifurcation is a special feature of chaos theory. Applied to historiography, the study of the space-time patterns in history, a bifurcation would be a significant historical event. When you look at a histomap, a bifurcation should just jump out at you.

For example, let's look at Hull's histomap, in figure 1. The vertical bar in the center is an exemplary bifurcation, the conquest of Alexander the Great. In a decade he conquered most of the known world. All of the separate strands of different cultures were united by him personally, so all the horizontal rivers of culture join that vertical bar. Upon Alexander's death his empire disintegrated, so the vertical bar breaks up into more rivers. This was a double bifurcation.

4. Millennia as the Epochs of History between Bifurcations

If world cultural history is punctuated by quantum leaps, then there must be periods of gradual change in between the major bifurcations. These we call *epochs*. The division of the whole of history and prehistory into epochs is a subjective process, and many such divisions, or *schemes*, have been proposed. We will now review several of them.

4.1. *An Archeoastronomical Scheme*

Ancient skywatchers followed the histomap of the zodiac. The major bifurcations were marked by the passage of the vernal equinox from one zodiacal constellation to another. These events occur roughly every 2,200 years, and were very important in early cultures.[2] Within the recent millennia of the Holocene Interglacial, here are the dates:

- 10,500 B.C.E., Leo; 7,900 B.C.E., Cancer; 6,500 B.C.E., Gemini
- 4,500 B.C.E., Taurus; 1,900 B.C.E., Aries; 100 B.C.E., Pisces
- 2,500 C.E., Aquarius

4.2. *My Scheme of Three Epochs*

In my book *Chaos, Gaia, Eros*, a scheme of three epochs is proposed, with major bifurcations:

- 10,000 B.C.E., the agricultural revolution
- 4,000 B.C.E., the discovery of the wheel
- 1972 C.E., the chaos revolution

4.3. *William Irwin Thompson's Scheme of Four Epochs*

William Irwin Thompson is one of the leading cultural historians of our time. His approach to world cultural history, which is both cultural and mathematical, has a division into four periods which he calls *cultural ecologies*. Associated with each is a characteristic mathematical style, or *mentality*. These, with beginning dates, are:

- 4,000 B.C.E., the riverine cultural ecology, with the arithmetic mentality
- 500 B.C.E., transcontinental, geometric
- 700 C.E., oceanic, dynamic
- 1972 C.E., biospheric, chaotic

A comparison of these three schemes is shown in figure 2.

4.4. *What is a Millennium?*

Originally, the millennium meant a particular period of one thousand years, which was to follow a great bifurcation, according to an apocalyptic doctrine of the ancient Hebrews.[3] When the coming of Christ was thought to signal that event around the year 1 B.C.E., the end of the millennium (that is, the apocalypse) was to fall around the year 1000 C.E. It did not, but the concept persisted in groups knows as revolutionary millenarians.

> The millenarians believe that the end of this world, and of historical time,
> is at hand. A new world, and a new time, will be inaugurated, usually

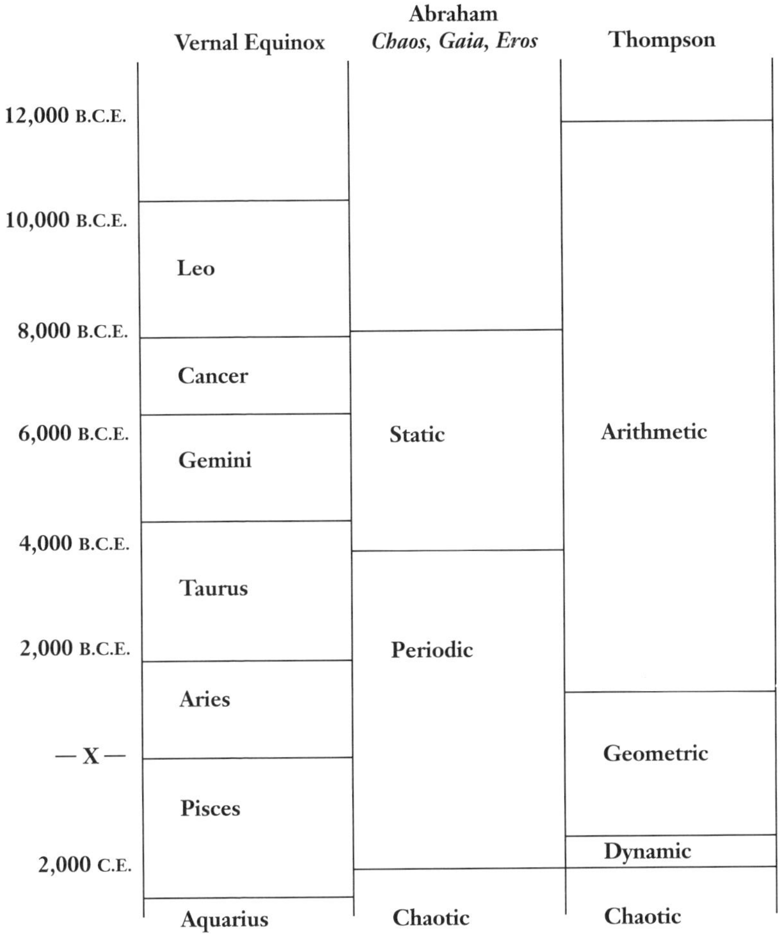

Figure 2.
Comparison of Schemes for the Holocene Interglacial.

through the agency of a messiah: a saviour or deliverer. There will be many tribulations and mighty conflicts. The forces of evil will gather themselves up in a last bid for victory. But the good will triumph. The new era—the millennium—will be a time of peace, plenty and righteousness.[4]

For the purposes of this talk, I am pirating the word *millennium*, and appropriating it as a synonym for *epoch*. It has no longer any implication of a period of one thousand years.

Thus, we now have a catastrophic bifurcation from the Periodic millennium to the Chaotic millennium, according to me; from the Oceanic millennium to the Biospheric millennium according to Thompson; or from the Modern to the Transmodern, according to Ray. Whatever you call the epochs, all agree that we are now in a bifurcation—one which is the largest so far, according to Laszlo. As William Irwin Thompson writes,

> In our global development, we have moved from the ancient arithmetic mentality to the classical geometrical mentality to the modernist dynamical mentality and now finally to the new chaos dynamical mentality, a mentality that is based on the new sciences of complexity, on the new art forms that cross one genre with another, and on the new multidisciplinary sciences such as Lovelock's geophysiology that give us a biospheric vision of our new planetary cultural ecology.[5]

But in addition to characterizing the dominant mathematical style of the coming millennium, *the chaos mentality is able to model the great transformation itself.* This is my main message here: Chaos theory can help us to understand our unique experience in this special moment of history, at the dawn of a new millennium. *Chaos and the millennium!*

5. Education for the Chaos Millennium

Chaos and the millennium is a very important subject. It is very appropriate for this time, and it has crucial implications for education in general and for honors programs in particular. The school system is where the future is actually created, and honors programs provide a special opportunity to teach new paradigms. So here is something for us to do: the reformation of education on all its levels, to address the future, and to create a society which has a sustainable future.

New programs are badly needed which integrate world cultural history, the new branches of mathematics, and the willful creation of the future. Chaos theory must be rescued from the fringes of academia and brought into the center of our schools and universities. Curricular reform in our schools, and integrative programs such as honors programs in our universities, provide opportunities for the renewal of our outworn educational system, and the creation of a viable future.

Notes

1. See John Sparks, *Histomap of World History*.
2. See Giorgio de Santillana and Hertha von Dechend, *Hamlet's Mill*.
3. See Cohn, *The Pursuit of the Millennium*.
4. Krishnan Kumar, *Utopianism*, 7.
5. William Irwin Thompson, *Coming into Being*, 241.

Bibliography

Abraham, Ralph. *Chaos, Gaia, Eros*. San Francisco: Harper San Francisco, 1994.

Cohn, Norman. *The Pursuit of the Millennium*. Fairlawn: Essential Books, 1957.

De Santillana, Giorgio, and Hertha von Dechend. *Hamlet's Mill: An Essay on Myth and the Frame of Time*. Boston: Gambit, 1969.

Eisler, Riane. *The Chalice and the Blade*. Cambridge: Harper & Row, 1987.

Hull, Edward. *The Wall Chart of World History: With Maps of the World's Great Empires and a Complete Geological Diagram of the Earth*. Facsimile edition. Dorset Press, 1988.

Kumar, Krishnan. *Utopianism*. Buckingham: Open University Press, 1991.

Laszlo, Ervin. *The Age of Bifurcation: Understanding the Changing World*. Philadelphia: Gordon and Breach, 1991.

Sparks, John B. *Histomap of World History*. New York: Rand McNally, 1931.

Thom, René. *Structural Stability and Morphogenesis: An Outline of a General Theory of Models*. Trans. D. H. Fowler. Reading: W. A. Benjamin, 1975.

Ray, Paul H. "The Rise of Integral Culture," *Noetic Sciences Review* (Spring 1996), 4–15.

Thompson, William Irwin. *Pacific Shift*. San Francisco: Sierra Club Books, 1985.

————. *Coming into Being: Artifacts and Texts in the Evolution of Consciousness*. New York: St. Martin's Press, 1996.

Zeeman, E. C. *Catastrophe Theory: Selected Papers, 1972–1977*. Reading: Addison-Wesley, 1977.

Acknowledgements

I am grateful to my colleagues of the General Evolution Research Group and the Lindisfarne Association for the collegial sharing of ideas over the years, to Courtney Sale Ross for awakening me to the possibilities of elementary education, and to Russell Spring for bringing Paul Ray to my attention.

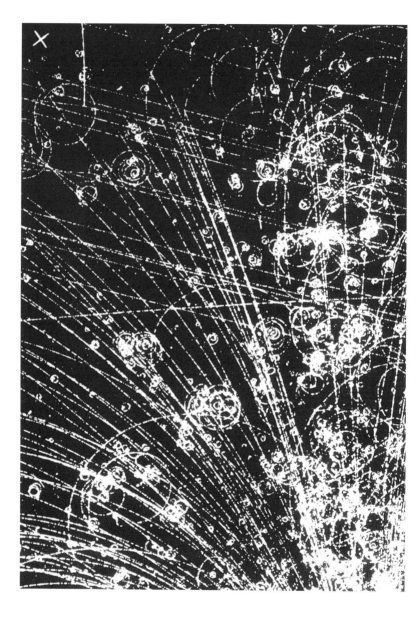

Is Anything the Matter?

Roger S. Jones

ACCORDING TO MODERN SCIENCE, the material objects of our everyday experience aren't made out of anything at all. There's no stuff there. There's no there there. Twentieth-century chemists and physicists have convinced most of us that the world is made out of atoms, but what are *they* made of? Atoms themselves surely must consist of some kind of stuff and substance, right? Wrong! Stuff and nonsense is more like it.

There are no hard little balls or even fuzzy atoms whizzing around in space and time. Matter isn't concrete at all. In fact, there is no scientific support whatsoever for the quaint idea that rocks and water and air are made out of any primal substance. The ultimate scientific description of the material world is a complete mathematical abstraction—a kind of potentiality for existence, which is itself so theoretical and ideational that even in principle it can never be detected or measured, let alone seen or felt. You may see and feel a rock, but according to science, there's nothing there. Modern physics, the most successful, quantitative, and "hard-nosed" scientific theory in history, offers no materialistic explanation for the physical world. In fact, science cannot substantiate matter.

Matter, Matter, Everywhere

Before we explore the viewpoint of modern science, we should consider why we have any notion of matter in the first place. The explanation seems obvious: Experience demands it. If there is no ultimate tangible substance, then why doesn't your fist pass right through the table when you bang on it? And isn't it patently clear that diamond is hard and water is wet? Such commonplace qualities seem true enough to our senses of sight, hearing and touch. But the notion that there is some kind of stuff or matter behind our sensations and experiences is a pragmatic construct of the mind—a complex of beliefs, which we conjure up to make sense of and negotiate our way in the world of experience.

When my fist stops at the table top, or when I grasp a book between my thumb and fingers, I am not actually feeling anything like "hardness" or "solidity." These are terms I apply to the combined sensations of pressure, smoothness, and muscle tension in my fingers and hand. I attribute my sensations to some external source—a table or a book, which I assume has just the appropriate characteristics to justify my experience. I say the book is "hard" and "takes up room," which accounts for my physical feelings. In fact, all the commonly *perceived* characteristics of matter, such as "solidity," "wetness," "rigidity," "pliability," and "softness," are simply unconscious mental constructs or inventions that we ascribe to our sensations to create a convenient and efficient mental image of a world that can account for our experiences. Without such constructs and beliefs, we would be overwhelmed by a deluge of random, chaotic, meaningless sensations with no rhyme or reason.

As philosophers and thinkers have known for thousands of years, there is no empirical or theoretical way to prove that matter actually exists. And since the very idea of tangible matter and even materialism itself—the theory of a substantive basis of "reality"—are nothing but mental fabrications, then neither science nor any other system of thought is under any obligation to dispose of the idea of matter as substance before offering other theories that can account for experience. Furthermore, as we shall see, modern science does have a theory to explain our experiences of the "physical" world, and that theory is based on purely mathematical abstractions. Thus we should recognize materialism as a convenient aid, a mental construct, a metaphor, and nothing more.

Quantum Rules

The starting point for the scientific study and exploration of matter, its properties and behavior, is the modern and very unintuitive science of quantum physics. You might expect this most fundamental of all the sciences of matter to be the ultimate guarantor of materialism. On the contrary, at its deepest level, quantum physics may be the supreme advocate of idealism.

According to quantum physics, all matter is reducible to elementary particles and forces, such as electrons, photons, and magnetic fields. The fundamental quantum description of these elements involves highly mathematical entities, variously called *wave functions* or *state vectors.* This doesn't mean that electrons and photons are waves or states or anything else that we can picture in space and time. The quantum wave function is a pure mathematical abstraction, which can be coaxed into giving us limited information about an electron, but which itself is not an electron by any stretch of the imagination. It would be just as incongruous to expect the word "pig" to bear any resemblance or physical similarity to the animal of that name. The wave function of an electron is the ultimate and only source of knowledge about an electron that science gives us. It is an abstract and intangible form of knowledge, but it is all we have.

It is tempting to think that the quantum description of an electron may very well be abstract, but that the electron itself is perfectly real and tangible. But here the truly radical and unintuitive aspect of quantum physics foils us. For quantum physics restricts all possible *scientific* information or knowledge about an electron to what may be deduced from its wave function. And the equations of quantum physics never deal with or describe atoms or electrons directly, only their wave functions. What an electron or photon may be apart from its wave function is a true scientific mystery. Beyond the mathematical wave functions of quantum physics, there are no pictures, concepts, or further information of any kind to be learned about elementary particles from science. Like the "raiders of the lost ark" we may use the magical laws, but we can never peer inside the box. If there is a tangible electron, it eludes scientific description.

More to the point, there is now concrete experimental evidence that rules out the very assumption of hidden or unknown information beyond the laws of quantum physics. Suppose, for example, you assume there exist unobservable aspects of photons that affect their behavior in ways that exceed or transcend the rules of quantum physics. Based on these assumptions, you may predict how the spins of a pair of photons are correlated. Such predictions have been directly contradicted by experimentation. It is the predictions of quantum physics—and not of any hidden photon theory—that always prevail in the laboratory. Quantum physics and its experimental consequences exclude the possibility of any "hidden" photon or electron. There is no matter underlying the wave function.

And yet, without any tangible electrons or atoms, quantum physics can rationalize "physical reality" and human experience. To explain the properties of diamond or water, the quantum physicist invokes the wave function of the atom. Atomic wave functions are abstract patterns of potentiality that have, as it were, a kind of mathematical incompressibility and persistence. When atoms are combined into bulk matter, the incompressibility of the wave functions is extended and amplified into properties that we experience, for example, as solidity and wetness. Thus, concreteness is a consequence of abstraction. Your fist is prohibited from passing through the table by abstract mathematical laws, just as traffic laws prohibit you from passing through a red light. But we're getting ahead of the story.

Quantum physics, like all the exact sciences, begins from postulated mathematical equations that arise spontaneously in the human imagination. These equations can be used to make predictions that may be tested experimentally or lead to new discoveries. Thus the predictions can be checked against reality, and the more correct predictions there are, the more faith we have in the source equations. But although the equations can be proven wrong by experiment, they can never be proven ultimately correct. They are mathematical statements about abstract concepts, which typically do not correspond to anything in our everyday experience. The equations are simply the sources of our predictions, and we hold on to them as long as they are fruitful.

What's the Alternative?

As you contemplate the irrationality of quantum physics, you may well be tempted to reject such a hypothetical and seemingly absurd science. Physicists are the first to sympathize. Richard Feynman said that anyone who thinks he or she understands quantum physics clearly doesn't. One never really understands quantum physics; one simply learns to live with it. And its mathematical complexity and level of abstraction are notorious and the bane of every physics student. But none of this makes the slightest difference, because quantum physics is also renowned as the most precise and accurate theory in the history of science. It consistently and infallibly makes the most subtle and exact predictions about the "material" world, and in addition it has given us the laser, the microchip, the CAT scan, the superconductor, and similar inventions of enormous and prodigious influence on our civilization. With all due respect to Albert Einstein, who could never accept the quantum world view, the rejection of quantum physics simply is not an option for a contemporary scientist.

Of course, one may look outside of science. This might well require rejecting materialistic science altogether as an explanation of the physical world. What would that mean? Is the world merely an idea, a fiction, an illusion? How could such things ever be proven?

On the other hand, any theory that contradicts science is unlikely to gain many supporters. Anyone willing to reject quantum physics simply has no scientific leg to stand on. And, if quantum physics cannot rationalize matter, what else can? But, if science can rule out a substantive or material basis of matter, then that would make an ideational theory of physical reality far more compelling. Not a proof perhaps, but certainly food for thought. Modern physics and idealism seem like strange bedfellows indeed.

In any case, quantum physics shares with all of science the ability to explain how, but not why, the world works as it does. That may seem insufficient to us, but it also represents an ultimate limit to scientific knowledge. While acknowledging these limits, let us now try to understand the intangible nature of matter within the scientific framework.

Information Theory

The wave function of an electron can provide qualified information about what we detect or measure in any empirical observation of an electron. It can tell us, for example, what we may learn experimentally when we look for an electron. This is the only kind of information quantum physics can give us—the result of an actual observation. It cannot tell us what an electron is doing, or even whether or not it exists, between our observations. In this sense, quantum physics gives a clear answer to the proverbial question—does a tree falling in a forest make any noise when no one is there? The answer is no. In fact, quantum physics does not even guarantee the existence of the tree or the forest when we're not looking. For this reason, quantum physics is often referred to as a theory of information, rather than a theory of nature. It tells us what we may *know* about things, but not what they are or how they do what they do. If there is a bag of tricks, we can never open it.

Suppose we wish to observe an electron. The wave function can tell us, for instance, what the chances or the probabilities are of finding the electron in some particular location. There may be a 10% chance of finding it at location A and a 30% chance of finding it at B. If we look for an electron under the same conditions 100 times, we would find it about 10 times at A and 30 times at B. The results aren't exact because we are dealing with probabilities, not certainties. But because of the law of averages, the more cases we observe, the more accurate the predictions will be. Life expectancy tables can scarcely be applied at all to ten people, but the tables become extremely accurate for 250 million.

Physicists often represent this information about the electron pictorially (not the electron itself, but the information about the electron) in the form of what's called a *probability distribution*. It illustrates how the probability for finding the electron is distributed through space—10% here, 30% there, and so on. If we represent a probability distribution graphically, it is a picture of information, not a picture of an electron.

A Game of Chance

A more familiar example of a probability distribution is one we might use in representing gambling probabilities—for the game of craps, for instance. Craps is based on the different odds for throwing various number combinations with a pair of dice. There are 36 possible combinations of the numbers on two dice—six numbers on the first, and for each of those six, there are six possible numbers on the second. Thus, there are six times six or 36 possible combinations. But there aren't 36 distinct numbers or totals you can throw—only 11 (2 through 12). And because some of those totals can be thrown in several different ways, they have different odds. There's only one way to throw "snake eyes," or 2, and that's with a 1 on each die. There are two ways to throw a 3: a 1 and a 2 and a 2 and a 1. There are three ways to throw a 4: a 1 and a 3, a 2 and a 2, and a 3 and a 1. Thus the odds for snake eyes are one chance in 36 or 1/36. The odds for a 3 are 2/36 and for a 4 are 3/36. And so on. A 7 has the highest odds, 6/36. Then the odds begin to decrease. An 8 can be thrown in five ways: as a 2 and a 6, a 3 and 5, a 4 and a 4, a 5 and a 3, and a 6 and a 2. Thus, the odds for 8 are 5/36. Finally, since "box cars" or 12 can be thrown in only one way, a 6 and a 6, it has odds of 1/36.

We often describe craps, roulette, and black jack as games of chance and luck. But there is little luck involved in the long-term gambling odds. The huge success of a Las Vegas is the direct result of the mathematics of probability and the law of averages, whose predictions are precise enough to guarantee billions in profit for any gambling casino with a good statistician.

Now we could represent the probabilities for the game of craps graphically by plotting the odds for each of the dice totals—2 through 12—against the totals themselves. We would plot 1/36 against 2, 2/36 against 3, 3/36 against 4, and so on. Continuing, we would plot 6/36 against 7, 5/36 against 8, and eventually 1/36 against 12. If you actually graph such a plot, you can connect the plotted points with two straight lines that reach a peak at 7 and slope down on either side to 2 at one extreme and 12 at the other. This tent-like figure represents the probability distribution for the game of craps. It shows how the odds for craps are distributed against all the possible throws of the dice. It is a picture of certain information about the game of craps, but in no sense is it a picture of the game itself.

If some extraterrestrial anthropologist were studying gambling practices on Earth and had no information about craps other than its probability distribution, he, she (or it) would not have the foggiest idea of what a craps table or a pair of dice actually look like. In fact, exactly the same odds and the same probability distribution would apply to two "wheels of fortune," each of which can spin through the numbers 1 to 6. The anthropologist could tell nothing about the physical nature of the game of craps from its probability distribution. Exactly the same is true of an electron: its probability distribution tells us nothing about its ultimate nature, if any.

A probability distribution is a representation of information, but not a picture of anything physical or material. The odds for the game of craps is an abstraction. You cannot find the odds on the table or in the dice. Gambling odds are not physical, but mathematical—an abstraction. They are calculated from observing and thinking about gambling. They provide a description of the outcome of many cases, or the chances of a particular case occurring. But odds and probability distributions are simply forms of information and not physical things themselves. The map is not the territory. Neither is an electron's probability distribution in any sense an electron or even a picture of an electron.

What Is an Electron?

The chances of finding an electron somewhere in space can be represented as a probability distribution. Other information about an electron, such as how fast it is moving or how much energy it has, can also be represented by probability distributions. As we have seen, these distributions portray abstract information about an electron, but in no sense do they represent the electron itself. And quantum physics strictly limits the scientific information about an electron to such abstract forms. We can ask where an electron is and how fast it is moving, and quantum physics enables us to calculate the probabilities for the various possible answers to these questions. But when we actually search for an electron, either we will find an electron at a certain location or we will not. We will not find a probability. We will find an electron moving at one speed or another, but we will not directly observe the probability of its speed.

What do we actually observe when we detect an electron, you may wonder. We measure a certain constellation of properties—mass, charge, spin, location, speed, energy, momentum, etc., which uniquely characterizes what we call an electron. This unique constellation of properties is the signature of the electron, as it were, but certainly is not the electron itself. Footprints, fingerprints, and even DNA traces may seem to identify a criminal, but they are not the culprit. We cannot send footprints to jail.

The properties of an electron are measured indirectly but quantitatively and are represented by numbers, each of which has a certain probability. Thus each measured property is a specific numerical value from a probability distribution. And that, according to quantum physics, is what a "physical" or "material" electron is. Nothing more. Nothing tangible. An electron is a characteristic collection of numbers from a group of probability distributions. In poker, a "full house" is also a characteristic collection of numbers from a group of probability distributions, but you can never empty out a full house or rent one.

Wave Functions

Furthermore, all of these probability distributions are derived from a wave function, which is the most fundamental source of information we have for the electron. And the wave function or state vector is even more abstract and less physical than a probability distribution. It is a mathematical representation of the potential manifestations of an electron—its mass, charge, spin, etc. The wave function is prior to, or more basic than, the probability distributions, which may be derived from it. The wave function itself is neither the electron, nor its probability, nor anything whatsoever physical about the electron.

The wave function isn't the rabbit in the hat. It isn't even the chances of pulling a rabbit or a pigeon out of the hat. It is the potentiality of all the possible rabbits, pigeons, and other apparitions that may be pulled from the hat.

The wave function represents all the ways an electron may manifest itself in an observation. It is not any one of these manifestations, but rather all of them taken together. In fact, the wave function is decidedly nonphysical, for it represents all possible manifestations of an electron, which are mutually contradictory. An observed electron cannot be in several places at once, and yet the electron's wave function represents *simultaneously* all the possible places an electron can be, not to mention all the speeds, energies, etc., that the electron can have. Furthermore, a wave function cannot ever be measured, detected, or observed under any circumstances. It is a complete mathematical abstraction, and ironically is most often represented by imaginary numbers, which are themselves mathematical abstractions that cannot directly represent "physical reality."

It's Immaterial

Thus, quantum physics provides no materialistic basis for the physical world. Its totally hypothetical abstractions, its patterns of potentiality, its nonphysical, unobservable wave functions are the only representations of electrons (or anything else) that quantum physics provides us with. They are completely immaterial, unpalpable and ideational. At the most basic level in quantum physics, an electron is nothing but an idea, a collection or array or pattern of abstract and imaginary numbers that suggest the idea or potentiality of what an electron may be or do. There is nothing meaty, solid, hard, impenetrable, or resistive about the quantum electron. Between our observations, it cannot even be said to exist. How it gets from one manifestation to another—how it makes its "quantum jumps"—we cannot know. Quantum physics does not answer such questions. In fact one may say that such questions are not within the province of science, which tells us only the results of actual experimental observations, but not how they come about or even how they are possible.

To explain materiality and tangibility, science begrudges us only abstract equations, laws, and principles. When we delve into the nature of matter with the tools and concepts of modern science, we find no corporeal atoms, no hard little particles, nothing material at all, but only "such stuff as dreams are made on."

All the "evidence" of our senses and experiences cannot guarantee any material basis of reality. In fact, science refutes it. But that does not alter our experience. Rather, it forces us to reinterpret it. It makes us bite the bullet, and then admit its atoms are more fanciful than real. Rocks will still feel hard and water wet, but we must entertain the thought that our minds—or Mind—are somehow involved in conjuring our experiences. For if mathematical abstraction and ideas are at the core of experience (or reality, if you prefer), then where do those ideas and equations reside? What is the realm or expressive instrument of idea and abstraction? What other than mind? Contrary to its reputation, science may force us to reject materialism and to embrace instead an ideal or spiritual foundation for matter. We may just have to take quantum physics at face value and recognize in it the best argument we have that the world is an idea.

Earthrise from Moon.

Magnificent Desolation

DANA WILDE

BEFORE I SAY what happened to the Moon, let me tell you what Parmenides said about reality. He was born in the Greek city Elea, in southern Italy, in the last decades of the sixth century B.C.E. Socrates when very young talked with the elderly Parmenides, and speaks of him in Plato's *Theaetetus* as a "being whom I respect above all . . . a 'reverend and awful' figure." Socrates expresses the fear that no one understands exactly what Parmenides was talking about.

Parmenides' words have tumbled down the ages to us in a collection of fragments, most of which sound more like Orphic sayings rather than part of a coherent rational philosophy. But one of the main threads in the longer fragments is fairly simple and, to a literal-minded reader, self-evident. Parmenides says that *what is, must be*, and that *what is not, cannot be*. What difficulty Socrates might have had with remarks like these is not immediately clear. If you are grasping them, these sentences sound exactly the same, logically, as sentences like "blue must be blue" and "colors other than blue cannot be blue."

They are of course a little more complicated. Parmenides suggests straight up that the two sentences actually refer to two ways of understanding the world. One way assumes that everything that *is* exists and any understanding of truth and reality comes through this assumption. The other way assumes that *what is not* is knowable despite its non-existence, and that an understanding of truth and reality can come through understanding *what is not*. Parmenides flatly says that "no information comes back" from this latter way. "You cannot know nonexistence."

This also seems obvious enough.

But as Socrates well knew, it is not really obvious. The truth of

Parmenides' statements hinges completely on what you take to be real. If you take the material world to be real, then any object of your five senses is part of *what is*, and you can assume that accurate information about reality comes through them. This, in general, is the view of science as it has constructed itself in the last 400 years. Knowledge is derived from repeatable observations of and experiments with the materials of the universe. Anything that is not experimentally or observationally verifiable is not real and is not inquired into or even spoken of. For example, many scientists ignore reports of UFOs because there is no repeatable, verifiable evidence that UFOs—as opposed to airplanes, meteors or swamp gases—even exist. Or more interestingly, some cognitive psychologists avoid discussions of "consciousness," as though it does not exist.

But despite the instructions of science, it is not necessary to take the material world as the final reality of the cosmos. This view is most clearly represented, perhaps, in the Hindu view that the material universe is an illusion, or a shadow of reality, called *maya*. The material existence, or actual physical nature, that we perceive is called *prakriti*. The illusion itself is made of tensions between three qualities of existence called the *gunas*—roughly speaking, the qualities of inertia, restlessness, and balance. Material reality is not as we perceive it; it is made of qualities rather than material substance.

This diverges a little from Parmenides, but is nonetheless similar to what he says. For Parmenides also introduces, in his fragments, the difference between *being* and *becoming*. In other words, *what is* timelessly and always *is* whatever it is; it has being. The material world, on the other hand, is in a constant state of flux; it always changes and becomes something else. Because it is always becoming something else, it is never anything. It never *is*, but always *becomes*. The becoming is an appearance only, like a shadow, which is an absence of light— nothing appearing over something. The appearance is an illusion; it *is not*.

And so to Parmenides and Hindus, the material world is not, finally, *what is*. Its existence is not the existence we perceive, and so to believe that what we perceive is *what is* is an error. Plato later developed this by saying that a material object is *an image* of reality, and is not the being, or *what is*, of the reality itself. No information about reality comes back from *what is not*. The material world we perceive is not real; it is an illusion of change, flux, transience.

Now in the words of Plutarch, Parmenides was "an ancient naturalist," and we should not understand that he denied our experience of the material world. But if matter is only an image of *what is*, then what does Parmenides say *is* real? An answer is in one of his cryptic fragments: "to think and to be are one and the same." If you are at all familiar with Plato, you can see from this that Socrates took Parmenides very seriously. This one sentence encapsulates a key element of everything Socrates says about reality: the noetic world—of thought and ideas—is *what is*, and the rest is an illusion, like the play of puppet shadows on the wall of a firelit cave.

The implications that unfold from Parmenides' simple point that "*what is* is and *what is not* is not" constitute a logical swamp of contradictions, paradoxes, and strangeness. Neither Parmenides himself, nor Plato, nor Plotinus, nor any philosopher, up to and including the philosophers of quantum physics (who have had to treat quantum implications about reality in some of the same terms) have solved the logical difficulties. They agree that the human mind plays an important role in shaping the world. They disagree about what the world, or reality, actually consists of—in the same way that most readers of this essay, at this very moment of reading, are disagreeing with or muddled by the propositions about "reality" bobbing up and down in these pages.

We quite naturally, in this situation, expect science to help us keep our heads above water. For the past four hundred years it has instructed us that reality is constituted by objects composed of matter or, in a more refined version, energy. The intangible things of the unconscious mind, like emotions and thoughts, and even life itself, result from complex chemical reactions and exchanges of energy. Invisible and untestable notions like "the spirit" or "God" do not, in conventional scientific terms, exist and are not normally investigated by reputable scientists. In a sense science has tacitly followed

Parmenides' advice by excluding from its range of investigation what scientists believe *is not*.

"Nature will respond in accordance with the theory with which it is approached," noted the physicist David Bohm in 1980. If we theorize that the physical world is real and God is not real, then the physical universe will seem real to us, whether it is or not. If we theorize further that the physical world is an accumulation of essentially inert, lifeless objects, and that the objects themselves are accumulations of smaller lifeless objects, and the small objects are further accumulations of even smaller objects, where the smallest of all the objects are merely whirling and creating by their energy, motion and association the illusion of larger objects, then it will seem that the universe is essentially an accumulation of inert, lifeless, meaningless objects. According to Bohm's principle, if we approach the world as an accumulation of lifeless objects, then the universe will respond as an accumulation of lifeless objects.

This is exactly what modern science, as it is commonly practiced and understood, has found. According to one highly-refined mathematical understanding of the physical nature of the universe, which accounts for the properties of matter and antimatter and the universal law of the conservation of energy, the total energy in the universe is zero. Or more tangibly, every object, with only one or two exceptions, that astronomers have studied in space has been assumed or proven to be inert and lifeless. Even the Viking biology experiments on the surface of Mars, which were very hopefully designed, ended up to be at best ambiguous, but in the judgment of most scientists, nearly conclusively negative: most agree that there is no evidence of anything alive on Mars. We assume Mars is, like the rest of the extraterrestrial universe, lifeless. Maybe there will be evidence of life on Titan, but given the scientific assumption that the universe is composed of lifelessness, the prospects are not good. More likely, the robot space probes will find nothing on Titan, either.

It begins to look like conventional science has not really followed Parmenides' advice. Parmenides said that "to think and to be are one and the same." What comes into being and goes out of being—in other words *prakriti*, nature, material reality—is not *what is*. Science's objects of study, the accumulations of the material universe, are the fluctuating components of the world of becoming. Science is engaged, from this point of view, in the massive analysis of an illusion.

Some eminent scientists have addressed this proposition obliquely, by suggesting that science's range might be limited. Arthur Eddington pointed out that science examines only one aspect—the material aspect—of all that exists, and that other aspects of existence cannot be understood or even approached with scientific methods. He gives the lucid example of the impossibility of science ever explaining what is funny in a joke. His point is that in some unknown way, reality does not inhere solely in material substance. There is another range of reality.

But scientists like Eddington have not set the main course for science as it is popularly understood, practiced, and utilized. We commonly think of science as the answer to all our troubles and questions, which we in turn think of as primarily material. Your intuition that God might exist is, for example, a psychological impulse; your psychology is a product of complex, highly-evolved chemical and electrical actions in your brain. That is to say, your intuition, like your whole existence, is an illusion. It is not *what is*, and since *what is not* cannot be, it is essentially nothing.

Parmenides flatly states

> That Nothingness exists will never break through.
>> Withhold your mind from that way of inquiry.
> But don't let fashion force you to travel
>>> the empirical road either
>> using the blind eye for instrument
>>>> the ringing ear and the tongue.[1]

To Parmenides, reality is your intuition and thought, not the illusions of sight and sound and crafty verbal manipulation. Parmenides' advice was to approach nature with the theory that what is *is*. *Maya* and *prakriti* are only appearances; the timeless qualities, which manifest themselves as thought or mind, shape the world as we perceive it. Nature responds in accordance with the theory with which it is approached. If the material world is all, then all is nothing. This cannot be. No information comes back from this way.

* * *

What the Moon actually is has interested people for millennia, at least. In pre-Christian times the celestial bodies were not just divine, but in some views the divinities themselves. The Moon, being close, bright, and highly regular in its phases and position, was thought to influence the Earth in many ways, and so was thought to be a cosmic power with an identity and being, in different aspects, of its own.

The ancient Greeks were interested in what the heavens were actually made of and how they were structured, and they propounded as many theories of the Moon as any other planet. Parmenides himself indicated our modern understanding of moonlight:

> nightshining
>   round earth
> a wanderer with borrowed light

Others thought the Moon was merely a stone. Some thought it was a stone whose pores leaked light from the heavenly world. Opinion differed on whether the Moon was flat or spherical. Aetius reported that the Pythagorean, Philolaos, had said the Moon was Earthlike and supported plants and animals fifteen times larger than terrestrial plants and animals.

Others explained that, like all the objects in the sky, the Moon was made of the celestial fire, a pure, ethereal fire as opposed to the material fire found on Earth. This belief was held widely well into the Renaissance, and provides one of the main metaphors in Dante's celestial cosmology. On leaving Eden at the top of Mount Purgatory to embark for heaven, Dante and Beatrice pass through a final purifying wall of fire into the sphere of the Moon.

In the fifteenth century, da Vinci thought the changes he detected in the Moon's surface appearance were caused by clouds rising from water. With inferences like this, modern, inductive, observational science begins. Galileo, looking through his telescope, changed the world's lunar theories for good. He thought the dark areas he saw were literally large bodies of water, and he called them "seas." In 1651 Giambattista Riccioli followed Galileo's lead when he mapped and named the dark areas as bodies of water, for example, Lacus Somniorum, the Lake of Dreams, and Mare Tranquillitatis, the Sea of Tranquillity (Apollo 11's landing site). He named craters after philosophers and scientists, and his nomenclature became generally accepted. But he thought the names merely apt conventions. For religious reasons, he believed neither water nor inhabitants existed on the Moon. Riccioli's Christian conviction was a direct descendant, coming down through Aristotle, St. Augustine, Dante, and other religious thinkers, of the sense that the stars and planets are made of a divine, immaterial substance.

As the methods of objective science gained authority, the Moon's divinity dissolved. Reputable eighteenth-century astronomers conjectured that the Moon was Earthlike and had an atmosphere and grew plants. An early nineteenth-century German astronomer speculated that the rilles, long cracks in the Moon's surface, were roads, and announced at one point that he had discovered a lunar city. Soon afterward, the astronomers Beer and Madler explained the Moon's surface features in detailed geological terms, and the modern view of a dead, rocky Moon settled into place.

To be sure, no one was unequivocally certain about the Moon's deadness. Peculiar changes of light, for example, that could not be objectively explained, continued to occur on the Moon. A reddish light glows in some craters from time to time, unpredictably. Astronomers call these glows "transient lunar phenomena," but have no idea what they are. They still occur, unexplained, today. Astronomy textbooks give the general feeling that the glows are illusions of some kind that are either minor physical peculiarities or more likely don't concern science at all.

We do know, now, that the Moon is a lifeless ball of rock. Shortly before Apollo 11 landed on the Sea of Tranquillity in July 1969, most scientists were reasonably certain that the Moon was airless and waterless, rocky rather than icy. Apollo 8 had flown around it ten times at Christmas of 1968 and said so. The astronauts described pretty much exactly what the scientists expected they would.

Only the fine details were still uncertain. For example, there was concern that the Moon might be harboring alien microbes with the potential to cause mass infection on the Earth, so mission planners quarantined the astronauts after the first few Apollo landings. Some geologists were concerned that Moon rocks suddenly exposed to oxygen in the spacecraft might burst into flames. At least one reputable scientist was convinced that the Moon was covered with a very light powder, into which Neil Armstrong, Buzz Aldrin, and the *Eagle* would disappear forever.

But in general the most conventional theories were borne out. *Eagle* landed on firm soil. The astronauts found only rocks and dust. Gravity was low. Nothing moved that the astronauts did not kick up themselves. The Moon's mountains and plains *looked* different from any Earth landscape, but this too was generally predictable. Armstrong reported that the landscape appeared amazingly sharp and clear because of the lack of atmosphere, but he found it difficult to judge sizes and distances because there was nothing familiar for comparison. In brilliant sunlight the rolling land was tan-colored, and in the shadows of rocks and hills it was ashen gray. To Aldrin, coming down the ladder shortly after Armstrong, everything seemed somewhat disorderly, but peculiarly precise. It was an emptiness of rock and dust, lifeless. And yet the shapes affected them, and Armstrong said, "It has a stark beauty all its own." A few minutes later Aldrin framed the oxymoron-like fragment: "Magnificent desolation."

This is exactly what the scientists, and any one conversant with postwar science and astronomy, expected. The Moon corresponded exactly to the theory with which it was most closely approached.

* * *

Every observation, rock and bag of dust the Apollo 11 astronauts picked up in their 2 1/2 hours of poking around on the Moon's surface was important to the scientists. The astronauts' bodily responses, conditions, and functions were of great interest. What the astronauts thought and experienced while on the Moon was of less importance.

Most of the literature on the astronauts' personal, inner responses focuses on their feeling of being surrounded by beauty and desolation. All the Apollo astronauts, with few exceptions, apparently, were greatly affected by the sight of the blue, cloud-swirling Earth rising over the Moon's horizon. For the most part, not much more is made of the astronauts' inner experiences.[2]

This is because, except in clinical psychological terms, the astronauts' thoughts are of little interest to science. But Aldrin's oxymoron might be of considerable interest to Parmenides or Socrates. Aldrin had a deep sense that the world around him was desolate, which is to say, empty; it was nothing. He was there to scrutinize, as closely as he could in only a few hours, what some inner sense was telling him is not all of what is. At the same time, he and Armstrong both experienced a sense of tremendous beauty. The surface of the Moon is desolate yet magnificent.

Between desolation and magnificence, surely magnificence is of greater interest because it clearly *is: it is the quality of the experience of desolation.* Magnificence—or in Socratic terms, Beauty—is not the rocks and craters themselves, it is not the Earth rising over the tan aridity of the Moon. "To think and to be are one and the same." Magnificence indicates the existence, not of the rocky Moon, but of the mind that is making sense of the Moon.

The Apollo scientists, however, were intent upon the desolation. They wanted to know about the color of the rocks, their variety, the shape of landscapes, the measurements of gravity, and whatever else the public will never know about. The Moon is an object, an accumulation of lifeless substances that have undergone geological activities and have lain silent and locally inert for billions of years.

It's as though, after four hundred years of figuring and refiguring, we have focused our attention on one aspect of reality, decided it is

what is, and systematically excluded all other aspects as *what is not.*
Even though it is plain even in the mouth of the second man to step
foot on the Moon that what is generally held to be *not* is in fact
expansively *what is.* And even though it is plain that what is generally
held to exist, does not absolutely exist: it is an illusion created by
swirling electrons, whose own existence is only marginally verifiable
by mathematical equations and streaks of light on photographic film.
The technological achievements of science are spectacular: medicine,
transportation (trips to the Moon!), housing, electric lighting, food
storage, information processing and transmission, weapons, and so
on. But science has also explicitly denied that other spectacular ranges
of human experience are even real. There is no God. A dream is an
evolutionary survival mechanism. Science cannot explain the humor
in a joke, and does not seek to because humor is not objective; in a very
real scientific sense, humor is not real.

It was inevitable that the Apollo astronauts would find a lifeless
Moon. In theory they could not find anything else. One wonders what
Parmenides or Socrates would have found, if they had been able to go
there. It would have included what Aldrin described, but would have
radically differed because they would have approached the Sea of
Tranquillity with a completely different theory of reality. They would
have seen a reality indescribable and perhaps unbelievable to us. They
might have told stories of guiding goddesses and firelit caves.

In one sense, we think of our time as a tremendous Golden Age of
human existence. The rise of scientific reasoning prompted philosophers to name the eighteenth century the Age of Enlightenment, and
all through the twentieth century, science has been confidently
described as the most accurate and successful method for explaining
and theorizing about the universe ever devised by human beings.
Given the astonishing material comforts we now have, even in parts of
poor countries, there is much circumstantial evidence to support the
validity of this description. Parmenides the naturalist would surely be
impressed. Our material lives seem magnificent.

In another sense, we think of our time as degenerate. The most
horrible wars and most extensive atrocities against human beings and
the planet itself have been conducted in the last two hundred years. A

general degeneration of moral sensibilities is described again and again, everywhere in the Western world. People in the industrialized world are bored, angry, and resentful even though they have more material comforts than any human beings in any time. Our inner lives seem desolate.

If science has indeed been investigating illusions, as Parmenides' ideas suggest, then it has been returning to us more illusions. If any of this is true, then centuries from now (if they exist in human terms), historians might describe the age of science as the Great Dark Age of humanity when the knowledge of *what is*—the magnificence experienced by Buzz Aldrin, the thought or mind spoken of by Parmenides, Plato, Plotinus, the Vedas, Christ—was systematically eradicated and replaced by the illusory knowledge of *what is not*—the desolation.

* * *

When the Apollo 14 astronaut Stuart Roosa visited Nepal in 1975, he talked to some schoolchildren about his flight to the Moon. One of the kids asked, "Who did you see there?" Roosa answered, "No one. There is nothing there."

Later he learned that one of the teachers took the child aside to clarify what Roosa had said. The teacher told the child the astronaut didn't know what he was talking about. For as all Nepalese know, the Moon is where the souls of the dead go. It could not be true that "nothing is there" because Heaven is there.

Stuart Roosa and his wife felt bad about this after it happened. They wished they had been briefed more thoroughly beforehand about the culture they were visiting. This means, presumably, that Roosa felt he could, given adequate information, have framed an answer to the child's question that created the illusion that Roosa did indeed believe he had seen, on the Moon, something. Even though he thought he saw nothing.

In the age of science, the belief that Heaven is in the Moon seems quaint. From another perspective, the belief that you can solve all your problems if you can just acquire enough facts, also seems sort of quaint.

Speaking and thinking are the same as *what is*. This does not mean, however, that we invent our own reality. Both Parmenides and Neils Bohr roughly agree on these points. Parmenides declares categorically that *what is*, is, and that *what is not*, is not. This is not a matter *decided* by thought, but shaped by thought. Bohr says quantum physics indicates that an observer's mind plays a role, complementarily, in the results of an experiment. But this does not mean the mind re-formulates the structure of molecules.

There are illusions and there are truths about reality. The natural world is (apparently) an illusion of some kind. It is an image, science explains, formed by subatomic particles. In Plato's terms, this description is nearly as far away from reality as it's possible to be, and still not be in the (non-)realm of *what is not*. Closer to the truth will be a correct opinion of the nature of the object. This includes the object's image as a starting point (which is probably what Parmenides the naturalist meant), but also the actual object of knowledge, which is the essential being of the thing. Probably, in the same way that we can't know exactly what or where an electron is, we can't objectively know essential being. We are faced with our own theories and descriptions. To speak is to think.

Science is an intellectual edifice made of words. It is a vast, incomprehensibly-detailed description of physical objects and events together with theories about the objects and events. If you tried to grasp all of science whole, in your mind, you would come up against a swamp of inconsistencies, logical contradictions, unexplainable peculiarities like lunar transient events and appearing and disappearing subatomic particles. You would find almost nothing about your actual inner experiences of beauty, conscience, courage, temperance, evil, and so on; most scientific discussions of them would divert from the actual experiences and refer to them as chemical activities or as symbols without concrete reality.

It all sounds very desolate. It gives you a desolate feeling, as though you had looked directly at the surface of the Moon and seen nothing. No one is there.

Notes

1. Quotations of Parmenides are from *Parmenides and Empedocles: The Fragments in Verse Translation*, translated by Stanley Lombardo (San Francisco: Grey Fox Press, 1982).

2. There are, of course, exceptions. Edgar Mitchell during the return journey of Apollo 14 experienced a contemplative or mystical state of consciousness, and later founded the Institute of Noetic Sciences. It was clear to him, apparently, that what happens in the mind is at least as important as what happens to the body. See his book, *The Way of the Explorer* (New York: Putnam's, 1996).

Soul Loss and Soul Making

KABIR HELMINSKI

THE GREATEST TRUTHS and aspirations are perpetually at risk of being subverted from their highest possibilities. We see tendencies arising these days which are rationalized through a spiritual rhetoric yet lack a spiritual center and which therefore are at the mercy of distortion by the ego and its narcissistic demands. This is especially true when there is any opportunism, any possibility of telling the ego what it wants to hear, rather than telling the Truth. These can take the form of celebrity spirituality, quantum affluence, psychological polytheism, mythological paganism, mystical eroticism, ego-empowerment, get-what-you-want-mysticism. Each in subtle and not so subtle ways misplaces the center, and is therefore out of balance.

So many new beginnings have come and gone, leaving behind a trail of disillusionment and pain. Well intentioned efforts are always in danger of narrowly missing their mark and continuing on a deviated trajectory. Small errors of judgment and metaphysical principles become the twofold and threefold compounding of errors.

Our postmodern world has seen a profound disillusionment with the Judeo-Christian monotheistic tradition, as well as with the scientific materialism that largely superseded it. This disillusionment has become so thorough among some people that we are seeing a reaction against these worldviews in the name of the "new." At the root of this reaction may be a wish to restore a lost wholeness, to heal a deep division within the psyche.

While reactions against religions which have abandoned their own wisdom tradition or against a science which could not respond to the needs of the soul are understandable, and to some extent justifiable, the reaction is in danger of being so extreme and unbalanced that it denies what has been known and practiced by authentic wisdom traditions for countless centuries. If Western culture has been ill, then psychological polytheism and other regressive cultural currents are not the remedy, but signs of a hypersensitive immune system, or, in other words, an allergic response.

Perhaps the most important contribution that any authentic wisdom tradition can make is that of establishing the quality of discernment based on clear spiritual criteria. This metaphysical clarity can be a spiritual compass in our ever-changing cultural environment, and can lead us beyond metaphysics to a deepening experience of the inward reality of the human being.

Considering the waves of invented spiritualities and pop psychologies which besiege us, I feel it is appropriate that some of their tendencies be made more explicit and seen in the light of traditional spirituality and the monotheistic perspective. In some important respects, many of these self-applied remedies further the illness. I approach these issues neither in the name of a "monolithic monotheism" nor any form of "orthodoxy," but from a wish to do justice to and preserve the attainments of those whose exploration of the Divine Imagination has not been in vain.

Within the broadly tolerant culture of our time, few people seem to have much passion or conviction about metaphysical principles. If the Prince of Darkness himself were to offer a workshop at one of today's growth centers, there would very likely be any number of people who would give him a fair hearing and perhaps find quite a few ideas to agree with, before going on to the next lecture or workshop. This willingness to consider anything is one of the naive virtues of our time, but if this openness does not lead to some developing certainty based on inner knowing, we are lost in the shifting sands of conjecture.

Often, the new spiritualities appear on the scene as if humankind had never faced the essential problems of human existence before. I do not wish to demonize these approaches or their proponents, but I believe truth and error sometimes stand very close together. Eventually, however, truth does stand out from falsehood, although we may have wasted precious time and resources for not having discerned one from the other earlier.

The Imaginal Power of the Soul

It is a common enough notion that modern humanity is suffering from a loss of soul which can be traced to the quantification and intellectualization of reality.

The development of soul depends on our understanding of what the soul is and what its possibilities are. What has to be restored is the presence of soul and its imaginative powers, but souls can be sick or healthy; souls can be created in this "vale of soul-making," and souls can also be lost.

The prevailing Western culture, especially of the last century or so, has recognized only two forms of knowledge: the concrete/sensory and the abstract/conceptual. We have sense impressions and we have ideas. The proposition "wheresoever you look, there is the Face of God" would be viewed as neither a statement of sensory fact, nor as a valid hypothesis deduced from sensory experience, but as a statement of the religious imagination. According to our cultural prejudices, whether the statement is inspiring or entertaining, it is imaginary, and what is imaginary is not real.

That existence can be imagined to be the "Face of God" signifies a way of perceiving which depends on a psychospiritual power which has more or less atrophied in modern humans. We have to rediscover it in order to know the value of the knowledge it offers. This psychospiritual power has been called the Active Imagination and its field of perception is neither the world of abstract impersonal concepts nor the world of sensory data, but the imaginal world (*mundus imaginalis* in Latin, or *alami mithal* in Arabic).

This "active imagination" is a term used by classical Sufis who represented a metaphysics of pure monotheism in which only God, i.e. the Self, is real, while the "I" that separates itself from this unified reality is unreal.

The mundus imaginalis is a level of reality in which "meanings" are embodied as images which have a kind of autonomous existence. The alami mithal is an "interworld" in which visions, which are simultaneously meanings, are experienced by a psychospiritual faculty, the active imagination, or what Sufis would simply call the "heart." It is important to realize that this level of perception was reliably available only to those souls which were to some extent "purified." In its mature functioning it was certainly not a conceptual, intellectual, or merely symbolic experience, but a visionary one of the kind that many Western psychospiritual explorers touch only rarely in their life, but which is the natural medium of mature mystics. It is not uncommon for a Sufi to ask another, "Did it happen in the tangible world or in meaning (*mana*)." Regardless of whether the experience of the active imagination is in a "dream" or in wakefulness, it has the quality of profound significance.

For some, whom I will call the psychological polytheists, the mundus imaginalis is the playground of "the gods." They have appropriated the concept of the interworld for very limited purposes. The mundus imaginalis is not to be unlocked by either fantasy or intellect, but by the purified heart, understood here as a subtle but penetrating cognitive faculty of mind beyond intellect.

When it is proposed that modern man has lost his soul, one meaning is that we have lost our ability to perceive through the Active Imagination which operates in an intermediate world—an interworld between the senses and the world of ideas. This Active Imagination is the imaginative, perceptive faculty of the soul, which cannot be explained because it is itself the revealer of meaning and significance. The Active Imagination does not produce some arbitrary concept standing between us and "reality," but functions directly as an organ of perception and knowledge just as real as—if not more real than—the sense organs. And its property will be that of transmuting and raising sensory data to the purity of the subtle, spiritual world. Through the Active Imagination the things and beings of the earth will be made incandescent. This imagination does not construct something unreal, it unveils the hidden reality. It helps to return the facts of this world to their spiritual significance, to see beyond the apparent and to manifest the hidden.

The function of this power of the soul is in restoring a space that sacralizes the ephemeral, earthly state of being. It unites the earthly manifestation with its counterpart on the imaginal level, and raises it to incandescence. Isn't this what is sought by most of those who are drawn to paganism, mythologies, and mystical eroticism?

Reinventing the Soul

One of the ideas that has gained some currency is a reinvention of the meaning of "soul." Soul has commonly meant one's essential, spiritual identity, one's deepest self. Yet according to this reinvented view, soul is somehow contrasted with or opposed to Spirit.

In some forms of this view, the soul has become a catchall term for deep, moist, feminine, imagistic energies that love to taunt, distract, and otherwise harass the rigid, self serious ego and the well-meaning, but rather dry and all-too-highbrow spirit. Yet this "soul," at the same time, is also understood as the key to meaning, love, religious concern. Sometimes it seems that all that is left over for poor old spirit is but an impersonal bird's-eye view of all the messy stuff of life.

It is difficult to argue with concepts and categories that are often amorphous and self-contradictory. Is the matter of soul so beyond definition, beyond principles, that we can only make poetic lunges at meaning which lead to no particular conclusion? It may be that soul cannot be confined by anyone's definitions and is fundamentally a mystery. Nevertheless, the idea of "soul" has a history within Western spiritual tradition.

The Neoplatonic heritage to which most Western spiritual thinkers must trace their idea of soul can be read very differently. According to Plotinus, for instance, the human "soul" was originally free and supersensuous, but turned its gaze earthward and bodyward and so fell into this earthly existence. Having lost its original freedom, its fulfillment will consist in "remembering" its condition prior to this involvement with flesh and the material world. The true self which consists of *logos* and *nous*, pure knowing and reflection, later became obscured or veiled by the animal appetites and the desire to fashion material. As a preparation for visionary contemplation, this true soul must first go beyond the conceptualizations of the philosophers, and then must purify itself of the contamination of the body and its sensuality. Even this, however, is not the final stage. Union with the Divine can only be known through ecstasy, namely when the soul is taken out of itself and reaches identity with Spirit.

It is not among the realized saints of Spirit that we find dryness and denial of the earthly, but among the "pharisees," and certain academics and religious professionals. The saints by contrast are the first to meet the salt of the earth on their own terms. This is what Spirit does, in addition to lifting the human being up. It is not Spirit which denies the validity of earthly existence, both its pleasures and suffering, but that indulgent hedonism, which is more likely to be the outcome of psychological polytheism's Felliniesque concept of soulfullness. Psychological polytheism conceives the psyche's basic structure to be an inscape of personified images. Through the lack of a true center, it diminishes and trivializes the human soul by reducing it to the terms and level of the social disease of our time: psychic fragmentation. Mysticism would propose that this is not the psyche's basic structure or nature, but only a superficial layer of the psyche. Beyond this psychological menagerie lies a deeper selfhood which alone can give order and meaning to life.

Doesn't it strike anyone as strange that the psyche should be composed of an inner pantheon of ancient literary creations, as if such a pantheon were an objective personification of the human psyche? Why select one mythology out of all the world's many mythologies and give it central importance, especially considering that it was probably supplanted many times over by later "myths" that were more alive and of much wider application? The return to mythology is a narrowing of our consciousness on an archaic and idiosyncratic soap opera, which is not to say that some human psychological truth can't be found in it. But just because the human psyche creates characters does not necessarily mean that the human psyche is determined by the characters it created.

Yet a pure monotheism need not be monolithic nor abstract. Zoroastrian monotheism had its angels: an angel of the earth, angels of the mineral and vegetable worlds, an angel of feminine wisdom, an angelic counterpart for each human soul. Islam, the matrix within which ecstatic Sufism arose, has its Divine Attributes, which fall into the two categories of gentleness and rigor, intimacy and awe, hope and fear. Although Plotinus did not reject polytheism out of hand, he saw the "gods" as manifestations of the One Divine. Historically, however, his successors deviated further and further until their polytheism degenerated into superstition, magic, and theurgy, which are distractions from the One Spirit and Unity of all existence. Psychological polytheism could contribute to a similar degeneration.

What distinguishes psychological polytheism from monotheism is not its willingness to admit diversity; rather, it is that polytheism has no center. Polytheism is a not an uncommon state in the modern world, an unconscious and chaotic idolatry of appearances, a fragmentation and disintegration of the psyche, which is a living Hell. It is the state of the one whose identity is always shifting, a dissociation of voices and images absorbed from the mass media, an identity without integration. A comedian like Robin Williams, who can shift persona in mid-sentence, is an entertaining example of psychological fragmentation; at least he makes us laugh. Some would have us believe that we are nothing but a menagerie of animals and mythological figures, and that any integration around a center is a ploy and fantasy of the ego.

One of Jung's contributions to our understanding of the psyche is the discovery of autonomous complexes (archetypes) that create drives and produce images and stories that seem to have lives of their own. These archetypes are relatively independent of the conscious ego and are sometimes opposed to it. Jung, however, believed in a central and essential archetype, the Self, which is the unifying principle of all other archetypes. For Jung, all archetypes were in service of the Self, and the end of conscious development is a harmony between ego and Self.

It is true that our greatest disease in this postmodern era is "the loss of soul," but this is not necessarily because we have denied the image-making capacities of the psyche (our culture is dominated by images), nor because we have denied ourselves a soulful sensuality (we live in the era of unrepression), nor because we live at such a spiritually transcendent height. We have lost our soul, our interiority, within the artificial and unnatural conditions we have accepted as everyday life, which requires an extraordinary sense of purpose to sustain that interiority. We have set in motion forces which have their own oppressive momentum oblivious to the rhythms of the human soul. As a result, we have surrendered to compulsive and stressful living, and have seen our attention fragmented. More and more, these unnatural conditions have driven us toward more unconscious sensuality and materialism in a blind effort to grasp something real.

Psychic Fragmentation and Spiritual Minimalism

As we are pulled into the future, our developing technologies shrink time and space, while increasing information. More and more information and fantasy is available and it is available more easily and cheaply. Whether we gain access to this new world of fantasy, instant shopping, and pornography by cable in Atlanta or through a "satellite walla" in a Calcutta slum, old boundaries are dissolving and new "realities" are beckoning.

Satellite television, VCRs, computer networks are offering us a world of entertainment and distraction, most of it created and controlled by commercial producers whose main interest is to make profits. In traditional, premodern societies, culture developed out of whatever sacred framework the tribe or community shared. Such sacred frameworks were the repository of wisdom and experience and of the needs of the unconscious. Today's mass culture is created by marketing departments who are seeking to hold people's attention by any means possible, regardless of whether what is communicated affords any personal, social, or spiritual benefit.

Our subconscious dream life has now been exteriorized through the omnipresence of surrealistic images and sounds. It could also be proposed that the entertainment environment is degrading our subconscious psyche by indiscriminately, if not perversely, catering to our appetites and egoism.

We may be creating psychic ghettos in which a poverty of human values, an unemployment of creative powers, and an overcrowding of inner space lead to gratuitous violence, atrophy of will, and addiction to mind- and heart-numbing entertainment. Just as the sociological ghetto is the outcome of our dark side of economic exploitation and social injustice, leading to the fragmentation of the family and community, so with the new psychic ghetto of inner world decay.

The perverse individualism we have accepted as normative is based not so much on the human being as the center of the universe, but on human egoism having usurped the wholeness of the human mind. Many human problems are rooted in the slavery of the human ego to a formless, unconscious, selfish search for individual pleasure which becomes increasingly a numbing addiction.

This tyranny of the ego is the direct result of the abandonment of the principles of transformation, sacred to all traditional wisdom cultures, involving sacrifice, love, presence, humility, and surrender to the Way of the Universe.

It may seem unfashionable, untimely, or politically incorrect to offer a prophetic voice at this time, but perhaps we need a reminder that many "civilizations" before us have perished through their own excesses, the loss of control of their own selves, their transgressions of common sense, harmony, and balance.

Not all choices and developments in an individual human life or in a society's life are necessarily the healthy self-correcting, self-regulating powers that may sometimes be found in a healthy or nearly healthy psyche. Sometimes the unconscious (heart) has the power to guide, heal, and redirect the conscious (ego), but this exteriorized dream world we are living in may be the nightmare of a collective mental illness.

If so, what are our possibilities and choices? The conscious self can make certain decisions and choices which reflect upon the health, and, might we say, purity of the unconscious. In the past, these choices would have been informed by the collective wisdom of the culture, a wisdom which included such values as humility, self-respect, patience, sacrifice, and self-awareness. But then the culture might have been the product of some wisdom and not of mere marketing. Hearts need education and refinement just as the body needs exercise and modera-

tion. While a large percentage of our planet's population is malnourished, a large percentage of industrial culture is overfed and toxic.
Likewise, to the extent that we do not incorporate some conscious
principle of transformation, some uplifting agency, our souls are
malnourished and toxic, our hearts are numb, and our wills are
atrophied.

Perhaps what is called for at this time, more than anything else, is a
spiritual minimalism, a reliance on the principle of less is more: less
distraction, less cynicism, less entertainment, less pleasure seeking for
its own sake, less indiscriminate consumption of information and
fantasy, and more inner silence, more concentration upon our own
nature and being, more unmediated sharing of each others' simple
human presence, more development of our innate human qualities of
friendship, nurturing, awareness, sensitivity, humbleness, and awe.

The outer dream that surrounds us may be the manifestation of our
own psychic fragmentation. It may be less an embodied vision than a
broadcast, commercially sanctioned schizophrenia. When the heart
has been awakened and refined, its dreams are freed from neurotic
subjectivity and become more objective, symbolic, and inspired.
These are obviously not the dreams our consumer culture is dreaming.
It doesn't take a brilliant observer to realize that the quality of our
dreams has been becoming more morbid and perverse even in the
relatively tiny span of recent decades. How will we wake from this
disturbed sleep? Are these the symptoms of an illness that will finally
be acknowledged? Where would we find the collective will to commit
ourselves to our own recovery?

The Soul as Unifying Center, Presence, Interior Space

If there is a realm of soul it is this: presence, which is the attribute
of the Self, the center of the being, and which as center can integrate
all the levels of the human being. Presence is a faculty that operates at
all levels of being and which also makes the mundus imaginalis
intelligible, but only if we have "presence" on that level of refinement,
which may only be achieved by not being dominated or ruled by
sensual concerns—which is not the same as denying or repressing

them.

The psychological polytheists often attack a caricature of spiritual work—which is not to say that such caricatures do not exist and thrive in the marketplace—which focuses on the transcendent at the expense of the immanent. It is true that there are pathologies of spiritual aspiration. But the realization of the spiritual is always allied with a realization of our own humanness in humility. It is the helplessness of our human situation, our weakness in relation to our subconscious complexes that lead us to surrender to the wholeness of the Self. While the unconscious may produce complexes that challenge the autonomy of the ego, the soul is precisely that unifying presence and interiority which experiences and reconciles our finite humanness and our spiritual transcendence. Both the ego and the unconscious complexes, on the one hand, and Spirit, on the other, are held within the embrace of presence.

All true spiritual work is based on the unity of these different aspects of our being. An alternative to the conception of the human being proposed by psychological polytheism and other regressive pathways, and one more consistent with the highest wisdom traditions, would be the following model, which is based on three essential factors combining to form a whole. The terms that must be used in English are, unfortunately, somewhat vague and imprecise. By defining our terms, however, we can give these terms a more exact meaning within the context of our studies.

1) The "ego" (or natural self, eros), a complex of psychological manifestations arising from the body and related to its survival. It has no limit to its desires, but it can supply the energy necessary to aspire toward completion, or individuation.

2) The "spirit" or "spiritual self" (essential self, essence, *logos*, *nous*), the center which is capable of conscious reflection and higher reason and is in communication with the spiritual world. The essential self can help to guide the natural self, limit its desires to what is just and reasonable, and, more importantly, help it to see the fundamental desire behind all desires: the yearning to know our Source. It can help

to establish presence on all levels of our being.

3) The "soul," sometimes called "the heart" (including the psychic functions, active imagination, presence), and interior presence which includes the subconscious faculties of perception, memories, and complexes, and which can be under the influence of either the ego or the spiritual self. When we speak about involving ourselves "heart and soul" we are speaking about this aspect of ourselves. Living from the heart, having a pure heart refers to a deep condition of spiritualized passion. Losing one's soul refers to a condition of having the soul dominated by material, sensual, and egoistic concerns. Such a "heart and soul" is veiled, dim, unconscious. The heart is the prize that the "animal self" and "spiritual self" struggle to win, but when it is dominated by the "animal self" it is not truly a heart at all.

4) The "individuality" (the result of the relationship of the other three). When the spiritual self has been able to harmonize with the natural self, and "heart and soul" have been purified, then the human being exists as a unified whole, fully responsive to the divine, creative will.

One way to conceive of this model is as three successive layers. The outer layer is the "natural self" which contains the deeper level of "the soul" within which is contained "the spirit." If the soul, as presence, is not in place, there cannot be a relationship between the natural self and spirit.

We are not the first people on earth to attempt to understand the human soul and its purpose in the universe, nor are we necessarily the best prepared or the most mature. The principles of the Way are neither so mysterious nor complex. Essentially the work means transforming the ego, the desire nature. Some religious traditions have proposed weakening the ego and the body in order to experience the spiritual self, but weakening ourselves is denying what we have been given. A more complete way is to strengthen the essential, spiritual self, purify the heart and bring ego and eros into harmony with it. Only a strong and healthy individuality can reach completion, or gnosis. The individuality needs strength and passion to reach spiritual completion.

Both the spiritual self and the body have their needs. The body needs to be cared for, nurtured, trained, and exercised. It should not be allowed to dominate the heart. The more the animal side dominates, the more the heart is weighed down. The more the spiritual self predominates, the more lightness and spirituality we feel, the more our desires are in harmony with the Divine will. Such a person will be content with relatively little in the material world, whereas a person dominated by their ego's desires will never have enough sex, pleasure, *serenity* money, or power. All of existence is the manifestation of Spirit in a vastly colorful and real array. The soul and its imaginative power is that which experiences Spirit, unless, of course, it only experiences the body and its emotions.

Psychological polytheism seems to overlook the degree to which the unconscious complexes may also be related to the ego. The ego, then, in a desperate attempt to assure its own survival at the expense of the wholeness of mind, can produce unconscious complexes of nightmarish power. One suspects that what is sometimes meant by soul may be the deep voice of eros/ego, of hedonism, of narcissism, of simple indulgence.

Perhaps, real healing and real wholeness on the individual level is when we operate as a whole, when we are not in disabling conflict, emotionally or physically. On the spiritual level, health is realizing that we are integral to this universe, not a part of it, not a microcosm of it, but coextensive and consubstantial with the Whole, the true Center. The awakened soul is characterized by presence of heart. Through its purified imaginative powers, the awakened soul raises earthly and ephemeral facts to the level of spiritual incandescence. By virtue of its reconciling power it brings about a loving marriage between the natural self (ego/eros) and spirit.

The world is a place for fashioning the soul, in the sense that soul is not given to us automatically, despite our assumptions to the contrary. Our interiority, our presence, must be created from within the distractions and forgetfulness of everyday outer life, from within the constant clash of pleasure and pain, happiness and loss. Our soul is a space for our experience; it makes the difference between being nominally alive and consciously alive. It makes a real connection possible between the ego and Spirit.

Ideal Beauty and Sensual Beauty in Works of Art

APHRODITE ALEXANDRAKIS

IT IS A FACT THAT CERTAIN OBJECTS are set apart by particular cultures and considered to be aesthetic objects, and are considered as having that interest alone. In this case, aesthetic interest is consequently directed to some objects and not to others. Philosophers of art often try to clarify the nature of this aesthetic interest by asking what makes some objects and not others valuable in this peculiar way. Frequently, however, this "aesthetic interest" toward "aesthetic objects" varies from one civilization to another. In fact, sometimes, aesthetic interest seems not to be present. For example, though the Egyptians appreciated fine craftsmanship, their sculptures and paintings were seldom placed for the benefit of spectators, but were instead hidden away in the darkness of tombs. They did not seem to have distinguished their perceptions of art from their religious and political attitudes, nor did they view art as presenting special problems. As a result, "aesthetic interest" had not been developed or felt amongst people.

The Greeks, on the other hand, did make this distinction, though not as clearly as it has been made in modern times. Bosanquet, in his *History of Aesthetic*, calls a passage from Homer "one of the earliest aesthetic judgments that Western Literature contains." Homer says that on the shield of Achilles made by Hephaestus, *"the earth looked dark behind the plough, and like to ground that had been ploughed although it was made of gold; that was a marvelous piece of work!"* This Homeric exclamation of aesthetic admiration gives rise to aesthetic questions, such as the question of appearance versus reality and the relationship between the image and the actual object that it represents.

But Homer marked only the beginning of this distinction of aesthetic interest and aesthetic object. Democritus (460 B.C.E.) was the first philosopher to work out a full theory of the relativity and subjectivity of secondary qualities, as contrasted with the properties of the atoms. Note that before Democritus, Parmenides (500 B.C.E.) had titled the two halves of his great poem "On Truth" and "On Seeming" (opinion). A second development in Greek culture, the symbolic invention of poetry and music by the gods, helped prepare the way for full-fledged aesthetic inquiry.

A little later, Plato began the debate over the role of the arts in a good society, a debate that continues even today. Presently, the debate over what is considered obscene and pornographic, and the elimination of such works from exhibiting in art galleries, has been a center of attention for various professionals in the field. Also, a great deal of attention has been paid to the impact of explicit sexuality and violence on the young. And today, just as in Plato and Aristotle's time, there are professionals making claims either for or against the influence of violence and immorality in television, film, and art on the behavior of youth. The current debate mirrors the dispute between Plato and Aristotle over what is good and bad art, and on whether beauty involves moral or aesthetic elements only.

This short essay's aim, however, is not to determine what is moral or immoral in the works of art from Plato's time to the twentieth century, but rather to make the distinction between the Platonic notion of *ideal beauty*, and Aristotle's notion of *sensual beauty* in works of art. I will therefore not address the issue of the proper role of art in society. But since I will be referring to sensual art I would like to first mention a few things about pornography in order to clarify its sharp difference from *sensual art* and art in general as I see it.

A few years ago, an exhibit of photographs caused an enormous stir and led members of Congress to place restrictions on the support provided by the National Endowment for the Arts to all artists. This exhibit was not only considered pornographic, but it was also seen as an insult to the public and their religious beliefs. Here, I would like to point out the following distinction: I think that even though pornography is of a sensual nature, art works of a sensual nature may not be pornographic. Pornography is exactly what the term denotes, and has nothing to do with artistic expression or art in general. Pornographic pictures stimulate sexual desires and lead to lustful thoughts. Contrary to what some may believe, I think that an artist, through his or her art works, should not be expected to move the viewer or reader to tears, laughter, indignation, or compassion. Instead, the viewer should be led into admiring something both mentally and visually beautiful—perhaps something like Clive Bell's "significant form." Consequently, the viewer's thoughts get stimulated and awaken a wonder or understanding of what is beauty and the beautiful; an intellectual satisfaction and appreciation.

In order to distinguish *ideal beauty* from *sensual beauty*, the term beauty must first be defined. Instead of comparing and contrasting the many definitions of beauty, I will refer to beauty as I understand it to be defined. This does not suggest by any means that I invented the theory of beauty myself. But through years of thinking about it and studying it, I have pulled together my own ideas and understanding of beauty. My approach to the understanding of beauty is formalistic, perhaps Platonic, and is therefore based on certain objective principles. All objects and things, whether artificial or not, have a form or specific configuration—a *schema*—an outline, that the object's appearance depends on. The exactness, balance, coherence, and interrelatedness of the object's lines and shapes will result in rhythm and harmony. One may ask "Yes, but what is form?"—a question for which there are numerous answers. It all depends on how one thinks about and envisions form. My understanding of form, and what immediately comes to my mind when I think of it, is the *whole*. But how do we look at an art object as a whole? A whole is such because it is made of individual parts, such as lines, shapes, color, texture, that are well balanced, have a continuous rhythm, and result in harmony. A good example would be Raphael's *School of Athens*. If the proportions of the various parts of an object's composition are the proper ones, then there is balance. Proportions are based on geometry and have the correct measurements. The correct proportions will reflect a good, positive impression to the viewer whether the art object is a painting, sculpture, or architecture. In other words, the object, or art work, has symmetry.

The second element to look for is *rhythm*. Rhythm is found in properly distanced repetitious lines, curves, shapes, and color. This may easily be detected in *The School of Athens* by noticing the repetition of motif—arches, lines, reliefs, sculptures, gestures, etc.

Finally, the third objective element to look for in a work of art is *harmony*. The word harmony means much more in Greek than it does when translated into English. When harmony refers to sculpture, painting, or to a poem, it means the rhythmical, balanced flow of lines, curves, colors, or words, from one part to another. But harmony means much more than this: among other things it means "fitting together," that everything is where it belongs. It also means calmness. But there are several degrees of harmony. The highest degree will be achieved by having the above qualities, plus a feeling of calmness that beautifies even more the art object itself. When all three elements— harmony, rhythm, and symmetry—are present in a work of art, they form a complete whole and they create a harmonious effect that leads to beauty. It was the combination of harmony, rhythm, and symmetry that gave Greek classical sculpture of the fifth century B.C.E. its serene, aloof, lofty, moral, and ideal appearance and meaning. A good example of this is the *Zeus of Artemision*. The contemplation of the formal qualities ends up causing the viewer to feel aesthetic satisfaction, that is, a mental kind of peaceful pleasure. This special, aesthetic pleasure is the result of appreciating the objective elements with disinterested- ness. This is reflected in what Plato said in the *Philebus* 51C–D:

> The beauty of figures (*schematon kallos*) which I am now trying to indicate is not what most people would understand as such, not the beauty of a living creature or a picture; . . . is something straight, or round, and the surfaces and solids . . . things like that are beautiful not, like most things, in a relative sense; they are always beautiful in their very nature, and they carry pleasures peculiar to themselves which are quite unlike the pleasures of scratching.

Similarly in *Philebus* 64E, Plato adds, "the qualities of measure (*metron*) and proportion (*symmetron*) invariably . . . constitute beauty and excellence."

What do all these have in common? The pure tone or hue, the straight line, the face and figure of Agathon, the Greek Krater, or temple? They have unity, regularity, and simplicity. All these qualities together make the whole harmonious. These qualities give the object an ideal character and they are the constituents of beauty. Appreciation of these qualities causes aesthetic pleasure, meaning in this context the pleasure of hearing music and poetry or seeing beautiful forms.

For Plato, this kind of pleasure ranks among the higher and finer pleasures available to a good man and a good citizen. Accordingly, he says, "the love of the beautiful is the love of the good." As a consequence, the Greeks made the noblest creations of artistic genius and exemplified beauty and grandeur in a concrete form. How did they succeed in this? There are several good reasons, too lengthy to address here. But in general they succeeded by following principles such as simplicity and purity of form, truth to nature, nobility of form, and majesty of expression—qualities that still command the admiration of the world. Pure form is therefore the essential quality that constitutes ideal art. It is important to understand, however, that pure form is not accidental. It is the result of the mind's thinking process; it is rational. As Hegel pointed out, "the beauty of art is the beauty that is born— born again, that is—of the mind . . . for such a fancy must at least be characterized by intellectual being and by freedom." The formal elements are therefore present in the artist's mind during creation.

The contemplation of the formal elements leads to the realization of ideal form. This in turn results in aesthetic appreciation, which is a peculiar kind of emotion. Aesthetic emotion therefore has nothing to do with feelings such as happiness or sadness. Instead, it is a peculiar feeling a viewer (or reader) experiences as a result of the realization and appreciation of the presence of lines, shapes, and colors, and their interrelationship that yields a unity, which in turn forms a whole. The subject matter plays no role at all, for if it did, it would have not been formal art, and the art work would have appealed to the senses as such.

The fact that ideal beauty is based on, and is reflective of the formal elements, does not necessarily mean that sensual beauty must lack formal elements. I call a sensual work of art one whose subject matter has been painted or sculpted realistically or even naturally. In this case, usually, the effect of the composition, or perhaps even the goal of the artist is not of an intellectual or spiritual nature, but of a rather realistic or naturalistic subject. One such example would be any eighteenth-century French Rococo painting by Watteau, Boucher, and others, or even Rodin's *The Kiss*. A certain hue, combination of colors, a particular pose, or expression may be painted or sculpted in a way expressing sensuality with emphasis on texture and emotion. Hence, sensual art is preoccupied with the physical, rather than the spiritual or intellectual, and therefore it appeals to the senses. It may even suggest sexuality, but this should not be confused with pornography. Although Plato's student, Aristotle, agreed with Plato that art is an imitation, he accepted sensual art. Contrary to Plato, he developed a positive attitude about the emotions aroused by art. Aristotle's presumption for accepting sensual art was of course that the formal (objective) elements were present as well. He believed it is the artist's fusion of thought and sense that produce the imitation that he is working on, i.e. rationality and emotion.

To summarize, I tried to illustrate the distinction between two kinds of beauty: ideal beauty and sensual beauty. Ideal beauty, the beauty of form, arises from properly combined formal (objective) elements such as harmony, rhythm, and symmetry, expressed in the proper combination and proportion of lines, shapes, and color. Sensual beauty's subject matter is presented realistically through sensuous colors and realistic expressions. Like ideal beauty, sensual beauty also includes the formal elements, but this is not its primary focus of attention. Finally, there are no degrees of beauty in formal or ideal beauty. Something is either beautiful, or it is not. On the contrary, sensual beauty's degree of beauty depends on the viewer and the subject matter.

Socrates and the Art of Dialogue

ROBERT APATOW

And if the questioner were one of the wise logic choppers who argue only to win, I would say to him: "My position has been stated; if I do not reason correctly, it is your job to take hold of my statement and refute it." However, if such people should wish to enter into a dialogue with each other as friends, like you and I are now, it would be necessary for them to be somewhat more gentle and to answer each other in a manner more appropriate to the dialectic. And equally important, it is the more dialectical approach not only to answer the truth but also to answer by means of those things which the questioner would agree he does know. I will then also try to speak to you in this way. So reason with me.

—Socrates, from Plato's *Meno*

IT IS THE GENIUS of a culture to transform a natural human activity into a spiritual art. The particular genius of the ancient Greeks was to transform communication into the art form they called *dialogos*. Although its principles are generally not recognized today, the knowledge of the art of dialogue has been preserved in the writings of Plato, which present the work of its greatest master, Socrates. Plato's works are a literary and idealized representation of the kinds of dialogues that actually took place between Socrates and many of the famous teachers and personages of classical Greece. The dialogues concerned philosophical questions like: What is Excellence? (*Meno*) What is Justice? (*The Republic*) What is Love? (*Symposium*).

The practice of dialogue is not limited to discussions of philosophy, but can be used to seek the truth in any personally significant discussion. The word "dialogue" literally means "through logos." In ancient Greek *logos* means "word," but also "reason," because the

Greeks recognized that all reasoning takes place through words. Simply put, then, to have a dialogue is to share reasoning.

When we enter into a dialogue with another person we relate through mind and gain a precious opportunity to reach genuine understanding. Understanding is not a physical thing, but is a spiritual power that brings souls into a state of unity; for understanding is the very bond of friendship, and the greater the understanding, the more intimate the bond.

This intimacy is achieved because unlike everything else in the physical world, thoughts are private, and so when we express our thoughts in words to another we express our minds and reveal who we truly are. Understandably, this is a fearful activity because in this revealing there is a risk that what we express may be rejected or judged as false. However, as in all things, the degree of risk is commensurate with the potential for benefit and growth. For as Socrates says, it is by the discovery of what is not true that our souls are liberated and most truly benefited.

The ancient Greeks were keenly aware of the dangers that false thinking could lead us to individually and socially. The ancient poets dramatized this most vividly in the great works of tragedy. And although they revealed that the root of all tragedy could be found in false beliefs, it was the work of philosophers, like Plato and Socrates, to bring humanity this art which functions as a means to liberate humankind from the grave danger of ignorance. Socrates called his art a kind of *midwifery* because through questioning he was able to deliver false beliefs from the souls of men and through dialectical questioning reveal their truth or falsity.

Socrates practiced his form of midwifery according to the definition of a classical art, a power or knowledge that is used to benefit others. We still use this idea of art in reference to things like the pilot's art of navigation or the healer's art. One practices the art not for one's own benefit but for the benefit of the subject who is in need of the art. For example, the healer does not practice his art of healing for his own benefit, but for the benefit of the patient. According to the principles of an art, the healer is paid for his time and not for his knowledge.

Socrates, however, never requested fees for his company, but believed he was called by the gods to help benefit his fellow citizens.

Socrates' life is an ideal for us today. In himself and with others, Socrates practiced dialogue as a means of seeking wisdom and testing the soul for the presence of any falsehood. He practiced dialogue in the spirit of friendship and compassion; and yet when he encountered hostility he was able to keep his cool and bring a manner of sincerity and directness that usually enabled the dialogue to continue, despite the aggressiveness of his interlocutor.

Many in Athens became quite suspicious of Socrates and the kind of life he led. In fact, Socrates reports that there was a long-standing prejudice against philosophers in his day. There were also a significant number of important Athenian citizens, who after encountering Socrates in dialogue, were angered because they were shown publicly to think they knew when they really did not know. Finally, three of these citizens brought Socrates to trial and charged him with corrupting the youth, not believing in the city's gods, and introducing new and strange divinities into the city. Socrates was found guilty and then put to death. At the end of Plato's *Phaedo*, the dialogue that narrates Socrates' last day, one of Socrates' friends says: "This was the end of our comrade, a man, as it appears to me, of all those we had known in that time, the noblest and the wisest and the most just."

Through the work of Plato, we have inherited the ancient art of dialogue that Socrates displayed in his life. By studying Socrates' life and these philosophical principles, we have the opportunity and responsiblity as lovers of truth to bring light into a world that is dominated by the darkness of ignorance. Today when philosophy is often considered useless or of no practical value, the Socratic commitment to reason, friendship, and truth-seeking is an ideal that all philosophers can strive to share and communicate.

The Spiritual Art of Dialogue for Today

In the Platonic dialogue called *Meno* (see quote above), Socrates explicitly presents the basic principles for the activity of dialogue, which I have adapted as a model and standard for contemporary

practice in my recent book *The Spiritual Art of Dialogue*. According to
the model, I have defined dialogue in the following way: *A dialogue is
a discussion that focuses on a certain question in which the participants join
together as friends to seek out the truth by following the logos.*

1. Focused Question

There are many forms of discussion, dialogue being one special
form. The most common form of discussion is what we can call
conversation. In a conversation people express different views on a
range of subjects without concern for where the conversation goes and
what twists and turns it may take. Often a conversation stays on a
particular subject because it is considered important or interesting,
but it doesn't necessarily have to. In order to have a dialogue, the
speakers must make a shared and conscious decision to enter into
dialogue, because a dialogue is a conscious endeavor. A dialogue
begins with a specific question or issue for exploration and aims to
remain on this path. Of course, within a dialogue, there are times when
an interesting side issue may arise. If the dialogists choose to follow the
direction of the side issue, then they do so consciously, and this is
termed a *digression.*

2. Search for Truth

People join in dialogue in order to search for the truth. Therefore,
the participants must trust that the truth of the issue exists. The
opposite approach is that of the skeptic, who claims that the truth
cannot be discovered. Whereas the skeptical approach closes us to the
investigation and search, the truth-seeking approach makes us active
and eager in our search and more open to possibilities. Even in the
discussion of the most difficult issues, it is the desire for and trust in a
genuine answer that must guide us in dialogue. In the search we do not
abandon our own questions and concerns, but we do put aside our
unsupported doubts.

3. Friendship

We can enter into this discussion as friends or competitors. Competitors enter into dialogue to win. Friends enter into dialogue

because they seek the truth. When competitors enter into a discussion, it is not called a dialogue, but a debate. In a debate, competitors no longer maintain the goal of truth, but instead utilize any means to win a war of words. In a friendly dialogue it is of no concern who is right or wrong; the only concern is for the truth. Dialogue demands the spirit of friendship because dialogue is a kind of relationship that demands a spirit of care and concern, trust, understanding, and fairness from its participants.

4. Follow the Logos

Follow the logos means following the word. The dialogists must follow the word, because the word is the expression of the speaker's mind and the very means of communication. The logos, therefore, must be articulated and agreed upon. This means that the participants must clearly define key terms and articulate the principles of reasoning they appeal to when they make their argument.

For a dialogue to maintain its integrity, speakers and listeners must remain true to the words spoken. This goal requires that speakers try to express what they mean and for listeners try to listen attentively and not interpret the words that are heard. Interpretation is the process whereby ones adds or subtracts ideas from what one reads or hears. In this process one changes the very meaning of what is said, and the integrity of the communication is lost. Following the logos is perhaps the greatest challenge of dialogue.

The Process

The process of dialogue can be likened to a game with its own area of play defined by the time and space set aside and the agreement to the four principles. A specific question or issue is established by the participants who then take on the roles of *questioner* and *answerer*. The *answerer* presents his or her opinion and the questioner then asks questions that draw out the position so that it can be most fully understood, perhaps revealing the position's underlying assumptions. The roles then may be switched, if there is another position to be explored, or the dialogists can explore the question together starting without a position and sharing the desire to discover an answer.

Since the goal of dialogue is explication and understanding, arguing and debating are eliminated. Some of the possible results of a dialogue are the following: 1) greater understanding of each others' positions; 2) a shared appreciation of larger questions that need to be explored; 3) the shared recognition that one of the positions is false or inferior. On the other hand, if certain difficulties or differences block the achievement of one of these goals, those specific issues can become the subject of another dialogue.

The Ideal of Dialogue

This model we have presented functions as an ideal for our dialogues. By taking on this model in a conscious manner, we set out a standard for our discussions, a standard that is agreed upon and clear to all the participants. In the sphere of interpersonal communications, where emotions and one's own false projections often block the path to understanding, the shared commitment to a standard for dialogue brings an important element of objectivity to which each of the participants can appeal. Therefore, despite whatever disagreements may exist in the content of the discussion, dialogic partners can be united by their shared commitment to the ideal of the dialogue.

Most of the concerns we may have about dialogue in general, or in a particular dialogue, can be resolved by an appeal to one of the four principles outlined above. The key to using this model successfully is the willingness to express your concerns to your dialogic partner. For example, if you fear that your words will not be taken seriously or that you will be laughed at for what you say, you can appeal to the principle of friendship. If your partner has committed to this principle, then he or she should recognize what kinds of behavior are appropriate between friends. At the same time, it is important to recognize that we may violate these principles on occasion, so dialogists must also extend an appreciation of human limitations and look toward the four principles to help get the dialogue back on track.

As humans we all share the gift of words and reasoning, and inasmuch as this gift is a power, it has the equal ability to divide us through disagreement or unite us through understanding. In dialogue, we are challenged to present our own thoughts into words where they can be seen most clearly and evaluated most objectively. From the sincere questioning of our friends or lovers, we gain the opportunity to practice true philosophy and look within, rise above the limitations of our personal beliefs, awaken the highest part of the mind, free ourselves from what is false, and discover what is true. In the spirit of ancient philosophy, dialogue is a path towards personal growth in concordance with the eternal quest to fulfill the ancient Delphic exhortation—*Know Thyself.*

On Philosophical Midwifery: A Selection from Plato's Theaetetus

TRANSLATED BY ROBERT APATOW

SOCRATES: The art of the midwives is very great, but nonetheless, it falls short of what I do. For women do not give birth to images sometimes and true offspring at other times. It is not easy to make this kind of distinction. But if midwives were to judge the true and the false, it would be their greatest and noblest deed. Don't you think so?

THEAETETUS: Yes, I do.

SOCRATES: All that belongs to these midwives also belongs to my art of midwifery, but my art does differ in these respects. I practice midwifery on men and not women, and I examine the offspring of their souls, and not their bodies. But the greatest part of our art is to be able to test in every way whether the thought of a youth that is born to light is an image and falsehood or a genuine offspring and true. And there is also this which I share with the midwives. I am childless in wisdom, and what the many reproach me with is true; I ask others questions but I do not answer at all myself about anything because I have no wisdom. The reason for this is as follows. The God requires me to be a midwife, and so he prevented me from giving birth. I am therefore not at all a wise man, nor does there exist any kind of enlightened discovery in me being born as an offspring from my soul. And although those who associate with me at first appear sometimes very ignorant, all of them after continuing on in this relationship with me, that is, those with whom the God allows me to relate, make marvelous growth, as they themselves and their friends recognize. And it is clear that they are never learning anything from me, but they discover and give birth to many beautiful learnings by themselves and from themselves. And in truth both the God and myself are responsible for the delivery. And here is the proof. Many who are ignorant of this have attributed the delivery of these beautiful learnings to themselves and have scorned me and have persuaded themselves to leave sooner than was needed; and by leaving they have aborted their remaining offspring on account of their bad relations, and through their bad nurturing have also killed the offspring delivered by me; they have made falsehood and images more important than truth, and so in the end have shown themselves ignorant to themselves and to others. One of these is Lysimachus' son, Aristeides, and there have also been many others. When they come back again in need of the relationship with me and do remarkable things to get it, sometimes my daimon comes and prevents me from relating to them, but at other times, it allows it and again these people continue their growth. And, of course, the ones who associate with me have the same experience in giving birth. They go through the throes of labor and become filled with puzzlement both night and day, much more than those whom the God blocks me from associating with. My art is able to both rouse and cease the throes of labor, and those who are pregnant are affected accordingly. Sometimes, though, Theaetetus, there are some who do not appear to me to be pregnant at all, and since I know that they are in no need of my art, in a very kindly manner, I arrange a relationship for them. With the help of the God, I most satisfactorily place them in relationships that I believe are likely to benefit them. Many of these people I have given to Prodicus as students, and many to other wise and divine-sounding men. Now, I have explained this at length to you, my beautiful boy, for this reason. I suspect that you are in the throes of labor with something and in need of giving birth to it, as indeed you yourself suppose. Bring yourself to me as to the midwife's son and to my maieutic art; and the questions I ask eagerly answer however you are able. And when in my examination of what you say I lead to birth an image and untruth and I lift it away from under you and discard it, don't be savagely angry, like a mother protecting her first born. For there have been many already, oh marvelous youth, who were so angry at me that they were altogether prepared to bite me when I took away some foolishness from them; and they did not think that I did this because of my concern for them, since they were far from knowing that no god has bad intent towards man, nor do I perform this function with any bad intent. But it is the law of my very nature never to yield to falsehood nor to hide the truth.

Footprints on the Threshold

CHRISTINE RHONE

"The Science of Imagination is also the science of mirrors."
—Henry Corbin

IT ALL BEGAN with a walk in springtime on the Ridgeway, one of the oldest roads in England, a prehistoric track that runs many miles along the chalk spine of the White Horse Downs. Suddenly, as I advanced, I felt a sort of pulling sensation in my heart. This was a familiar signal that something was about to happen. As I rounded the bend, Silbury Hill came into view, its pyramidal shape like a gigantic Christmas pudding cooked by a green daemoness. On the flat-topped summit appeared a thick column of smoky white light, an aura crowning the hill and rising skyward. I knew then that there was some work to do here, that this was the place.

I returned to the Ridgeway again in early February at the time of Imbolc, when the first veil of spring is lifted with the coming of snowdrops. That morning, I had seen a fox darting fast across the road. Hours later I was startled by a sound behind me and stood still as a pack of beagles ran past, followed by a formal hunting party of some forty riders. Some hunters in Landrovers offered me a lift, but I went on by myself, walking rhythmically, my cape whipped by the wind. In the gray slanting light, the torn shapes of the clouds became a ship of ghosts, fatally wrecked, as the hunting party disappeared in pursuit of the glories of their old country traditions. The dogs had seemed so clean and educated, they had been almost smiling. I smiled to myself, mirroring them in my own pursuit of something fleeting.

The still water of the West Kennet canal was veiled in glassy patches of ice. The trees along the towpath were dusted green with lichen. All around, one could walk for miles among ancient earthworks and barrows, fields strewn with standing stones, along footpaths and byways, threading in and out of view of Silbury Hill and Avebury, the largest stone circle in Europe. The whole landscape seemed sculpted, but by whose hand? The crests of hills and ridges were as full of meaning as any earthwork, the difference between the created and the natural more a question of wording. Every summer the slopes became a showplace for local crop circle art, or else an elusive message board of non-human origin. The entire place is an arena where dreams and waking run races, swifter than time, and where the power of the Imagination outstrips all.

I stopped on the canalside at the Barge Inn for some warmth and wiped my muddy shoes. The ceiling was painted with a mandala of folklore figures and crop circle glyphs. What was the message of the column of light on Silbury Hill, I wondered. What was the work to do here in the Avebury area? How could I enact my admiration of this threshold place? To admire a thing is to reflect an image of it within oneself, to become its mirror. But I wanted to find a way to admire it unintrusively, almost secretly, without attempting to lift the veil, to remain on the threshold myself. Into this temple I would not barge. That was basic.

The column of light could be seen as a symbolic axis mundi or perhaps the base of a pillar of an invisible temple joining heaven and Earth. If the base of the pillar were reflected corporeally, this would be the feet. These could be used not to conquer distance and possess the place, but to touch its edges, encompass it, turn round it admiringly, orbit the magnetic attractiveness of the column of light at the center.

Checking my map, I saw that the pathways to which I had been instinctively drawn suggested the shape of an enormous footprint. The remaining parts of the outline could be found on the map by looking at the smaller byways more closely. If I walked its contour, my feet would become both an image and a mirror of foundation. I could draw the image with my footsteps, in an act of admiration that would seem as ordinary to passersby as would a rambling beagle.

The footprint was some sixteen miles in perimeter. The right side was the Ridgeway, and the heel, the earthworks along the Wansdyke.

The left side was composed of small roads and pathways going up through Beckhampton over Windmill Hill and beyond to a ruined stone circle at Lambourne Ground. The toes began there and went through Winterbourne Bassett and back up to the Ridgeway. The overall shape was as close to a rough print of a right foot, or the sole of a right shoe, as was possible while remaining within the confines of pathways currently marked on the map. I returned to Avebury in June to walk the outline of the footprint to celebrate the solstice, when the sun is said to stand still, and made my way among green paths and trees where floated white islands of elderflowers.

Half a year later, toward the winter solstice, I was in South India traveling on a dirt road, the edge of my dress still stained with the rusty red mud of the monsoon rains. My companion that day was an ecologist from Switzerland, who had agreed to accompany me for a couple of days to the Karthigai Deepam festival, a ritual pilgrimage up the holy hill of Arunachala. Children stared at his light hair as we drove through the tiny villages that dotted the rough plateau. The landscape was scattered with immense boulders, some balanced precariously on the tops of great outcrops of rock, the remainders of an ancient and heavily eroded chain of hills. The spirit of the place was austere and grave, a long tone opening in a deep silence.

For years I had been drawn to come to this holy hill. In the hermitage at its foot, I found unexpectedly that Avebury and Arunachala were connected. This link is in the story, told in the Puranas, of the hill's origin. It is said that Vishnu, the preserver, and Brahma, the creator, began to quarrel one day about which one of them was the greater. The dispute caused the universe to fall into chaos. Shiva, the destroyer, saw that the two had succumbed to delusion. Filled with compassion, he manifested as a colossal pillar of light to settle the argument, and proclaimed that the greater god would be the one who could find its beginning or end.

Vishnu took the form of a boar and began to burrow to find the base. After aeons of digging, he declared himself ready to submit to Shiva, his delusion destroyed. Brahma meanwhile had taken the form of a swan and had flown ever higher to find the summit, his frustration increasing the farther he went. Then he saw a mountain flower drifting down. He asked the flower where it had come from. "From the summit," it said. Exhausted and irritated, Brahma resorted to trickery. He asked the flower to vouch for him in front of Shiva, when he would claim that he had succeeded in getting to the top. The flower consented to the lie. Vishnu and Brahma went before Shiva. Vishnu bowed down to him with humility, while Brahma pretended to prostrate, aware that Shiva could see right through him. Brahma confessed. Shiva forgave him. Then, because the effulgence of the column of fiery light was too dazzling to behold, Shiva transformed himself into the hill of Arunachala.

Unlike other places sacred to Shiva, the hill is not the abode of the god, his dwelling, but is his very body. It is revered as the first and primordial lingam, and is one of the most ancient and sacred of all India's many holy places. Sri Shankara spoke of it as Mount Meru and considered it so sacred he could worship it only from afar. For Ramana Maharshi the hill is the heart of the Earth, the spiritual center of the world. Viewed from the side of the hermitage, it is a symmetrical hill flanked by two, almost equal foothills, said to be like the Self between two thoughts. It is always auspicious to circumambulate Arunachala, about an eight mile walk, and this should be done slowly and mindfully "like a pregnant queen in her eighth month." It is never more auspicious to do so than at Karthigai, in November or December, at the time when the constellation of the Pleiades (*karthigai*) is in conjunction with the full moon.

My companion and I were lucky enough to find a hotel room with an unobstructed view of the hill just opposite, and a good one of the street below, where from late afternoon on, pilgrims from near and far streamed in, mostly barefoot. Men wore muted, baggy lungis, while women appeared in saris of impossibly splendrous color contrasts. Less fortunate perhaps was that in the street below was a vendor selling tapes of mantras, which were played at full volume, non-stop, for several days.

Overnight, the number of pilgrims in town had swollen to 200,000. We found our way to the base of the hill and began the 2,600 foot climb, which is meant to be done strictly barefoot. The going was very slow with so many people on the path. It took hours to reach the top. When we reached the summit, the space between bodies was reduced to nothing. Pilgrims were packed solid, front to back, all inching forward in a mass. The smell of sacrificial ghee was overpowering in places. I was seized with a moment of panic, suddenly wishing I could escape. I looked over my shoulder, but it was obvious that I could no longer go back down against the incoming tide of pilgrims. There was no other choice but to let go into the crush. As the crowd crept to a certain point, each pilgrim was given a little packet, the movement of the many arms outreaching as unified as that of a centipede negotiating a pebble. The packets contained pellets of camphor to be deposited into a huge black cauldron that was placed at the mouth of the downward path.

At dusk, from the hotel balcony, we watched the lighting of the great cauldron of camphor. The beacon flame gleamed gold, as night washed in deepening shades of blue and wrapped the hill in indigo. Distant points of light, little lamps held by the evening pilgrims threading their way to the crest, drew a thin line of spangles on the hill's body. The next day my companion returned to his wife, who had been unable to come with us, having injured her knees chasing undisciplined cows across too many Alpine meadows. We all shared a peaceful drink together, under the green, shaded universe of a banyan tree.

We talked about Sri Lanka. I would have liked to go there and see Adam's Peak, but they were in pursuit of other things. On its summit there is a footprint shape in the rock, a goal of pilgrimage for three of the world's major religions. The Christians see it as the imprint of Adam's first step out of paradise. The Buddhists honor it as the sole of Buddha and the Hindus that of Shiva. I thought of the column of light and how the image linked Avebury and Arunachala. My friends departed to pack for Sri Lanka, leaving me with my own thoughts.

Footprints seemed everywhere in the picture, sketched roughly onto my map of the Avebury area, those of many shoeless pilgrims on the old Tamil mountain, and Adam's mark on Sri Lanka. There were also the feet that are the units of distance measure. To make the proportions of the human body a unity in all distances is to include our corporeity as part of the universal scheme. Human embodiment, our Adamic nature, is thus interwoven with the harmony of the spheres and we find our home, our hearth, within the expanse of light years. If Adam's foot brings a measure of earthly things into a universe measured in terms of light, we find relationship with all of these things as we pursue the trails of our own kinds of paradise.

With every step we take, our foot casts upon the ground a momentary shadow, bringing with its touch a swift and total eclipse of all light. In this dark midnight, and in an instant of oneness and recognition, the foot marries its own shadow and, from this act of intimacy, leaves something of itself behind. So the footprint acts magically as a link to its creator, the sole of our foot leaving an impression of our lunar nature and of our soul.

Our steps are measures of the Earth's body, and through these measures, the Earth makes known to us her laws of gravity and grace. By grace and gravity we walk in dynamic balance, our return to Earth's possession inevitable, our fate sealed in our every movement, as every human heel is marked with the mortal cord of Achilles, imprinted with the vulnerability of Orion.

Our feet follow the desire of our eye, so we chase our dreams and visions. In the circle of the stars, the giant foot of the constellation Orion forever strides across the river of Milky Way stars in pursuit of the apples of his eye, the fleeing Pleiades. The geometry of the eye shows us plainly that it is the mirror of the universe. The perfect circle of the iris is the quintessential geometry of the heavens. In this circle where the universal orb is drawn upon our body, and is drawn into it, like an open mouth that eats the sun, sleeps the goddess Iris, messenger of the gods before Hermes, she of the rainbow bridge, wing-footed mistress of colors and of all dreaming.

The bridge of Iris is one joining vision and foundation, eye and foot, or geometrically speaking, it is the union of the circle and the square. This is an image of the temple, the place of contemplation, and is implicit in our bodies in the simple act of standing. As the iris of the eye and the dome of the head represent the heavens, so the feet stand for the square of Earth, easily illustrated if one stands feet parallel, a short distance apart. To move from this position and to walk in contemplation is to imprint our admiration on the body of the Earth. When we go in admiration, we walk in measure with foundation, and thus we make our footprints steps of light upon the threshold of a place where the whole universe shines, undivided and unbroken.

Science: Method, Myth, Metaphor?

AMY IONE

KARL POPPER once asserted that the aim of science is to find satisfactory explanations of whatever strikes us as being in need of explanation. His point was that it may be naive to speak of the "aim" of science, for clearly different scientists have different aims.[1] Scientists also offer more than one explanation of how science fits within the culture-at-large. For example, at present, the physicist David Peat suggests that the maps of science have reached so high a degree of abstraction and sophistication that they have lost their deeper meaning and connection to the world in which we live. Peat urges we recapture something of the living quality in ancient mythology.[2] The cosmologist Joseph Silk, on the other hand, infers that science retains this living quality when he says that the creation story as now told through the Big Bang might be regarded by those who follow us as a late twentieth-century myth, one similar to the creation stories of antiquity.[3] All scientists, however, do seem to agree with the assessment of the astronomer Martin Rees. As Rees points out, the success of the Big Bang does not mean we should not question it. Like all scientific theories it remains falsifiable. In time we may find that the theory was simply comparable to adding a new epicycle to the Ptolemaic model.[4]

Ideas like these, which reflect on the place of science in human life, have always existed within the scientific community. This paper focuses on how this kind of idea informs human consciousness and influences scientific development and speculation. Using the formation of the Presocratic, Ptolemaic, and Copernican cosmologies as a counterpoint to today's science, this paper considers scientific devel-

A shorter version of this paper was delivered in the science and epistemology session at the "Tucson II" conference, "Toward a Science of Consciousness," sponsored by the University of Arizona, Tucson, Arizona, April 8–13, 1996.

opment and speculation in four ways. First, the discussion explores the Greek discovery of the mind and science. Then the emphasis moves to illustrate how scientists have merged preconceptions and prejudices with our ability to ask questions and our inventiveness in stabilizing scientific models. Third, the motility of scientific speculation is shown and the evidence that scientific inquiry cannot be isolated from other approaches to life is introduced. The paper concludes that scientific studies combine method, myth, and metaphor and thus all of us benefit in developing a comprehensive grasp of how cultural beliefs and human consciousness impact scientific investigations and why the scientific method continues to change the face of science as scientists continually question and reevaluate their assumptions.

1. The Greeks

The development of Western scientific techniques is usually associated with the Greeks. The intriguing aspect of this is that the ancient Greeks were not a cold-hearted and detached people so much as a people passionately engaged in seeking to *rationally* answer the questions life posed. In fact, it was this passion to know more that led them to see the world as a question to be answered. Their efforts to answer the questions that we ask as we live also compelled them to seek to define the underlying principle of the *cosmos* and nature.[5]

Four aspects of the Greek experience particularly stand out. First, the early Greeks were trying to explain *all things* by one of several principles—themselves being considered as among these *things*.[6] Second, the Greek experience and the Greek "discovery" of the mind were not limited to *an* individual's perception of the world but, rather, moved into individual consciousness while, *simultaneously*, becoming a part of how a people communally redefined their perspective on living. Third, in the process of trying to explain nature, they discovered their personal identities to a larger degree. This point cannot be emphasized strongly enough, for it was not the intention of the Presocratic natural philosophers to deify logic and objectivity.[7] Nor was it their intention to lay the foundations for science and philosophy. Their hope was to form a ground for better living. They saw reason as a way of exploring (among other things) whether there was consistency within life, and how humans were—or could be—involved with what their lives contained. Finally, dialogue was the technique the Greeks used in their pursuit of knowledge. This relational method of exchanging ideas became a key component of Western theology and science. No doubt, if the ancient Greek tradition was never broken in the West it was because the Greek dialogue served as the foundation for the supernatural theology of Christianity.[8] It is also at the heart of the methods we find in Modern thought.

A. *The Greek Discovery of the Mind*

The organic and finite worldview of the Homeric religion, which emerged around the eighth century B.C.E., seeded the dialogue that led to the Greek discovery of the mind. Homeric culture is aptly described as one that moved the Greek culture out of a Dark Age into a vision of life in the sun. Homer's epics provided the religious foundation for this Olympian belief system and its basic premise was that life in the sun was beautiful, although painful, but, nonetheless, always moving as it should.

Gilbert Murray notes that the Homeric religion was a step in the self-regulation of Greece.[9] In Murray's opinion, as a religion it attempted, and failed, to bring order into chaos, moralize the cruel and socially-offensive aspects of the old rites and rituals, and to create a social organization for the community. The Olympian religion did, however, succeed in generally permitting progress by not only encouraging obedience to virtues but also *urging* humans *to use* their power of thought, daring, and endurance. These attributes were thus engaged and focused on defining proper living and purging the more humanly degrading aspects of the old religions.[10]

What stands out here is that the Homeric vision, despite the Homeric negation of the possibility, was actively seeding the development of the self-aware mind by creating a more effective means for education and a code for social order. The religion was also planting the seeds that would broaden discussion about nature (*physis*), autonomous identity, social place, and social function. This was because the

Homeric tradition began to codify the oral tradition, or to define what was "known" and what was "believed." The key point here is that while moving into a proactive framework the Olympian religion both moved beyond the "darkness" of the early religions and, simultaneously, was representative of them. "To parody the words of Anaxagoras, 'In the early religions all things were together, till the Homeric system came and arranged them.'"[11]

Let me emphasize that the evolution of Homeric culture was subtle, as is evident when we examine how the culture seeded the idea of personal autonomy. Initially, as E. R. Dodds has pointed out, the Homeric concept of personal ego was virtually undeveloped.[12] Many have also noted that the quality of Homeric consciousness was almost like being hypnotized or in a dream state.[13] Contextually this meant that the Homeric human had no unified concept of what we would call "soul" or personality. Rather, in the Homeric world, unsystematized, nonrational impulses and the acts resulting from them tended to be excluded from the self and ascribed to an alien origin.[14] Thus, the people did not see their shortcomings self-consciously, partially because the Homeric epics encouraged a passivity of surrender to experience that was accomplished through the use of the emotions and motor reflexes. Let me stress that it was through this instinctive activity of surrender that the people were educated and socialized to know the mores of the traditions:

> When confronted with an Achilles, we can say, here is a man of strong character, definite personality, great energy and forceful decision, but it would be equally true to say, here is a man to whom it has not occurred, and to whom it cannot occur, that he has a personality apart from the pattern of his acts. His acts are responses to his situation, and are governed by remembered examples of previous acts by previous strong men. The Greek tongue . . . [at this point] . . . cannot frame words to express the conviction that "I" am one thing and the tradition is another; that "I" can stand apart from the tradition and examine it; that "I" can and should break the spell of its hypnotic force.[15]

Yet, and despite the fact that the concept of an independent identity was foreign to the Greek mind, the Homeric stories offered a means for people to reflect on questions concerning nature, identity, and being. Initally the stories brought ideas that were alien to the people into their minds and the cultural environment. In effect, the stories acted like metaphors in the following way: First, on hearing the stories the Greeks were exposed to ideas that were not actually a part of their worldview. Then, through discussing the content of the stories they were able to conceptualize possibilities outside of their experience interpersonally. I cannot emphasize strongly enough that this was an experiential endeavor, one which gave them the experience of holding two frames of reference simultaneously and eventually this experience brought about what we would call Greek rhetoric.

How the initial experience worked is best explained through looking at an example from the *Iliad*. In the *Iliad* we find Achilles wrestling with an unsolvable contradiction. On the one hand, he wants to do his duty and fight with his companions. On the other hand, he is not permitted to join them. Achilles reflects on his predicament, and his ruminations offered people an example of what it meant to reflect on the nature of one's place and function as a member of the group, as follows:

> Achilleus weeping went and sat in sorrow apart from his companions beside the beach of the grey sea looking out on the infinite water. . . . Never now would he go to assemblies where men win glory, never more into battle, but continued to waste his heart out sitting there, though he longed always for the clamour and fighting.[16]

This reflection was believable in the context of the poem because Achilles was part god by birth.[17] According to Greek mythology *only* a god, or someone who had the blood of a god, could actually *consider* place and function in the immobile Homeric culture, where roles were defined by birth and reinforced by the community.[18] Achilles' parentage thus gave him the legitimacy to question how he could want to fight with his companions and not be permitted to do so. His situation and his questioning of it in turn exposed people the possibility that "I" could be one thing and the "tradition" could be another.

In sum, through considering questions like whether Achilles' conflict was a part of a cosmic justice—or more aptly seen as injustice—people engaged in a process of differentiating possibilities and considering what individual beliefs and group acceptance meant in the scheme of things. Let me emphasize that this was a long process and it was only over time that individual and cultural changes were apparent. Eric Havelock offers a wonderful description of how this change in human consciousness added a level of individualized awareness not previously apparent in the Western psyche:

> [S]ome time towards the end of the fifth century before Christ, it became possible for a few Greeks to talk about their 'souls' as if they had selves or personalities which were autonomous and not fragments of the atmosphere nor of a cosmic life force, but what we might call entities of real substances . . . as late as the last quarter of the fifth century, in the minds of the majority of men, the notion was not understood, and . . . in their ears the terms in which it was expressed sounded bizarre. Before the end of the fourth century the conception was becoming part of the Greek language and one of the common assumptions of Greek culture.[19]

Four exceptional aspects of this cultural exercise are important to this discussion. First, as mentioned above, the method the Greeks used resulted from a group process that was also particularized in the experience of many individuals. Second, there was no predefined model in the Greek experience that the people could turn to help them frame the idea of autonomous personhood. It was precisely because *there was no existing model for their "model"* that they *created a new way* of perceiving the world, and in the process of creating this new way of seeing the world, they allowed it to come into existence.[20]

Third, the process differed from the kinds of revelations we find in religious thought. This too can be attributed to the Greek emphasis on dialogue. Although the Greeks often credited their insights to divine origin, their process was more dynamic and more relational than direct revelation. Their exchange did not *confirm* revealed insights so much as it helped them to develop new ways of seeing their relationship to the world. Concepts emerged as abbreviations of their insights. These concepts, in turn, enhanced their interpersonal communication because the concepts gave the Greeks a shorthand that enabled them to cover more territory. Again, these concepts were not objectively discovered nor objectively invented—*for there were no aims involved*. The new way was effected in the process of revealing itself.

Finally, and possibly most noteworthy in terms of our world today, is that it would be nonsensical to separate the religious and the scientific in looking at this early Greek process. The Greeks of this period believed their gods still lived *in* the world. Humans were perceived to differ from gods only because they were mortal.[21] The Greek gods loved and hated, helped humans, harmed humans, and appeared among them as they did so.[22] These gods had created neither matter nor humans. Humans and matter, like the gods, were infused with spirit and divinity—because it was assumed that *all* was by nature divine. It would have been nonsensical to them that it could be otherwise. Thus their emerging conceptual language, like their polytheistic culture, included both the intuitive and the spiritual in its essence.[23]

This conceptual union is particularly evident in the Greek view of the *cosmos*. The *cosmos* at this point was seen to be unified, divine, self-organizing, and dynamic. Perceived as alive, the *cosmos* was presumed to have both a physical and a biological nature. This view of reality would be called a cosmobiology or a living-systems view of reality today.

Moira was the word used to connote the self-organizing process, presumed to be the nature of everything that exists.[24] As an impersonal principle, and thus not to be confused with "God," *Moira* represented the life principle which governs the *cosmos*, keeps order, assigns limits, and designs each fate (*moira*) in the sense that all have a proper place and a proper function within the organic self-regulation. This means that *Moira's* microcosmic counterpart, *moira*, comprises all particulars in relation to this self-organization—be they human life, cities, rivers, horses, etc. Every particular *thing* has its *moira*. The key point here is that the concept attempted to contextualize that a two-in-one quality was the nature of the whole. One could also say that *Moira/moira* was believed to include the overall dynamic, the whole, the parts that comprise the whole, and the changing functions of both the parts and the whole.[25]

It was when the natural philosophers (e.g., Thales, Anaximander, Heraclitus, and Parmenides) began exploring the nature of *Moira* that the foundations for Western cosmology, ontology, and epistemology began to take form.[26] Three ramifications of their initial probings must be emphasized.

First, their active method of questioning was born in the Homeric tradition. In addition, it was limited to a select group, despite the way the aristocratic Homeric worldview came to define the cultural mind and the formal design of the culture. Moreover, the conclusions of these few defied the community's views and frequently overlooked the value of many of the treasured, redeeming, and nurturing qualities of the general populace. This means that even while being adopted by the culture, the new ideas were creating a conflict with the sense of security—and identity—provided by the old, and known, religious tradition.[27]

This cultural polarization is important to acknowledge today as many people challenge the value of science and the reductionistic logic that resulted from the process of differentiation. If I may editorialize, it is critical to see the limitations in the "discovery" of science; but we do ourselves a disservice if we use these limitations as reasons to romanticize the holistic, two-in-one quality of premodern cultures, like the Homeric culture. This kind of romantization often fails to acknowledge that there were real incentives for the people who did so to look more closely at their culture. Clearly, being regularly forced to face the violence, murder, and lack of civility evident in many traditional rituals and practices provided a legitimate reason to try to see beyond life as it was known.[28] Given the overall situation, it is really not surprising that many saw reason, differentiation, and logic as positive additives to life:

> The medieval plan of burning heretics alive had not yet been invented. But the history of uncivilized man, if it were written, would provide a vast list of victims, all of them innocent, who died or suffered to expiate some portent or *monstrum* . . . with which they had nothing whatever to do, which was in no way altered by the suffering, which probably never really

happened at all, and if it did was of no consequence. The sins of the modern world in dealing with heretics and witches have perhaps been more gigantic than those of primitive men, but one can hardly rise from the record of these ancient observances without . . . feeling within him that the lightening of this cloud, the taming of this blind dragon, must rank among the greatest services that Hellenism wrought for mankind."[29]

Second, the Presocratic use of dialogue and logic came to define the scientific method. In saying this I cannot stress strongly enough that the nature of their enterprise does not correlate with key prejudices about scientific practice today. For example, their efforts to analyze the world "as if it were objective" represented an attempt to share information in a way that would take them beyond cultural assumptions, individual biases, and prejudices in general. Their efforts were not a rejection of religion or of anything that *we* would call the humanities. These kinds of idea do not even fit within their cultural mind. The Presocratics simply wanted to reach beyond the unverifiable narrative of myth. Their efforts were not *impersonal* so much as *interpersonal*. Stimulated more by passion than skepticism, they believed there was a *value* in reaching beyond accepted understandings of reality.[30]

Third, as both Havelock and Dissanayake point out, in Homeric Greece, as in prehistoric societies generally, and in preliterate groups today, political and social institutions were necessarily transmitted and preserved in an oral tradition, or a memorized "encyclopedia" of the information that was considered essential for the perpetuation of the group.[31] In the Homeric tradition the identification with the oral performance was how the social code was kept in place. Learning was *embodied* through how the rhythm of the poetry encouraged a state similar to hypnosis. This state encouraged a total involvement with the sounds, sensations, and emotions transmitted to human lives through their embodying of the poetic experience.

B. *Plato and the Beginnings of Cosmology*

It is with Plato that we find the oral tradition moving into a literate and visual framework.[32] This conceptual change, which was problematic from the beginning, became more problematic over time. Briefly, while the early natural philosophers had established a rational counterpoint to the Homeric story when they studied *physis*, Plato brought reason (*logos*) and divinity (*theos*) together and defined what became the underlying assumptions of Western cosmology, creativity, duality, theology, philosophy, art, and science. Philosophically, Plato also revolutionized the Presocratic method by systematizing it, defining it, and rejecting its organic foundations. "Plato was the first who used the word 'theology,' and he evidently was the creator of the idea. He introduced it in his *Republic*, where he wanted to set up certain philosophical standards and criteria for poetry."[33]

What I want to emphasize is that theology for Plato still *included* science and philosophy, and his science was *unlike* that of the natural philosophers who proceeded him. The Presocratics, who are especially relevant because they bridged the Homeric and Platonic cultures, only *appear* to take a non-theological position ontologically if we compare them with contemporary views. It cannot be stated strongly enough that the Presocratic focus on nature did not negate the divinity of the world and had nothing to do with religion or theology. Their world *is* divine and undifferentiated rationally. Through posing questions they began to put the cosmos into a context that facilitated them in gaining a deeper and a broader insight into the particulars of nature (*physis*). Factoring in that when the Greeks began enlarging their conceptual awareness they did not see themselves as independent personalities—but rather as functioning parts in relation to a whole—highlights that rationale and differentiation were useful in developing a sense that each one of us could offer different insights about life and reality. In addition, while the natural philosophers concentrated on facts ascertainable by the senses and wanted to see beyond the myths, Plato distrusted the senses and created his own myths to explain his "vision," using dialogue as a philosophical technique.

The impact and limitations of Plato's philosophy have been well-documented. In sum, Plato's rational solutions to social problems encouraged manipulating human consciousness and emotions in order to turn people toward his system, which he saw as turning people toward the Good, for he saw his system as the Truth. There were four key elements within this: 1) Plato's philosophy was grounded within a living systems, or cosmobiological philosophy, as well as being a *reaction* to this kind of philosophical foundation.[34] 2) As noted earlier, Plato helped precipitate the change from an oral to a literate tradition.[35] 3) Plato's view was dualistic. The human world was represented by Plato as the cave, where shadows appeared to be real. The real was actually within a divine and transcendent realm which included the archetypal forms and the mathematical symbols. 4) Finally, although Plato's philosophy included his concern with how the oral tradition manipulated human consciousness and emotions, he was oblivious to the fact that he too adopted manipulative tactics in his rational philosophy.[36]

Plato's cosmological model, which was based on reason and geometry, integrated his philosophy into the cultural milieu. The model itself offers some perspective on how the Greeks in general brought their realistic and visionary views together.

Using the circle as a symbol of harmony and perfection, the cosmological model assumed that any valid physical model of the cosmos could only be perfectly stated if it used circular celestial trajectories, or a combination of circles. While there is reason to believe that the spherical theory of the universe was first advanced by the mystic Pythagoras, and that he may have been inspired by Babylonian, Egyptian, and Eastern philosophies, it is in Plato's *Timaeus* that the first geometrical cosmology is given for the "music of the spheres." Eudoxus, Plato's pupil, mapped the first design for this spherical universe,[37] which eventually became the circular Ptolemaic cosmology.[38] The circularly-based Ptolemaic cosmology was, in turn, used until the beginning of the seventeenth century when Kepler realized that planets move in elliptical, not circular, orbits. In many ways all of the models intertwined with the various individual and cultural prejudices.[39]

2. From the Hellenistic Era to the Modern Era

The Hellenistic period followed on the heels of Plato and Aristotle and changed the foundationally optimistic and aspirational focus which germinated the earlier period into one of synthesis. Scholars have offered diverse insights about what the relationship between reason and spirituality during this period meant and how it took form. Gilbert Murray, for example, claims the West lost its vitality when the Hellenistic quest for *ataraxia* (peace of mind) subdued the mood and the tone of the population:

> Any one who turns from the great writers of classical Athens, say Sophocles or Aristotle, to those of the Christian era must be conscious of a great difference in tone. There is a change in the whole relation of the writer to the world around him. The new quality is not specifically Christian: it is just as marked in the Gnostics or Mithras—worshipers as in the Gospels and the Apocalypse, in Julian and Plotinus as in Gregory and Jerome. It is hard to describe. It is a rise of asceticism, of mysticism, in a sense, of pessimism; it is a loss of self-confidence, of hope in this life and of faith in normal human effort; a despair of patient inquiry, a cry for infallible revelation; an indifference to the welfare of the state, a conversion of the soul to God. It is an atmosphere in which the aim of the good man is not so much to live justly, to help the society to which he belongs and enjoy the esteem of his fellow creatures; but rather by means of a burning faith, by contempt for the world and its standards, by ecstasy, suffering and martyrdom, to be granted pardon for his unspeakable unworthiness, his immeasurable sins. There is an intensifying of certain spiritual emotions; an increase of sensitiveness, a failure of nerve.[40]

Responding to this idea of a failure of nerve, E. R. Dodds suggested it was not so much a failure of nerve as a fear of freedom.[41] Dodds says it was this fear of freedom which stymied the original impulse which had birthed the Greek awareness of a separate individuality that was not *simply* a part of a larger unity. Dodds asserts that the medieval Christian world formed as it did because of how the Greeks failed to include an adequate instrument for *actually* understanding, much less controlling, the importance of that which was not reasonably understood—that which went on below the surface or below the threshold of consciousness.

Weighing these two viewpoints and others, Peter Brown asserts that contemporary scholars are imposing modern factors in their conclu-

sions.[42] In Brown's opinion, before we talk of anxiety and disillusionment as pervasive and distinguishing features of the period, we must
ascertain whether we are using the standards of antiquity or our own.
In his words, "Disillusionment assumes illusion, and ancient men kept
themselves studiously free of illusions about what life could offer
them."[43]

All who study this period, however, do seem to agree that the
Hellenistic world was exceedingly different from the one preceding it
and that even by the second century C.E. the difference was not so
much the rising influence of Christianity as it was the cultural mood
in general. Probably this is because the pagans and Christians actually
agreed on many things.

Perhaps the best example of this is how both pagans and Christians
viewed personal fulfillment in hierarchical terms. When people observed that some pagans and some Christians "found" spiritual suste-
nance, while others merely *aspired* to this sense of spiritual wholeness,
both Christians and pagans concluded that some were elect.[44] This
belief that those who felt fulfilled were closer to divinity encouraged
a hierarchical social structure, which of course eventually came to be
the governing body of the Church.

It is imperative to acknowledge that this hierarchy on earth gradually came to mirror the hierarchical Platonic cosmology. Gradually is
the key word here. Initially, the Platonic cosmological picture had
come into the cultural imagination subdividing space into levels of
reality while retaining the general cultural perception that the whole
structure was the expression of a divine order. It depicted the earth as
a globe suspended in space at the center of a system of concentric
moving spheres. This order was felt to be beautiful, worthy of worship,
and alive or informed by a living spirit. Three points are critical in
conceptualizing the cultural evolution. First, again, initially the whole
cosmos was believed to be alive. Second, it was also assumed to be
interdependent, linked by *sympatheia*.[45] Third, and most important
when looking at the historical story, it was because the assumed
mutuality between the parts and the whole did not seem to be reflected
in human life that the people began to question it. For example, given
the many inexplicable aspects of life, especially the tragic ones, people

could not ascertain why it was assumed there was an equality between the human and the divine. Clearly the divine was higher and more powerful!

Both pagans and Christians increasingly accepted the dualism of the Platonic cosmology, where the celestial and terrestrial realms were separate and operated under different laws. The apparent inequality of the parts and the whole led the dualistic model to stabilize with the assumptions that 1) the *locus* of "divine power" was supernatural and 2) the higher celestial realm was the realm of the Divine order. This divine order was also presumed to differ from the evident nature of human life. I cannot state strongly enough that the supernatural was not only a different realm, it was also a different substance from the natural—even when they were philosophically defined as a unity. Experientially, this view placed the realm of science within the physical world and the realm of religion in some metaphysical relationship to the physical world. The translation of these ideas into the social context resulted in a culture that was progressively withdrawing divinity from the material world and, in effect, changing the human relationship to divinity.[46]

Again, it must be emphatically stated that this belief in levels of reality was neither specifically Christian nor specifically pagan. Nor was it specifically Western. The key point here is that when this cultural idea emerged in the West, it created the consensual view that there was an antithesis between the celestial and terrestrial worlds. Again, the terrestrial world was increasingly seen to be that of mortals.

Two points stand out here. First, as the people discussed the ideas it became increasingly difficult to see the human spirit as equal to that of the divine and it became easier to ask if matter *was* spirit and to see them as different, allowing ideas of a supernatural to be tied into ideas of incarnation and divinity, and ideas about bringing the spiritually elect into "power." Second, this situation weighed in favor of Christianity becoming the preferred worldview because of the desire for a defining philosophy much like what the Christian belief represented to the people of that period. It is critical to recognize this so as to acknowledge that the religion was not simply imposed on the populace when Constantine became a Christian and officially established Christianity as the state religion in 313 C.E.

Actually, four psychological conditions favored Christian growth. First, the refusal of Christianity to concede any value to alternative forms of worship was considered a *strength* at this time, not a source of weakness. The knowledge that one was on the "right" path not only offered a sense of security, it relieved believers of the burden of continually weighing and judging alternatives. According to Christianity, since there was one—irrevocable—choice, the road to salvation was clear. In addition, Christianity gave the people a new kind of certainty. Believers had a sense of place and a sense of belonging because the institutionalized beliefs offered a universal code for living. Second, because Christianity made no social distinctions, in principle it was open to all. Third, in a period when life on earth was increasingly devalued and feelings of guilt were widely held, Christianity held out the promise of a better inheritance in another world. Finally, the benefits of becoming a Christian were *not* confined to the next world. A Christian community brought its members together in this world by offering a way of life.[47]

In sum, science, the cultural cosmology, and the social system reinforced particular beliefs. In the overall cultural context these ideas favored a model like the Christian Church because both pagans and Christians alike wanted some kind of overriding *religious* vision that would feel coextensive with their lives. They wanted a social structure that would give them a sense of meaning and this search for meaning brought diverse views together. In fact, if any cultivated person of the second century had been asked to put in a few words the difference between the pagan view of life and the Christian one, the reply would probably be that it was the difference between *logismos* and *pistis*, between reasoned conviction and faith.[48] By the fourth century, the situation had changed. On the one hand, Christianity had—through theology—added rationale to its beliefs and the rational pagan focus had added faith to compensate for a lost vitality.[49] What is key within this is that pagans felt spiritually drained. Their loss of vitality was a sharp contrast to the emotional commitment found among Christians. It was because Christianity had become a religion that people were willing to die for—and did die for—that Christianity appealed to the people. Christianity was judged to be a religion worth living for.

3. The Invention of the Modern Worldview

Christian supremacy began to be challenged around the twelfth century when social contradictions as well as emerging views on law and governance began to subtly erode Church power.[50] Eventually the religious monopoly on life and belief gave way to secular views, allowing the people a greater degree of individual choice and autonomy. Cultural revisions, moreover, aligned with scientific, religious, and philosophical revolutions. The interpenetration of all these revolutions is perhaps easiest to see through looking at the cosmological revision.

Paul Dirac, one of the pioneers of quantum physics, once said that the great breakthroughs in physics always involve giving up some great prejudice. In the case of Modernism it was the assumption that any valid model of the cosmos needed to presume all orbits were circular. This proved to be an implicit assumption—one never questioned—rather that an operative law. As it turned out, the ongoing contextual debate that had developed in regard to earth-centered and sun-centered theories was resolved with the discovery that the planets had elliptical rotations.[51] This perception gave the system a new look, and a precision never evident in any of the many circular cosmologies— including the Copernican heliocentric theory. The earth-shattering nature of this can only be appreciated contextually and in relation to why the earth-centered view of the universe had become predominant.

As noted earlier, Claudius Ptolemy, a Egyptian-born Greek astronomer and geographer who lived in Alexandria in the second century C.E., proposed the first plausible explanation for complex celestial motions. His earth-centered description, based on the Platonic cosmology, stated that the earth did not move and that the stars and planets moved around earth. Ptolemy's model also resolved the occasional *retrograde*, or backward, motion of planets. This was a tremendous accomplishment because retrogradation was perhaps the greatest scientific challenge of that time.

The concept of retrograde means that while most of the time a planet like Mars appears to move from west to east across the background of stars, every so often the planet's motion is retrograde: that is, for a few weeks it appears to slow, stop, and reverse direction with respect to what appears to be a fixed background. This was critical to the study of the heavens because the movement of the planets needed to be *explained* theoretically. Ptolemy's model,[52] using the mathematical tools of the epicycle, eccentric circle, and equant, was viable and successfully predicted planetary motions, eclipses, and a host of other heavenly phenomena with relative accuracy, despite its complexity. While ultimately challenged in the Renaissance by alternative models, Ptolemy's geocentric theory was one of the longest-lived scientific theories ever derived. It prospered for 1500 years and, as time went on, the longevity of its use was one of the reasons often given to validate it.

In analyzing the long-term acceptance of the geocentric model I must stress that it survived because it seemed to match the appearance of the world more closely than the other options proposed. We often forget that many ancient and medieval natural philosophers had suggested the universe was heliocentric or sun-centered. For example, the Presocratic Anaximander (611–548 B.C.E.) postulated a heliocentric universe, as did Aristarchus, a Pythagorean astronomer who was born in 310 B.C.E. Their ideas were rejected, however, because the geocentric cosmologies appeared to work—at least to some degree—and the heliocentric theories did not seem to fit as well with reality as it was known and experienced.

The empirical evidence clearly indicated that the sun moved around the earth in a circle. One could see this every day, for the sun rose every morning, traveled across the sky, and then set in the evening. In addition, people could not feel the earth move. Also, when objects were dropped, they fell straight down, as if the earth were standing still and nothing seemed to get left behind as a result of earthly "movement." These experimental perceptions of earthly centrality were also supported by the religious views. It was "known" that the earth was the center of the universe, just as humans were central to God's plan. Knowing, too, that divinity lived in another realm, because some people were "closer" to divinity, came to strengthen the overall cultural and earth-centered perception because people could see the duality. One need only look at the stars in the heavens to see that they appeared fixed, as if they followed one set of laws, the divine laws; while another set of laws was operative on earth, where things changed.

As noted above, it was the precision offered by the elliptical rotations that convinced scientists they should adopt the sun-centered system. The story that has come down to us is that it took Kepler six to ten years to deduce the pattern that he used to create the elliptical formula.[53] Kepler derived the elliptical formula after studying data about the physical world that had been compiled by the astronomer Tycho Brahe from over twenty years of observing the movements of the planets.

Once Kepler perceived the elliptical formula he was able to use the information to mathematically define it. Adding empiricism, logic, and efficiency to his insight in turn allowed him to define the cosmic pattern so that phenomena fit together in a way that had not previously been perceived, at least not in any kind of logical way. It must be emphasized that first Kepler had the insight and then he was able to concisely *correlate* what had previously been only a massive amount of *unrelated* information. The exceptional aspect of this is that the elliptical model was a radical departure from the principle of uniform *circular* motion which had been considered *self-evident* and *inviolable* from the earliest times. This innovative quality cannot be emphasized enough. Nor can the precision the mathematics brought to the picture:

> The numerous observations made by Tycho Brahe, with a degree of accuracy never before attained, had in the skillful hands of Kepler revealed the unexpected fact that Mars describes an ellipse ... the genius and the astounding patience of Kepler had proved that not only did this new theory satisfy the observations, but that no other hypothesis could be made to agree with the observations, as every proposed alternative left outstanding errors, such as it was impossible to ascribe to errors of observation. Kepler had, therefore, unlike all his predecessors, not merely put forward a new hypothesis which might do as well as another to enable a computer to construct tables of the planet's motion; he had

found the actual orbit in which the planet travels through space.[54]

Again, let me emphasize that once the implicit pattern—the pattern that none had previously perceived—became explicit, the elliptical idea was in a position to change cosmological assumptions and the cultural dialogue. What had not even existed in a metaphysical context, now became defined in relation to the physical world. In short, *once* the explicit description evolved, the cultural dialogue *expanded* to include ideas on orbits that were *not* circular. For example, David Fabricus, a clergyman and amateur astronomer who maintained a correspondence with Kepler from 1602 through 1609, wrote Kepler:

> With your ellipse you abolish the circularity and uniformity of the motions, which appears to me the more absurd the more profoundly I think about it. . . . If you could only preserve the perfect circular orbit, and justify your elliptic orbit by another little epicycle, it would be much better.[55]

The larger point is that men like Descartes, Kepler, and Newton, who are often accused, often applauded, for bringing forward the ideas that led to what many now say is a godless model without life and spiritual consciousness, were deeply religious men, trying to assert something vitally and deeply alive within them, something they often equated with God. If we can believe their own words, they did not separate science and religion in their minds, in their hearts, or in their consciousness—despite the fact that their ideas came to be connected with "materialism," "physicality," and the loss of human centrality in the cosmic picture.

For example, when Kepler conceptualized the mathematics he needed to describe the three basic laws that bear his name, he joyfully credited God, saying,

> I thank thee, Lord God our Creator, that thou allowed me to see the beauty in the work of creation; I exult in the works of thy hands. See, I have completed the work to which I felt called; I have earned interest

from the talent thou hast given me. I have proclaimed the glory of thy
works to the people who will read these demonstrations, to the extent
that the limitations of my spirit would allow.[56]

As Kepler's words indicate, he saw his insights as a revelation. Thus,
despite the fact that Kepler's laws are frequently said to be the first
"natural laws" in the modern sense, they were derived in an effort to
define the perfection of God's creation. Moreover, Kepler's commitment to God's perfection was so strongly aligned with the cultural
prejudice that cosmic perfection could only be defined using "circles"
that *he, too, subscribed to the circular ideal*. This was why when Kepler
discovered that planetary orbits were *elliptical*, he had a hard time
accepting this possibility. Yet, eventually, the simplicity and the clarity
of the new design won him over.

Newton, who was also a deeply religious person, used Kepler's
innovative insight as the foundation for his laws. His cosmological
design was infinitely more revolutionary that Kepler's insight, for
Newton's Laws allowed much that had formerly been defined as if it
was of the supernatural to be defined in relation to the natural world.
This is the beauty of the Newtonian model, which redefines what had
been seen as two realms, heaven and earth, each with its own pattern,
as one.[57] Describing the celestial and terrestrial domains as a unity also
brought astronomy and physics under one set of laws.

Yet, again, Newton, who defined the framework which eventually
took God out of the physical workings of phenomena, studied nature
in order to more fully understand God and God's creation.[58] Newton's
revised cosmological model offered *him* a means to more effectively
speak about God's presence and omniscience by pointing to God, the
Creator he believed we could never know. Let me emphasize that it
was because Newton used God as the keystone for his theory of
everything that it *retained* the spiritual dualism of Christianity. Clearly
Newton's dualism assumed that a Creator God was a part of the overall
unity. It was the metaphysical assumption that was needed by Newton
to articulate that there is an objective reality created by an unchanging,
absolute—God. As Newton wrote:

God is the same God, always and everywhere. He is omnipresent not *virtually* only but also *substantially*; for virtue cannot subsist without substance. In him are all things contained and moved, yet neither affects the other; God suffers nothing from the motion of bodies, bodies find no resistance from the omnipresence of God. It is allowed by all that the Supreme God exists necessarily, and by the same necessity he exists *always* and *everywhere*. . . . As a blind man has no idea of colors, so have we no idea of the manner by which the all-wise God perceives and understands all things. . . . for all our notions of God are taken from the ways of mankind by a certain similitude, which, though not perfect, has some likeness, however.[59]

* * *

In other words, while the physical world, *res extensa*, may have authored God's demise, the scientific activity of Galileo (1564–1642), Kepler (1571–1630), Descartes (1596–1650), Huygens (1629–1695), and Newton (1642–1727), and most of the other mathematicians who are credited with bringing this about sought—and expected to find— broad, profound, immutable, and *God-created* rational principles either through intuition or immediate sense perception. Thus the irony within the birth of Modern science is that it was in affirming God and God's perfection in the eternal language of mathematics that the "godless mechanistic" model we ascribe to Modernism became possible. The model *needed* God. God was the point of origin. God was the creator of the symbols used in the model to speak about God's creation and the eternal realm. He was also the symbol that had been created to designate a Creator. Therefore, His realm was assumed to be complete, and was assumed to be beyond human cognizance and the nature of the world in which we conduct our lives.

These philosophical paradoxes, which framed the birth of Modernism, can be attributed to a few cultural factors.[60] First, the Renaissance approach was developing ideas that differed from Church assumptions, but it still reflected the educational base and the logical approach of medieval scholastics.[61] Second, Renaissance symbologies came to celebrate God's supremacy in impersonal Platonic terms. Thus they assumed that "the knowledge at which geometry aims is the knowledge of the *eternal*,"[62] which was, of course, perfect and *outside* of the natural imperfection of the earth. This means that the revised symbolic language of mathematics, being scientific, philosophical, and *outside* of the redefined realm of nature, was not applied to relationships that existed between spirit, nature, and the individual on earth—which still were defined as somewhat inferior to that which was purely divine.[63]

To be sure, science was freed to pursue the now spiritless and valueless matter of the physical world and this revised framework allowed scientists to pursue science without having problems with the religious authorities. But now there were other problems. One problem was that the same God supported the scientific philosophy and the religious philosophy and the two did not align. Another problem was that science still assumed God had set the mechanistic universe in motion. He, however, was reduced to a point of reference in the model. He became *only* the metaphysical force behind the world. He retained His position of authority because He was defined as the origin. He was the first cause. He was the reason for the cosmos, The Author of Nature. Yet, all in all, He was a stillborn God.[64] He had set the universe in motion and then became almost unnecessary to how the mechanistic universe functioned.

Three points need to be emphasized before turning to the twentieth century. First, ironically, it was the very mathematical foundation that made it possible to expand our understanding of the cosmos that also made the model more a religious than scientific one. During the Middle Ages the mathematical symbols had been placed in the divine realm, the belief being they had been created by God. Second, faith per se was not put aside in the minds of the people. What changed was the focus of human experience. Finally, the turn toward earthly concerns could as easily be attributed to social conditions as it could be attributed to the revised cosmology. Events such as the plagues which ravaged Europe in the fourteenth and sixteenth centuries had led people to ask questions like: Why does the Church have no power to stop the horror of this deadly disease? The people answered these kinds of questions actively, trying to find more effective ways to address their lives. More to the point, after the disease killed more than one fourth of the population of Europe, it was painfully clear that the medieval religious approach was completely ineffective in doing anything about this kind of disaster. Every technique and all of the symbols known to the medieval world were employed in the attempt to control the plagues—prayer, ecstatic mysticism, scapegoating, medicine based on sympathetic magic, and so forth. The continuation of the massive death, however, led people to conclude that if the culture was to be able to address and survive catastrophes like the Black Plague, people needed better methods for studying how to understand and control their world.

4. The Twentieth Century

Environmental factors and emprical knowledge of course changed as time moved on and today we are again living in a transitional era. I would suggest that we are too close to the challenges surrounding us to accurately perceive how the culture is in fact changing. Our legacy has yet to formalize.

Perhaps what is most evident from our vantage point is that science has again been dramatically revising long accepted assumptions about reality. In my opinion, just as the naked eye of premodern cultures gave way to the telescopes and microscopes that revised, expanded, reduced, and formed the Modern vision of reality, Modern ideas are being replaced and somehow what is taking their place is "connected" to our global and "post"-Modern vision. I have deliberately written "post"-Modern so that I can underline that postmodernism as a philosophy is a Western construct that distorts the actuality: we are becoming "post"-Modern because Modernism was a Western point of view, belonging to a particularly triumphant epoch, and we are trying to learn how to live effectively in a world where Western and non-Western traditions interpenetrate to a larger degree.

The challenge of becoming a global community includes bringing Western, non-Western, premodern, modern, and postmodern views of reality into some kind of working relationship. Clearly, the nature of the problem has led people all over the world to intensely take up questions debated by cultures throughout time. Is one vision preferable for all or does this kind of universality diffuse traditions and identity? Does a universal vision allow diversity within the community? Do technologies help or harm the human community? How do religious technologies best relate to and interface with scientific technologies? Should we trust our senses or do they deceive us? How can we best address social and ethical concerns? Can science help us answer these kinds of questions?

Consciously reflecting on the dialogue surrounding these questions, I am as struck by the passion within the dialogue as I am by how adept we are at developing many, often contradictory, versions of reality. Reviewing the versions offered shows that many have turned to twentieth-century scientific theories to help frame new possibilities and to recontextualize old ones.[65]

Science has, of course, encouraged these new visions of reality by virtue of having revised its conclusions about reality. For example, now, in the twentieth century, we no longer see ourselves in a static Newtonian universe where absolute time and absolute space are accepted assumptions. Instead, we have quantum complementarity in our expanding omnicentric universe. Euclidean geometry, once believed to be a perfect fit with physical reality, has proved to be limited. As a result, we have developed other geometries, often more facile in dealing with the multidimensional reality we have come to know. Yet, even given these revisions, social solutions and personal concerns continue to challenge human consciousness.

Considering that "we" are very much a part of the problem, it seems prudent to consider that, since Plato, the West has offered endless philosophies to comment on how science interfaces with society as well as on how individuals and cultures interpenetrate. If one aspect of the story can be generalized, it is that individuals and groups frequently spawn elegant and appealing theories about everything under the sun that in turn become problematic when they are mapped onto societies.[66]

This also affects subcultures, like the scientific community. In science the vision of one "truth" has often encouraged what Thomas Kuhn calls "normal science." During a period of normal science the community of scientists practice (or learn) one overriding metaphysic that becomes how reality is seen to such a large degree that people overlook whatever falls outside of the idealized picture.[67] While I believe Kuhn oversimplifies some key elements, I still agree with the essential feature of his idea that vision frequently narrows during periods where scientists are pretty much in agreement. As Karl Popper has pointed out in response to this idea, the problem here is that integration into this kind of scientific community does not speak about what science can be so much as how people learn to be scientists.[68] I would quickly add that scientific training does not always encourage creative investigation so much as it encourages a particular kind of focus, one which really trains technicians. When coupled with scientism, this kind of scientific culture can effectively perpetuate itself *and* close off options for genuine creative envisioning of new possibilities while doing so.[69]

This kind of culturally-biased and politically-correct harness is not nearly as hard to challenge as many spiritual solutions. Spiritually-based societies often encourage believers to frame their understanding of life and experience in accordance with the vision of a chosen tradition. Being subjective, intersubjectively validated, and integrated into the social system as "truth," this kind of perspective encourages the one-sided vision the Church brought to society in the Middle Ages. Integration in this kind of society requires the kind of political correctness that made it difficult to bring new ideas into the vision of the Church.

In sum, narrowly defined perspectives have a great deal of difficulty questioning their favored assumptions. As a result, they lack the capacity to factor in that learning, as an ongoing, intergenerational, and creative process, includes *grappling* with *all existing* metaphysics on an ongoing basis. It is because this kind of narrow focus is 1) present in both spiritually-based and scientific communities; 2) often encouraged to a greater degree than a "creative" orientation; and 3) born of human consciousness that my final point is how science uses method, myth, and metaphor.

5. Method, Myth, Metaphor

Turning first to method, I would assert that to suggest science has a method can too easily miss the art of science: the floundering that precedes a discovery, the alertness needed to see another possibility, and the process of translating the discovery into something others can access.[70] Since, in science, the insight is incomplete if the scientist does not offer it in a way that allows others to comment on it, replicate it, and often improve on it as well; the implication that there is a method one can use that will lead to some kind of discovery or understanding is misleading. It diffuses the emergent quality of invention—so actively a part of scientific creativity and so necessary for discovery.

If it sounds as if I am suggesting that science has no method and simply invents myths, likely tales, this is not my intention. Rather, I am inferring that for many who engage in science, the subjective and the categorization processes interface, much as they did in the experience of the Presocratics. The effort of the scientist is not only reductionistic, because it includes *using* insights—and insight is the critical skill in scientific invention.

Scientific insights are meaningless unless they are combined with technical virtuosity and a passion to know more about how the world is connected. This passion includes the quality of myth, for it includes the desire to explain the world to a greater degree. However, unlike many cultural myths which are often harder to see,[71] scientific myths are explanations that are under constant scrutiny by those who believe in science the most! Science is science because it encourages an ongoing discourse and the refinement of ideas in light of new information.

This point must be emphasized if we are to see *learning* as an ongoing and critical component of scientific speculation and development. Yet even learning is a complicated activity. It can mean learning by rote and it can mean developing the ability to expand one's frame of reference. The latter approach continually changes the conceptual basis (biases?) and can be compared to Kepler's realization of elliptical orbits, which differed significantly from how people had *learned* to see, believe in, and reinforce the Ptolemaic geocentric system for 1500 years.[72] The larger point is that Kepler's insight was able to *add* information to the cultural discussion and offered a means others could use to move to another level when discussing possibilities.

I see this enlargement of our shared body of knowledge as closely intertwined with how we use metaphors. As I showed earlier, in the Homeric culture ideas outside of the cultural experience became a part of the people's experience through the attempts of the people to grapple with their foreign nature. These metaphors came into being experientially, as a result of a desire to understand something "mysterious" to a greater degree. Like all metaphors, they were created in the sense that we use a metaphor to say *this*, when we mean *that*, because we cannot say what *this* is directly. In the Homeric world, however, metaphors were not purposefully created so much as they were social constructions. Like all metaphors, the Homeric metaphors allowed people to reconstruct information. The new form in turn made something formerly mysterious more accessible to others. Scientific metaphors—whether used in theories, thought experiments, or whatever—are not an exception to this description. They make information more explicit to us. Yet, even when under the umbrella of so-called "objective" science they are potentially problematic because they are closely intertwined with our intentions and values.

If a culture values confirmation of "the" preexistent cultural truth, whether it be a scientific, philosophical, or religious truth, it is a different kind of science, philosophy, and religion than one which continually probes for more effective ways to reconstruct information. I am proposing that the latter approach equates with keeping an open mind. It encourages an ongoing reevaluation of what is "known" and what is "believed."

"Heart" may inevitably be very much a part of this, for science includes who we are. Stuart Kauffman, a biologist affiliated with the University of Pennsylvania and the Sante Fe Institute, captured this in his introduction to *The Origins of Order*, a biologically based study of self-organization and selection in evolution:

> Like many other books by scientists, this one is ineluctably auto-biographical. It witnesses one mind's sense of mystery. The famous physicist Wolfgang Pauli is said to have remarked that the deepest

pleasure in science comes from finding an instantiation, a home, for some deeply felt, deeply held image. I share this odd sense. . . . The greater mystery, after all, is not the answers that scientists contrive, but the questions they are driven to pose. Why? Why this question rather than another? Why this search, hope, despair, rather than another?[73]

In sum, perhaps it is because the existence of the universe cannot be sensibly disputed that our questions about how it works and whether it "came to be" are intriguing. Exploring the answers humans have proposed, we find that scientists have not been able to reduce their investigations to objective methodology, despite their desire to engage in "unbiased" inquiry. It is with this in mind that I am led to conclude that all of us can benefit from developing a comprehensive grasp of how cultural beliefs and human consciousness impact scientific investigations and why the refining process that science uses continues to change the face of science as scientists continually question and reevaluate their assumptions.

Notes

1. David Miller, ed., *Popper Selections*, 162.

2. F. David Peat, *The Philosopher's Stone*, 14.

3. See John Noble Wilford, "Big Bang's Defenders Weigh Fudge Factor, a Blunder of Einstein's, as Fix for New Crisis."

4. Martin Rees, *How Much Cosmology Can We Really Believe?* Hitchcock Lecture, University of California, February 28, 1995.

5. See H. D. F. Kitto, *The Greeks*, and Bruno Snell, *The Discovery of the Mind in Early Greek Philosophy and Literature*.

6. It seems imperative to differentiate here between the Greek perception of *being a thing*—at their point of consciousness development—and that of Descartes in the seventeenth century. For the Greeks, the idea of being a "thing" does not correspond to the Cartesian idea of being spiritless matter. Rather the Greeks' perception of each individual as a "thing" meant that each was a part of the larger, breathing, vital, organic whole. The key points being that the Greeks had not yet discovered a self-conscious identity and did not "objectify" nature. These points will be expanded as this paper develops.

7. Werner Jaeger, *The Theology of the Early Greek Philosophers*, 1–38.

8. Jaeger, *The Theology of the Early Greek Philosophers*, 2.

9. See Gilbert Murray, *Five Stages of Greek Religion*.

10. Murray, *Five Stages of Greek Religion*, 59–75.

11. Murray, *Five Stages of Greek Religion*, 199.

12. E. R. Dodds, *The Greeks and the Irrational*, 6–18.

13. See Eric C. Havelock, *Preface to Plato*, and Julian Jaynes, *The Origin of Consciousness in the Breakdown of the Bicameral Mind*.

14. See Dodds, *The Greeks and the Irrational*. The Greeks had a word for these nonrational impulses that were supposedly alien in origin, *atê*, which is a temporary state that sometimes clouds or bewilders and moves an individual or the group away from a clear or a normal vision, state of being, or perception. The Homeric worldview said, *"Delusion [Atê] is the eldest daughter of Zeus, the accursed who deludes all; her feet are delicate and they step not on the firm earth, but she walks the air above men's heads and leads them astray"* (*Iliad* 19.91–94, Lattimore translation).

15. Havelock, *Preface to Plato*, 199.

16. Homer, *Iliad*, 1.349, 490 (Lattimore trans., 68, 72).

17. His mother, Thetis, was a goddess. His father, Pelius, was a mortal.

18. "[T]he strongest moral force which Homeric man knows is not the fear of god, but respect for public opinion, *aidos*: . . . In such a society, anything which exposes a man to the contempt or ridicule of his fellows, which causes him to 'lose face,' is felt as unbearable" (Dodds, *Pagan and Christian in an Age of Anxiety*, 18).

19. Havelock, *Preface to Plato*, 197.

20. Bruno Snell, *The Discovery of the Mind in Early Greek Philosophy and Literature*.

21. See Richard Tarnas, *The Passion of the Western Mind*, and W. K. C. Guthrie, *The Greek Philosophers: From Thales to Aristotle*.

22. This is evident in the Greek language where their word *theos*, for example, is usually translated as god and is a predicative. Thus, *theos* was a quality to the Greeks, (i.e., God is not love, but love is a God). It is also important to remember that the gods of the Greeks were of the earth. See Tarnas, *The Passion of the Western Mind*, 470.

23. Until the time of Xenophanes (*c.* 570–475 B.C.E.) it was assumed that anthropomorphic gods existed. The gods, moreover, coexisted with metaphysical ideas like the *apeiron* of Anaximander, which suggested an unlimited ground for the *cosmos*. Xenophanes formulated the religious universalism that in later antiquity and Christianity became an essential feature of God in any "true" religion. See Jaeger, *The Theology of the Early Greek Philosophers*, 38–54.

24. Not to be confused with the three fates or *Moirae*, who were a later development.

25. Essentially, Homeric *Moira* could be equated with the Indian idea of *Ritam*, the Chinese *Tao*, and other ancient principles of the cosmos which refer to an organic, just, dynamic, self-organizing, and self-correcting principle.

26. See Guthrie, *The Greek Philosophers: From Thales to Aristotle* and F. M. Cornford, *From Religion to Philosophy*.

27. E. R. Dodds suggests the Greek Enlightenment and the absence of universal education was instrumental in creating an environment that divorced the beliefs of the intellectuals from those of the people, to the detriment of both. Dodds says that the first signs of this regression appeared during the Peloponnesian War, and were doubtless in part due to the war. Then cracks appeared in the fabric and disagreeably primitive things poked up here and

there through the cracks. Dodds believes this led the intellectuals to withdraw further into a world of their own and the popular mind was left increasingly defenseless as a growing number relapsed with a sigh of relief into the pleasures and the comforts of the primitive. See Dodds, *The Greeks and the Irrational*, 250.

28. Despite how many like to romanticize non-Western and premodern cultures, social problems are neither particular to the West nor the result of Modernism. See Robert B. Edgerton, *Sick Societies: Challenging the Myth of Primitive Harmony*.

29. Gilbert Murray, *Five Stages of Greek Religion*, 36–37.

30. See Havelock, *Preface to Plato*, and Guthrie, *The Greek Philosophers: From Thales to Aristotle*.

31. See Havelock, *Preface to Plato*, and Ellen Dissanayake, *What is Art for?* (Seattle and London: University of Washington Press, 1988).

32. See Havelock, *Preface to Plato*, and Ellen Dissanayake, *What is Art For?*

33. Jaeger, *The Theology of the Early Greek Philosophers*.

34. "The city, then, is best ordered in which the greatest number use the expression 'mine' and 'not mine' of the same things in the same way . . . For example, if the finger of one is wounded, the entire community of bodily connections stretching to the soul for 'integration' with the dominating part is made aware, and all of it feels the pain as a whole, though it is a part that suffers, and that is how we come to say that a man has a pain in his finger. And for any other member of the man the same statement holds, alike for a part that labors in pain or is eased in pleasure . . . the best-governed state most nearly resembles such an organism" (Plato, *Republic* 462D).

35. See Havelock, *Preface to Plato*, and Dissanayake, *What is Art For?*

36. It should be noted that in its final form Plato's society decreed, "The principal thing is that none, man or woman, should ever be without an officer set over him and that none should get the mental habit of taking any step, whether in earnest or in jest, on his individual responsibility: in peace as in war he must live always with his eye on his superior officer, following his lead and guided by him in his smallest actions . . . in a word, we must train the mind not even to consider acting as an individual or know how to do it" (Plato, *Laws* 942AB).

37. "Plato, though fully aware of the impressive number of astronomical observations made by the Babylonians and Egyptians, emphasized that they

had no underlying or unifying theory and no explanation of the seemingly irregular motions of the planets. Eudoxus, who was a student of the Academy . . . took up the problem of 'saving the appearances.' His answer is the first reasonably complete astronomical theory known to history" (Morris Kline, *The Loss of Certainty*, 24).

38. Ptolemy himself is quite explicit about why the idea of circular integrity must be foundational: "We believe that the object which the astronomer must strive to achieve is this: to demonstrate that all the phenomena in the sky are produced by uniform and circular motions." Ptolemy also makes it clear why astronomy must renounce all attempts to explain the *physical* reality behind it: "because the heavenly bodies, being of a divine nature, obey laws different from those to be found on earth" (Quoted in Arthur Koestler, *The Sleepwalkers*, 77).

39. Although Arthur Koestler's work bears a certain prejudice toward the humanities, his summary of how all of the models intertwined with the various individual and cultural prejudices was astutely stated in his book *The Sleepwalkers*. Koestler writes: "Plato had merely thrown out, in semi-allegorical language, a suggestion . . . it was Aristotle who promoted the idea of circular motion to a dogma of astronomy. . . . In Plato's world the boundaries between the metaphorical and the factual are fluid; all such ambiguities disappear as Aristotle takes over. . . . The God of Aristotle no longer rules the world from the inside, but from the outside. . . . Aristotle's God, the Unmoved Mover . . . is the God of abstract theology . . . Beyond the sphere of the moon, the heavens are eternal and unalterable. This splitting-up of the universe into two regions, the one lowly, the other exalted, the one subject to change, the other not, was to become another basic doctrine of medieval philosophy and cosmology. It brought a serene, cosmic reassurance to a frightened world by asserting its essential stability and permanence, but without going so far as to pretend that all change was mere illusion, without denying the reality of growth and decline, generation and destruction" (Koestler, *The Sleepwalkers*, 60–61).

40. Murray, *Five Stages of Greek Religion*, 117.

41. Dodds, *The Greeks and the Irrational*, 236–69.

42. See Peter Brown, *The Making of Late Antiquity*.

43. Brown, *The Making of Late Antiquity*, 5.

44. Brown, *The Making of Late Antiquity*, 11–12.

45. *Sympatheia* was a Stoic idea used to explain how all is interdependent rather than additive or independent. In this view the physical state is an organization of dynamic character, each element mutually sharing in the dynamic nature of the whole. This dynamic coexistence, or sympathy, is assumed to be a living organism because it mirrors the united structure of the living body. See Samuel Sambursky, *The Physics of the Stoics*.

46. ". . . [in] the period between Marcus Aurelius and the death of Constantine . . . the *locus* of the supernatural had come to shift significantly . . . What changed in no uncertain manner, however, between the second and fifth centuries, were men's views as to where exactly . . . 'divine power' was to be found on earth and, consequently, on what terms access to it could be achieved. In this period 'divine power' came to be defined with increasing clarity as the opposite of all other forms of power. The 'locus of the supernatural,' where this unique power was operative, came to stand for a zone in human life where decisions, obligations, experiences, and information were deemed to come from outside of the human community" (Brown, *The Making of Late Antiquity*, 8, 11).

47. Dodds, *Pagan and Christian in an Age of Anxiety*, 133–38.

48. Dodds, *Pagan and Christian in an Age of Anxiety*, 120.

49. Dodds, *Pagan and Christian in an Age of Anxiety*, 132.

50. See Toby E. Huff, *The Rise of Early Modern Science*, 228–34.

51. Within reasonable limits of accuracy, the fact that the orbit is an ellipse is hardly in doubt, except within discredited or at least unfashionable paradigms such as that of the earth-centered universe. The explanation of an elliptical orbit, however, depends upon the paradigm adopted. Within Newtonian mechanics, it is deduced from the existence of an attractive force between the planet and the sun; the mental image is that of a ball being whirled around on the end of an elastic string. Within Einsteinian relativity, the almost elliptical orbit is a consequence of the curvature of space-time, and the mental picture is of a ball rolling inside a funnel. Different mental pictures lead us to pose different questions. See Jack Cohen and Ian Stewart, *The Collapse of Chaos*, 362.

52. Ptolemy's cosmology described the physical picture by attaching the planets to small spheres rolling inside of larger spheres. This picture accounted for the discrepancies in motion and retrogradation and matched the observations as closely as possible. Whether these "spheres" were envisioned

by Ptolemy as cosmic structures or just mathematical models is still debated.

53. Einstein used Kepler's discovery of elliptical rotations to articulate how knowledge cannot advance from experience alone—for it builds on how the inventions of the intellect correlate with observed patterns. See Albert Einstein, *Ideas and Opinions*, 262–66.

54. J. L. E. Dreyer, *A History of Astronomy*, 392.

55. Quoted in Koestler, *The Sleepwalkers*, 352.

56. Quoted in Philip J. Davis and Reuben Hersh, *The Mathematical Experience*, 111.

57. Newton showed that basic laws of motion and gravitation can be applied to various situations in the heavens and on earth. The beauty of his laws is that the same quantitative relationships can be used in both domains.

58. See Koestler, *The Sleepwalkers*; S. Thayer, ed., *Newton's Philosophy of Nature: Selections from his Writings*; and E. A. Burtt, *The Metaphysical Foundations of Modern Science*.

59. In Thayer, *Newton's Philosophy of Nature*, 43–44.

60. The image of the machine would be good example of a cultural factor, for it was burgeoning and occupying, in an almost mysterious way, the imaginative space that formerly had been taken up by the image of God.

61. See Kline, *Mathematics and the Search for Knowledge*, and Burtt, *The Metaphysical Foundations of Modern Science*.

62. Plato, *Republic* 527B.

63. One could say that the Renaissance scientists were theologians with nature instead of God as their subject, and the transcendent God-created symbols held the unity together, despite the philosophical dualisms. In the medieval world there was the dualism of a realm of God and a realm of nature. Modern "dualism" was a more complexified dualism. In the Modern view, Cartesian duality supported two realms of Nature—one of spirit (which included mind) and one of matter. Of course this was necessary for God to remain supreme. And, of course, God's world continued to transcend both.

64. "Descartes has come after the Greeks with the naive condition that he could solve, by the purely rational method of the Greeks, all the problems which had been raised in between by Christian natural theology . . . what he did, at least in metaphysics, was to restate the main conclusions of Christian natural theology as if Christian supernatural theology itself had never existed. . . . the essence of the Cartesian God was largely determined by his philosophical

function, which was to create and to preserve the mechanical world of science as Descartes himself conceived it. . . . the God of Descartes was a stillborn God" (Étienne Gilson, *God and Philosophy*, 79–80; 87–89).

65. See Willis Harman, *Global Mind Change: The Promise of the Last Years of the Twentieth Century*; Jeremy W. Hayward, *Shifting Worlds, Changing Minds*; Gerald Holton, *Thematic Origins of Scientific Thought*; Thomas S. Kuhn, *The Structure of Scientific Revolutions*; Andrew Pickering, *The Mangle of Practice: Time, Agency, and Science*; Frederick Suppe, *The Structure of Scientific Theories*; and Frank J. Tipler, *The Physics of Immortality: Modern Cosmology, God and the Resurrection of the Dead.*

66. See Karl R. Popper, *The Open Society and its Enemies.*

67. See Thomas S. Kuhn, *The Structure of Scientific Revolutions*, and Karl R. Popper, *Quantum Theory and the Schism in Physics.*

68. See Karl Popper, "Normal Science and its Dangers."

69. Even still, light continues to break through. For example, systems theories and complexity theories were in fact invented to allow us to model nonlinear and ever-emerging possibilities within a living and multi-dimensional reality. When used to look at complex systems—like human life and human consciousness—they may offer a means for visualizing alternative options. Also, when combined with new techniques, such as computer modeling, these kinds of theories have the capacity to help us model information in ways that were not possible in earlier periods of science—when scientists were limited to theoretical and experimental modeling. According to Heinz Pagels, just as the telescope and the microscope changed our perspective of material reality, so does the computer because it allows us to manage enormous amounts of data and to simulate reality. Through these options we can process information in a new way. Thus the computer offers a unique window and a means to see all facets of reality differently. See Heinz R. Pagels, *Dreams of Reason.*

Areas of the electromagnetic spectrum that were unknown until the end of the nineteenth century (x-rays, gamma rays, radio waves, etc.) have also expanded our knowledge base. Through developing new tools capable of accessing these rays, scientists have gathered substantial empirical information about domains formerly invisible to our eyes, our microscopes, and our telescopes. See Amy Ione, "Defining Visual Representation as a Creative and Interactive Modality."

70. See Brewster Ghiselin, ed., *The Creative Process*; John Briggs, *Fire in the*

Crucible: The Self-Creation of Creativity and Genius; Amy Ione, "Multiple Discovery"; and Amy Ione, "Defining Visual Representation as a Creative and Interactive Modality."

71. The belief in one God seems to be the best and probably the most controversial example.

72. Child development is a good example of the kind of learning I am implying. A child does not simply build on ideas already learned, but repeatedly embodies new conceptual understandings. In doing so, she repeatedly reorients her relationship to life as previously known information is assimilated. Thus she uses newly discovered concepts to revise and reform her vision of reality.

73. Stuart A. Kauffman, *The Origins of Order*, vii.

Bibliography

Briggs, John. *Fire in the Crucible: The Self-Creation of Creativity and Genius*. Los Angeles: Jeremy P. Tarcher, 1990. Reprint. Grand Rapids: Phanes Press, 2000.

Brown, Peter. *The Making of Late Antiquity*. Cambridge and London: Harvard University Press, 1978.

Burtt, E. A. *The Metaphysical Foundations of Modern Science*. Garden City: Doubleday Anchor Books, 1954.

Cohen, Jack, and Ian Stewart. *The Collapse of Chaos*. New York: Viking, 1994.

Cornford, F. M. *From Religion to Philosophy*. Princeton: Princeton University Press, 1991.

Davis, Philip J., and Reuben Hersh. *The Mathematical Experience*. Boston: Houghton Mifflin Paperbacks, 1981.

Dissanayake, Ellen. *What is Art For?* Seattle and London: University of Washington Press, 1988.

Dodds, E. R. *The Greeks and the Irrational*. Berkeley: University of California Press, 1951.

——————. *Pagan and Christian in an Age of Anxiety*. New York: W. W. Norton, 1965.

Dreyer, J. L. E. *A History of Astronomy*. Cambridge: Dover, 1953.

Edgerton, Robert B. *Sick Societies: Challenging the Myth of Primitive Harmony*. New York: Free Press, 1992.

Einstein, Albert. *Ideas and Opinions*. New York: Dell, 1973.

Ghiselin, Brewster, ed. *The Creative Process*. New York: Mentor Books, 1952.

Gilson, Étienne. *God and Philosophy*. New Haven: Yale University Press, 1941.

Guthrie, W. K. C. *The Greek Philosopher: From Thales to Aristotle*. New York and Evanston: Harper & Row, 1950.

Harman, Willis. *Global Mind Change: The Promise of the Last Years of the Twentieth Century*. Indianapolis: Knowledge Systems, 1988.

Havelock, Eric C. *Preface to Plato*. Cambridge, Massachusetts and London: Belknap Press, 1963.

Hayward, Jeremy W. *Shifting Worlds, Changing Minds*. Boston: New Science Library, 1987.

Holton, Gerald. *Thematic Origins of Scientific Thought*. Cambridge: Harvard University Press, 1988.

Homer. *The Iliad of Homer*. Translated by Richard Lattimore. Chicago and London: University of Chicago Press, 1961.

Huff, Toby E. *The Rise of Early Modern Science*. Cambridge: Cambridge University Press, 1995.

Ione, Amy. "Defining Visual Representation as a Creative and Interactive Modality." In *Visual Representations and Interpretations*, R. Paton and I. Neilson, editors (Berlin: Verlag-Springer, 1999), 112–20.

——————. "Multiple Discovery." In *Encyclopedia of Creativity*, M. A. Runco and S. Pritzker, editors. San Diego: Academic Press, 1999.

Jaeger, Werner. *The Theology of the Early Greek Philosophers*. London: Oxford University Press, 1967.

Jaynes, Julian. *The Origin of Consciousness in the Breakdown of the Bicameral Mind*. Boston: Houghton Mifflin Company, 1976.

Kauffman, Stuart A. *The Origins of Order*. New York: Oxford University Press, 1993.

Kitto, H. D. F. *The Greeks*. Middlesex: Penguin, 1951.

Kline, Morris. *The Loss of Certainty*. Oxford: Oxford University Press, 1982.

——————. *Mathematics and the Search for Knowledge*. Oxford: Oxford University Press, 1985.

Koestler, Arthur. *The Sleepwalkers*. London: Hutchinson, 1959.

Kuhn, Thomas S. *The Structure of Scientific Revolutions*. Chicago and London: University of Chicago Press, 1970.

Laszlo, Ervin. *Evolution: The Grand Synthesis*. Boston: New Science Library, 1987.

Miller, David, ed. *Popper Selections*. Princeton: Princeton University Press, 1985.

Murray, Gilbert. *Five Stages of Greek Religion*. Garden City: Doubleday, 1955.

Pagels, Heinz R. *Dreams of Reason*. New York: Bantam Books, 1989.

Peat, F. David. *The Philosopher's Stone: Chaos, Synchronicity, and the Hidden Order of the World*. New York: Bantam, 1991.

Pickering, Andrew. *The Mangle of Practice: Time, Agency, and Science*. Chicago: University of Chicago Press, 1995.

Plato. *The Collected Dialogues of Plato*. Edith Hamilton and Huntington

Cairns, eds. Princeton: Princeton University Press, 1989.

Popper, Karl R. *The Open Society and its Enemies*. 2 vols. New York: Harper Torchbooks, 1962.

——————. "Normal Science and its Dangers." In Imre Lakatos and Alan Musgrave, editors, *Criticism and the Growth of Knowledge* (New York: Cambridge University Press), 51–58.

——————. *Quantum Theory and the Schism in Physics*. London and New York: Routledge, 1992.

Rees, Martin. "How Much Cosmology Can We Really Believe?" Hitchcock Lecture, University of California, February 28, 1995.

Sambursky, Samuel. *Physics of the Stoics*. Westport: Greenwood Press, 1973.

Snell, Bruno. *The Discovery of the Mind in Early Greek Philosophy and Literature*. Translated by T. G. Rosenmeyer. New York: Dover, 1982.

Suppe, Frederick. *The Structure of Scientific Theories*. Urbana and Chicago: University of Illinois Press, 1977.

Tarnas, Richard. *The Passion of the Western Mind*. New York: Ballantine Books, 1991.

Thayer, H. S., ed. *Newton's Philosophy of Nature: Selections from his Writings*. New York: Hafner Press, 1974.

Tipler, Frank J. *The Physics of Immortality: Modern Cosmology, God and the Resurrection of the Dead*. New York: Doubleday, 1994.

Whitehead, Alfred North. *Process and Reality*. New York: Free Press, 1929.

Wilford, John Noble. "Big Bang's Defenders Weigh Fudge Factor, a Blunder of Einstein's, as Fix for New Crisis." *The New York Times*, November 1, 1994, 7, 11.

Teaching Archaeoastronomy

GREG WHITLOCK

AMIDST THE STEEP CLIMB of technological progress, educational levels are sinking, threatening to leave society with a technological caste system of Brahmins and untouchables. The poor, illiterate, and disenfranchised see the gap widen between them and the technocrats; many feel that the consequences of science for their communities have been largely negative.

Science should have no ethnicity, no gender nor age. But saying that doesn't make it so. We need to work to create a multicultural context for science, to integrate it into the life of all people. One way is through archaeoastronomy.

Interest in ancient astronomy is a powerful means for promoting science in communities of all ethnicities, because it illustrates the universal character of science. Archaeoastronomy introduces scientific concepts to students and stimulates their inquiry into the pursuit of science. It reveals the connection between science and world views in different cultures. It puts present-day technological differences between societies into a world-historical context. And it helps to provoke thought regarding a much broader issue: the perceived disconnection between science and modern life.

In the humanities classroom, the role of astronomical observation in daily life can stimulate interest in science. In the science classroom, evidence of the equality of cultures and peoples can stimulate interest in multiculturalism. In this age as in the past, cosmology—the common ground of science, philosophy, religion, and myth—can create an interdisciplinary synergy.

The Science of the Whole

This reintegration is based on the assumption that science, in some form or other, is a universal activity. All people seek to discover meaning in human existence. Their yearning is the drive for an umbrella of illusions and pseudo-explanations. Culture is the result of any human endeavor to provide this meaning. Each culture constitutes a perspective from which individuals interpret the natural and social worlds. Nonetheless, complete difference between cultures has never been fully achieved; all cultures are related.

Multiculturalism combines this interpretation of culture with the principle of multiperspectivism: the idea that the truth is most closely approximated when the most perspectives are presented. Few people normally think of multiculturalism in the context of science, but there are important areas of overlap between the two. In science as in multiculturalism, a multitude of perspectives is a strong force; ultimately all forms of science, like all cultures, are related.

Though archaeoastronomy is a new field, it already has tremendous power as a tool for linking disciplines and cultures together. Colgate professor Anthony Aveni has defined archaeoastronomy as "the study of the practice and use of astronomy among the ancient cultures of the world based upon all forms of evidence, written and unwritten." Throughout history, human imagination has integrated the lights in the night sky into a larger view of human existence. The celestial lights have been recorded, noted, or remarked upon in an endless variety of ways, but the continuum of astronomical observation across cultures is indisputable.

Even though archaeoastronomy does not solve particular philosophical conundrums, it casts light on the methods whereby cultures attempt to do so. Aveni, one of the field's most philosophical thinkers, has distinguished two types of archaeoastronomy, "green" and "brown." So-called green archaeoastronomy, generally European, concerns itself entirely with astronomical alignments of ancient megaliths, buildings, and so on. So-called brown archaeoastronomy, practiced in the Americas, asks why people align structures astronomically. The brown variety seeks to integrate ancient astronomy into its cultural context, providing us with ideas about cultural history. An example is Linda Schele's work interconnecting Mayan astronomy with Mayan religion and philosophy.

By seeking to understand the purposes to which science is put, rather than seeking to judge ancient science by twentieth-century standards, a multicultural approach to archaeoastronomy avoids ethnocentrism. Ethnocentrism is a fallacy that takes one cultural perspective as universally valid. For example, even though the Sun-centered cosmology is a pivot in the history of modern science, most technologically undeveloped people do not need heliocentrism to explain events in their daily lives. Perhaps multiculturalism is no more (or less) than a temporary educational corrective for the ethnocentrism historically associated with science.

Ontogeny Replicates Phylogeny

"The most important lesson of archaeoastronomy" wrote astronomer Michael Seeds of Franklin and Marshall College, "is that humans don't have to be technologically sophisticated to admire and study the universe." The humans that Seeds referred to include our students as well as ancient peoples.

As I have used it in the classroom, archaeoastronomy puts Western, as well as Chinese, philosophy into a relativistic, multicultural context. It has stimulated students' interest in the physical sciences. I begin my Introduction to Philosophy course with a four-week study of the Mayan *Popol Vuh*, the earliest historical link between astronomy and philosophy. Subsequent topics include the cosmology of Heaven and Earth according to the Chinese philosophers Confucius and Lao Tzu, the cosmology of the Greek philosopher Plato, and the connection between Greek and Egyptian cosmology.

These topics give me the opportunity to introduce astronomical ideas such as the solar ecliptic, solstice and equinox, zodiac, phases of the Moon, motion of planets, Milky Way, and the precession of equinoxes. Even in the humanities, technical ideas and words don't have to be avoided in attracting students to science.

Students can readily identify with the perspectives of ancient astronomies, since they share the same geocentric image of the universe that results from earthbound, naked-eye observation. Just as astronomy developed historically from geocentrism to heliocentrism, our students' perspectives of the universe can develop. If, by analogy to biology, ontogeny replicates phylogeny, then we can use the history of cosmology to teach modern ideas to our students. Instead of just telling them that the Earth goes around the Sun, we can explain how, and among whom, this idea arose.

Despite the power of this approach, many educators give short shrift to pre-Copernican ideas, leaving students with the impression that modern science sprang sui generis from superior European intelligence—and, by analogy, that modern science issues forth from scientists like magic.

All modern forms of science, philosophy, and technology have deep historical roots. Because ancient astronomy was multicultural, the accumulated knowledge of astronomy, in the individual and in society at large, is multicultural. Ancient Egyptian and Greek astronomy are parts of a continuum of early scientific inquiry into the heavens, not the apex of a pyramid of ancient astronomies. Accomplishments of all cultures in science can be detailed as part of a course in the history of science. The once-forgotten Mayan and Aztec astronomy is a topic of great interest currently, though we should remember that India, Babylonia and China also undertook systematic observation.

A student interested in the history of science, through topics such as geocentrism or observational astronomy, may well continue into the study of physical science. As an example of a student in a humanities classroom crossing an interdisciplinary bridge, consider the following. One of my students became convinced that an undeciphered Mayan hieroglyph represented a comet. He researched occurrences of comets over Mesoamerica and was able to prove that, in fact, Halley's comet was seen shortly after the date inscribed in the text, unfortunately for his hypothesis. A month later, however, I read an announcement of the decipherment of the hieroglyph in question—as a comet. It was not Halley's, but a lesser known comet, that the Maya had seen. My student, stimulated by his inquiry, pursued a course in archaeoastronomy.

The progression from cosmology to early modern science is the great nexus of connections between the sciences and humanities, for no other reason than that they were in ancient times inseparable. Modern science has an organic relation to the entire history of humanity; its roots run deep, down to the first human inquiry. All cultures pursue scientific inquiry in some manner. Science, in turn, can and should marshal a colossal societal effort to improve the lives of all people.

Poliphilo and Polia Browsing the Ruins.

"Poliphilo likes ruins. He loves architecture. As Godwin points out, he is an architecture fetishist. . . ."

Oneiriconographia:
Entering Poliphilo's Utopian Dreamscape— A Review Essay

PETER LAMBORN WILSON

NEARLY TWENTY YEARS AGO when I was living in Rome, an Italian friend—a mystic student of alchemy—gave me the itinerary for a very strange little tour. It took two or three days to accomplish, and was limited to a small area some fifty miles north of Rome, in and around Viterbo. The tour focused on a series of Renaissance villas and gardens, built by various Roman aristocrats and princes of the Church as summer retreats (also included were Bagnaia, built for a Farnese, and the famous Tivoli, built for Cardinal d'Este), and linked by the fact that the architect, Giacomo Barozzi da Vignola (late sixteenth century), had worked for all or most of these patrons—who were roughly contemporary and all either friends or relatives of one another. The area seemed largely unchanged since the Renaissance (or even since the Etruscan period), and was at that time still relatively untouched by the blight of commercial tourism. Moreover, the architecture and landscape were uniformly exquisite. However, my itinerary was not meant solely to map an aesthetic experience. It was proposed as a puzzle, an esoteric mystery pilgrimage. There was something to be learned—some revelation—some transformation. I expected no less of my friend, the savant.

I have long since lost my notes from that trip, but I remember the highlights quite clearly. In the ancient little village of Soriano, there dominates an enormous and wonderfully mossy fountain, the Papacqua,

---

Hypnerotomachia Poliphili: The Strife of Love in a Dream by Francesco Colonna. The entire text translated for the first time into English, with an introduction by Joscelyn Godwin, with original woodcuts. London and New York: Thames & Hudson, 1999. Cloth, 476 pp., $70.00.

ΠΑΝΤΩΝ ΤΟΚΑΔΙ

Figure 1.
Papacqua Fountain, Soriano. Inset: Engraving from the French edition
of *Poliphilo* showing the "Mother of All" Fountain.

Figure 2.
Detail of the Temple of
Venus (top), *Dream of
Poliphilo*. Compare with
Temple of Venus by
Vignola, Villa Orsini,
Bomarzo.

designed for the Cardinal of Trente (fig. 1). Ruled by the figures of a reclining female satyr and her attendants—all leering, goatish satyrs and fauns—the Fountain centers "ideologically" around a huge, grinning representation of Pan himself, who is shown from the waist up as if he were walking through the very earth. Although the design of the Fountain is sophisticated and learned, the sculpture itself is slightly naive and almost rustic—which gives the archaic smiles of Pan and his companions an eerie profundity: a kind of weird, unpolished directness. No mere exercise in Classicism, the Papacqua has the presence of actual vision.

The villa and garden of Caprarola (designed by Vignola for a Cardinal Farnese) and the garden of Bomarzo (which contains a "Temple of Venus" by Vignola, built for a Duke Orsini) were the two focal points of the tour. Caprarola is one of the world's archetypal gardens: a *hortus conclusus*—paradisical, perfect. Greco-Roman mythological themes prevail. In fact, they predominate. In fact, there is not one Christian image *anywhere* in the Cardinal's house or garden. The eccentric and highly Catholic Queen Christina of Sweden (1626–1689) is said to have summed up her feelings about Caprarola thus: "It is as if our Savior had never breathed." Presumably she meant this as a criticism, not as praise—nevertheless, she seems to have hit upon the actual aesthetic of Caprarola.

Figure 3. "Sacred Forest," Villa Orsini, Bomarzo.

Photographs by Philip Greenspun.

As for Bomarzo, it gives the game away. Vignola's jewel-like Venus Temple (fig. 2) is the only work he did for the Duke Orsini, a mad hunchback and fanatical Hermeticist. The Duke designed the rest of the "Sacro Bosco" himself, and had the statuary cut by local stone-masons. The country folk called it the "Garden of Monsters" (fig. 3). Orsini took his images from emblem books, but twisted them toward the dark side—and whoever sculpted them was a self-taught genius of the bizarre. (I agree with the opinion that the same hand may be responsible for the Papacqua of Soriano.) A little house of marble is built with every angle and perspective askew, like a fun house in a carnival; a huge "Hell-Mouth" gapes open, wide enough to walk through; an elephant with a castle on its back crushes a man in its trunk; a turtle carries a chess-pawn with a nymph perched standing on it; a Herculean giant menaces the passerby with a club; a Siren with a split-fork fish-tail smiles seductively (fig. 4). Unlike Caprarola, Bomarzo was lost and forgotten until the 1950s, and when I saw it, the garden was still largely wild and overgrown, adding to its air of mystery, while softening its menace into a kind of surrealism. As with Caprarola, however, and Soriano, and other related sites, not one Christian image was to be seen in the "Sacred Forest" of Bomarzo. The key to the mystery of the tour was precisely an *absence*. Everywhere in Renaissance Italy one may see mythological themes mixed with Christian themes—pagan imagery is not hard to find. But on this trip, *Christianity* had completely vanished. Cardinals of the Church and Catholic noblemen had banished "Our Savior" from their own private worlds.

My friend the savant had a conspiracy theory about this mysterious absence. In his view, the tour he'd designed for me was meant to demonstrate the existence of a secret society of Hermeticists and neopagans who were not merely in love with Antiquity, but also in revolt against Christianity. I don't know if this view is shared by other scholars, but I found it quite persuasive. It's certainly clear that Neoplatonists like Pico della Mirandola and Marsilio Ficino, and occultists like Giordano Bruno, flirted with ideas and positions that ranged from mere heresy to outright apostasy—so why should there not have existed a secret cabal that, dissatisfied with toying, embraced them in their entirety? Hadn't I just seen an overwhelming load of

How could there not have been?

Figure 4.
Siren, Villa Orsini, Bomarzo (left). Woodcut of siren from *Poliphilo* (right).

circumstantial evidence for such a theory? On the poetic level, at least, I was convinced.

Years later, in the Bibliotheca Philosophica Hermetica in Amsterdam, I fell under the spell of a strange book: the *Hypnerotomachia Poliphili*, published in 1499 by the famous Aldine Press of Venice, and attributed to Francesco Colonna. One of the most prized of all incunabula for its exquisite printing and woodcuts, very few people actually *read* the *Hypnerotomachia*. It has a reputation for being long and exceedingly boring. About two-fifths of it was translated and published in 1592 in London; the translation by "R.D." is traditionally attributed to Sir Robert Dallington (1561–1637), a friend of Sydney and Essex. This rather badly-printed book, missing most of the woodcuts, has never received a modern edition. Instead, one may struggle with a facsimile,[1] which I first saw in Amsterdam and was later able to copy at the New York Public Library.

As soon as I began to read *The Strife of Love in a Dreame*, I discovered two things: first, that it was not boring in the least; and second, that I was at once plunged back into the world of Soriano, Caprarola and Bomarzo. Not only did I now realize that some of the woodcuts in the *Hypnerotomachia* must have been used as models in the Sacro Bosco,[2] but I also sensed immediately that I was reading myself into the very world that produced the evidence—architectural, sculptural, and botanical—of a conspiracy, a neopagan cabal in revolt against Christianity. If such a conspiracy existed, this book could have been or *must* have been one of the sacred texts of its conventicles. Not one of the emblems in the Aldine edition contains a single Christian image—despite the fact that Colonna was a Dominican monk. And, as I made my way into the thicket of R.D.'s translation, I came to understand that the text was not only *not* going to disappoint me, but in fact, it was going to *illuminate* the mystery of this absence. I had in my hands a veritable manifesto of the secret cabal I had been sent to discover, years ago, in the sweet countryside around Viterbo.

* * *

Unfortunately, the R.D. translation breaks off *in medias res* and leaves us dangling. An old French translation exists, and a modern Italian edition with copious notes,[3] both to be found in the Rare Book Room of the New York Public Library. I guess I could have sat there wearing white gloves for two years trying to decipher one or both of these. But luckily, I heard (from the editor of *Alexandria*) that Joscelyn Godwin, scholar of music and Hermeticism, had undertaken the gargantuan task of a complete English translation. For three years I waited, uneasily expecting to hear that Godwin had broken down under the strain.

But late last year—the 500th anniversary of the original publication!— Thames & Hudson unveiled Godwin's masterpiece. For the ardent Anglophone Poliphilophile, it would be no exaggeration to call this *the* publishing event of the demi-millennium. For one thing, Godwin's book looks uncannily like the original object. Folio-sized, large, and lavish—476 pages on fine paper—it is printed in a modern version (called 'Poliphilus') of the original typeface. Add to this the volume's being laid out in an elegant recreation of Aldine Press' exuberant juxtaposition of woodcuts and shaped bodies of type, and the Godwin *Hypnerotomachia* deserves to win some major award as a masterwork of both printing and literature.

In fact, despite the old French version, the annotated Italian edition, and a small mountain of scholarship, it could be argued that until 1999, a complete modern assessment of the work as literature remained impossible for all but a tiny elite. Given Colonna's bizarre Latinate

Veneto-Tuscan neology, this elite may actually consist only of one or two mad antiquarians—and Joscelyn Godwin. Moreover, given the probability that Godwin's version will fail to top any best-seller lists, or reap for him the reward he actually deserves for such mind-boggling exertions, he (and Thames & Hudson) must be thanked for a real donation to culture, and for self-effacing noble generosity.

Emerging after a week in the dream time of the Godwin *Hypnerotomachia*, it appears to me that the work can be seen as "fractal" in some strange way, such that even a tiny piece of it somehow infolds and recapitulates the whole. The "whole" itself, however, remains a kind of ruin, still indeterminate and unresolved. A book that cannot be finished cannot be "killed" by a final reading. My experience of R.D.'s fragment was colored by the notion of a neopagan cabal. Out of an uncountable number of possible readings, the one given to me was "political." When I first heard of Godwin's project, I wondered if a complete modern translation would constitute a disenchantment, a repudiation of my intuition. Not at all! A complete reading remains impossible—yet every page, every illustration, provides a hermeneutic opening, a fractal patterning, of the entire *Strife of Love in a Dream*. Godwin's version simply expands or inflates all possible experiences of the book, without exhausting any. The political reading remains more plausible than ever—along with dozens or hundreds of other readings. Each reader dreams, and each dream is unique.

* * *

If Colonna was a monk, he nevertheless appears to have been a rather dissolute, worldly, and quarrelsome one. Probably an aristocrat by birth,[4] he belongs in the same social category as the "conspirators" around Bomarzo, i.e., upper-class churchmen. He had a reputation as a "libertine"—but the sensuality and Epicureanism of the book bears no relation to the coldness of the eighteenth-century libertines, nor to the bawdy worldliness of, say, the *Decameron*. The most illuminating comparison might be with the paintings of Botticelli—*before* his "conversion" by Savonarola—such as the "Primavera" or the "Birth of Venus."[5]

This world is not merely sensual, but simultaneously magical, initiatic, and philosophical. Botticelli absorbed his "pagan" world-view from the Platonic Academies of Ficino and Pico, who read Plato through the lens of "Late Classical" Neoplatonism, Hermeticism, and theurgy. But the Renaissance Hermeticists' positive evaluation of sensuality and the material world is clearly not derived only from classical sources,[6] but rather it represents their own breakthrough into a world of "magical materialism"—a philosophy with political implications. The defense of the body against dualism and moralism constitutes the most radical plank in the platform of Renaissance neopaganism. By no means can the Hermeticists be considered simply as materialist precursors of "modern science," however. On the contrary, they were "pantheistic monists" in revolt against the Church and its "slander of the body," and in extreme cases, this position led to a sort of crypto-apostasy, replete with magic and neopagan ritual.

As Frances Yates never tired of pointing out, within the Reformation/Counter Reformation context, the Hermeticists represented a radical "third force" that is neither Catholic nor Protestant, neither humanist nor pietistic. A century after the *Hypnerotomachia*, the Rosicrucian manifestos articulated a political position inherent in Hermeticism from the very start: "radical tolerance" for all religions (including the "pagans, Jews, and Turks"), and a "universal religion" for an occult elite that was at once syncretistic, theurgic, mystical, and self-liberatory. Pico was excommunicated for this very same heresy, and Bruno was martyred for it.

Thanks to Dame Frances, we also know that in England the same ideas flared up—due in part to Bruno's visit there—in such circles as the "School of Night," which loosely included figures like Raleigh, Sydney, Dee, Marlowe, and Shakespeare. Whether or not "R.D." is Sir Robert Dallington, the *Dreame* is dedicated both to Essex and the memory of Sydney (Lucy Gent's introduction to the facsimile also traces its influence on Shakespeare and Drayton, among others), clearly placing it in this milieu. Not all of these men should be considered anti-Christian neopagans, of course—although Marlowe, the Faustian atheist, might be so considered—with his "Moses was a juggler" and other "Damnable Opinions." But the world they belonged to also had an underground or "shadow" realm, populated by heretics and cranks, spies,[7] and propagandists of illuminism: progeni-

SPIA

Figure 5.
Hermes as patron of
"Intelligence" from
Cesare Ripa, *Iconologia*
(1644).

tors of the later free-thinkers, conspiratorial Masons, Rosicrucian enthusiasts, and finally—William Blake.

To say that the Renaissance magi were "revolutionary" is not to imply that they were revolutionaries in any modern sense of the word. They were not. For the most part members of an educated elite, they betray no "class consciousness"—although there can be felt in their work a foretaste of what would later be called "Utopian Socialism" (in Bruno, for example, or Campanella and More). But they were very definitely *rebels*. Perhaps we could say that their proposed "uprising" was directed against the very structure of the "Cosmos": the "Ptolemaic world" of the medieval Church that seemed to suffocate them like a sealed tomb. Against the Church's monopoly of discourse they proposed a polysemy, a syncretism, an open circulation of cosmic imagery—and a *way out* of the enclosed reality of an orthodox dogma that was no longer a living faith. Like Protestants they rejected the mediation of hierarchy, claiming for themselves an "inner light"—but like Catholics they believed in the efficacy of image, ritual, and symbol. Whatever their political involvement (or non-involvement), they generated "thought experiments" about Utopia, and proposals for its achievement, at least on the level of the individual imagination. But alchemical ideals could be applied, in a kind of "Hermetic critique," to existing social conditions just as they were to spiritual ones. (Campanella and More did so explicitly, and the Rosicrucians envisioned distinct and radical reforms.) Hermeticism's real revolt was directed against the Church—but the Church was inseparable from "worldly" government. Gradually and to varying degrees the Hermeticists were drawn toward revolution.

Hermeticism developed, entered into a struggle for paradigmatic primacy with other philosophies and sciences, lost the struggle and went underground, surviving as an occult and "damned" alternative to more successful paradigms. Simply by losing its "war," Hermeticism was set to drift among other rebellious ideologies and tendencies— and to intermingle with them. In nineteenth-century France, the Hermeticists were divided into opposing political factions, both quite extreme: either reactionary magical monarchism or radical magical socialism. Examples of the latter camp would include Eliphas Levi (the ceremonial magician and socialist agitator), Charles Fourier (the "Utopian Socialist"), Gerard de Nerval, Flora Tristan, etc.[8] Other politically radical Hermeticists are not difficult to list, but the decisive name is Blake, heir to the entire Hermetic project, and progenitor of all modern visionary revolutionaries—at least in the English-speaking world. Blake's very existence allows us to *read back* a certain political tendency into the Renaissance, and to speak of what may be called a tradition of the Hermetic "Left."

The world of Poliphilo (the dreamer, the hero of the *Hypnerotomachia*) seems far removed from any such "political" considerations. Commentators may argue about the "true" interpretation of the text, but no one would deny that—at least on one level—it is self-enclosed, obsessive, fetishistic, intensely personal, and disengaged from the social (even from the "real") world—anything but overtly "political." But just as the hidden agenda of Soriano, Caprarola, and Bomarzo appears in the very absence of all reference to Christianity—an absence shared by our text—so it is the absence of all overt political discourse that defines the *politique* of the *Hypnerotomachia*. In other words, Poliphilo (Colonna) does not say that the social world should be so-and-so, or that the just ruler should do such-and-such. He is asleep, he is dreaming, he is himself gone from the daylight world of society, carrying with him into that other, new, alien world only one image from "back there"—that of his *absent* beloved, Polia. But the book is not simply a psychology of love—although it most certainly contains such a psychology. In fact, it must be stated at once that the *Hypnerotomachia* is, and was meant to be, a great many things simultaneously. For example, it is a disquisition on visionary architecture—

but architecture defines public space. Nothing could be more "political" than architecture. It is a discourse on Utopia, on the "No place" place (or *Eutopia*, the "good place") of imagination. But even the most outlandish and impractical Utopia is already an implied critique of existing social reality; nothing could be more political than Utopia. It is an alchemical handbook—but the goal of alchemy is self-liberation, symbolized here by the character of Queen Eleutherylida, or "Liberty." This *direct experience* of spiritual reality implies a necessary rejection of mediation and dogma,[9] which leads us again to the political.

The book is also a Neoplatonic treatise (though not strictly in the school of Ficino and Pico), and in fact, an apology for neopaganism. In the nineteenth century, Thomas Taylor could be considered a harmless eccentric for declaring himself a pagan, but in Renaissance Catholic Italy, it was a "burning" issue—as Bruno discovered. The publication of the *Hypnerotomachia* in 1499 can be seen as a deliberate provocation, but luckily for Colonna and the Aldine Press, the text was so obscure that no one really seemed to notice its full implications. The ithyphallic emblems (such as the "Triumph of Priapus" or the Triple Herm) caused a scandal, and it is now difficult to find a copy of the book in which the offending members have survived the Renaissance equivalent of "white-out." Indeed, R.D. ended his translation just before the Priapic Triumph, as if even the text alone would have been too hot for Elizabethan London. But centuries later, we can see the provocation clearly: a political gesture—in fact, the oblique manifesto—of an invisible insurrection.

If then we can accept the text as also an exercise in propaganda for a cause, however erudite and mystical, we shall be able to read the book on one possible level that may be called political, without in any way denying its many other facets. In this sense, our text—along with many other Hermetic texts—can be seen as a means of persuasion. The Renaissance magi had a very definite theory about the persuasiveness of the text and the image. This theory emerged from their study of the Egyptian hieroglyphs.[10] Basing their interpretation of the hieroglyphs on sources from Late Antiquity, such as Plotinus and the *Horapollo*, they developed a Neoplatonic reading that viewed the pictographs as archetypal rather than "alphabetic." Each hieroglyph contained or "was" the inner essence of the thing depicted, as well as being both an allegory of that thing, and a sign for its spoken name. Invented by Hermes, the hieroglyphs constituted a system of "magical writing," and to be able to read them would allow a kind of imaginal *projective semiotics*. The Hermeticists assumed that this projection would bypass the usual linguistic process, so that the archetypes would be able to impress themselves on the soul directly, so to speak, without the mediation of the discursive intellect. This "action-at-a-distance" defined the magic of hieroglyphs. The *initiated* reader of the hieroglyphs would receive not only this "subconscious" effect, but also the semantic context of the text—but everyone who saw the text would be influenced to *some* extent, whether they could "read" it or not. By applying their intuition to the hieroglyphs, the Renaissance magi (like the polymath Athanasius Kircher) hoped to "unscramble" Egyptian texts. In the end all of them failed, and their work has been buried in the trash bin of "early Egyptology" (not one single work by Kircher has ever been edited or translated)[11]—but in their heyday they believed they were very close to success. In fact, as Colonna realized, once one understood the *principle* of the hieroglyphs, one could invent them at will. The simple descriptions in *Horapollo* could be expanded into *emblems*, that is, image/text complexes structured like hieroglyphs. The emblems were both allegorical and symbolic—e.g., Hercules represented "strength," Eros "desire," etc.—and the scenes in which they appeared could be "translated" back into these words. But, Hercules was also Hercules, with all the mytho-magical symbolism associated with his tradition—so, each pictorial element in the emblem also worked on a non-verbal level of emotions, associations, and even dreams or the unconscious. Meanwhile, the image was usually accompanied by a text—sometimes one text in prose and one in poetry—that offered a "translation," or at least an interpretation, of the image: an "ideologization" or "alienation"—as Walter Benjamin noted—from the pure formalism of the image, to the "message" or hieroglyphic content of the image. In the most beautiful of all alchemical emblem books, the *Atalanta Fugiens* of Michael Maier, a further synaesthetic dimension was added with music (and the *ideal* emblem book would have smell and taste as well!). If Benjamin detected an air of *melancholia* that hangs over the emblem books, we might trace it to a paradox: the emblems were historically based on a failure of interpretation. The magi never managed to "translate" a single Egyptian text—and in a sense, the whole Hermetic project was a "failure" as well. But the *melancholia* itself—a psychic attribute of Saturn—was the very sign and seal of the ideal of creativity (as found, of course, in Dürer's famous print). On this level of "failure," the emblems were a success.

The emblem tradition—deeply influenced by the *Hypnerotomachia*, one of the first precursors of the genre—was entirely given over to propaganda in the sense that all emblems were "moral." Benjamin stresses the allegorical and moralistic aspect of the emblems, but if we concentrate on the specifically Hermetic emblems, we can admit that some "morals" are not moralistic at all, and that "alchemic polysemy" involves much more than a one-to-one translation of word-into-image, or vice versa. Books like the *Hypnerotomachia* are not only symbolic as well as allegorical, they are also *initiatic* texts. Concentration upon the images, meditation on the text and its relation to the images, and "inner work" on the self in light of the revelations and inspirations thus obtained, all allow the book, in a sense, to *replace* the "laboratory work" of alchemy—equating it, as it were—with an inner transformative process of directed imagination. Because the emblem is not merely discursive or lineal or completely accessible to reason, *because* the emblem is occulted, obscured, it needs to be penetrated on all cognitive levels simultaneously—inclusive of meta-rational levels of consciousness that lie beyond cognition in any ordinary sense. Precisely for these reasons, the emblem book becomes a process—or even a *performance*—in which the reader can achieve self-realization through the initiatory "magic" of the text.

Oddly enough, Benjamin never seems to have made the very obvious connection between the emblem books and modern advertisements—another of his obsessions. When he spoke of the "Utopian trace" in advertising he came close, but the full connection was finally analyzed by the late Ioan P. Couliano.[12] He pointed out the dark side—the "spectre" as Blake would say—of Renaissance Hermeticism, in that the very same hieroglyphic theory used in the cause of alchemic self-liberation could also be deployed in the opposite cause of *mind control*. Certainly the magi themselves were aware of this, and some of them were quite willing to experiment with it, either on behalf of their own neopagan propaganda—or on behalf of the highest bidder. One such Hermetic notion took hold of the imagination of rulers: the idea that the Egyptian obelisks were magic texts broadcasting the influence of pharaonic imperial power in public space (fig. 6). Western governments have been looting obelisks from Egypt ever since—the first being the Vatican—or else building their own, like the (Masonic) Washington Monument.[13] As Couliano pointed out, modern advertisers, PR flacks, spin doctors, disinformationists, propagandists, and "social planners" must be considered among the descendants and heirs of the Renaissance Hermeticists. The occultist revolutionaries—the Hermetic "Left"—may have failed to implement their Utopian politics by means of projective semiotics or hieroglyphic theory, but the advertisers have certainly succeeded. The tyranny of the Image has been universalized in our century. The cosmos of pan-capitalism has closed, like the Ptolemaic world of medieval orthodoxy, and all human relations are now mediated through the imagery of exchange—including the relation of the human and "Nature" itself, thanks to commercial bioengineering. In my view, one of the "burning" reasons to read the old Hermetic books is to recover hieroglyphic theory and reappropriate it for a critique of the Image, for a deeper understanding of the instrumentality of the Image, and for a self-liberation, for the "reader," from all projective

Figure 6.
Obelisk
designed by
Athanasius
Kircher for
Emperor
Ferdinand III.

semiotics. *In effect, we must ourselves write ourselves—or else be written.* The imagination is everywhere in chains—self-forged manacles as well as the restraints of consensus perception—under hypnosis, entranced, overpowered. Couliano's rather "Gnostic" point was that *knowledge* of Hermetic principles can free us from the malign Hermeticism of mediation. But theory is nothing without praxis, and the beginning of praxis is *to read*, to learn *how* to read—and how to write. As we read the *Strife of Love in a Dream*, we must not only learn *how* to read it, but simultaneously, also how to *recreate it imaginally* within ourselves—how to experience it as "inscribed" directly, how to "write" it in fact.[14]

Approached on such a level, the text is anything but boring! In fact, one of the first mysteries we must investigate is why everyone seems to have found it so dull.

* * *

The *Hypnerotomachia* has remained "one of the most celebrated, enigmatic, and unread books" in existence. Castiglione, in his *Courtier*, considered it to be long-winded, sarcastically referring to an "hour" of lovers' conversation, when spoken in the manner of *Poliphilo*, as being drawn out into what seems like a "thousand years."[15] "So often quoted and so little read,"[16] from a modern literary point of view it has been more often seen as "nonsensical,"[17] or as merely a curiosity. "[W]ritten in a florid and pompous Italian," it is teeming with "ornate and self-constructed words of Latin, Greek, and Hebrew origin," considered to be an obvious "display of the author's erudition."[18] Even Rabelais mocked Colonna for the "art-worship and belief in illusion" he found there.[19] Thus, from its first appearance to our own time, the *Hypnerotomachia* has been valued largely for its splendid woodcuts (which may have been designed by Mantegna) rather than for its text, which Benedetto Croce, as well, dismissed as a *bizzaria*.[20]

Reasons for this poor opinion of the book are not hard to imagine. For one thing, other peoples' dreams are always met with a strange resistance by our waking consciousness, which experiences such accounts as boring (or at the very least not as interesting as our own).

Moreover, the *Poliphilo*'s dream structure is not merely a literary convention, but quite essential to its interpretation. That is to say, it must be interpreted as dreams are interpreted—in a "hieroglyphical" manner—as we shall see. But if the text were simply and solely a dream narrative, or simply classifiable in some recognizable genre—any genre—then it would have no doubt found a place in the literary canon. The real problem of the text is that it violates expectations by shifting, looping, and interpenetrating itself through an almost endless set of literary categories, into a unique and unfamiliar form. For some readers, the resistance or unease caused by this "category problem" translates on the conscious level into boredom. Clearly the book is not a novel, since it bears no relation to "bourgeois reality"— but neither is it a romance, since it lacks any chivalric element. Its "plot" depends neither on a realistic representation of human relations, nor on a fantasy representation of wish-fulfillment. It is not an "epic" since it is written in prose, and contains no "national" or social element (despite a superficial resemblance to Dante, especially in the "Dark Forest" opening). The book cannot be called an allegory because it includes psychological reflection, and because its characters do not remain fixed in value (Poliphilo and Polia at least are "real" characters, even though they are also made to "stand for" certain ideas). Nor can we reduce it to the status of an alchemical handbook (with or without "Jungian" archetypes), except at the cost of an "erosion of categories"[21] and an impoverishment of interpretation.

It might be possible to say that the *Hypnerotomachia* is all of the above: dream, novel, romance, epic, allegory, Hermetic treatise, also an essay on art and architecture (an aesthetic tract), even a kind of emblem book, with emblems as elements in a narrative rather than simply a collection of image/texts. It might also be considered (as discussed above) to be a kind of manifesto for a spiritual movement with political implications. Although this last and least obvious of all the categories interests us most in the present reading of the text, it would be impossible to treat one such aspect in isolation. All of these levels are part of Colonna's deliberate "labyrinthian" structure, and cannot be disassociated from any attempt at interpretation. The text *moves* through all these categories in order to create its own *genus* and *species*—therefore, anyone who approaches the text with expectations about specificity of genre will be instantly repelled and disappointed.

One such obstacle for the reader of the original text would be its very language, Colonna's famous *pedantesca*, a gallimaufry of Tuscan, Venetian, Latin, Greek, and according to legend, Hebrew, Arabic, and Chaldean! (Though, as Godwin points out, there are only a few dubious bits of Hebrew and Arabic, and no discernible Chaldean.) The Rabelasian, Joycean, or even Carrollesque punning and "portmanteauishness" comes through in R.D.'s version, in which language itself sometimes seems to dream, boiling up such excited bits as "cataglyph," "eurythmy," "mustulent," "phane," "stilypode," "plemmyrules," "umbriphilous," "illaquiated," "gewgawes and gimmerie whatchets," etc. Moreover, R.D. had the advantage of being an Elizabethan and thus writing when English was still molten and protoplasmic, giving birth to itself. Godwin, in his preface, describes the dilemma that faced him as a modern translator: whether merely to translate the text, or attempt to "transcreate" it. The latter approach, he says, would result in such sentences as: "In this horrid and cuspidinous littoral and most miserable site of the algent and fetorific lake stood saevious Tisiphone, efferal and cruel with her viperine capillament, her meschine and miserable soul, implacably furibund." With obvious regrets, Godwin opts for the path of clarity, and gives us: "On this horrid and sharp-stoned shore, in this miserable region of the icy and foetid lake, stood fell Tisiphone . . ." (p. 249). Although at first I felt some disappointment that Godwin had not undertaken a true Poliphilic transubstantiation (Godwin himself mentions the danger of being "comprehensible but bland"), in the end I count myself among readers "relieved at the decision" to "honor every word of the original text" with a transparency that will allow me (some day!) to tackle the original with Godwin as guide. Certainly, Godwin's version is no mere trot. It has a deep elegance of its own.

Moreover, there are a number of "symbolic languages" at work in the text—the language of flowers and plants, the language of gems, the language of classical allusions (used structurally, as in old Chinese or Persian poetry), the language of music, and so on. Each of these systems provides yet another template, so to speak, that can be applied to the text, or peeled away from the text, like palimpsestic layers. In short, we can use the term *hallucinatory logothetism* to describe this style. A *logothete* (originally a title in the Byzantine Court) constructs a universe of words and then lives in it, as Barthes said of Sade, Loyola, and Fourier. In this sense we might speak of an interchangeability of words and images, so that the logothete is also an iconothete, like William Blake. I assume that the Surrealists took an interest in the *Hypnerotomachia*, which so uncannily foretells their obsessions with dreams, dream words, emblems and heraldry, alchemy, sexuality, anti-Christianity, and other Poliphilesque themes under the "sign of Saturn," or creative *melancholia*. Perhaps the most modern aspects of the book are its obsessiveness, fetishism, erotomania, experimental-ism, and its *sui generis* uniqueness. Colonna's disguise/revelation of authorship (an elaborate acrostic formed out of the first letters of each chapter), and the problematical identities of Poliphilo (author? hero?) and Polia (real? not real?), lend an air of deconstruction to the work that seems quite contemporary. In fact, perhaps the book can only really be read now, now that all the categorical expectations of "Western Culture" have been questioned or even discarded. We no longer feel anxiety when confronted with a text that makes no claim to be anything but itself; this is our modern "pleasure of the text," liberated from preconceptions, open to textual adventure—and at home with dissolution and madness.

Not that I wish to make any argument that seems to validate the book because of its modernity—especially since Colonna himself was so obsessed with *Antiquity*. The word *polia* can mean either "bright/shining" or "ancient." Poliphilo ("lover of *polia*") is therefore in one sense an antiquarian. Perhaps his obsessive browsing amongst the ruins of Antiquity can be compared with Postmodernism in some way. But these are not value judgments, pro or con. All I mean to say by this is that we are "at last" free simply to *read* the *Hypnerotomachia* without category-*angst* and therefore hopefully without boredom.

* * *

Poliphilo falls asleep in Treviso, near Venice, in the spring of 1467. In his dream he comes upon a large dark forest. He hears a voice singing and tries to follow it, but fails. Exhausted, he falls asleep within the dream (so that everything that comes after may be a dream within a dream, although Godwin's "map" of the plot does not suggest this). When he wakes again, he finds himself out of the wild, wolf-haunted wood and into culture—a deserted landscape of ruins.

Poliphilo likes ruins. He loves architecture. As Godwin points out, he is an architecture fetishist. He feasts his eyes on the antique landscape. His *scopophilia*, or love of "looking," constitutes a major theme of the book; Colonna seems to accept Vision as chief of the senses, in agreement with most classical and Renaissance theory. The Tyranny of the Eye alone might become oppressive, but our dreamer is no mere "sightseer" or tourist—we will learn that his other senses are no less acute. But now he gives vent to an ecstasy of the Antique, and his language takes on the vocabulary of an expert and connoisseur of architecture.

The entire landscape of ruined and half-ruined buildings and statues clearly constitutes a series of emblems. The weeds and briars growing around the ruins, the swifts flitting between the broken columns, the lizards "crawling among the overgrown stones": Nature itself reinforces the symbolism of the architectural space and its museum (or "musoleum") of images. The architecture fails to remind us clearly of Renaissance neoclassicism, despite Colonna's probable debt to Leon Battista Alberti and his *De re aedificatoria*.[22] Moreover, despite the great "spire" of the obelisk, there is also nothing particularly medieval about Colonna's architecture. Since he had never seen real Egyptian buildings, he could neither describe them nor instruct his artist how to depict them. The building style of the *Hypnerotomachia* can certainly be called "visionary"; it takes its place at the head of a long tradition of "eccentric" architecture typified by, say, Simon Rodia's Watts Towers in Los Angeles—or the "Garden of Monsters" at Bomarzo. But all visions, even the most original, must be based on some cultural matrix. In Colonna's case, the imaginal source belongs to the world of Late Antiquity, with its mélange of Greek, Roman,

Egyptian, and Oriental styles and religions. As Wind and Couliano both emphasize, the *early* Renaissance first came into contact with this *late* and rather "decadent" classical past, not with the "real" classical period of Plato and Aristotle so much as the twilight world of Iamblichus, the cults of Isis and Serapis, Theurgy, and the *Corpus Hermeticum*. This is the past ("*polia*") so lovingly recreated in Poliphilo's dream, and the key to its significance lies in the omnipresence of "Egyptian hieroglyphs."

Not only is the whole landscape-with-ruins meant as an emblem, the architecture itself is *inscribed* with emblematic imagery and rebus-texts. The *Dream* contains a map, and the coordinates of the map are the actual buildings and emblems seen in the dream. The map is also "drawn" with plant references, jewel references, perfume references, etc., in a complex *over-writing*, or palimpsestic technique of redundancy or over-determination, as well as camouflage and steganagraphy (secret coding). No doubt for Colonna each detail of the architecture was meaningful—he often gives exact measurements, as if the very proportions or symmetries were significant and decipherable. But lest we fail to interpret one level of the map, we are always given other series of coordinates with the same meaning. The principle in all cases derives from the *hieroglyphic theory* described above, in which Neoplatonism's collection of Egyptian fragments was sifted and resifted for patterns of illumination. Colonna was one of the first hieroglyphic obsessives of the Renaissance. He may have "cracked" *Horapollo* on his own, and taught himself to "write hieroglyphics," or he may have learned the secret from some teacher or book unknown to us. He influenced the whole subsequent tradition—for example, Pierio Valeriano, author of the highly influential *Hieroglyphica* (1556), met Colonna in Treviso when Pierio was sixteen.[23] Even such a later figure as Athanasius Kircher still regards Colonna as an "expert," and in the art world, Colonna's theories would still influence a Piranesi in the eighteenth century.

Poliphilo's thrill as he confronts the ruins, the excitement that drives his minute descriptions, arises from the realization of hieroglyphic theory (synthesized by *dreaming*) in the form of this vast and meaning-saturated landscape. It is clear that a *process* is underway, a voyage—a promise of becoming, of transformation. On one level, it will consist of a search for Polia, the lost/absent beloved, since many signs and symbols will speak of her and continually rekindle Poliphilo's desire and despair. But at the same time, it will also constitute an alchemical operation, a Hermetic initiation, in which Poliphilo as *materia prima* will undergo the stages of the spagyric art and attain realization of the Philosopher's Stone—that is, of Polia's love.

In the opening sequence of the *ruins*, for example, we have a series of images: the wolf, the ruins themselves, a huge black elephant carrying another hieroglyphic obelisk, and a gargantuan hollow Colossus into which Poliphilo descends, reaching the very bowels—images all suggestive of the alchemic stage of *nigredo*: blackness or dissolution. With his usual obsessive doubling and redoubling of images, Colonna recapitulates the whole series in a climactic encounter between Poliphilo and a dragon, who actually chases him into and through the great emblematic Gate of the Pyramid/Temple, causing him to lose himself in dark underground cellars, tunnels, and caves. We also see sculpted images of a Hell-Mouth much like the one at Bomarzo, a gigantomachy, a dedication "To the Ambiguous Gods," an allegory of Time and Loss, a sepulcher in which a King and Queen are shown, and various terrors of the labyrinth beyond the Gate—all symbolizing the same initiatic complex: despair and breakdown as the beginning of wisdom—the dark night of the soul.

Among the significant inscriptions on the Gate we find "*Nihil firmum*, Nothing Permanent," and in Greek and Latin, "To the Holy Mother Venus and her Son Amor, Bacchus and Ceres have given of their own substances." Thus the emblems themselves are seen as fluid, impermanent, uncertainly bordered, sharing each other's substance. The emblems are not simply a linear series, but also a set of "loops," or interpretations and recapitulations—"a net of jewels in which each reflects all," as the Oriental tradition would express it.

The original illustration of the Gate shows only the outline, but a later French edition "improved" on it by filling in the blank spaces with tiny versions of the scenes described in the text. Although this filling-in reduces the scope of the reader's imagination, it helps to realize how Colonna intended such illustrations and texts as *Memory*

Palaces. Each space left vacant in the ground-design is to be filled imaginally with memory-images, each of which can be "unpacked" or cross-referenced at will. In this way, one can not only memorize vast knowledge-systems but also *process* information, since the whole system is "alive" through the ever-fluid or mercurial imagination—in short, a magical epistemology, as studied by Frances Yates in her works on Bruno. In fact Yates believed that the *Hypnerotomachia* could be a matter of mnemotechnics "escaped from control and degenerated into wild imaginings."[24] I believe however that Colonna's system is very much under his control both as an artist and as a Hermeticist. The difference between his text and one of Bruno's more theoretical works is that Colonna's system is seen in *motion* (in narrative) and in *transformation* (as alchemy), rather than as a simple framework or file-index. Colonna is using the information he has memorized, translated into hieroglyphic complexes, and arrayed within an entire alternate universe of form and image—*using* it, not merely recording it. In Sufism, the "Stations of the Way" are often symbolized as caravanserais, or even palaces. (The *Hypnerotomachia* might be usefully compared with a work such as Nezami's *Seven Palaces*, another alchemical fantasy of architectural eros. Another fruitful comparison might be made with certain Taoist romances, or prose-poems describing visionary palaces, mountains, grottoes, etc.) The aesthetic result of this metaphor system is the creation of an *eros of space*. Not only is the architecture and its imagery devoted to an alchemical allegory of Love, Colonna himself is erotically fired by architecture, which for him, "is that cleare and perfect light,"

> which sweetly and with our unconstrained willes draweth our dimme sighted eyes to contemplate and behold the same. For none (unles it be he which of set purpose refuseth to behold it) but his eyes would dasell [dazzle] with continual desire to see it (R.D.'s version, pp. 57–58).

After all, this is dream architecture. Here the obelisk—which, to the ancient Egyptians, for example, represented a beam of sunlight in mathematical proportion—can be seen as reverting again from the condition of stone to the condition of light. The dream is not under the control of Poliphilo, but the *Poliphilo* is indeed under the control of Colonna. Or so it seems—after all, we find the symbolism coherent, not just "wild imaginings." But again, Poliphilo is not the only dreamer. Language itself is dreaming—hence the dream-like and portentous *significance* of all objects and events that gives the text its air of fetishism. The fetish is an object imbued with iconic power, over-determined in meaning, and saturated with desire. The goal of the text is *seduction*.

But what is the goal of the seduction itself?

* * *

Among other things, the seduction aimed at the reader includes (or is included within) a *theoria*, or "vision." Speaking loosely, this theory can be nothing other than the philosophy of Eros that also inspired Colonna's fellow Renaissance Hermeticists and Neoplatonists. The "Late" Classical origins of this theory (or group of theories) are elucidated succinctly by Couliano, and it would take us too far astray to repeat his outline here. But we should again emphasize that Colonna's "Neoplatonism" seems in no way directly influenced by that of Ficino or Pico. If the book was indeed written in 1467, then it could scarcely have made use of Ficino's first Hermetic foray (a translation of the *Pimander*) in 1463. As Couliano points out, this "escape" from Ficino's influence is "invaluable," since it allows a parallel development of Neoplatonic sources that is "personal, original, and inimitable."[25] Wind believes that "some of the best-informed scholars" are wrong to claim that "the *Hypnerotomachia* was conceived by an unphilosophical mind. The notion, deliciously phrased in the *Hypnerotomachia* . . . that matter has an appetite for form and rejoices in it, is indeed [not rigorously Thomistic]" but "occurs in Aristotle . . . : matter desires form 'as the female desires the male.'"[26] In other words, Colonna is neither a "rigorous" Scholastic nor a card-carrying Neoplatonist, but an "original" philosopher (or *crank*, depending on one's taste).

It is a paradox—or perhaps a contradiction—of Platonist thought that it can both value and devalue the "material world." Plato himself

Figure 7. Poliphilo with Nymphs at the Fountain of Venus.
"During the Renaissance, the radical elite came into contact with the
Neoplatonic 'defense of pleasure' . . . Those who were attracted to it,
however slightly, were justifiably suspect in the eyes of the Church."

adhered to a body/spirit dualism that led him to define the material
world as a bad shadow-copy of the world of spirit, or of the eternal
Ideas. The emanationist cosmogony of the Neoplatonists softened the
edges of the break between spirit and matter by extending the process
into a hypostatic series of ten demiurgic or angelic stages—but in the
end "matter" was still at the bottom of the series: flawed, imperfect,
longing for disembodiment. Faced with the radical Dualism of the
Gnostics, however, the Neoplatonists began a rear-guard defense of
the material world. As the site of theophany, "matter" will also find its

adherents amongst the Sufis. In fact, Ibn 'Arabi maintains that *oneness* cannot be contemplated except in *form*, in "many-ness," in the image, or in the "material object" itself. In this view, the material ("Earth") is not merely the bottom of the series but also its *center*. Oneness requires "Many-ness" in order to realize its ontological perfection: "I (Allah) was a Hidden Treasure, and desired to be known; therefore I created the world," as the *hadith* expresses it. Again in polemic with the Dualists, the Neoplatonists undertook (with much hesitation and equivocation) a defense of *pleasure*. Here again Sufi parallels are not difficult to find, nor is it hard to fall into a confusion of categories that the Sufis themselves (like other Occidental Christian counterparts) sometimes exacerbated in order to camouflage their deviation from orthodox doctrine. "Wine, music, and the beloved"—are these *topoi* meant to refer to allegorical conceits? (Wine=divine ecstasy, music=invocation, beloved=Sufi master, etc. ?) Or are they referring to forbidden material realities? Blood has been spilled over such niceties of literary analysis. Different Sufis propose different answers at different times—including the impeccably orthodox answer of "allegory." But the most subtle thinkers and poets of the "School of Love" (Ahmed Gazzali, Mahmud Shabestari, 'Iraqi, Ruzbehan Baqli, Hafez, etc.) often give the impression that *both interpretations are simultaneously true* (i.e., both "allegory" and "identity").

During the Renaissance, the radical elite came into contact with the Neoplatonic "defense of pleasure" and recognized it as catastrophic for Pauline dogma and Catholic morality. Those who were attracted to it, however slightly, were justifiably suspect in the eyes of the Church. In a sense, and taken to extremes, the Hermetic neopagans were proposing a kind of "Neoplatonism" that bore little or no relation to the "puritanism" of a Plato or an Augustine. They threatened to "turn the world upside down" by *restoring nobility* to "Earth," and a kind of primacy to matter itself. Nicholas of Cusa, a Hermeticist within the Church, swept away the Ptolemaic bottle shop with a grand gesture: the universe is *infinite*. Thus,

> Cusanus' effort, like that of Giordano Bruno, later his disciple, was directed toward the reevaluation of the metaphysical prestige of the

earth, hence of man—a prestige it had lost through Aristotelian-Ptolemaean cosmology. A fundamental reform of Christianity is envisaged in this new concept of the world.[27]

This new doctrine is nowhere explicitly expounded in the *Hypnerotomachia*, and this reticence is only to be expected, not only from fear of the Church, but more so because in Hermeticism, a doctrine must be expressed obliquely ("hieroglyphically") in order to be *effective* as a means of transformation. We as readers must play the active role of the dream-interpreter, not the passive role of the mere seeker of entertainment or edification. Unless we have "won" the meaning of the text for ourselves, we have simply failed to read the text. Above all, then, the textual *seduction* leads us to a method of reading, a hermeneutical exegesis as Corbin called it,[28] which is simultaneously an appropriation: an imaginal recreation of the text within ourselves as a "palace of memory" and working system of alchemical transformation. To read the *Dream* hieroglyphically is therefore to *write* it, to inscribe it within ourselves. In this sense, its "doctrine" will finally emerge only in our own responses to the symbolic set and setting of the narrative, as a series of organic *conversions* rather than merely intellectual perceptions. We must dream our way into the text and become Poliphilo's co-dreamers. And thanks to the "magic" of the text, which is not merely a stylistic mood but an *experimental science*, we are drawn by Colonna's persuasive seductiveness into the *beauty* of this world, wherein spirit and matter are one. Now we, too, have become figures in a landscape.

* * *

This landscape is both Utopian and eutopian. The architecture that appears within it recalls the strange Hermetic visionary objects that stand out against the bucolic landscape backgrounds of such alchemical emblem books as the *Atalanta Fugiens* (fig. 8). As Poliphilo penetrates deeper into Utopia, the wild forest of Nature and the ruins of Culture coalesce, or rather mate, in an ecstasy of sensual and

Figure 8. Utopian Landscapes from *Atalanta Fugiens*.

emotional pleasure. Again and again, the reader feels painted into the world of, say, Botticelli's "Primavera"—for example, the episode of Poliphilo and Polia in the meadow of adolescent lovers (177 ff). Expressed in words, as well as emblematic images, such Renaissance visions are freighted with literary references to Ovid on the Golden Age, and behind him Hesiod on the "Four Ages" and Pindar on the Hyperboreans.

As Yates pointed out in *Astraea*, the symbolism of the Golden or Saturnine Age *reborn* could have alarming political implications. A certain mystical messianism, which could attach itself to "progressive" monarchs or to ancient Rome-inspired republicanism, permeated the Hermetically-influenced elite circles of the Renaissance—and even the seventeenth century. (Freemasonry was likewise to have both a "left" and a "right" wing, both "conspiratorial.") The Golden Age was a radical concept because it implied egalitarianism, communal property, sexual "license," and other ancient rites and customs (as E. P. Thompson called them in *Customs in Common*). But the Golden Age could also be a "radical conservative" idea when it became the slogan of a power-seeking elite. Giordano Bruno reveals both sides of this Utopianism when he criticizes property, for example, but also speaks of the need to "manipulate" the masses for their own good.[29] Up to a point, all premodern revolutions were ideologically "backward-looking," since the very idea of progress in our modern sense of the term is missing, and social perfection was imagined as existing in the "past." Messianism, however, contains within it the seed of "progressive" thinking, since it does posit a *future* perfection. As for the Utopian ideal, even in its Ovidian, Pindaric, or Hermetic form, it continued to inspire radical thinkers well into the nineteenth century—and it may happen that we shall discover echoes of the *Hypnerotomachia* in the first manifestations of "modern socialism."

Of course, Colonna's "No-place" place represents the impossibilism of the dreaming subject, evoking by its very unreality the potential of "Perfectionism" (as J. H. Noyes, the American utopian socialist, called it), the notion that heaven on earth is both a spiritual and a political goal. This is the *praxis*, the inevitable completion of the theory of *Eros and Magic in the Renaissance*. To study the full implications of this emblem-landscape we should look ahead to the Rosicrucian manifestos.[30] The evocation of Utopia always carries with it the implied possibility of revolutionary realization.

* * *

Poliphilo finds the culminating version of eutopian space after his embarkation with Polia for the Isle of Cytherea, the magical Versailles of Cupid himself, laid out like a mandala (see Godwin's map, p. 475). But this magnificent climax has already been foreshadowed by the hero's initiatic experiences in the land of Queen Eleutherylida. Godwin translates the name as "free will," but it could also mean "Liberty" (or even, in Rimbaud's famous slogan, *la liberté libre*). The adventure begins at a fountain with a sculpted back wall showing the goddess of Nature sleeping under the gaze of an ithyphallic satyr (perhaps the inspiration for the Papacqua of Soriano). There he is discovered with five nymphs, representing the five senses, and conveyed by them to an exquisite crystal bath house. Poliphilo consumes a series of entheogenic substances, starting with water from the marble breast of the sleeping Nature-goddess ("Virgin's Milk," in alchemical terms). At the bath, the nymphs trick Poliphilo, first with a statue of a naked boy that piddles cold water in his face (boy's urine is also an alchemical commonplace). The giggling girls smear him with an unguent that gives him a raging, embarrassing erection, then another salve to cool him off. Then they invite him to Queen Liberty's feast, where foods and wines will be served, so magical that one might justly call them psychedelic.

Refreshed and given a new suit of clothes, Poliphilo now sets out with the nymphs for the court of the Queen. In front of the palace, they find yet another fountain (clearly the land of Liberty lives under the sign of mercuric fluidity), this one featuring a triplet of sphinxes with tangled serpentine tails, and the Three Graces themselves bearing intertwined cornucopias (fig. 9). Among the many fascinating "morals" and alchemical hints that could be gleaned from this structure, we might find Seneca's meditations on the Graces helpful in understanding Colonna's intentions:

"Why the Graces are three, why they are sisters, why they interlace their hands," all that is explained in *De Beneficiis* by the triple rhythm of generosity, which consists of giving, accepting, and returning. As *gratias agere* means "to return thanks," the three phases must be interlocked in a dance as are the Graces . . . for "the order of the benefit requires that it be given away by the hand but return to the giver," and although "there is a higher divinity in the one that gives," the circle must never be interrupted.[31]

Most emblemists follow the artistic convention of showing one Grace full-face, one half-face, and one turned away—since, as Pierio Valeriano explains in the *Hieroglyphica*, the giver gives "without ostentation," the receiver receives openly and shows gratitude, while the one who returns the benefit "hides the restitution but exhibits the benefit obtained."[32] Colonna's Graces are mirrored by the three sphinxes, expressing the dialectic as a mystery or hieroglyphic secret, and the horns of plenty indicate that the "giving" is done by and within the world of Nature's bounty, or lavish (triple) generosity. Again water spouts from the Graces' breasts, falling upon the heads of the dragons and passing through the mouths of the lions and harpies, in a reinforcement or over-inscription of the basic symbolism of the Graces. And all this serves to introduce Queen Liberty as the synthesis of the dialectic of Beauty, Love, and Pleasure.

The Queen's Court is designed around the theme of the astrological planets, and other heptads and multiples of seven. The Queen will occupy the seat of the Sun, which (as Charles Fourier and other Hermeticists have noted) is the visible god of the cosmos. The nymphs of the senses will take other planetary places, leaving Poliphilo the seat of Mercury (since, as M. Serres pointed out, Hermes is always the *guest*, the odd number). Six more nymphs make up twelve women in all—plus Poliphilo: a year of months, a zodiac of thirteen, a coven.

The Queen appears—gracious and beautiful, of course—her solar presence enhanced by gold and diamonds. After a polite questioning of Poliphilo, she invites him to his seat. All take their places, and now begins (with music) the ritual of the Court, the ceremony of the liberty of the senses—one of the most astounding and original of Colonna's

Figure 9.
Fountain of the Three Graces (left). Compare with the Goddess of
Nature (right), Villa d'Este, Tivoli.

imaginal artifices. The rite takes the form of an unbelievably elaborate
banquet, in which the Queen and her court are served by yet more
damsels, wheeling huge mobile fountains of perfume or mechanisms
for the dispersion of incense around the room, strewing the floor with
violets, etc. As the guests toy with gold balls of wire-work full of amber
("to the end [that] their hands, eyes, and senses should not be idle"),
a series of seven courses is served, each more rich and strange than the
last.

Now a cordial confection was presented, which I think I am right in
saying was a healthy compound made mostly of powdered unicorn's
horn, the two kinds of sandalwood, ground pearls in brandy set alight so
as to dissolve them completely, manna, pine-nuts, rose water, musk and

powdered gold . . . weighed and pressed out in morsels with fine sugar and
starch . . . six cuts of fattened, blinded capon, moistened with its own fat,
sprinkled with yellow rosewater mixed with orange juice, roasted to
perfection and then gilded all over. With this came six slices of snow-
white bridal bread, and beside it a sauce of lemon juice modified with fine
sugar mashed with pine nuts and the capon's liver, to which were added
rosewater, musk, saffron and choice cinnamon;

and so on, through partridge in crushed almonds, pheasant in egg yolk
and pomegranate sauce, peacock in sour green pistachio sauce, and a
dessert of dates ground with gold. All this accompanied by divine
wines and served on plates of emerald, beryl, jasper, and whatnot.

Charles Fourier would have loved this scene, with its quaint "Museum Orgy" atmosphere, its "gastrosophic" cookery, its bold defense
of the blissful luxury and exquisite pleasure that results from spiritual
liberation. Moreover, to read the passage as Fourier would have done
is already to answer a question about it that has puzzled the commentators. Why, if this be the ritual of *Liberty*, must it follow a rigid and
courtly formality—and why do some serve the banquet while others
enjoy it? How can this choreography of refined sensuality and apparent hierarchy be reconciled with the idea of *Liberty*? Indeed, how can
there exist a *Queen* of Liberty?

Fourier would explain that in Utopia (or "Harmony," as he called it),
ceremonial titles are bestowed on artists, musicians, chefs, and ge-
niuses of sexuality—masters or mistresses of all the Passions. It is in
actuality these aristocrats who serve all by virtue of the intensity of
their Passion, and if they are served in turn by all, it is with a voluntary
and amorous servitude, a kind of voluptuous and erotic joy. Moreover,
those who volunteer to serve today may be served tomorrow, and take
their turns at the high table—such is perfect liberty. When all Passions
are fully realized, they will mesh and organize themselves spontaneously for the luxury and pleasure of all. Desire (and realization) are the
only possible sources of freedom and order—which are not opposites,
but complements. There can be no doubt that Colonna believed this,
or something like it. The banquet of Queen Liberty is a vital key to
understanding the *politique imaginaire* of the *Hypnerotomachia*—a kind

of alchemical anarchism, or even "Utopian Socialism," always characteristic of the Hermetic "Left." In this alchemical exaltation of the body (or the "material bodily principle" as Bakhtin says), we find that body, soul, and spirit are "one" because they cannot be separated. And once again, in this Utopia of desire, we find ourselves present at Blake's "Marriage of Heaven and Hell": the *coincidentia oppositorum* beyond good and evil.

* * *

> "Aux beaux Esprits Qui
> Arresteront Leurs Yeux
> sur ce projets de plaisir sérieux"
>
> —*Le Tableau des riches inventions couvertes du voile des feintes Amoureuses, qui sont representées dans le Songe de Poliphile.* Desvoilées des ombres du Songe & subtilement exposées par Béroalde, *p. ii* [33]

Béroalde de Verville, who published his own French edition of the *Hypnerotomachia* (1600), invites us to read it as *lusus seriosus*, a "serious" joke or game, according to an old definition of alchemy. Donne and the English Metaphysicians used the word "wit" in a similar manner: "beautiful spirits" read with the I-sight of in-wit; they read *into* the text—and sometimes read something into the text that is "not there." They engage the text in a performative manner, as play, as mutability, as Bakhtinian "dialogue" rather than "dead letter." They recreate the text within themselves and make it their own. Béroalde has given us the key to such a performance of the *Dream of Poliphilo* in his *Recuil Steganagraphique*, an alchemical essay that serves as his introduction to the French translation. This deep reading of the book is given a hieroglyphical or emblematic dimension by a beautiful title-page, apparently designed at Béroalde's instruction, in which the inner structure of Colonna's text (rather than its outer narrative form) is illustrated (fig. 10).

Béroalde's boast—that he has unveiled the *Dream* of its shadows—

seems to annoy the art historians. Anthony Blunt says the Steganagraphic Note and Frontispiece "seem to have very little to do with the *Songe* and are . . . not in themselves important."[34] He calls Béroalde a libertine, and associates him with a group of similar minor writers:

> Socially this group was a relic of the chaos, material and moral, of the end of the Wars of Religion. Its members typified the Bohemian escape from the unpleasantness of the world into a doctrine which denied that there could be any positive standards for the conduct of life.

They "degenerated into anarchy" and were "attacked by the progressive writers of the period," an attack carried out "in the name of reason and common sense on the fantastic and affected culture" of writers like Béroalde.

Edgar Wind calls Béroalde's edition "debased," and accuses him of bringing the argument "down" to a (merely) alchemical level. He attacks Jung for the same kind of flattening of interpretation, which he calls "an erosion of categories."[35] This criticism might be justly applied to Jungianism, but I find the scolding of Béroalde rather puzzling. The alchemical level of the *Hypnerotomachia* will strike anyone as obvious, provided they've already read a few alchemical texts or even modern studies on alchemy. Even if Béroalde were mistaken to think that the alchemical level is the deepest or most important, surely it would be foolish of us to dismiss his interpretation as irrelevant or useless. In fact, a bit of reflection will reveal that his reading is not "merely" alchemical but also quite *literary*. Béroalde has something valuable to teach us about the structure of the *Dream*.

I have found two explanations of Béroalde's Frontispiece, one by a serious art historian (and spy!), Anthony Blunt, and the other by a serious scholar of Hermeticism, Adam McLean.[36] Oddly enough, neither of them seem to have followed Béroalde's own reading in the Steganagraphic Note. The "scenes" in the Frontispiece are not arranged in two columns, but in a clock-wise sequence, and contrary to appearances, the sequence does not begin at the bottom center with the sphere of Chaos, but at the bottom right. Here, according to

Figure 10.
The alchemical frontispiece to Béroalde's French edition of *The Dream of Poliphilo* (1600).

Béroalde, sits Jupiter enthroned as King of Crete, with the crescent Moon in his mouth and the Sun beneath his feet. He is reading a book

on the cover of which are depicted drops of water and flames of fire.
Behind him is the serpent Orthomander, whose breath and wings of
fire paradoxically coincide with its aquatic nature. Jupiter, who presides over the Triumphs of the *Hypnerotomachia*, here appears as the
reader/writer of the inner text, hiding that which is usually revealed
(Sun/Sulphur), and speaking (or eating) that which is hidden, nocturnal, and usually veiled by dream-shadows (Moon/Mercury). In a
sense, he stands for all the "I"s of the book: Colonna, Poliphilo, Polia,
the "God of Nature," the reader, the dreamer.

As Gaston Bachelard says somewhere: "The nocturnal assumes the
shape of an egg." Jupiter's lunar words begin with the enclosure of all
signs and symbols into a sphere or globe within a spherical enclosure:
a "yolk" within the cosmic egg. Within the yolk, joined like sperm and
ovum, are a drop of water and a flame of fire. The "white" of the egg
is chaos: fire, water, clouds, planets, all in structureless confusion—the
materia prima of the Great Work, that which can be found on any
dungheap, according to certain alchemists—matter itself. But the egg
is also an *athanor*, or alchemical vessel. Within it, a process has begun,
and chaos has been given a directionality and a temporality, indicated
by the tube or pathway that leaves the yolk towards the left. The chaos-
egg, like the entire structure of the Frontispiece, finds its place upon
a great cosmic tree: a myrtle, symbolic of Venus. As Hesiod says,
Chaos is the first of the gods, followed by Desire (Eros), then Earth
(Gaia), and "Old Night." (Night always precedes Day in all old
calendars and mythic time-systems.) Without attempting any facile
comparisons, we might note with interest that this sequence bears a
remarkable resemblance to certain concepts in modern "chaos theory,"
in which the random and indeterminate are given shape by "strange
attractors." Matter desires form: *chaos, eros, gaia*—but this is a *secret*,
veiled by the primordial nocturnality of the dream. Béroalde says:

> In the midst of the Chaos a small globe is happily indicated, and this is
> the supreme point of junction of all that is useful for our quest. This small
> space . . . on opening the store of its treasures, causes the two substances
> to appear, which are but a single one . . . from which emerges the scroll
> of destiny, extending evenly beyond the Chaos, after which it advances

in ordered fashion to its rightful end (McLean translation).

In other words, the mystery is always already achieved, and the "path," in a sense, is an illusion—although in another sense it is real because it is *our story*, our historical becoming.

The process in the athanor is divided into seven stages. The first is symbolized by the chaos-egg. The second is shown by the tree to the left, which grows out of fire. Daemons in the branches, according to Béroalde, cut them as they grow, and throw them down to feed the fire, so that the tree can grow more branches, *ad infinitum*. This probably symbolizes the alchemical *distillatio* in which the same substance must be repeatedly vaporized and condensed, circulating through a closed system toward ever greater subtlety, then reduced to ash and recombined again with fresh substance, and again distilled and sublimated, and so on.

The third stage is represented by a dragon-and-snake, intertwined and devouring each other (*not* the Ourobouros, as McLean suggests). Despite the violent imagery, this emblem represents an amalgam or *coniunctio* of Mercury and Sulphur, or "water" and "fire"—in other words, female and male, or sexual intercourse. (This interpretation is reinforced by the intertwined symbols of Mercury and Sulphur, which are shown in the chaos-egg as separate, but here as combined.) These forces "devour each other" because they become one, as Béroalde asserts—that is, in Love (including its manifestation as sexuality), the separation between consciousness and manifestation is erased: "Tantrik alchemy."

The fourth stage appears as a lion with its paws cut off, usually interpreted in alchemy as the fixation of the substance. The Green Lion can represent Mercury, which is thus fixated when it loses its liquid form as quicksilver in conjunction with Sulphur (the "cinnabar" of Taoist alchemy, a precursor of the Stone itself). Béroalde tells us that this is "the lion of love from the fairy mountain," so we can also interpret this emblem sexually as another conjunction. There may even be hints here about sexual fluids, such that the intertwined serpents produce one sort of fluid, and the lion's blood represents another sort, which—when combined—lead on to the next and fifth stage of the transformation.

The "scroll of destiny," which is also a pipe of fluid, leads on to the root of another tree where it pours into and fertilizes a butterfly-like cocoon. Herein, we are told, is born the worm that in time (note the hourglass to the immediate right) will become the Phoenix: a bird that is born, or reborn, out of its own ashes, like the alchemical substance itself—and thus attains the light of realization (or of perfected consciousness of the One, in Neoplatonic terms). But the sequence does not end with the light. Nature is not erased in pure spirit here, as in Dualism. Instead, Nature is *realized* in spirit, and spirit *in* Nature. This is the Mystery of Love according to Béroalde, and also according to Colonna. The Phoenix holds a strangely worm-like cornucopia, which bursts with the profusion of Nature—an expansion that mirrors the "ascent" of the Phoenix toward the light.

In the sixth stage, a single red rose falls from the cornucopia, representing the appearance of the elixir, or Philosopher's Stone. Five petals detach themselves from the rose (five drops of elixir? the five senses in their realized perfection?) and fall upon a dead tree trunk (i.e. the *projectio* of the Stone onto "base" metal, or Nature devoid of consciousness and life). These drops or petals seem to revivify the trunk and cause a new living branch to sprout. From this branch the elixir falls again in its final form: a water-flame drop, or "firewater," that drips and flows into a fountain, whereby the seventh stage is realized. As the elixir flows and recirculates through this very Poliphilian fountain, it rejuvenates the old god Janus (hence it is a "Fountain of Youth") who represents both end and beginning, and thus the liminal space or time between them—the "doorway" or threshold of the house, or the year. Thus the sequence has no final end, and this circularity may be symbolized by the curious fact that the "scroll" or pipe of destiny not only leads *out* of the chaos-egg, but also back *into* it as well.

Alchemy aside, Béroalde is the only literary critic of the *Hypnerotomachia* to note the vital thematic importance of fire and water for understanding its unifying structure, even on the "surface level" of the narrative. Scenes and episodes, and even characters, are classified by Colonna under these signs. For example, the Land of the

Five Senses and Queen Liberty belongs to the realm of water, and of fluid in general: mercuric, feminine, and highly positive. (Colonna and Béroalde are "feminists," at least on the Hermetic level where the feminine principle or "Sophia" outranks the masculine—and this, too, can be compared with the centrality of the Goddess in Hindu Tantra.) Later we shall come to scenes composed under the sign of fire, which can have negative connotations such as thirst, burning (with lust, for example), or destruction, but also the positive connotations of testing, strengthening, and enlightening. Both Poliphilo and Polia experience and represent both fire and water at different moments in the text, but the promise of their *coniunctio*, their becoming one in the pleasure of love, must be seen as the true *telos*, both of the narrative and of its "inner" or "secret" structure. If, on one level, the *Dream* is a study in the psychology of frustrated desire, it must be interpreted—like so much Sufi or Troubadour poetry—on other levels as well. From one point of view, frustration or separation from the beloved is a more "noble" state than satisfaction or union, since it helps to keep love alive and burning—and because the lover must do the will of the beloved in amorous servitude, even if that will manifests as separation. From another point of view, sexual union must be seen as the "higher" state, since it accomplishes for the subject(s) that *being/consciousness/bliss* which constitutes the "peak experience" of human life as represented by the *Dream*, whereby the cycle begins all over again from the beginning, in the chaos of becoming. If Béroalde and Colonna are "libertines," then so are Hafez and Dante (at least the "pagan" Dante of the *Vita Nova*). That which must be kept secret here (and above all, hidden from the Church) is the revelation not only that "God is love," but also that *Love is god*.

Béroalde's scroll or pipe of destiny makes an excellent metaphor for Colonna's treatment of time in the *Dream*. The scroll does not follow a straight-forward sequence of linear time but rather recirculates itself in and through time, in a series of operations that loops back upon itself in distillations or sublimations, and projections, in disappearances and reappearances. The *Dream* likewise violates its own "surface narrativity" in strange loops—for example, the dream within a dream, the endless digressions, or the confusion that interweaves dream time

with waking time in Part II of the book. Here, Poliphilo and Polia fade
in and out of daytime reality, sometimes wandering amongst the ruins
of the dream world and sometimes reliving their "real" lives in Treviso
in the mid-fifteenth century, where the real Polia may have died of the
plague.

In terms of space, Béroalde's "map" offers a means of understanding
the geography of the *Dream*, which "progresses" from one emblematic situation to the next in conceptual rather than dimensional space.
What appears on the surface as dream-logic or surrealism follows a
deeper logic or structure, that of alchemical or sexual transformation
and revivification. Moreover, Béroalde has clearly depicted the
neopagan message of the book in his Frontispiece and Note. (He even
lays claim to sources of wisdom outside the Church when he says, for
example: "Our Druids have left us, by a happy cabale, a ray of truth
... an archetype of beauty and the idea of form....") Not only are there
no Christian symbols in the alchemical system presented here, but
Béroalde specifically places the whole sequence under the aegis of
Jupiter, in the universe of Aphrodite. The Rosicrucian Manifestos
with their hidden agenda of magical revolution were already in
circulation around 1600, when Béroalde published his edition of the
Dream, and no doubt he included himself in the tradition of radical
Hermeticism that also embraced Colonna as well as the Rosicrucians.

In short, I believe that Béroalde de Verville was a close and
perceptive reader of the *Hypnerotomachia*, and more to be trusted than
his critics. The marvelous elusive and allusive "embeddedness" of the
imagery in his Frontispiece does critical justice to the dense *text* of
Colonna, to its ambiguity and perversity, and is not merely a *reductio*
or "erosion of categories." The *Hypnerotomachia* itself is a steganagraphic
text, a coding of hidden messages, obscured by the same hieroglyphic
method that promises to unveil or decode them. Like hieroglyphics,
the *Dream* states openly that which it seeks to communicate by hiding
it behind "pedantesqueries" and weird, unexpected anomalies, much
as the ancient Egyptians hid their wisdom in plain sight by emblema-
tizing it in the forms of vultures and baboons. In order to "explain"
Colonna, Béroalde presents us with yet another coded message.
Encoding/decoding/recoding becomes a single operation. Fire and

water are antagonists, but which, secretly, can also be made one. Meaning itself is antinomian—*caveat lector*. A mystery to be solved— or dissolved—in the *fluiditas* of time's "unspace."

* * *

Mention has been made of Godwin's "map" or schematic analysis of the structure of the *Hypnerotomachia* (preface, xviii). He says that Book One begins with Poliphilo in the "real world," and takes him into the dream world (perhaps a *double* dream, as I noted above). After numerous adventures he joins Polia—although at first he doesn't quite recognize her—and visits Cytherea, where they are "married" (although Colonna never uses such a word) by Cupid himself. After this climax, the nymphs of the Isle, in Book Two, beg Polia to tell her side of the story, "and this forms a separate narrative within Poliphilo's dream," as Godwin says. She tells her family history, describes the plague, her cure, her consecration to Diana, Poliphilo's ardent wooing of her, and her cruel rejection of him. Since this is the "real world" Polia is describing—the world outside the dream—what are we to make of its pagan setting? Is Polia actually a nun in "real life"? In Treviso in 1467? Clearly a structural difficulty has arisen, and it gets worse. Polia tells how Poliphilo actually dies of love in front of Diana's altar. Polia hides the body, then undergoes a set of nightmare visions of Cupid and Venus punishing girls who refuse to love. She repents. Meanwhile, Poliphilo is experiencing "near death" visions of the mysteries of Venus and Cupid. Polia rushes back to the temple and revives him with her tears. They then vow themselves to Venus in an elaborate ceremony (another "marriage").

Now back in Cytherea, in dream time, Polia concludes her narrative and the nymphs depart. Polia and Poliphilo embrace—but Polia dissolves in his arms like a ghost (with some hints of *coitus interruptus*). According to Godwin, "[b]ack in the real world, Poliphilo awakes from his dream to the nightingale's song" (and the text is dated "kalends of May 1467"). Polia's epitaph, composed (or spoken?) by herself now follows; she addresses Poliphilo and tells him: "Alas, cease. A flower so dry never revives. Farewell."

It appears that the structure of the book is by no means as clear as it seems in Godwin's "map."

* * *

From one point of view, the "strife of love in a dream" has ended as an alchemical marriage. Poliphilo is the spirit, Polia the soul, united in love. But from another point of view, both Poliphilo and Polia may be dead (of love, of the plague, of the plague of love). From yet another point of view, *la vida es un sueña*—or as the very title of the book tells us:

HYPNEROTOMACHIA POLIPHILI,

ubi humana omnia non nisi somnium esse docet

(where it is taught that everything human is but a dream).

The measure of Colonna's greatness—and strangeness—is that all three perspectives are valid. The *Dream* works on all these levels, and on others as well. Any school of psychology could find its own interpretation, but the Hermeticists were also "correct" in their alchemical reading. The Ruins could stand for the disintegration of Colonna's psyche in a fantasy of wish-fulfillment that is nevertheless perpetually postponed. Or they could signify the ancient wisdom of the Hermetic sages, now shattered and suppressed by the Church— so that only the "lover of Antiquity" might hope to reassemble the shards and lost codes into a coherent message. Or they could signify the alchemical *nigredo*. Or they could be interpreted as signs of the disjunctures and fragmentations of the text itself, of language itself as "ruins," of language dreaming itself. The *Hypnerotomachia* resists final interpretation—it cannot be "enclosed"—and if the commentators have hitherto experienced this resistance as an aesthetic failure, I believe that we can at last accept it as a kind of surrealist brilliance. Our own culture has fallen into "ruins," and in a sense we inhabit the landscape of Colonna's dream. Poliphilo speaks to our condition, and even suggests a possible escape-route from the labyrinth of our melancholy.

Specifically we have argued that among its many levels, the text functions as a political discourse. Colonna not only rejected the entire teaching of the Church, he also leveled a severe critique at all Dualist or "Gnostic" tendencies within Neoplatonism. Over and over again he insists on the "material bodily principle" as the basis for any valid spirituality. Like Fourier, he believes that *passion*—desire and sexuality—constitute the only possible force for the reconciliation of personal freedom and social harmony. The purpose of Hermeticism, in Colonna's view, is not an escape from the body into a mental realm of pseudo-mysticism, but rather an alchemical "re-entry" into the body as the perfected subject of Love.

As the prophet of his own faith, Colonna proposes a religion of the body, of sexuality, of "Nature." He is too subtle, too "psychological," to offer a simple manifesto of revolt against Christian morality (and also too clever)—but the deep reader of the text cannot fail to notice its true intent beneath the hieroglyphic mask of the alchemical dream. Like Blake or Whitman, he asserts the body of Nature as the sole divine principle, and the human body as its primary focus. In this sense, although we have heard recent disquisitions on the "death of Nature," we can accept no final disappearance while the body persists in its becoming. Technology has replaced the Church as the enemy of nature, but like the Church, it has never succeeded in carrying out a final enclosure. Capital may achieve the suppression of the body, just as bioengineering may succeed in eradicating human sexuality—but not without a final revolt. "Nature" is something that can be defended—and even "restored." In this resurrection of the body, Colonna's text gains its full significance.

For Colonna, this political agenda implied a religious foundation, and clearly paganism for him was not merely a source of allegorical figures. The Three Graces, for him, are not a "vestige of the Trinity" but a genuine living triad, verified by direct vision. Venus, Cupid, Hermes, Priapus, even the nymphs and satyrs, are more than figures in some neoclassical landscape; despite the ruination of Antiquity, they live and breathe for Colonna (and for his brilliant artist). A careful reading of his book will convince us of the real possibility of a "neopagan conspiracy" in Renaissance Italy—and perhaps more than one secret society devoted to Colonna's agenda, or something similar. If this Hermetic *politique* never emerged openly in history, despite the best efforts of Bruno and the Rosicrucians—if it was submerged in the crisis of the Reformation, Counter-Reformation, and the wars of religion—nevertheless it existed as a genuine "third force," and claimed the loyalties of some of the most brilliant intellects and talents of the era. And perhaps, it is not yet defunct even now.

By analogy with the Freemasons and their "Invisible College," we might say that Colonna and his fellow conspirators proposed an Invisible Revolution. It was invisible because it never emerged, but it was also invisible because of its chosen strategy. The "hermetic" is also in one sense the hidden or unseen. Hermetic propaganda was highly visible, in that it took the form of art—of illuminated books, of obelisks and statues, and gardens of monsters. But Hermetic art holds something back—it reveals and conceals with one and the same gesture. According to hieroglyphic theory, the image acts simultaneously on both a conscious and an unconscious level—hence its "magic" power. Inasmuch as all art does this, all art is "political." But Hermetic art offers a further dimension: it contains in itself the key to the unconscious level, to the unseen, so that the active intellect and imagination can penetrate the image and appropriate its hidden wisdom. It presents a mystery precisely so that the mystery can be unveiled and overcome, so that one can be released from the mystery itself. Hermetic art is an enchantment into freedom, or rather into the "work" that can be carried out only by the human spirit for itself. Enlightenment can only be given if it is received—and recirculated. It can only exist in process, in becoming. It is unseen because it is everywhere, and yet visible only to itself.

In a world that suffers from the tyranny of the Image, and from a kind of malign Hermeticism, we might perhaps make use of the potential "Hermetic criticism" and "hieroglyphic theory" proposed by *The Strife of Love in a Dream*. We seem to need a method that can liberate us from the image by the image: a theory of the Unseen, and simultaneously a theory of Reembodiment. The cornerstone for such *theoria*, at least inasmuch as Colonna's contribution is concerned, has now been laid by Godwin's superb translation. Not a single "problem" of the text has been solved, of course. But thanks to Godwin, the work can begin. Poliphilesque pleasures await a new self-chosen elite of deep readers.

Notes

1. Francesco Colonna, *Hypnerotomachia, The Strife of Love in a Dreame* (1592), trans. R.D.; introduction by Lucy Gent (Delmar, NY: Scholars' Facsimiles and Reprints, 1973).

2. Needless to say, I was not the first to realize this! A brief search turned up the following confirmation: Emanuela Quaranta, *Incantesimo A Bomarzo* (Firenze: Editioni Sansoni Antiquariato, 1960); and Emanuela Kretzulesco-Quaranta, *Les Jardins du Songe—"Poliphile" et la Mystique de la Renaissance* (Paris: Société d'Edition "Les Belles Lettres," 1986); also Jacqueline Theurillat, *Les Mystères de Bomarzo et les jardins symboliques de la Renaissance* (Geneva: Les Trois Anneaux Genève, 1973). In English, for comparisons see Claudia Lazzaro, *The Italian Renaissance Garden* (New Haven: Yale University Press, 1990).

3. Edited by Giovanni Pozzi and Lucia Ciapponi, 2 vols. (Padova: Antenore, 1964. Reprint, 1980).

4. For an account of his life, see George Painter, *The Hypnerotomachia Poliphili of 1499: An Introduction to the Dream, the Dreamer, the Artist and the Printer*, 2 vols. (London: Eugrammia Press, 1963).

5. Edgar Wind, *Pagan Mysteries in the Renaissance*, 2nd ed. (New York: W. W. Norton, 1968). Despite his disdain for Hermeticism, Wind provides an excellent context for reading the *Hypnerotomachia*, and some useful insights as well.

6. According to E. Wind, Pico and Ficino sometimes distort Plato and the Neoplatonists in order to turn their anti-material bias and moralism upside down into a new doctrine. "It is curious to observe Ficino twisting Plato's clearly derogatory passage [on 'divine drunkenness'] into a positive argument on divine *voluptas*" (*Pagan Mysteries in the Renaissance*, 61 n. 31; see also 278). But it is precisely those points where the Renaissance magi diverge from their classical sources that mark their most original thoughts. The "defense of pleasure" was a truly revolutionary doctrine.

7. Bruno, Marlowe, and Dee all either spied or worked on ciphers, propaganda, and disinformation for Walsingham, Queen Elizabeth's spy-master. Dee's code-name, believe it or not, was "007"! Hermes, of course, is also the god of "Intelligence."

8. See my *Escape from the Nineteenth Century* (Brooklyn: Autonomedia,

1998), especially the essay on Fourier, and the essay on "The Shamanic Trace" ("Nineteenth-Century Escapism"). See also A. Faivre, *Access to Western Esotericism* (Albany: State University of New York Press, 1994), especially Part I, 44–47; and J. H. Billington, *Fire in the Minds of Men: Origins of the Revolutionary Faith* (New York: Basic Books, 1980).

9. Of course, not all alchemists were heretics—but the Church generally considered them as such, and certainly many of them were freethinkers, gnostics, or syncretists.

10. See my article on Horapollo, "Speaking in Hieroglyphics," *Alexandria* 3 (1995), 307 ff.

11. For example: *Prodromus Coptus sive Aegyptiacus* (Rome, 1636); *Obeliscus Pamphilus, hoc est, Interpretatio nova & hucusque intentata hieroglyphici* (Rome, 1650); and especially *Oedipus Aegypticus, hoc est, Universalia hieroglyphicae*, 3 vols. (Rome, 1652–54). The only modern study of Kircher known to me is Joscelyn Godwin's *Athanasius Kircher: A Renaissance Man and the Quest for Knowledge* (London: Thames & Hudson, 1975).

12. *Eros and Magic in the Renaissance*, trans. M. Cook, foreword by Mircea Eliade (Chicago: University of Chicago Press, 1987).

13. See Peter Tompkins, *The Magic of Obelisks* (New York: Harper & Row, 1981), for an entertaining illustrated history of the obsession.

14. This is the process referred to in Sufism as the "Shower of Stars"—see my study of the dream book tradition, *"Shower of Stars," Dream & Book: Initiatic Dreaming in Sufism and Taoism* (Brooklyn: Autonomedia, 1996). As we shall see, it is precisely the *dream* nature of the text that allows this hieroglyphic self-inscription.

15. Helen Barolini, *Aldus and His Dream Book: An Illustrated Essay* (New York: Italica Press, 1992), 102. Barolini herself calls the text "prolix," 97.

16. Wind, *Pagan Mysteries in the Renaissance*, 104.

17. Andrew Lang (in his preface to the 1890 facsimile of R.D.'s translation), cited by L. Gent, *Hypnerotomachia, The Strife of Love in a Dreame* (1592), vi.

18. Erik Iversen, *The Myth of Egypt and its Hieroglyphs in European Tradition* (Princeton: Princeton University Press, 1961/1993), 67. Despite his lack of sympathy, Iversen is essential for an understanding of Renaissance hieroglyphic theory.

19. Andrew Lang (in his preface to the 1890 facsimile of R.D.'s translation),

cited by L. Gent, *Hypnerotomachia, The Strife of Love in a Dreame* (1592), xv. Rabelais, however, also mentioned the book with respect, as did Erasmus.

20. Barolini, *Aldus and His Dream Book: An Illustrated Essay*, 98.

21. The phrase is Wind's, *Pagan Mysteries in the Renaissance*, 215 n.

22. Barolini, *Aldus and His Dream Book: An Illustrated Essay*, 105. Alberti discussed "Egyptian letters" and may have been Colonna's first source. See also Liane Lefaivre, *Leon Battista Alberti's Hypnerotomachia Poliphili: Re-Cognizing the Architectural Body in the Early Italian Renaissance* (Cambridge: MIT Press, 1997). Lefaivre has argued that the author of the *Hypnerotomachia* was not Francesco Colonna, but in fact Leon Battista Alberti. Her strongest argument rests on a large number of references and quotations from Alberti in Poliphilo's narrative—but this could be attributed to influence rather than identity. Otherwise, her evidence is circumstantial. For example, the *Hypnerotomachia* uses an eye as a hieroglyph, and Alberti's personal emblem was an eye with wings—but no *flying* eye appears in *Poliphilo*. Moreover, she fails to explain away the famous acrostic identifying Colonna as the lover of Polia, merely remarking that Alberti must have used the name as an "alter ego." To complicate matters, yet another Francesco Colonna has been championed as the true author (a Roman aristocrat, a younger contemporary of Alberti)—and Alberti himself worked for the Colonna family. Lefaivre has certainly demonstrated that the authorship of the book remains problematic, but I do not believe she has proven the case for Alberti. But she has succeeded in establishing the architectural brilliance of Poliphilo as well as his architectural fetishism, showing that on several occasions he actually makes love to buildings—one of which (the Temple of Venus) responds with a veritable architectural orgasm.

23. Iversen, *The Myth of Egypt and its Hieroglyphs in European Tradition*, 70. In Milan I was able to consult two editions of Valeriano: an Italian version (Rome: Giuseppe Iacomo de Franceschi, 1581) with several Mayan codices added as frontispieces, and a Latin version (Venice: Antonio and Iacabo de Franceschi, 1604). The influence of the *Poliphilo* is very clear in this beautiful work, and also in Cesare Ripa's fine *Iconologia* (Padua, 1618), published with a preface by Mario Praz and edited by Piero Buscaroli (Milan: TEA Arte, 1992).

24. Yates, cited in Couliano, *Eros and Magic in the Renaissance*, 42.

25. Couliano, *Eros and Magic in the Renaissance*, 40–41.

26. Wind, *Pagan Mysteries in the Renaissance*, 104 n.

27. Couliano, *Eros and Magic in the Renaissance*, 24. Or, as Bruno put it, "*Natura est deus in rebus*": Nature is god in things. See *The Expulsion of the Triumphant Beast*, trans. A. D. Imerti (New Brunswick: Rutgers University Press, 1964), 235.

28. His translation of the Arabic *ta'wil*, meaning the tracing of a thing back to its source—as in the interpretation of Koranic terms, for example.

29. He does both in the *Expulsion*. See p. 145 for "socialism," p. 149 for a rather "Nietzschean" passage, etc.

30. *The Chemical Wedding of Christian Rosenkreutz*, attributed to J. V. Andreae and published in 1616, was almost certainly directly influenced by the *Hypnerotomachia*. See the excellent translation by Joscelyn Godwin (Grand Rapids: Phanes Press, 1991).

31. *De Beneficiis* 1.3, cited in Wind, *Pagan Mysteries in the Renaissance*, 28. Colonna could well have read this passage.

32. Wind, *Pagan Mysteries in the Renaissance*, 32.

33. A Paris, chez Matthieu Guillemot, au Palais, en la gallerie des prisonniers, 1600. (The French translation republished by Béroalde first appeared much earlier, and along the way it had acquired some interesting extra woodcuts.)

34. "The *Hypnerotomachia Poliphili* in Seventeenth-Century France," in *Journal of the Warburg Institute*, 1.2 (1937).

35. Jung drew the attention of Linda Fierz-David to the *Hypnerotomachia*, and supplied a preface for her study, *The Dream of Poliphilo*, trans. M. Hottinger (New York: Pantheon, 1950). Fierz-David's work does indeed suffer from Jungian reductionism, and from a curious prudishness (she uses the censored version of the "Triumph of Priapus," for example).

36. *The Silent Language: The Symbols of Hermetic Philosophy* (Exhibition Catalogue, Bibliotheca Philosophica Hermetica, Amsterdam: In de Pelikan, 1994), 30.

Memorials

A. H. Armstrong (1909–1997)

A. H. ARMSTRONG was both a Christian Platonist and the leading scholar of Plotinus in the English speaking world, if not the whole world. His important works include, on the recommendation of E. R. Dodds, a seven volume translation of the *Enneads* for the Loeb Classical Library; *An Introduction to Ancient Philosophy*; *The Architecture of the Intelligible Universe in the Philosophy of Plotinus*; editor and contributor, *The Cambridge History of Later Greek and Early Medieval Philosophy*; numerous articles written from the 1930s to 1990s, many of them gathered in two Variorum volumes, *Plotinian and Christian Studies* and *Hellenic and Christian Studies*. His article, "The Divine Enhancement of Earthly Beauties," originally an Eranos lecture delivered in Ascona, Switzerland, is probably the best general introduction and analysis of Greek and Platonic religious and aesthetic sensibilities from the beginning to the end of classical antiquity.

Armstrong was educated at Cambridge University, and should be counted among the greatest of the "Cambridge Platonists," as was Alfred North Whitehead in the earlier part of the twentieth century. After several teaching positions, and service on Malta during World War II, he became Gladstone Professor of Greek at the University of Liverpool, a position he held until 1972. From 1972–1982, he was Professor of Classics at Dalhousie University in Nova Scotia, where he taught several exceptional students, who are now actively engaged in Neoplatonic studies. Another significant contribution was his foundation there of the journal *Dionysius*, for the study of Christianity and Late Antiquity. In 1982, he retired to the town of Ludlow, Shropshire. He remained active in scholarly circles; even after a stroke limited his mobility he continued to publish and to communicate with other scholars.

Hilary Armstrong "kept the altars of Plotinus warm" in an era when metaphysical ideas of any kind were all but ridiculed in Anglo-American philosophical circles. Nor did he favor the "letter" of Plotinus over the "spirit." Certainly, no contemporary or recent scholar and/or "Plotinian mystic" has even come close to his faithfulness to both. He himself made it clear that we have long ago left behind the era in which those who understood Plotinus were not the best philologists; and those who knew Greek well, failed to understand the philosopher they were engaging.

Today, partly because of the mystical revival of the last four or five odd decades, and because of the increased interest in religious ideas, his work remains more relevant than ever. In addition to his major contribution as translator and exegete of the *Enneads*, Armstrong published significant work on the historical (and contemporary) problems of religious pluralism and tolerance. This has led to confusion in certain circles. Since A.H.A. was subtle and avoided strong dogmatic language, his critics have often failed to "hear" him. As he himself pointed out, even some of the most learned and sophisticated people "repeat the same (dogmatic) intellectual pattern again and again" and simply miss the point of things that move outside of that pattern.

Originally a member of the Church of England, in which his father was a minister, Armstrong became a Roman Catholic for several decades, until serious disagreements with the Catholic Church precipitated his return to the Anglican Church. He remained a Christian, but he was open to the valid religious expressions of other traditions. For example, the "Temple of Greco-Roman Isis" in our world that he would actively honor, if he should come upon it, would be a Hindu Temple. Temperamentally opposed to dogmatism, intolerance, and triumphalism of any kind, he insisted that "it is permissible to disagree" on religious and philosophical issues. He believed, with the tolerant fourth-century Roman Senator Symmachus, that there cannot be only one path to the highest mystery. As he liked to put it: "I'm a *non uno itinere* . . . man. " He would have preferred that the Christian

Church had not been established in the fourth century, which has led to the historical disaster of "imperial dogmatic Theodosian Christianity," which was seriously challenged, historically speaking, only recently. In fact, A.H.A. went so far as to speculate on an "alternate history" in which Julian had a longer reign, and, furthermore, a long lived successor. This would not have ended Christianity; but perhaps it would have prevented the establishment of a Church supported by the power of the state.

In philosophical theology he favored the "way of unsaying" or "apophasis," commonly known as "negative theology": the One is not this, not that, and it is not not this, not not that. In the end all of our formulations, including our negations, must be negated. Hence, all dogmatic formulations are at best provisional. More seriously, that they led to people being hurt or killed was intolerable. The modern Christian, thought Armstrong, should be an "Idoloclast" but also an "Iconodule." Furthermore, he considered the Church's "churchiness," and therefore neglect of the natural world, one of the culprits in our current environmental crisis. The natural world, in the tradition of the Byzantine Maximus Confessor (the "medieval Teilhard de Chardin") as well as that of Plotinus, is to be welcomed as a theophany that reflects the transcendent Plotinian realities of One-Intellect-Soul. Armstrong thus identified himself with the Platonic tradition that gives positive valuation to the body, the sensible world, and to nature.

Armstrong was also a great admirer of the poet William Blake, whom he considered a Neoplatonist in certain respects; he thought that W. B. Yeats was a "theurgic Neoplatonist" in the tradition of the fourth-century anti-Christian emperor Julian's guru, Iamblichus. Interestingly, A.H.A also much admired Julian himself. Indeed, he thought that he was one of the last to get both a traditional classical and a traditional Christian education. But he accepted both major elements of our "inherited conglomerate," whereas Julian accepted only the former. A.H.A.'s religious sensibility was modern yet in close touch with traditions from late antiquity. At times it seems perhaps closer to the original Greek than most.

Armstrong could at times be humorous about his thorough familiarity with Hellenism. One noted Christian scholar of Greek thought once told him that in the end one must either choose Augustine or Plotinus. "Very well then," he replied, "I have chosen Plotinus." Thus, Plotinus remains available to Christians.

In regard to a group of "archetypal psychologists" in London, who were enthusiastically commending to him the post-Nietzschean "revived god" Dionysus, he wrote, "don't they know that they are talking about an old friend of mine?" In fact, he was highly suspicious of such modern revivals, and attributed most of them to German speculation that distorted the historical reality of Greece. Apollo and Dionysus, the Greeks knew, were together at Delphi.

Of great importance to contemporary students of religions is Armstrong's insistence that Neoplatonism is the best way for a Westerner to approach and to appreciate Eastern religions. It has largely been forgotten that in the early twentieth century many scholars held that Plotinus was directly influenced by Indian thought. Armstrong himself, however, was one of the scholars that showed that this was probably not true. Nevertheless, Neoplatonism, in part because of its compatibility, is of crucial importance in the philosophical discussions between East and West. Armstrong, then, was also a pioneer in this regard. Although he was seriously involved in religious and spiritual concerns, he eschewed the title of guru and always claimed to be "of the college, rather than of the coven."

Hilary Armstrong was a generous friend to many of his students and colleagues, often helping them with their professional careers and engaging in lively personal and intellectual debate—not only about purely academic questions. In the last years of his life he continued this for the most part through an exceptional correspondence, now no longer the norm in our cyberworld. He will be deeply missed.

—JAY BREGMAN

Marie-Louise von Franz (1915–1998)

THE LATE MARIE-LOUISE VON FRANZ embodied in both her life and in her writings the spirit of Jungian psychology. For sixty-five years she lived in relationship with the mysterious inner part of the personality called the unconscious. From that relationship flowed lectures, articles, and books that remain the most brilliant explication and expansion of C. G. Jung's theories. Though the Jungian world currently suffers from splits and conflicts, and though there are many who relegate von Franz to the past, there is little doubt that both her spirit and her writings continue to guide those truly invested in the process of becoming whole, the process known as individuation.

Dr. von Franz first met C. G. Jung in 1933, when von Franz was still a young student. Dr. Jung, a gourmet chef, had prepared a delicious soup and then began to lecture Dr. von Franz and other students present about the nature of his psychology. Among other stories, he recounted the experience of a woman who imagined that she had been to the moon. Jung commented that when the woman returned from the moon she was quite changed. Von Franz said, "you mean, when she acted as if she returned from the moon." Jung replied, "I mean when she returned from the moon." Von Franz went away believing that either she or Jung was quite mad. She never told me which conclusion she accepted, but she soon became a serious student of Jungian thought.

After obtaining her doctorate in 1940, von Franz began to seriously work with Jung not only as a student but also as a collaborator. Her first major work on alchemy was *Aurora Consurgens*, written as a companion piece for Jung's masterwork *Mysterium Coniunctionis*. Jung and von Franz planned to publish these works as one volume, until a publisher objected. Many critics argued that *Aurora Consurgens* was incomprehensible. Stung by such comments, von Franz presented a series of lectures on alchemy at the C. G. Jung Institute in Zurich, which later became her book *Alchemy*. This book in its simplicity and erudition is perhaps the best introduction to both alchemy and Jung's understanding of it. However, for the serious student of alchemy, *Aurora Consurgens* is a fit companion for *Mysterium Coniunctionis*. In addition to these two works, von Franz later wrote a little book entitled *Alchemical Active Imagination*, a study of the practice of active imagination as illustrated in the writings of the great alchemist Gerhard Dorn.

Von Franz was interested in many things besides alchemy and much of her reputation rests on her authoritative work with fairy tales. She told me that she spent ten years almost exclusively in the study of fairy tales and from this work she developed an uncanny ability to interpret dreams. Her many writings on fairy tales include such works as *An Introduction to the Psychology of Fairy Tales*, *Problems of the Feminine in Fairy Tales*, *Shadow and Evil in Fairy Tales*, and *Archetypal Patterns in Fairy Tales*. These works not only illustrate the Jungian method of interpretation and amplification but also reward the serious student with insights into the nature of symbols and the symbolic expression of the collective unconscious. Moreover, through her understanding of these symbols, she revealed much about the workings of archetypes in ordinary life and in the process of individuation. No one interested in the study of dream interpretation, regardless of their orientation, can afford to ignore the writings of von Franz on fairy tales.

Jung so respected her abilities that he didn't hesitate to give her tasks that were, to say the least, onerous. When his wife died before she was able to complete her lifelong study of the Holy Grail, he asked von Franz to complete that work which resulted in the book, *The Grail Legend*. Of even greater significance, Jung came to believe at the end of his life that number was a key to understanding the mysterious ordering principle of the universe. Too old to study the archetypal nature of number in depth, he asked von Franz to undertake this work. Her studies culminated in the publication of the book *Number and Time*. Of all her books, this is by far her most difficult work. Yet, in her own mind, it was one of her most important efforts. She told me that one hundred years from now only this book would still be remembered. She also told me that a source of great pain for her was the inability of her colleagues to grasp her main points about number and its ordering effects. I sympathize with both her pain and the incomprehension of her colleagues.

As she grew older, von Franz grappled with the meaning and experience of death. She came to believe that something of the personality survived death. In her work *On Dreams and Death*, she not only discussed this probability but also opened the door to the possibility of transpsychic experience. Allowing for the feasibility of a reality beyond the psyche, von Franz has created fertile ground for the student of today. If we build on this possibility we are no longer bound to accept the strict equation of psyche and spirit, but can explore the worlds of the spirit in their own right. I suspect that her work on death is even more significant than her work on number.

Dr. von Franz was not only a prolific writer, but also a teacher and an analyst. I had the privilege of experiencing her in both of these roles. She was a brilliant lecturer and her classes were always filled to overflowing with students eager to hear whatever she happened to be lecturing on. She was tough on her students and intolerant of questions that seemed to her either shallow or ill thought out. Since she would confront her students and force them to think through their own questions, engaging her in the classroom could be a formidable experience. She was equally formidable as an analyst. If she thought her client was unwilling to change or face a difficult issue, she would not hesitate to stop the analysis until the client demonstrated the courage to go on. I often left my sessions with her deeply shaken and sometimes relieved that I had another analyst who patiently explained to me how to understand the deep insights into myself she had uncovered. But I learned more from watching her interpret dreams than from any other class I could have taken.

Perhaps most importantly for those who knew her personally, she was a living model for the process of individuation and for the spiritual connection to the self. One felt in her presence something numinous and awesome. She could seem on the surface the most ordinary of women, but one always sensed the wellspring of spiritual energy that flowed from her innermost center. She never hesitated to express herself and what she believed to be true. Shortly before I returned to the States from Zurich, she said to me that when I lectured or wrote I must not concern myself with whether my audience agreed with me or even understood what I was trying to say; the only important thing was to say what I felt. In this, as in so much, I have tried to follow her example.

—JEFFREY RAFF

About the Contributors

Ralph Abraham holds a Ph.D. in mathematics from the University of Michigan and is professor emeritus of mathematics at the University of Santa Cruz. He taught at Berkeley, Columbia, and Princeton before moving to Santa Cruz and has held visiting positions in Amsterdam, Paris, Warwick, Barcelona, Basel, and Florence. A pioneer in the field of chaos theory, he is the author of over twenty books, including *Chaos, Gaia, Eros* (HarperCollins), and is director of the Visual Math Institute.

Aphrodite Alexandrakis is professor of philosophy and humanities at Barry University and has published in the area of Platonic and Neoplatonic aesthetics. In 1997 she received the Barry University Outstanding Faculty Award and in 1999 the Sister Jeanne O'Laughlin Scholar Award. She is the recipient of two National Endowment for the Humanities fellowships and lives in Coral Gables, Florida.

Robert Apatow has a Ph.D. in philosophy, is a philosophical counselor, and has taught at the college level. He is the author of *The Spiritual Art of Dialogue* (Inner Traditions, 1998).

Jay Bregman teaches in the history department at the University of Maine. He has written on the connections between Neoplatonism and the religions of Late Antiquity, especially in the work of the "philosophe-bishop," Synesius of Cyrene, and the ecstatic Neoplatonic theologian, solar worshipper, and Roman emperor, Julian. He also has a long-standing interest in the influence of Neoplatonism on later thinkers. At present he is editing the proceedings from the 1999 conference held at Vanderbilt University on "Platonism, Neoplatonism, and American Thought." He is also writing a book on

Neoplatonism in North America for Kees Bolle's Hermeneutics and History of Religions series at Penn State Press.

David Fideler is editor of *The Pythagorean Sourcebook and Library*, the founder of *Alexandria* and Phanes Press, and holds a Ph.D. in philosophy and the history of science and cosmology. He has taught at the university level and and over the past several years has been a frequent speaker at scholarly conferences. Having discovered that he is an epistemological pluralist, he has returned to music, and recently had several pieces for piano and cello performed in concert. As a writer and educator, his work has focused on exploring the relationships between cosmology, philosophy, myth, and culture.

Philip Greenspun contributed the photographs of the "Garden of Monsters" at the Villa Orsini on pages 402–3. He is a photographer, educator, computer scientist, chairman of ArsDigita, and author of *Philip and Alex's Guide to Web Design* (Morgan Kaufmann). Color enlargements of his Villa Orsini photographs can be viewed at *www.photo.net/italy/between-rome-and-florence.html.*

Kabir Helminski is a Shaikh of the Mevlevi Sufi order, which traces its origin back to the thirteenth-century mystical poet Mevlana Jalaluddin Rumi, and is director of the Threshold Society (*www.sufism.org*) with his wife Camille. He has published translations of Rumi and other Sufi poets, and is the author of *Living Presence: A Sufi Way to Mindfulness* (Tarcher) and *The Knowing Heart: A Sufi Path of Transformation* (Shambhala).

Amy Ione is an artist, writer, and an international lecturer on topics related to art, science, and culture. Her background includes international exhibition of her art work, consulting for venues such as the San Francisco Exploratorium, teaching the history of science at the university level, an art commission from the City of San Francisco, and many publications including an invited contribution on "Multiple Discovery" for the *Encyclopedia of Creativity* (Academic Press, 1999). She lives in Berkeley, California and is currently coauthoring a book on art, cognition, and vision.

Roger S. Jones is a Morse Alumni Distinguished Teaching Professor Emeritus of Physics and Astronomy at the University of Minnesota, where he taught and worked for thirty-two years before retiring in 1999. Because of his interest in popular and conceptual science education, he often lectures and offers courses on physics, its relation to the arts and humanities, its philosophical implications, and its cultural influences. He has written two books—*Physics as Metaphor* and *Physics for the Rest of Us*—that present physics from a conceptual, critical, and humanistic point of view and explore its inner meaning.

E. C. Krupp is the author of many articles and books on archaeoastronomy including *Echoes of the Ancient Skies: The Astronomy of Lost Civilizations* (Harper & Row), *Beyond the Blue Horizon: Myths and Legends of the Sun, Moon, Stars, and Planets* (Oxford University Press), and, most recently, *Skywatchers, Shamans, and Kings: Astronomy and the Archaeology of Power* (John Wiley, 1997). Dr. Krupp is the director of the Griffith Observatory in Los Angeles (*www.griffithobs.org*), travels frequently to sites of archaeoastronomical interest, and writes a monthly, illustrated column of astral lore, myth, and history for *Sky & Telescope*, "Rambling Through the Skies."

Christina Linsenmeyer-van Schalkwyk is a cellist and has worked as a violin maker. She holds a degree in music from Colgate University and a diploma in violin making and restoration from North Bennet Street School in Boston. She has performed with the Boston Civic Symphony, played in chamber music groups, and is currently working on a Ph.D. in musicology at Washington University in St. Louis.

Doug Mann, Ph.D., teaches in the philosophy department at the University of Windsor in Windsor, Ontario. His main interests are social and political philosophy, continental thought, cultural studies, and the philosophy of history. He has published over twenty articles in a variety of journals in all his fields of interest.

Joseph W. Meeker is a human ecologist with a Ph.D. in comparative literature, and masters and postdoctoral studies in wildlife ecology and comparative animal and human behavior. He has worked as a ranger and field ecologist in Alaska, Oregon, and California; as a broadcaster on television and National Public Radio; and has taught at the University of California, the University of Alaska, and Union Institute, where he is a core faculty member in the graduate school. He is the author of several books including *The Comedy of Survival: Literary Ecology and a Play Ethic* (third edition, University of Arizona Press, 1997). His research into comedy and play is an exploration of the relationships between humanity and the natural world, and seeks to bring science, literature, and philosophy together for a more comprehensive and friendly understanding of the meaning and dynamics of living systems.

F. David Peat holds a Ph.D. in physics from the University of Liverpool and is the author of over seventeen books. Recent publications include *Infinite Potential: The Life of David Bohm* (Addison-Wesley), *The Blackwinged Night: Creativity in Nature and Mind* (Perseus), and, with John Briggs, *Seven Life Lessons of Chaos* (HarperCollins). David Peat lives in Pari, Italy—a medieval hilltop village overlooking the Tuscan countryside—and can be found on the Web at *www.fdavidpeat.com.*

Jeffrey A. Raff, Ph.D., is a psychologist, Jungian analyst, and member of the International Association of Analytical Psychology. He has taught seminars, workshops, and classes on Jungian psychology and mysticism all over the United States and in Europe, and has been a student and teacher of alchemy for thirty years. His book *Jung and the Alchemical Imagination* is forthcoming from Nicolas-Hays in the fall of 2000.

Christine Rhone is a writer, translator, and artist interested in ancient cultures and landscape symbolism. Her article "Plato, Athena, and Saint Katherine: The Education of the Philosopher" appeared in

Alexandria 3, and her translations include Jean Richer's *Sacred Geography of the Ancient Greeks* and Antoine Faivre's *Theosophy, Imagination, Tradition*, both published by the State University of New York Press.

Theodore Roszak is professor emeritus of history at California State University, Hayward. His most recent book is *The Gendered Atom: Reflections on the Sexual Psychology of Science* (Conari Press), a study of gender-bias in the theory and practice of science. His other nonfiction works include *The Making of a Counter Culture*, *The Cult of Information*, *The Voice of the Earth: An Exploration of Ecopsychology*, and the recently published *America the Wise: The Longevity Revolution and the True Wealth of Nations* (Houghton Mifflin), a comprehensive study of the cultural and political implications of our society's lengthening life expectancy. His fiction includes *Flicker* (Bantam Books) and the award-winning *Memoirs of Elizabeth Frankenstein* (Random House and Bantam Books).

David Ulansey is a historian of religion specializing in the religions of the ancient Mediterranean and a professor in the Philosophy, Cosmology, and Consciousness Program at the California Institute of Integral Studies. He is particularly interested in the mystery religions, Gnosticism, ancient cosmology, and the relationships between religion, myth, and the evolution of consciousness. Dr. Ulansey is author of *The Origins of the Mithraic Mysteries: Cosmology and Salvation in the Ancient World* (Oxford University Press), as well as numerous articles in publications ranging from *Scientific American* to the *Journal of Biblical Literature*.

Greg Whitlock teaches philosophy at Parkland College and Eastern Illinois University and has written on such diverse philosophers as Malcolm X, Nietzsche, and Confucius.

Dana Wilde holds a Ph.D. in literature and has taught at the University of Maine, the American University in Bulgaria, and has lectured on astronomy. His writings have appeared in *The North*

American Review, *The Magazine of Fantasy and Science Fiction*, *Alexandria*, and other publications. He is teaching in China under the auspices of a Fulbright Grant and his book *Infinities: The Inner Dimension of Outer Space* will be published by Phanes Press in 2001.

Peter Lamborn Wilson was affiliated with the Imperial Iranian Academy of Philosophy in Tehran, explored Persia and the Orient between 1968 and 1981, and is the author of many books and articles on Sufism, including *Scandal: Essays in Islamic Heresy* and *Sacred Drift: Essays on the Margins of Islam*. Recent publications include *Ploughing the Clouds: The Search for Irish Soma* (City Lights, 1999), and, from Autonomedia, *Pirate Utopias: Moorish Corsairs and European Renegadoes* (1995); *"Shower of Stars," Dream and Book: The Initiatic Dream in Sufism and Taoism* (1996); and *Escape from the Nineteenth Century and Other Essays* (1999). He lives in New York and teaches each summer in Boulder, Colorado at Naropa University's Jack Kerouac School of Disembodied Poetics.

List of Subscribers

THE FOLLOWING INDIVIDUALS have made *Alexandria* 5 a reality by joining THE ALEXANDRIA SOCIETY, the sole purpose of which is to support our publications program. We thank these individuals for their generosity and support, which has made this forum possible.

Semi-Divinity, $500
Ellen Burstyn
Phil Lesh
Katherine Neville
Haven O'More

Patron, $250
A. Jay Damon
Thomas Hampson
R. Dennis Walton
Roger Harman Weeks
Thomas D. Worrel

Benefactor, $100
Anonymous (1)
Ann Ashworth
Luana Coats
Bob Culley
Frances M. Evans
Ignacio L. Götz
Alvin Holm
Avona L'Cartier
Sidney Lanier
Doss McDavid
Patricia J. Middleton, M.D.
Lorna D. Mohr
Constance S. Papson Johnson
James B. Robinson
Dr. Sersuya

Brenda Spencer
Julian Watson
Thomas Willard

Sustainer, $75
Steve Bass
Hall C. Burbage
Leroy Clark
Derek Gilman
Joscelyn Godwin
Meredith Hardin
Ann Knight
Rosa McGehee
Sondra Ford Swift
Allison Talarico

Supporter, $50
Anonymous (2)
Richard A. Adams
Norman Anderson
William R. Bacher
Delton I. Baerwolf
Nancy B. Barohn
Thomas Beckett
Elizabeth J. Bissell
H. Avoise Blackway
Dr. G. J. Bosman
Jay Bregman
Thomas Merton Brightman

Dean Brown
Richard Brown
Cornelius Bull
Joseph Caezza
David D. Campbell
John Carey
Champions of the Rose
Walter R. Christie, M.D.
Tom Condon
George Contos
Armand Courtois, Sr.
Michael Crisp
Carl Daggett
Robert & Elsbeth Diehl
William Dillon
Harry Doumas
William Downey
James Englemann
Jacques H. Etienne
Ellen Faith
Antoine Faivre
Brett Forray
Karen Gardner, Ph.D.
Pam Giese
Geoffrey Gough
Julia Grabel
Andrew Green
Sara & John Michael Greer
Mickey Bright Griffin
Denton E. Hall
Ken Harbour
Patty A. Hardy
Helen Henry
Richard M. Higgins
Karl F. Hollenbach
Albert Jacobbe
Robert Kaladish, M.D.
Marianna Kaul-Connolly
Scot Kelly
Julia Kirk
Hannah Kodicek
Maurice Krasnow, Ph.D.

William M. Kuhn
Clem Labine
T. Jerome Layfield
Gerald F. Leska
Bruce MacLennan
Thomas Mansheim
Kevin A. Mc Carthy
Jo Gayle McClellion
Jack Meier
Donald Melchoir
Ralph Metheny
M. Joy Mills
Dr. John Mizenko
Alexander Moshos
D. D. Nelson
Charles Newlin
Jane Olinger
Scott A. Olsen
Charles E. Pasley
Barry Popik
Karen K. Prince
Rebecca C. Reath
Philip S. Schuman
Jay Sherry
Mark Siegeltuck
Göran Svarvell
Toby Symington
Mary M. Tius
Erol Torun
John T. Walker
John Walker, IV
Gerry Wapple
Richard Ware
Anthony Watson
Andrew White
Beatrice S. Wittel

Member, $35
Anonymous (2)
Pasquale Accardo
Frederick C. Adams
Dave Akerman

Jo Alexander
Jerrold E. Allen
Anton A. Armbruster
Rev. Steven A. Armstrong
Ralph Ashbrook
Jo Ashenden
Peter Assezbergs
Marz Attar
Steven G. Ayre, M.D.
Chris Bache
Alexander Bardosh
Sarah Batchelor
Janet Bayliss
Chester L. Behnke
Jack Behrman
Don E. Benson
Owen C. Benson
Liza Berdnik
Jacob Bialos
Rudolf A. Binnewies
Claude Bird
Marco Bischof
Lorraine Black
R. E. Bliss
Carolyn Bliss Spurlock
Liliane Boardman
Jeanine Bourdon
Mary Branch Grove
Kenneth B. Breese
Russell Brehm
Jeanne Bresciani
Jacki Brook
Francis P. Broussard
Dennis Brown
Barbara Brucken
J. H. Bruening
Richard Brzustowicz, Jr.
Rose Mary Byrne
Tom Cabot
Carol Camp
Bonnie Campbell
James Earle Canfield

Lucia Capadilupo
Toni Cardona
Mary Kathleen Carroll
Donna May Chien
J. Richard Christian
Leigh Christopher
Christi Clogson
Ruth A. Coates
Pamela Cole
Bill Collins
Christopher Michael Collins
John Robert Colombo
Theony Condos
Mariana Kaul Connolly
Vincent J. Cornell
Tadd Cowing
Joseph Coyle
Paul Craven
Andrzej Czubernat
Elizabeth Dancoes
Frederick A. De Armas
Lynne De Gerenday
Dante Deamicis
Lance deHaven-Smith
Nancy Denton
Jon Dependal
Jonathan Paul DeVierville, Ph.D.
J. A. Diaz
Michael Diaz
Adam Dietrich
Katherine Dimma
Robert Dobie
Frank E. Dougher
Elizabeth Downs
Jill Draper
Anne Kari Dreyer
Arthur Durant
Susan Ehrlich
Brian David Ellison
Claude Epstein
George Eraclides
Jose Esparza

Joel Fairbanks
David Fankushen
Robert Ferguson
Gwen Ferguson
Fetzer Institute
Sally Finch
Aaron Fitzgerald
V. H. Flach
F. G. A. Fluitsma
Josep Fortiana
Marie Fountaine
Farida Fox
Rev. Leonard Fox
Norman Frank
D. Moreau Franklin
Marco Frascari
Jeffrey I. Friedman, D.C.
Diane Gaboriault
John Gacher
Michele Gagnon
Robert Galbreath
Prof. Dr. Helmut Gebelein
Dimitrios Geroukaulis
Jeff Gorvetzian
Phillip Graham
Dr. Sydney R. Grant
Diana Gray
Vincent J. Graziano
Mark Greene
J. A. Grimes
Joseph Groell
James Haberland
John Haddington
Dr. Hans T. Hakl
Craig A. Hanson
Jeff Hardee
Jack Hardie
J. Patrick Harrington
Mary Ann Hawk
Harold Hays
Elena Heckathorne
Don Hecke

S. C. Hedger
David Height
Fritz Heinegg, M.D.
Kevin Heinold
Pamela Hemingway
David Henderson
John W. Henry
Fran Hergoth
P. J. Herro
Patricia Herron
Miguel Herschberg
Delbert Highlands
Fran Hill
Harold Hodges
Larie Holenes
Diane Holland
George Hollenback
J. W. F. Holliday
Alice O. Howell-Andersen
Charles Hudson
Lee Irwin
LaVerne Isenburg
Morten Jellestad
Joseph Jenkins
Jane Jensen-Holmer
Robert Jimison
Evangelyn D. Johnson
Norris Johnson
Roger S. Jones
Louis N. Jones
Perry Jorgensen
David Joy
Dr. Roger W. Jung
Christopher Kaiser
Gregory Kamm
Neil H. Kaufler
Jean Keating
Chad Keiffer
Scott Kelley
Margaret Kerns
C. V. Khomutov
Michael Kiggans

Sean Kinnevy
Richard M. Kline
Jon Knebel
Vaksdal Knut
P. M. Koch
Olga Kokino
Mary Kolodny
Art Kompolt
John J. Kottra, M.D.
Randy Lee Kremer
Rowena Pattee Kryder
Lorene Kuimelis
Dianne Kynaston
M. Lakshmanan
Nelson E. Lamborn
Charles Larry
John A. & Adeleen Leaman
J. Douglas Lee
Chris Lemoine
Monica R. Lewis
Max Licher
Paul D. Lidstrom, M.D.
Donald Lindsay Holms
Sue Lovell
Ana Lucia Sampaio Faras
Cesar Lugones
Timothy Lutzweit
Frannie Lyon
William Maccrea
James MacLellan
Shimon Malin
Carolyn Mallison
Perry D. Manack
Andrew Manze
Adam M. Marshall
Jennifer A. Marshall
David E. Mathieson
Carolyn A. McColley
Howard W. McCoy
Bonita J. McEnaney
Robert McGahey
E. J. McInnis

Thomas McKnight
Dr. James L. McNamara
David W. Meany
Eric Medalis
John Meeks
David Melton
George M. Melvich
Ciaran Mercier
Metaekdotiki, Ltd.
Jim Meyers
Melanie Mineo
Ralph B. Montee
Alvin Moore, Jr.
Gary Moring
Elise Murphy
Richard Myers
Jorge Najera
Jeremy Naydler
Deanna J. Neider
Stuart Nelson
Richard Nelson
Paul Newall
Vanya Nick
Dan Niehaus
David Nikias
Daniel C. Noel
W. Nookadu
Jan Noyen
Vivenne O'Reagan
Phillis O'Rourke
Laura Obendorfer
Daniel Oberti
Ronald Olson
Gordon M. Onslow Ford
Stephen Overy
M. Curt Paddock
Richard Palcanis
Jon Parks
David Pellegrino
Peter B. Pellier
Patti Perleberg-Owen
Sabra Petersmann

Richard Pickrell
Francis I. Pierce
Kelly Piette
Susan Pope
Frances W. Porter
Lynn Quirolo
John Ratliffe
Hermann Paul Rechten
F. Marion Redd
Christine Rhone
David Richards
Bob Richardson
Jack Riesenbeck
Michael Rigby
Nicholas Romas
Alan Rosenus
Stanford K. Rossiter
Elisabeth Zinck Rothenberger
Andrew E. Rothovius
Mossman Roueché, Jr.
Ramona Rubio
George K. Russell
Peter Russell
Gerald Rutt
Octavio Salcedo
Val Savenko
Helen Schell
Michelle Majerus Schmidt
Al Schmoeller
Mark Schuber
Gloria Y. Schwartz
Henry Seale
Shirley Self
Jane Seligson
Robin Van Löben Sels
Elizabeth Sewell
Gregory Shaw
Rev. Milton R. Shaw, Ph.D.
Robert Siefer
David Skrbina
Kate Smith-Hanssen

John Sokol
Dr. Michael G. Sollenberger
Ruben Soto
Alissa Springer
Barton Stanley
Crystal Star
Roger Steed
Pamela Steel
Joanna Stewart
David Stobbs
Carol Stoddard
Jon T. Strehlow
Gerd Stumpf
Ray Styles
Joseph H. Sulkowski
Terrence M. Sullivan
Linda Sussman
Marilyn C. Sutcliffe
David Sweet
Beverly L. Taylor
Beverly Taylor
Cailean & Raphael Taylor
Russell Teague
Terrance Teis
Siemen Terpstra
Scott Thayer
Rev. A. H. Thelander
Gretchen Thometz
Charles Tilden
Doris Tillman
Rev. Shawn Tracy
Michael Treat
Mary M. Tufano
David Tuggle
Janis Tupesis
Ann K. U. Tussing
Hal Tynan
Rick Uphaus
Douglas Urbina
Knut Vaksdal
Peter Valentyne

Lerie Alstad Van Ells
Susan Victor
Kay Vigiletti
Rod Wallbank
Jim Walsh
Leor Wanner
Rosemary Warner
Daniel N. Washburn
John Waystuffe, III
Garnet Lee Webb
Peter Weeda
Edward Weise
B. Robert Welton
Marc A. Wessels
James West

Mary Anne Westover
David White
Vickie White
Elisabeth Whitten
Gary R. Whittle
Dr. Jay G. Williams
Norman Williams
Virginia T. Wilson
Edgar Winger
Will Wood
Edith Wood Forgy
John Wootten
Lorraine Yee
Cathleen Conley Young

ALEXANDRIA

ALEXANDRIA 1 • "Revisioning the Sacred for Our Time" by Kathleen Raine • "The Orphic Mystery: Harmony and Mediation" by Lee Irwin • "Hymns of Orpheus: Mutations" by R. C. Hogart • "Michael Maier's Alchemical Quadrature of the Circle" by John Michell • "The Eternal Feminine: Vladimir Solov'ev's Visions of Sophia" by Kristi A. Groberg • "Embodying the Stars: Iamblichus and the Transformation of Platonic Paideia" by Gregory Shaw • "Galaxies and Photons" by Dana Wilde • "Esotericism Today: The Example of Henry Corbin" by Christopher Bamford • "The Waters of Vision and the Gods of Skill" by John Carey • "The Path Toward the Grail: The Hermetic Sources and Structure of Wolfram von Eschenbach's *Parzival*" by David Fideler • "The Creation of a Universal System: Saint-Yves d'Alveydre and his Archeometer" by Joscelyn Godwin • "Aspects of Ancient Greek Music" by Flora R. Levin • "A Plotinian Solution to a Vedantic Problem" by Michael Hornum • "Gnosticism, Ancient and Modern" by Arthur Versluis • "Hekate's Iynx: An Ancient Theurgical Tool" by Stephen Ronan • Reviews and more • Paperback, 384 pages, $25.00

ALEXANDRIA 2 • "The Museum at Alexandria" by Edward Parsons • "A Note on the Muses" by Adam McLean • "Bibliotheca Alexandrina: The Revival of the First Universal Library—A Report from UNESCO" • "Alexandria: Past, Present, and Future" by Eric Mueller • "Hypatia of Alexandria: Mathematician, Astronomer, and Philosopher" by Nancy Nietupski • "The Life of Hypatia" from *The Suda* • "The Life of Hypatia" by Socrates Scholasticus • "The Life of Hypatia" by John, Bishop of Nikiu • "Psychedelic Effects and the Eleusinian Mysteries" by Shawn Eyer • "The Science and Art of Animating Statues" by David Fideler • "The Alchemical Harp of Mechtild of Hackeborn" by Therese Schroeder-

Sheker • "The Fish Bride" by Jane Thigpen • "An Introduction to the Monochord" by Siemen Terpstra • "A Note on Ptolemy's Polychord" by David Fideler • "Mysticism and Spiritual Harmonics in Eighteenth-Century England" by Arthur Versluis • "Mentalism and the Cosmological Fallacy" by Joscelyn Godwin • "Printing, Memory, and the Loss of the Celestial" by Arthur Versluis • Gerhard Dorn's "Monarchy of the Ternary in Union Versus the Monomachia of the Dyad in Confusion" • "Imago Magia, Virgin Mother of Eternity: Imagination and Phantasy in the Philosophy of Jacob Boehme" by Hugh Urban • "The Castle of Heroes: W. B. Yeats's Celtic Mystical Order" by Peter Cawley • "The Availability of the One: An Interpretive Essay" by Michael Hornum • "The Magic of Romance: The Cultivation of Eros from Sappho to the Troubadours" by Christopher Bamford • "Seating Arrangements in Plato's *Symposium*" by Robin Waterfield • "All Religions are One" by William Blake • "The Dolphin in Greek Legend and Myth" by Melitta Rabinovitch • "Sacred Geography of the Ancient Greeks" by Christine Rhone • "The Cosmological Rorschach" by David Fideler • "Reports from Hyperborea" by John Henry • Reviews and more • Paperback, 440 pages, $25.00

ALEXANDRIA 3 • "Harmony Made Visible" by Michael S. Schneider • "The Alchemy of Art" by Arthur Versluis • "Ecopsychology in Theory and Practice" • "The Divine Sophia: Isis, Achamoth, and Ialdabaoth" by Lee Irwin • "Ruminations on All and Everything" by Peter Russell • "The Strange Case of the Secret Gospel According to Mark: How Morton Smith's Discovery of a Lost Letter of Clement of Alexandria Scandalized Biblical Scholarship" by Shawn Eyer • "Knowledge, Reason, and Ethics: A Neoplatonic Perspective" by Michael Hornum • "Delphi's Enduring Message: On the Need for Oracular Communications in Psychological Life" by Dianne Skafte • Anatolius "On the Decad" • Two Letters of Marsilio Ficino • "Cosmologies" by Dana Wilde • "The Invisible College" by Anthony Rooley • "Reviving the Academies of the Muses" by David Fideler • "Plato, Athena, and Saint Katherine: The Education of the Philosopher" by Christine Rhone • "The School of Wisdom" by Jane Leade • "Education in the New World Order," a trialogue by Ralph Abraham, Terence McKenna, and Rupert Sheldrake • "The Teaching Mission of Socrates" and "A Note on Myth, the Mysteries, and Teaching in Plato's *Republic*" by Ignacio L. Götz • "Reflections on the Tarocchi of Mantegna" by Oliver T. Perrin • "Speaking in Hieroglyphics" by Peter Lamborn Wilson • "Three Exemplars of the Esoteric Tradition in the Renaissance" by Karen-Claire Voss • Ships with Wings • "Apuleius in the Underworld" by John Carey • "Astronomy, Contemplation, and the Objects of Celestial Desire" by David Fideler • Reviews and more • Paper, 494 pages, $25.00

ALEXANDRIA 4 • "The Cosmic Religious Feeling" and "Science and Religion" by Albert Einstein • "Science and the Beautiful" by Werner Heisenberg • Thomas Moore and Suzi Gablik in conversation on "Soul and the World" • "Retrieving an Ancient Ecology" (art by Christopher Castle) • "Deep Form in Art and Nature" by Betty and Theodore Roszak • "Ecomorphology" (art by Gordon Onslow Ford) • Two Poems by Betty Roszak • "Cosmology, Ethics, and the Practice of Relatedness" by David Fideler • "Cultivating Ecological Design Intelligence" by Stuart Cowan • "Neoplatonism and the Cosmological Revolution: Holism, Fractal Geometry, and Mind in Nature" by David Fideler • "Egos, Angels, and the Colors of Nature" by Robert Romanyshyn • "The Contemporary Christian Platonism of A. H. Armstrong" by Jay Bregman • "The Theology of the Invisible" by Bruce Nelson • "The World Religions and Ecology" by Joseph Milne • "The Information War" by Hakim Bey • "Philosophical Counseling" Kathleen Damiani • "Novelty, the Stop, and the Advent of Conscience" by David Appelbaum • William Irwin Thompson speaks out on "Life, Lindisfarne, and Everything" • "Jung and the Myth of the Primordial Tradition" by Andrew Burniston • "The Lost Spirit of Hellenic Philosophy" by Christos Evangeliou • "Drinking with the Muses" by Thomas Willard • "Claiming a Liberal Education" by Stephen Rowe • "How to Host a Philosophical Banquet" by Plutarch • "Words of the God: Ancient Oracle Traditions of the Mediterranean World" by Lee Irwin • "Hermeticism and the Utopian Imagination" by John Michael Greer • Reviews and more • Paperback, 440 pages, $25.00

To order, enclose cost plus $4.00 shipping for the first item, 50¢ each additional. Make your check payable to Phanes Press. Major credit cards accepted.

Phanes Press • PO Box 6114 • Grand Rapids, Michigan 49516 • USA

STAR MYTHS
OF THE GREEKS AND
ROMANS: A SOURCEBOOK

Theony Condos

Star Myths of the Greeks and Romans:
A Sourcebook. Translation and
commentary by Theony Condos.

THE NIGHTLY APPEARANCE of the stars, their arrangement in the sky, their regular risings and settings through the course of the year, have been a source of endless wonder and speculation. But where did the constellations come from, and what are the myths associated with them?

Star Myths of the Greeks and Romans is the most comprehensive work ever published on the forty-eight classical constellations. Included in this handbook are the only surviving works on the constellation myths that have come down to us from antiquity: an epitome of *The Constellations* of Eratosthenes—never before translated into English—and *The Poetic Astronomy* of Hyginus. Also provided are accurate and detailed commentaries on each constellation myth and complete references for those who wish to dig deeper. This book is a comprehensive sourcework for anyone interested in astronomy or mythology—and an ideal resource for the occasional stargazer.

Paperback, ISBN 1-890482-93-5, $18.95.
Published by Phanes Press
www.phanes.com